THE MASTER MUSICIANS

BRITTEN

Series edited by Stanley Sadie

The Master Musicians

Titles available in paperback

Berlioz *Hugh Macdonald*
Brahms *Malcolm MacDonald*
Britten *Michael Kennedy*
Bruckner *Derek Watson*
Chopin *Jim Samson*
Grieg *John Horton*
Handel *Donald Burrows*
Liszt *Derek Watson*
Mahler *Michael Kennedy*
Mendelssohn *Philip Radcliffe*
Monteverdi *Denis Arnold*
Purcell *J.A. Westrup*

Rachmaninoff *Geoffrey Norris*
Rossini *Richard Osborne*
Schoenberg *Malcolm MacDonald*
Schubert *John Reed*
Sibelius *Robert Layton*
Richard Strauss *Michael Kennedy*
Tchaikovsky *Edward Garden*
Vaughan Williams *James Day*
Verdi *Julian Budden*
Vivaldi *Michael Talbot*
Wagner *Barry Millington*

Titles available in hardback

Bach *Malcolm Boyd*
Beethoven *Barry Cooper*
Elgar *Robert Anderson*
Handel *Donald Burrows*

Schubert *John Reed*
Schumann *Eric Frederick Jensen*
Schütz *Basil Smallman*
Richard Strauss *Michael Kennedy*

In preparation

Bartók *Malcolm Gillies*
Dvořák *Jan Smaczny*

Musorgsky *David Brown*
Puccini *Julian Budden*

THE MASTER MUSICIANS

BRITTEN

Michael Kennedy

OXFORD
UNIVERSITY PRESS

OXFORD

UNIVERSITY PRESS

Great Clarendon Street, Oxford OX2 6DP

Oxford University Press is a department of the University of Oxford.
It furthers the University's objective of excellence in research, scholarship,
and education by publishing worldwide in

Oxford New York

Athens Auckland Bangkok Bogotá Buenos Aires Cape Town
Chennai Dar es Salaam Delhi Florence Hong Kong Istanbul Karachi
Kolkata Kuala Lumpur Madrid Melbourne Mexico City Mumbai Nairobi
Paris São Paulo Shanghai Singapore Taipei Tokyo Toronto Warsaw

and associated companies in Berlin Ibadan

Oxford is a registered trade mark of Oxford University Press
in the UK and in certain other countries

Published in the United States
by Oxford University Press Inc., New York

© Michael Kennedy 1981, 1993, 2001

First paperback edition 1983
Revised 1993

The moral rights of the author have been asserted

Database right Oxford University Press (maker)

First published in paperback by Oxford University Press 2001

British Library Cataloguing in Publication Data

Data available

Library of Congress Cataloging in Publication Data
Kennedy, Michael, 1926–
Britten / Michael Kennedy.
p. cm.—(The master musicians)
Includes list of works (p.), bibliographical references (p.), discography (p.), and index.
1. Britten, Benjamin, 1913–1976. 2. Composers—England—Biography.
I. Title. II. Master musicians series.
ML410.B853 K45 2000   780'.92—dc21   00–057119

ISBN 0–19–816479–3

1 3 5 7 9 10 8 6 4 2

Typeset by Selwood Systems
Midsomer Norton, Avon
Printed in Great Britain
on acid-free paper by
Butler & Tanner Ltd
Frome and London

Preface

I belong to the generation which witnessed Benjamin Britten's career from its meteoric early brilliance to the courageous last years of struggle against illness. His music was an essential part of our lives, a continuous counterpoint to all the other activities of the crowded years. Each new work was a landmark. Some of them were easy to accept from the outset; others were perhaps underrated or misunderstood. I have written this book partly in expiation of my own misunderstandings at certain periods, but mainly as a celebration of the joy his music has brought to me for over forty years.

For I think of his music principally as a bright star amid the encircling gloom of our century. Of course it has its sombre side, for he understood the failings of humankind, but on the whole it is the music of light. Leonard Bernstein has spoken of 'something very dark' in Britten's music, adding, 'There are gears that are grinding and not quite meshing and they make a great pain' — a singularly inapposite metaphor, it seems to me, for if ever there was a composer whose music engaged the gears smoothly it was Britten. The darkness is undoubtedly there, for, like us all, he had his inner doubts and misgivings. Unquestionably he was, like every great artist, dissatisfied and unhappy; he frequently looked both. But if he was, as the fashionable approach has it, 'tortured' and 'anguished', it was not, surely, because his life was in any sense tragic. He was loved by his family and friends and by one friend particularly; he lived most of his life in seclusion in chosen surroundings; he made music with people as gifted and dedicated as he was; in his twenties his music was taken up by three great conductors; he had few material worries; and he enjoyed wide-spread recognition of his work from the public. Even his heart operation and illness, cause for grief and compassion though they were, brought him further evidence of the devotion of his circle; and one of them has said that Britten himself believed that 'people died at the right moment'.

Any future writer on Britten's life must inevitably acknowledge, as

I do, the indispensable source-material contained in *Benjamin Britten: Pictures from a Life 1913–76*, edited by Donald Mitchell and John Evans (London 1978). Another treasure-trove of material to which I am indebted was the three broadcast features *Britten: the Early Years,* written and presented by Donald Mitchell. To Mr Mitchell himself, Britten's official biographer, I offer my thanks for his helpful attitude to my book. He has put me right, from his specialized knowledge, on several points of fact and many of detail. The diaries of Lord Britten are the copyright of the Britten Estate, not to be reproduced without written permission, and I am therefore grateful to the Executors of the Estate for allowing me to quote from extracts already published. I am also grateful to the Executors for permission to quote from Lord Britten's letters, speeches, articles and interviews, and for their ready co-operation in the provision of many of the illustrations. Numbers 1, 2, 5, 6, 8, 9 and 14 are here reproduced by courtesy of the Britten Estate. In the case of number 4, the copyright of the music is vested in Boosey & Hawkes Ltd.

I owe a particular debt to the Secretary to the Estate, Miss Rosamund Strode, for her advice, help and patience in answering my queries and for her hospitality on my visit to the Aldeburgh archive. Sir Peter Pears has also answered my questions and I am indebted to him for his frankness. Mr Eric Crozier, too, was most kind and helpful. I gratefully acknowledge permission from Britten's principal publishers for reproduction of music examples from his works (Boosey & Hawkes Music Publishers Ltd: nos 1–18, 21 and 23; Faber Music Ltd: nos 19–20, 22 and 24–30), and from the editors of *The Times, The Daily Telegraph, The Guardian, The Observer, The Sunday Times, The Musical Times, Music and Letters,* the *Spectator,* the *New Statesman* and *The Gramophone* for quotations from reports and articles which first appeared in their publications. I am grateful to Faber and Faber for permission to quote short extracts from *Britten* by Imogen Holst and from *Themes and Conclusions* by Igor Stravinsky; and to Faber Music Ltd., London, and Faber and Faber for permission to quote from Lord Britten's *On Receiving the First Aspen Award*. I wish especially to thank Mr Ray Crick for the comprehensive discography which he has compiled for my book, Dr Joyce Bourne for help with research, Mr Joseph Ward for lending me his letters from Britten, Mr Anthony Friese-Greene for lending me a photograph, and Mrs A. Wragg for typing my manuscript. Finally I would like to thank all the performers of Britten's music, past and present, who have made this book possible.

September 1980   *M.K.*

Preface to the 1993 edition

In the twelve years since this book first appeared, there have been several major additions to the Britten bibliography which no future study of the composer can fail to take into account. *A Britten Source Book* (1987) reveals the astonishing extent of Britten's juvenilia and provides a chronologically exact record of his creative and performing life. In the first two volumes of *Letters from a Life* (1991), with further volumes to follow, Donald Mitchell and Philip Reed have published extracts from Britten's diaries and a selection of his letters which, together with the editors' copiously informative notes, supply what almost amounts to an autobiography. Christopher Headington's *Peter Pears* (1992) is a sympathetic and detailed account of the tenor's life and career and tells us much about his relationship with Britten. Finally, Humphrey Carpenter's *Benjamin Britten* (1992) is a massive and diligently researched biography which pulls no punches in its analysis of its subject's personality and proclivities. In the face of all this evidence, an author of a book which preceded it might well feel that his only course was to 'turn skies back and begin again'. However, my short study was primarily concerned with Britten's musical life and his music. Fascinating as are revelations about his personal dealings and relationships, his compositions and his place in British musical life are what will carry his music down the ages. So for this new edition, I have taken the opportunity to add a chapter on works performed and/or published since 1983 (when the book first appeared in paperback), to correct some facts, to expand the list of works and bibliography, to include a few significant biographical points and, in the light of twelve years' further listening, to modify a few opinions. I would like to express my gratitude for further help to Rosamund Strode, Paul Banks, and Donald Mitchell, and to Ray Crick for his thorough revision of his discography to take account of compact discs.

For this reprint the Bibliography and Appendix C have been brought up to date. Once again I owe thanks to Ray Crick for completely revising the Discography. Thanks are also due to Judith LeGrove and the Britten–Pears Library for their help and co-operation.

March 2001   M.K.

Contents

Illustrations

'It is quite a good thing to please people, even if only for today. That is what we should aim at – pleasing people today as seriously as we can, and letting the future look after itself.'

Benjamin Britten, 1964, on receiving the Aspen Award.

1

Suffolk childhood

On the evening of 23 February 1934, the BBC broadcast a performance of *A Boy Was Born*, a new set of choral variations for unaccompanied voices by the twenty-year-old Benjamin Britten. Thus, on the very day of the death of Edward Elgar, who had hoped he might be the first English composer to be raised to the peerage, as poets, painters and actors already had been, there was broadcast to the nation music by the man who, forty-two years later, was to achieve what Elgar had been denied. This juxtaposition of the names of Elgar and Britten in the opening lines of a book about the latter is no mere predictable quirk of this particular author; in any list of the half-dozen greatest English composers they may reasonably be expected to appear, and common to their careers to a striking degree were an early indifference and hostility to their music from the British academic musical establishment, followed by adulatory and highly partisan championship by immigrant writers and musicians and by British royal and aristocratic circles. As if to compensate for the rough beginnings, honours were showered on them in their middle age. Yet the causes of the early antipathies were different. Elgar suffered by reason of his class and religion; Britten because he was a pacifist and homosexual. Both, of course, were not at first forgiven for the superiority of their music to that of their rivals, and both knew that, notwithstanding the heart-warming appreciation from thousands of their fellow-countrymen, they were working in a country which, as Britten said,[1] 'has for years treated the musician as a curiosity to be barely tolerated... The average Briton thought, and still thinks, of the arts as suspect and expensive luxuries.' How one wishes, he said, that the 'basic philistinism of this country would wither away'.

There is another parallel to Elgar in Britten's life. Just as Elgar thrived creatively only when working and living in the countryside around Worcester, so Britten could say of Suffolk: 'I am firmly rooted in this glorious county...'[2] 'I find as I get older that working becomes more and more difficult away from that home.'[3] Edward Benjamin Britten was born on 22 November 1913, the feast of music's patron

St Cecilia, at 21 Kirkley Cliff Road, Lowestoft, Suffolk. He was the youngest of four children born to Robert Victor Britten, a dentist, and his wife, Edith Rhoda (*née* Hockey). The others were Barbara (b. 1902), Robert (b. 1907) and Elizabeth (Beth) (b. 1909). The house faced the North Sea, but the first sound Benjamin remembered hearing was not that of wind and waves or the cry of gulls but the explosion of a bomb dropped by a Zeppelin on a field near by. His terror was assuaged by the comforting of his nurse, Annie Walker (later Mrs Scarce).

Robert Britten senior, besides being a skilled dentist, was well liked by his patients, no mean achievement in that profession. He was not a musician, but he liked the domestic music-making which his wife encouraged and never wanted to own a gramophone or wireless in case they prevented it. (That his younger son inherited this attitude to machines is shown by his remark, 'If I say the loudspeaker is the principal enemy of music, I don't mean that I am not grateful to it as a means of education or study, or as an evoker of memories. But it is not part of true musical experience.'⁴) His principal contribution to his children's wider education was to read Dickens and other authors to them, to take them sailing, and to show them the pleasures of long walks in the Suffolk lanes. Edith Britten was an amateur soprano. She held 'musical evenings' at home and sang German Lieder, arias by J.S. Bach, Handel, and Mozart, and English songs. She was honorary secretary of Lowestoft Choral Society, and when professional soloists came from London to sing in *Messiah* or *The Creation* she invited them to come and stay at the Brittens' home. Benjamin listened to their practice. He was given his first piano lessons by his mother when he was five, but she had involved him at the age of three in his first theatrical production, a performance of an adaptation of Kingsley's *The Water Babies*. She played Mrs Do-as-you-would-be-done-by, and Britten remembered wearing skin-coloured tights, that his hair was 'madly curly' and that he tried desperately to remember his lines as Tom the water-baby. Family theatricals, with Britten as playwright, composer and producer became a regular occurrence in the nursery with the big rocking-horse at No. 21.

Britten began composing when he was five, 'hundreds of dots all over the page connected by long lines all joined together in beautiful curves', but soon he was writing 'elaborate tone-poems [for piano] usually lasting about twenty seconds, inspired by terrific events in my home life such as the departure of my father for London, the appearance in my life of a new girl friend, or even a wreck at sea'.⁵ When he was six or seven Britten wrote a play called *The Royal Falily* [*sic*] which includes his first incidental music.[6] Having been impressed by the recent death at the age of thirteen in January 1919 of Prince John, fifth son of King George V and Queen Mary, Britten began his play with the prince's illness. In Scene 2 the child dies and the King and Queen lament accordingly:

Q. (crying) Oh ... John's dead. Poor me.
K. Oh. How.
Q. He was ill.
K. Oh.
Q. Yes.
K. Why was he ill.
Q. Of course he had fits.
K. Oh, oh, oh.
Q. Why, why.
K. My toe-toe and roe-roe
    (song to these words).

His first school was at Southolme, a pre-preparatory school run by Miss Ethel Astle, who also taught him the piano so successfully that he could soon act as accompanist to his mother. At the age of eight he was composing prolifically, working before breakfast so that his music did not interfere with schoolwork. 'I wrote symphony after symphony, song after song, a tone-poem called *Chaos and Cosmos*, although I fear I was not sure what these terms really meant.'[7] He remained fond of his Longfellow setting *Beware!* composed at this time, while he drew on some charming *Walztes* [*sic*] for piano, written in 1923–5, for parts of the *Simple Symphony* for strings (1933–4). In 1923 he entered South Lodge preparatory school. It was but a short walk from his home so he was a day-boy, but for weeks on end he was at home only to sleep. He was good at his lessons, especially mathematics, and very keen on games. Few great English composers have shown much interest in our greatest game, cricket, but Britten was an exception, at any rate in his youth. In his last year at South Lodge he was captain of cricket and when he was twenty he went back there for a game occasionally, writing in his diary for 5 April 1933: 'I go & play cricket with South Lodge boys... Great fun; have a glorious knock, making 33 & eventually retiring with bust bat! Not stylish cricket, tho'.' In later life he continued to play tennis. Yet his family said later that he had not been given much chance of survival after a severe bout of pneumonia when he was three months old. Doctors feared that he might never be able to live a normal life, and he himself spoke of having a 'wonky heart' in childhood.

It was about 1923 when he began viola lessons with Audrey Alston, of Norwich. Soon he was writing music for strings, marking details of bowing and using some of the rare Italian directions, such as *mancando* (dying away) which he had learned from Stainer's *Rudiments*, given to him on his ninth birthday. There was no musical life at school, therefore much of his musical education was undertaken solo, by studying scores. When the family spent a day in London, the big treat for 'Bennie' was to browse through miniature scores at Augener's before deciding which to buy. One day, in the local music shop, he came across Holst's *Song of the Ship-builders*, one of four part-songs for children composed in 1910. This excited him. But of deeper significance was his visit to the Norwich Triennial Festival in 1924 when he heard Frank Bridge conduct his suite *The Sea*. The ten-year-old boy was, to use his own words, 'knocked sideways'.[8]

Frank Bridge

Frank Bridge was born in 1879. He was a pupil of Stanford at the Royal College of Music from 1899 to 1903 and from 1906 to 1915 was viola-player in several string quartets, including the Joachim, Grimson and the English. In these years, too, he was active as a conductor, for instance with the opera company organized by Marie Brema at the Savoy Theatre, London, in 1910. His chamber music won Cobbett prizes in 1905, 1908 and 1910 and he was classified among the English 'pastoral' school. His *The Sea* dates from 1910–11. In all his work, professional craftsmanship is apparent and his song 'Love went a-riding' has achieved something like popularity. In the years after the First World War, he showed himself more aware than his contemporaries of developments in Europe. Schoenberg and other members of the Second Viennese School influenced his harmonic thinking in such works as the impressive cello concerto, *Oration* (1930), the third and fourth string quartets (1926 and 1937), the violin sonata (1930) and, above all, the piano sonata (1921–24) and second piano trio (1929). His *Enter Spring*, for orchestra, was performed at the 1927 Norwich Festival, and again young Britten was in the audience and profoundly impressed by 'a riot of melodic and harmonic richness'.[1] Britten's viola teacher, Mrs Alston, knew Bridge well and then arranged for her young pupil to meet him. What followed is best told in Britten's words:

> We got on splendidly, and I spent the next morning with him going over some of my music... From that moment I used to go regularly to him, staying with him in Eastbourne or in London, in the holidays... This was immensely serious and professional study, and the lessons were mammoth... Often I used to end these marathons in tears, not that he was beastly to me but the concentrated strain was too much for me... This strictness was the product of nothing but professionalism. Bridge insisted on the absolutely clear relationship of what was in my mind to what was on the paper. I used to get sent to the other side of the room; Bridge would play what I'd written and demand if it was what I really meant... He knew he had to present something very firm for this stiff,

naïve little boy to react about... In everything he did for me, there were perhaps above all two cardinal principles. One was that you should try to find yourself and be true to what you found. The other – obviously connected with it – was his scrupulous attention to good technique, the business of saying clearly what was in one's mind. He gave me a sense of technical ambition.[2]

This emphasis on 'good technique' was perhaps the greatest lesson Britten learned from Bridge. 'I badly needed his kind of strictness', he wrote. 'His loathing of all sloppiness and amateurishness set me standards to aim for that I've never forgotten. He taught me to think and feel through the instruments I was writing for.' Thrilled by Holst's *The Planets* and Ravel's string quartet, Britten experimented with a freer harmonic style and showed Bridge a passage containing a series of major sevenths on the violin. Bridge pointed out that the violin did not vibrate properly with this interval: it should be divided between two instruments.

Bridge also broadened Britten's knowledge of the musical scene. His diary for the end of April 1928 mentions long morning lessons with Bridge, buying records of Ravel's *Introduction and Allegro* for harp, flute, clarinet and string quartet, and attending a 'wonderful Beethoven concert' at the Royal Albert Hall (Sargent conducting the *Choral Fantasia*, the B flat piano concerto and the *Mass in D*). Together they heard the first performance of Holst's *Hammersmith* (orchestral version) and the first London performance of Walton's *Belshazzar's Feast* (25 November 1931). They heard the first English performance of Stravinsky's *Symphony of Psalms* (16 November 1931) and 'when everyone around was appalled and saying how sad about Stravinsky, Bridge was insisting that it was a masterpiece'. For the first time, Britten saw how an artist lived: 'I heard conversations which centred round the arts; I heard the latest poems discussed, and the latest trends in painting and sculpture. Bridge was not intellectually over-sophisticated, perhaps, although well-read and full of curiosity, but he had a circle of highly cultured friends.'[3] But there were cakes and ale in this relationship: explorations of the Sussex Downs, with Bridge driving the car badly; a trip to Paris with Mrs Bridge; shrimping parties on the beach near Friston; and Britten reversing roles by coaching Bridge at tennis ('his was wild and unconventional; I considered mine rather good and stylish').

In one other important area Bridge influenced the boy Britten for life: 'A lot of my feeling about the First World War ... came from Bridge... Though he didn't encourage me to take a stand for the sake of a stand, he did make me argue and argue and argue. His own pacifism was not aggressive, but typically gentle.'[4] The first collision arising from this came in his last term at South Lodge in July 1928. In an end-of-term essay on 'Animals', Britten wrote an impassioned criticism of hunting and extended this to include all organized cruelty, particularly war. Even though he was head boy and *Victor ludorum*, he was in disgrace. His essay received no marks, the first time such a sign of magisterial disapproval had been registered. A happier event in the same month was his setting of four French poems by Hugo and Verlaine, for soprano and orchestra, as a present for his parents on their twenty-seventh wedding anniversary.

His first day at public school, Gresham's at Holt, Norfolk, also taught him what to expect from his elders. He was walking over the playing-fields when a man who he discovered later was the music-master stopped him and said: 'So you are the little boy who likes Stravinsky!' Nevertheless he enjoyed the atmosphere of Gresham's, which was 'liberal' and 'progressive'. Boys with conscientious objections to joining the Officers' Training Corps were not held up to ridicule but were given extra time for games. At school concerts Britten was heard as viola player and pianist and some of his compositions were performed. He was by now having piano lessons from Harold Samuel in London. The earliest works he allowed to be published were written at Gresham's, the setting for voice and piano of Belloc's *The Birds*, composed in June 1929, and the beautiful anthem for unaccompanied chorus, *A Hymn to the Virgin*, written while he was in the school sanatorium in July 1930. Both were revised in 1934, but the anthem had its first performance at a Lowestoft Musical Society concert in St John's Church on 5 January 1931, together with the carol *I saw Three Ships*, published in 1967 as *The Sycamore Tree*. Bridge made his contribution to *The Birds*: 'I had a terrible struggle with this before finding what has been called "the right ending in the wrong key". Bridge made me go on and on at it, worrying out what hadn't come right, until I spotted that the cycle of changing keys for each verse needed such an ending.'[5]

Britten won an open scholarship for composition to the Royal College of Music and left Gresham's in July 1930. The adjudicators were Vaughan Williams, John Ireland and S.P. Waddington. During the summer holidays, he was at a tennis party in Lowestoft and was asked by another guest what career he would take up. 'I'm going to be a composer,' he replied. 'Yes,' said his questioner, 'but what else?' More ominous was the *sotto voce* remark which Ireland said was made by S.P. Waddington at Britten's college scholarship examination: 'What is an English public schoolboy doing writing music of this kind?'[6]

Britten described his R.C.M. composition examination on 22 July 1931 as 'absolute farce... Of course they look at the wrong things...' The examiners on that occasion were Vaughan Williams, Waddington and Edgar Bainton.

3

At the College

Asked by Murray Schafer in 1961 if he had happy memories of his student days at the R.C.M., Britten replied: 'They don't seem very happy in retrospect. I feel I didn't learn very much.'[1] This will come as no surprise. He had, after all, had concentrated composition lessons for three years from a composer who was himself consolidating a highly chromatic, though not actually atonal, later style. He had been taught to think instrumentally, to acquire technical skill, and to investigate contemporary avant-garde works. 'Not nearly enough account was taken of the exceptionally gifted musician', Britten said. 'When you are immensely full of energy and ideas you don't want to waste your time being taken through elementary exercises in dictation.'

The director of the College at this date was Sir Hugh Allen, whose musical orientation was in the direction of Vaughan Williams rather than of anyone more outlandish. Vaughan Williams himself was still a professor of composition at the R.C.M. and at the height of his powers as a composer, having completed *Job* in 1930 and being about to begin his F minor symphony. To those out of sympathy with him, his outlook was regarded as parochial rather then merely nationalist, but this is a misjudgement. He was not opposed to continental influences, having himself benefited from study with Ravel as much as from contact with English folk-song, but he believed passionately that a composer must be a national composer before he could be cosmopolitan. His own struggle, like Holst's, had been to free his style not so much from foreign influence as specifically from the Teutonic influence which had, for instance, subjugated his teacher Stanford's natural gifts. He was, therefore, unsympathetic not only to Schoenberg and Hindemith, Berg and Webern but to Strauss and Reger. He also distrusted brilliance in any form, including technical virtuosity for its own sake, and he held the opinion that Bridge's music was 'the deepest abyss of the result of writing "effectively"'.[2] Everything one knows of Vaughan Williams sustains the conviction that he would never have made the 'English public schoolboy' remark. He used to recall that

Britten went into the room for his examination with a bundle of compositions under his arm. 'Is that all?' Vaughan Williams asked, with a twinkle. Britten blinked and replied: 'Oh no, I've got two suitcases full outside'. Vaughan Williams was an individualist of strong and rugged musical character and therefore a dangerous model for younger composers. Bridge, at any rate, suggested that Britten should go to John Ireland for composition and to Arthur Benjamin for piano. Ireland found him 'very industrious', but Britten realized in his first week that he was far in advance of his fellow-students.

Not only were entrance standards to the R.C.M. lower then than now, there was much less corporate life. Lodging at first in Prince's Square, Bayswater, and later with his sister Beth at 173 Cromwell Road, Britten attended his two lessons a week and spent the rest of the time practising and composing in his room. During his time at Gresham's, his musical gods were Beethoven and Brahms; it was 'a red letter day' when he was given the full score of *Fidelio* on his fourteenth birthday. But now he was spreading his wings and turning away from the nineteenth century. He discovered Mozart and Schubert and, later, Purcell and the English madrigal composers; this led to sharper conflicts with Bridge, whose approach was largely nineteenth century and German. Also, at the age of twenty, Britten naturally tended to rebel. Now, when Bridge played some chords his pupil had written and asked if that was what he meant, the answer tended to be 'Yes, it is', to be countered by the grunted retort 'Well, it oughtn't to be'. It was about this time, too, that he discovered Mahler. He had been encouraged to regard him as long-winded, formless, self-indulgent. 'And so', he wrote in an American magazine in February 1942,

when I was at a concert soon after leaving school, specially to hear an exciting new piano concerto, and saw from the programme that I had first to hear a symphony by Mahler, I naturally groaned in anticipation of forty-five minutes of boredom. But what I heard was not what I had expected to hear. First of all, in spite of a slack, under-rehearsed and rather apologetic performance, the scoring startled me. It was mainly 'soloistic' and entirely clean and transparent. The colouring seemed calculated to the smallest shade, and the result was wonderfully resonant. I wasn't bored for one of its forty-five minutes, whereas I was for every one of the fashionable new concerto's twenty-three. The form was so cunningly contrived; every development surprised one and yet sounded inevitable. Above all, the material was remarkable, and the melodic shapes highly original, with such rhythmic and harmonic tension from beginning to end. After that concert, I made every effort to hear Mahler's music, in England and on the continent, on the radio and on the gramophone, and in my enthusiasm, I began a great crusade among my friends on behalf of my new god – I must admit with only average success.

Britten twice won the Ernest Farrar composition prize (£7) at the R.C.M., in 1931 and 1933, but during his time there only one of his works was performed at the College, although the Patrons' Fund scheme existed to promote rehearsals of students' orchestral compositions. This was the *Sinfonietta*, op. 1, for chamber orchestra, on 16 March 1933, six weeks after its first performance elsewhere. One of his fellow-students, the oboist Evelyn Rothwell (later Lady Barbirolli) remembers playing through some Britten works and how fascinated he was by some chords which she produced from her instrument 'for fun'. Bridge tried to persuade the college authorities to include Britten's works and 'intervened angrily when I couldn't get a performance of two choral psalms I'd written... Vaughan Williams claimed that the singers weren't good enough, to which Bridge retorted that it was up to the R.C.M. to have a chorus good enough'.[3] Yet this was the period from which Britten's first fairly mature compositions date. The string quartet in D, which he revised in 1974 and allowed to be published in 1975, was composed in May 1931;[4] the *Sinfonietta* was composed between 20 June and 9 July 1932, followed by the *Phantasy Quartet*, op. 2, for oboe; the choral variations *A Boy Was Born*, op. 3, were written in 1932–3 and two part-songs in June 1933. 'I had to go outside to get my music played,'[5] Britten wrote. One 'outside' was the enterprising series of concerts promoted at the Ballet Club (later Mercury) Theatre by Anne Macnaghten and Iris Lemare with such stalwart instrumentalists as Ralph Nicholson (violin), Sylvia Spencer (oboe), and Richard Walton (trumpet). Britten's posthumously published *Phantasy String Quintet* and his three two-part songs to poems by Walter de la Mare were performed in this series on 12 December 1932. The quintet was the first Britten work to be broadcast, on 17 February 1933, in a performance by the André Mangeot Ensemble. On 31 January 1933 Miss Lemare conducted the first performance of the *Sinfonietta* in a programme which also included works by H.K. Andrews, Finzi, Grace Williams and Gordon Jacob. The *Phantasy Quartet*, dedicated to Leon Goossens, was broadcast on 6 August 1933 with Goossens as oboist, and two part-songs to words by Wither and Robert Graves were sung at the Ballet Club on 11 December 1933. At this last concert three movements were performed from an uncompleted suite for string quartet which Britten called *Go play, boy, play*. His diaries show what a struggle he had with this work, which was intended as a series of portraits of school friends. A ballet score composed in 1932 which he was invited by M. Montagu-Nathan to submit to the Camargo Society, founded in 1930 to invigorate ballet in Britain, was returned to him.

Britten's musical education advanced more rapidly outside the college, particularly at BBC studio concerts conducted by Frank Bridge which he attended and through listening to broadcasts and attending the BBC Symphony Orchestra's enterprising concerts. Thus, in January 1933 he found Delius's *On hearing the first cuckoo in spring* 'a miracle', as he wrote in his diary, and was thrilled by Tchaikovsky's 'wonderful' *Francesca da Rimini*. On 8 February of that year he found Schoenberg's *Variations* 'rather dull' but met the composer afterwards. On 8 March Berg's *Three Fragments from Wozzeck* were 'thoroughly sincere and moving', while Mahler's Fourth Symphony conducted by Webern on 23 March was like 'a lovely spring day' while seeming 'a mix-up of everything one has ever heard but it is definitely Mahler'. Most important of all, in November he heard Schoenberg's *Pierrot Lunaire*: 'What a work – the imagination and technique!... I revelled in the romanticism of it'.[6]

Britten had been irritated when the R.C.M. had rejected his suggestion that the college library should have a score of Schoenberg's *Pierrot Lunaire*. But worse was to follow. In his last year as a student (he became A.R.C.M. on 13 December 1933) he won a small scholarship for travel abroad. Bridge had encouraged his interest in the music of Alban Berg and Britten wanted to use his scholarship to study with Berg in Vienna, especially after he heard the concert performance of *Wozzeck* conducted in London by Adrian Boult on 14 March 1934. 'When the college was told,' Britten recalled,

> coolness arose. I think, but can't be sure, that the Director, Sir Hugh Allen, put a spoke in the wheel. At any rate, when I said at home during the holidays 'I *am* going to study with Berg, aren't I?' the answer was a firm 'No, dear'. Pressed, my mother said, 'He's not a good influence'... There was at that time an almost moral prejudice against serial music... I think also that there was some confusion in my parents' minds – thinking that 'not a good influence' meant morally, not musically. They had been disturbed by traits of rebelliousness and unconventionality which I had shown in my later school days.[7]

Britten quelled his disappointment, and perhaps signalled the official end of his student days, by looking through his childhood compositions and, on 23 December 1933, beginning to put them into the form of a *Simple Symphony* for string orchestra which he dedicated to his viola teacher, Audrey Alston, and conducted at its first performance by the

Norwich String Orchestra in Norwich on 6 March 1934. His *Phantasy Quartet* had been selected for performance at the International Society for Contemporary Music's festival in Florence on 5 April and Britten went to hear the performance. He had to return home when he received the news that his father had become gravely ill; in fact he had died on 6 April, but Britten did not know until he reached home three days after. Whether because of this bereavement or because of restlessness after completing his formal education, Britten at this time found it difficult to compose with a sense of purpose and continuity. He spent the summer at Lowestoft. Among those who sunbathed on the beach with the Britten family was the composer E.J. Moeran, who perhaps discussed their mutual interest in folk-song with his younger companion. Britten had for long been a keen student of folk-song arrangements and one of his life-long enthusiasms in this field began on 3 March 1933 when he listened to a broadcast and wrote in his diary '... two brilliant folk-song arrangements of Percy Grainger – 17 come Sunday, & Father & Son, knocking all the V. Williams and R.O. Morris arrangements into a cocked-hat'.[8] Other names come into Britten's life at this time, Howard Ferguson, the pianist and composer, and Antonio Brosa, the violinist, both friends of Bridge, and the teacher and critic Henry Boys, three years older than Britten, whom Britten met while he was at the R.C.M. and who encouraged his interest in Schoenberg and Stravinsky. Britten's prowess as a pianist was becoming known; he worked hard at a recital he gave in St John's Church, Lowestoft, on 9 July 1934, partnered by the organist, C.J.R. Coleman. Together they performed the first movements of the Schumann and Tchaikovsky (B flat minor) concertos and Britten's arrangements of Bridge's *Moonlight* (from *The Sea*) and the finale of Mozart's E flat symphony (No. 39). Britten's solos were the slow movement of Beethoven's *Appassionata* sonata, Schoenberg's *Six Little Pieces* and Debussy's *L'isle joyeuse*. It was very hot and Britten played in 'just tennis shirt & trousers'. He wrote his *Te Deum* in C in July and in October the piano suite *Holiday Diary*, dedicated to his teacher Arthur Benjamin. The orchestrated version of his *Te Deum* received its first performance on 27 January 1936, at the Mercury Theatre when the conductor was Reginald Goodall, with Britten playing first viola. Nine years later, Goodall was to conduct the first *Peter Grimes*.

The *Sinfonietta* was broadcast during the year and was reviewed in the August issue of *The Musical Times* by William McNaught, aged fifty-one in 1934.

'This young spark is good company for as long as his persiflage remains

13

fresh, which is not very long', he wrote. 'To do him justice, his *Sinfonietta* closed down in good time. One hopes earnestly that he is aware of the nature of his present phase – a kind of programme-music phase, of which the programme is 'See how knowing I am, how much wiser than my years' – and that he intends sooner or later to use his exceptional talent for the working out of a different story, the gist of which is 'You will like this'.

The patronizing, schoolmasterly tone of this notice was a factor in contributing to Britten's obsessive hatred of critics generally and his scorn for their views.

This attitude had its genesis in his reaction to a notice by Christian Darnton, assistant editor of the magazine *Music Lover*. Reviewing the de la Mare songs performed at the Ballet Club Theatre on 12 December 1932, Darnton described them as good but added that they were 'reminiscent in a quite peculiar degree of Walton's latest songs' (the *Three Songs* to words from Edith Sitwell's *Façade* first performed in London on 10 October 1932). Writing twenty years later,[9] Britten said that this notice had

> damned them entirely – as being obvious copies of Walton's... This is silly nonsense. The Walton songs are brilliant and sophisticated in the extreme – mine could scarcely have been more childlike and naïve, with not a trace of parody throughout. It is easy to imagine the damping effect of this first notice on a young composer. I was furious and dismayed because I could see there was not a word of truth in it. I was also considerably discouraged.

In the same article he complained that, over the previous twenty years, 'my critics do not seem to have changed much. Of course, some have been more welcoming (about 50 per cent, at a guess), but practically all have been unobservant, if not actually inane... In every piece I have written, in spite of hard work, there are still passages where I have not quite solved problems. Not once have these passages been noticed, nor, of course, suggestions made as to how I could have improved them.' The question is begged of whether he would have welcomed lessons in composition from the critics. In any case, any young composer might have counted himself fortunate to be reviewed so favourably by so senior a critic as A.H. Fox Strangways, who, writing in *The Observer* about the first public performance of *A Boy Was Born*, referred to its 'endless invention and facility' as a mark of mastery, not of superficiality, and added: 'He rivets attention from the first note onwards: without knowing in the least what is coming, one feels instinctively that this is music it behoves one to listen to, and each successive moment strengthens that feeling.'

If Britten was wounded by that criticism, it could have been only from use of the word 'facility'. For too long it has been supposed that writing music came easily to Britten, that he could just dash a work on to paper, but composition was a painfully hard labour for him in his boyhood and youth.[10] In later years, although things still went wrong sometimes, he learned to think problems out in his head before committing music to paper, as Mozart and Schubert must surely have done, but the diaries he kept as a young man show how he wrote, rewrote, came to a full stop and started again, in such works as the *Frank Bridge Variations* and *A Boy Was Born*. Works with which he was dissatisfied he discarded ruthlessly. Concentration and acute self-criticism were his watchwords, as they are of all the great composers, for he found that writing music never got easier; and he resented the critic's power perhaps to damn or dismiss after one hearing (and possibly an inadequate performance) the travail of months or years.

4

Auden & Co.

In October and November 1934 Britten used his travel scholarship to go with his mother to Paris, Munich, Basle, Salzburg and, most important of all, Vienna. Berg was away, so the frustrated would-be pupil did not meet him, but friendship began with the conductor and writer Erwin Stein. While in Vienna, Britten began his *Suite*, op. 6, for violin and piano. On his return to London, he attended a Macnaghten-Lemare concert at the Wigmore Hall on 17 December at which three movements of the *Suite* were played by Henri Temianka and Betty Humby (who later became the second Lady Beecham) and the first public performance of *A Boy Was Born* was given. He added two movements to the *Suite* by June 1935[1] and during the year completed the twelve children's songs with piano, *Friday Afternoons*, op. 7, which he wrote for, and dedicated to, his brother Robert and the boys of Clive House preparatory school, Prestatyn, of which Robert Britten was headmaster.[2] Choir practice there was on Friday afternoons. In this year he also composed two short pieces for oboe and piano called *The Grasshopper* and *The Wasp*. These were dedicated to the oboist Sylvia Spencer, but were not publicly performed until after Britten's death.

True to the reply he had given at the Lowestoft tennis-party, Britten was determined to earn his living through composition. He now had a flat in north-west London, No. 559 Finchley Road, sharing it with Beth. The opportunity came in April 1935 to write music for the GPO Film Unit where the leading figure was the Scottish-born producer John Grierson (1898–1972), who gathered round him such talented film-makers as Paul Rotha and Basil Wright. An entry in Britten's diary for 27 April 1935 shows that he was first approached, at the suggestion of Edward Clark of the BBC, by the film director Alberto Cavalcanti, who offered him a commission for music for *The King's Stamp* documentary. 'I had to work quickly', Britten wrote later, 'I had to write scores for not more than six or seven players, and to make those instruments make all the effects that each film demanded. I also had to be ingenious and try to imitate, not necessarily by musical instruments but in the studio, the natural sounds of everyday life.'[3] There could not have been a better apprenticeship for the future composer of chamber opera. On 4 July 1935, Britten first met Wystan Hugh Auden, the poet, who was then teaching at a preparatory school at Colwall, near Malvern. They liked each other, and a further bond was that Auden, who was six years older than Britten, had been at Gresham's. 'Auden was a powerful, revolutionary person', Britten recalled later.[4] 'He was very much anti-bourgeois, and that appealed.' He stimulated Britten's interest in poetry, particularly that by Donne and Rimbaud. Auden and the artist William Coldstream were also working with the GPO Film Unit. In 1935 Britten wrote music for sixteen short documentary films, including *C.T.O., Conquering Space, The Savings Bank* and *The King's Stamp*. Before joining the unit's permanent staff at £5 a week in the following March, he had collaborated with Auden in two celebrated short films, *Coal Face* and *Night Mail*, the latter showing how the mail was sorted on the night train from London to Edinburgh. Auden's poem is brilliant and Britten's music ingenious. At one point for a train sequence in *Coal Face* he invented a *musique concrète* effect well ahead of its day: wishing to reproduce the sound of a train going through a tunnel and coming nearer, he recorded a cymbal clash and reversed the soundtrack so that the fading vibrations became louder. He also used a combination of sand-paper and wind machine to imitate a train-noise. Playing the percussion parts in these film sessions was James Blades, who was later to act as Britten's consultant for many of his percussion parts. He remembered Britten as a 'slim, shy young man' but that every member of the orchestra 'found plenty to keep them busy and interested in young B.B.'s score'.[5] In 1936 Britten and Auden collaborated again in *The Way to the Sea* for Strand Films.

Through his new associates, Britten was drawn to the edge of a circle of avant-garde writers and artists, mostly of left-wing views, some of them Communists, all of them disillusioned by unemployment and the British Government's attitude to the dictators. The 1930s, as the poet Stephen Spender has said, was the last period in which the individual believed he had a chance to influence events. Spender also admitted that to his and his friends' identification with the working-class and Communism at that time, there was a homosexual side. Auden and his friend Christopher Isherwood were homosexual, so was Britten. In recent years, since homosexuality ceased to be a criminal offence between consenting adults, several men, notably Isherwood, have written openly of their promiscuous homosexuality. Britten never wrote or spoke a word about his private life in this way or any other respect; he was a very private person and kept his intimate life to himself. One respects this; but the fact of his homosexuality cannot be evaded. It is also difficult to resist the conclusion that the British critical establishment, with its perennial puritanical leanings, made Britten's homosexuality the scapegoat for all they could not admire in his music.

One of the Left-wing sproutings to which Auden's circle contributed was the Group Theatre. The chief producer was Rupert Doone (1903–66), a former dancer in Diaghilev's company, and Britten became musical director and resident composer. Among the scenic designers was John Piper, whom Britten had first met at a concert in 1932. Britten composed incidental music for productions of *Timon of Athens* (1935), the *Agamemnon* of Aeschylus in a translation by Louis Mac-Neice (1936), *Out of the Picture* (MacNeice, 1937), *The Ascent of F.6* (Auden and Isherwood, 1937), and *On the Frontier* (Auden and Isherwood, 1938). Of these, the best-known is perhaps *The Ascent of F.6*. After the first night, 26 February 1937, Britten wrote: 'After the show we all have a good party at the theatre & then feeling very cheerful we all sing (all cast & about 20 audience) my blues as well as going thro' most of the music of the play! Then I play & play & play, while the whole cast dances & sings & fools, & gets generally wild.'[6] This 'blues', to Auden's lines 'Stop all the clocks', was written in June of that year for Hedli Anderson, a member of the original cast (who later married MacNeice) – the first of several cabaret songs composed with this singer in mind. In 1936 Britten also wrote incidental music for a Left Theatre production of *Stay Down Miner* by Montagu Slater, who eight years later was to write the libretto of *Peter Grimes*.

It is becoming increasingly difficult at this remove to re-enter the world of the 1930s, in which the young and generally Left-wing artists regarded it as part of their 'social commitment' to become involved, both in their life and in their work, in the political events of the period. Thereby, in most cases, they set up difficult tensions and frictions for themselves in having to reconcile the public side of their art with their private inclinations, a dichotomy which affected Britten for the rest of his life. In 1936 Auden, brilliant and intellectually arrogant, was like a comet streaking across the impressionable Britten's sky. Examining himself in his diary at the start of 1936, Britten, while noting that he was 'having a lot of success but not a staggering amount of per-formances', wrote of his 'bad inferiority complex in company of brains like Basil Wright, Wystan Auden and William Coldstream.'[7]

Britten did not become as politically committed as some of his friends, because he was too involved with music. For all that, he read

Karl Marx during 1936 – 'hard going, though edifying'. But there can be no doubt that his sympathies were most deeply aroused by anything connected with pacifism. 'I disbelieve profoundly in power and violence',[8] he said in 1961. In 1936 he wrote the music for a three-minute film, *Peace of Britain*, directed by Paul Rotha for Strand Films. The British Board of Film Censors withheld its certificate for a time, on flimsy grounds. The film took no political line except that it was better for nations to negotiate than to fight. 'The fuss caused ... is colossal', Britten wrote in his diary. 'Never has a film had such good publicity.'[9] But the most significant event for Britten in 1936 was his signing on 3 January of an exclusive contract with the publishers Boosey and Hawkes. This was through the enterprise of Ralph Hawkes (1898–1950), chairman of the firm and a considerable talent-spotter, and it gave Britten a valuable measure of financial security in addition to a ready outlet for his music such as Walton enjoyed with the Oxford University Press.

In February of this year he worked, again with considerable struggles, on a revision of the three movements from the suite for string quartet *Go play, boy, play* which had been performed over two years earlier. They were performed on 25 February by the Stratton Quartet and were, according to Britten's diary,[10] received with sniggers and in a 'pretty cold silence'. Moreover they provoked a 'stinker' of a notice from J.A. Westrup in *The Daily Telegraph*.

On 6 March 1936, in a broadcast recital, Brosa and Britten gave the first complete performance of the *Suite*, op. 6, and Britten accompanied the Swiss-born soprano Sophie Wyss in songs by Mahler and Walton and his own *The Birds* – so another important name enters the story. Miss Wyss had been told of Britten's talent by the South African pianist Adolph Hallis. She and her husband invited him to lunch with them at the Café Royal. Britten had already heard her sing Milhaud's cantata *Pan et Syrinx* at a London concert to which he had gone with Constant Lambert, and this had given him new ideas about use of the high voice. He asked her, at their first meeting, if she would sing the work he was writing for the Norwich Festival (*Our Hunting Fathers*). 'Benjamin Britten seemed as if he were from the Olympian land of *Pan et Syrinx*', Miss Wyss said over forty years later.[11] 'He never seemed to need to learn anything. He knew it all by instinct. He played piano accompaniments with the ease and grace of someone who had given a lifetime to the piano. He knew what extra little effects could be conjured from each instrument.' The *Suite* was chosen for the I.S.C.M. festival at Barcelona, where Brosa and Britten played it on 21 April, its first concert performance. It was on this trip that Britten began his friendship with another composer, ten years older than he, Lennox Berkeley, who had also been at Gresham's. At the festival he heard the first performance of Berg's Violin Concerto on 19 April. Three months later the Spanish Civil War began. Adolph Hallis ran a series of concerts and for one of them, on 15 December 1936, he commissioned from Britten a set of variations for oboe and piano, *Temporal Variations*, which were completed three days before the event. Perhaps this led to an unsatisfactory performance, for Britten was not happy about the work, withdrew it and presumably forgot it. Its revival has shown it to be one of the strongest of his works of this period.

Another fruitful if erratic friendship, with the poet and playwright Ronald Duncan, had begun in 1935. Britten had written a march for brass and percussion, *Russian Funeral*, which Alan Bush conducted at the Westminster Theatre on 8 March 1936. His first collaboration with Duncan was in 1937 on a *Pacifist March*, for the Peace Pledge Union, the pacifist organization founded by the Rev. Dick Sheppard, vicar of St Martin-in-the-Fields. Other examples of what Britten called his 'useful' music in 1937 were in several GPO films, including *Calendar of the Year* and *The Line to the Tschierva Hut*; he wrote the music for his only feature film, the murder mystery *Love From a Stranger* (directed by Frank Vosper, with Basil Rathbone, and important in this context because the score was conducted by Boyd Neel), and he wrote incidental music for two BBC feature productions, *The Company of Heaven* and *King Arthur*, the latter produced on St George's Day 1937 by D.G. Bridson. Britten's setting of an Emily Brontë poem in *The Company of Heaven* was almost certainly the first music he composed especially for the voice of the tenor soloist Peter Pears.

The principal composition of this period, however, was the symphonic cycle for voice and orchestra, *Our Hunting Fathers*, to a text devised by Auden. Britten and Auden first discussed collaborating on a song-cycle 'about animals' on 2 January 1936. Some of the text was compiled by March and on the 23rd of that month Britten showed it to Frank Bridge. 'He is impressed,' Britten wrote in his diary. 'Also find he is very sympathetic towards my socialistic inclinations, in fact we are in complete agreement over all – except Mahler! – though he admits he is a great thinker.'[12] In their choice of text, about the relationship of man to animals, Auden and Britten not only satirized the 'huntin', shootin', fishin'' segment of English society but indulged in sharp political comment through the symbolism implicit in the song 'Rats away!' The plague of rats was all around Britten as he composed this work – Italy reducing Abyssinia to ruins, the Fascists rehearsing in Spain for the Second World War. Britten began composition of the cycle on 13 May 1936. As usual, he found that composition did not come easily. His diary tells a rueful tale of frustrations with the 'Rats away' movement and of 'getting stuck' in the middle. But the whole work was completed on 23 July while he was on a working holiday at Crantock, Cornwall, living in a chalet in the grounds of the house of Ethel Nettleship, sister-in-law of Augustus John, where he was joined by Lennox Berkeley. Sophie Wyss travelled down to see the finished score and sing it through. In the radio talk already quoted, she told how they would work together, Britten urging her on 'to do the almost impossible, then he would go out in the garden and play French cricket with my ten-years-old son. Finally we would all dine together and he would talk with bitter humour about the way the world was drifting to war.'

On the day he finished the score, Britten recorded in his diary that it was 'Rather a beastly day – spoilt by Spanish news. There has been a lot more fighting & the Government doesn't seem entirely on top – there seems to be a lot of dirty work going on – rich people outside helping those bloody fascists. I actually finish the score of H.F. working till 11.30 at night – owing to these disturbances I don't work well & I'm very doubtful about the end'.[13] Next day in spite of more bad news, he confesses to being 'exhilarated at having finished Hunting Fathers. Spend day numbering pages, doing titles, index, cueing, general expression tempo marks etc. – which is good fun, especially as I am at the moment thrilled with the work.'[14]

Our Hunting Fathers was first performed at the Norwich Festival on 25 September 1936, with Britten conducting the London Philharmonic Orchestra, in the same programme (but after a ninety-minute interval) as the first performance of Vaughan Williams's Skelton choral suite *Five Tudor Portraits*. The Norwich audience had a bad day. Vaughan Williams's settings of what were then considered to be the bawdy poems of Skelton caused the elderly Countess of Albemarle to turn purple in the face and walk out, loudly exclaiming 'Disgusting', while the text of Britten's work contained a dance of death indicting those – many of them among the Norfolk gentry – who killed animals for pleasure. Sophie Wyss, over twenty years later,[15] remembered that 'the orchestra behaved like naughty schoolboys, not understanding Britten's musical idiom. Dr Vaughan Williams was at the rehearsal and reproved them and they pulled themselves together and gave a fair performance.'

Frank Bridge, who was at Norwich, did not like the way Britten's vocal writing had developed. 'But he was very sweet about *Our Hunting Fathers*', Britten said.[16] 'He didn't really like it, but he defended it. Later he gave me a long talking-to about the scoring, which he thought didn't work (he liked the approach to the individual instruments). He was severe on the last movement as being too edgy, and in the end I did change it.' Edwin Evans, writing in *The Musical Times* of October 1936, found the last movement 'extended out of proportion to the rest'. He described the work as 'clever almost to a fault ... teasing, irritating and enjoyable according to how you take it'. This at least was more sympathetic than *The Times*: 'His audience shares with him some sense of music or humour, or both, to which we are strangers... His earlier works have made their mark and perhaps this one will. Or, if it is a stage to be got through, we wish him safely and quickly through it.' Evidently the Olympian 'we' of *The Times* were not amused.

An influence on *Our Hunting Fathers* undetected by *The Times* was that of Shostakovich. A by-product of Britten's film-music activity was an invitation early in 1936 to write criticism of two concerts for the first issue of a magazine, *World Film News*. At the first, in February, Ansermet conducted Stravinsky's *Oedipus Rex* and in March Albert Coates conducted a concert performance of Shostakovich's opera *Lady Macbeth of the Mtsensk District*. The former Britten described in his diary[17] as 'tremendous... A most moving & exciting work of a real inspired genius.' Of *Lady Macbeth* he wrote: 'There is some terrific music in the entr'actes. But I will defend it through thick and thin against these charges of "lack of style"... There is a consistency of style & method throughout. The satire is biting and brilliant. It is never boring for a second – even in this form... The "eminent English Renaissance" composers sniggering in the stalls was typical. There is more music in a page of Macbeth than in the whole of their "elegant" output!'

Not many twenty-three-year-old English composers in 1936 were under the spell of Shostakovich and Mahler, but Britten's *Russian Funeral* march is impressive testimony of their fruitful influence on him. When Adrian Boult conducted the first London performance of *Our Hunting Fathers* on 30 April 1937, Britten wrote in his diary: 'They do my *Hunting Fathers* very creditably – I am awfully pleased with it too, I am afraid. Some things don't satisfy me at the moment – but it's my Op. 1 all right'.[18]

5

America

In 1937 Britten wrote three major works apart from his 'documentary' music. The year began badly, with the death of his mother on 31 January and with the departure in the same month of Auden to Spain to drive an ambulance. 'It is terribly sad and feel ghastly about it, tho' I feel it is perhaps the logical thing for him to do – being such a direct person. Anyhow it's phenomenally brave.'[1] Britten's attitude to the matter may be inferred from his earlier diary entry (1 December 1936): 'Wystan Auden arrives at teatime... It will be nice having him, if I can conquer this appalling inferiority complex that I always have when with vital brains like his. After dinner he tells me he's decided to go to Spain after Xmas & fight – I try to dissuade him, because what the Spanish Gov. might gain by his joining is nothing compared with the world's gain by his continuing to write; but no one can make W.H.A. alter his mind.'[2]

Britten's emotional void was filled two months later by the growth of friendship with a man he had met briefly in 1934 and who was to be his constant companion for the rest of his life and an artistic collaborator on an almost unparalleled scale. This was the tenor Peter Pears, born in 1910, and educated at Lancing College, Hertford College, Oxford, and the R.C.M. He was a pupil of Elena Gerhardt and from 1934 to 1937 was a member of the BBC Singers. Britten's mother was a dominating, powerful personality, determined that her younger son should be a great musician, the 'fourth B' after Bach, Beethoven and Brahms. Yet Britten told a friend in 1964 that he could remember nothing about her. This same friend significantly noted that Pears's singing voice was 'fantastically similar to that of Mrs Britten'.

In 1937 Pears was living in Charlotte Street, Soho. A friend of his was a *Times* journalist and violinist, Peter Burra, who had been at Lancing with him. Britten had met Burra in Barcelona in 1936 (*Mont Juic* is dedicated to his memory) and spent time with him and Pears after his mother's death. In April 1937 Burra was killed in an air crash near Reading and Britten helped Pears to sort through Burra's papers. 'And that', Pears said, 'was that'. He and Britten gave their first recital together (neither remembered where[3]) later in 1937. In May Boyd Neel, who had met Britten during the filming of *Love from a Stranger* and whose string orchestra, formed in 1933, was the first chamber ensemble of the day, invited him to compose a work for the orchestra's visit to the 1937 Salzburg Festival. Britten began the score on 6 June. Ten days later, Neel wrote,[4] the complete work was sketched out – a set of ten variations on a theme taken from Bridge's second *Idyll* for string quartet. 'In another four weeks it was fully scored for strings as it stands today, but for the addition of one bar.' The score is dated 12 July 1937 and is dedicated 'to F.B. A tribute with affection and admiration'. The first performance was on Radio Hilversum on 25 August. It was first played in public in Salzburg on 27 August – Pears but not Britten attended – and was a triumph. The work established Britten's international reputation, being played fifty times in less than two years in Europe and the United States. The first London performance was at the Wigmore Hall on 5 October 1937. The *Variations on a Theme of Frank Bridge* was the first major fruit of Britten's prentice years in documentary films. He could work hard and fast; he was thoroughly professional and adept in using limited resources; and he was able to absorb many and various influences and convert then into an individual style. This expertise and professionalism worried many English critics, such as J.A. Westrup, who wrote that the solving of technical problems appeared to occupy Britten 'to the exclusion of musical ideas'. Constant Lambert, on the other hand, while 'unmoved' by Britten's music, acclaimed him as early as January 1936 as 'the most outstanding talent of his generation and I would always go to hear any first performance of his'.

In the autumn of 1937 Britten bought The Old Mill at Snape, Suffolk. It had been converted from a windmill in 1933–4. There he completed the set of songs with piano, *On This Island*, to poems by Auden and dedicated to Christopher Isherwood. This was broadcast for the first time on 19 November 1937 by Sophie Wyss, accompanied by Britten. It, too, met with Bridge's disapproval in part. 'He got me to change the opening of "Let the florid music praise", the first song . . . Originally it began with a downward glissando on the piano. He hated that and said I was trying to make a side-drum or something non-tonal out of the instrument; on the piano, the gesture ought to be a musical one. So I rewrote it as the present downward D major arpeggio.'[5] Bridge, as ever, was a shrewd and knowing mentor. The poems Britten set were selected from Auden's *Look Stranger!*, published in 1936, which had greatly excited Britten. The complexity and novelty of the language and the brilliance of the verbal imagery were both challenge and obstruction, and Britten found particular difficulty with 'Let the florid music praise!' This had to be a new kind of English song and the contemporary models were of little use to Britten. Pears, writing in the Mitchell-Keller symposium in 1952, points out that most British composers of the 1930s were still dwelling creatively in Housman's Shropshire or Shakespeare's Arden.

At Snape too Britten completed a work begun during the Crantock holiday of 1936. This was *Mont Juic*, a suite of Catalan dances for orchestra written in collaboration with Lennox Berkeley. The first two movements were by Berkeley, the third and fourth by Britten. The first performance, a broadcast, was on 8 January 1938.

Britten left his London flat and settled fully in The Old Mill in April 1938. There he worked on his piano concerto, completing it on 26 July and playing it to the American composer Aaron Copland, who spent a weekend there. Copland was struck by the 'obvious flair for idiomatic piano writing' but had reservations about the musical substance, a shrewd judgment. Britten was soloist in the first performance at a Queen's Hall Promenade Concert conducted by Sir Henry Wood on 18 August. The movements were given in the programme as 1. *Allegro molto e con brio*, 2. *Allegretto, alla valse*, 3. *Recitative and Aria* and 4. *Allegro moderato, sempre alla marcia*, but Britten simplified them to 1. *Toccata*, 2. *Waltz*, 3. *Recitative and Aria*, 4. *March*. In 1945 he substituted an *Impromptu* for the third movement, 'using only material contemporary with the rest of the work (notably from incidental music to a BBC play *King Arthur*) and some of the figuration from the earlier movement'.[6] During the autumn and winter of 1938 Britten composed a short unaccompanied choral setting of a poem *Advance Democracy* by Randall Swingler (1909–67), a poet who was on the staff of the Communist *Daily Worker* (now *Morning Star*) and later became its literary editor. This formed part of the music for a film of the same title produced by the Realist Film Unit in 1938. He also wrote incidental music for J.B. Priestley's morality play *Johnson Over Jordan*, which opened in London in February 1939. Also to this time belongs music for two BBC productions, *Hadrian's Wall* (with Auden) and *The World of the Spirit*, a feature broadcast on 5 June 1938 for which Britten wrote an extensive choral and orchestral score. Trevor Harvey conducted the latter, with Sophie Wyss a soloist. Otherwise Britten's main preoccupation was with *Ballad of Heroes*, op. 14, for high voice, chorus and orchestra, to a text by Swingler and Auden. This was completed in March 1939 and performed in the Queen's Hall on 5 April at a festival of 'music for the people'. Constant Lambert conducted. The work honoured the Britons who had been killed fighting in the International Brigade in Spain. The Auden verses in the Scherzo are those which the poet had written in Britten's score before leaving for Spain; now they had an extra significance for Britten himself:

> Good-bye to the beautiful birds on the wall,
> It's good-bye, dear heart, good-bye to you all.

Never again was Britten to make such an overtly political statement in music.

The works of 1938–9 were composed against a background of intensifying international tension and economic depression. The Munich crisis of September 1938 was followed in the spring of 1939 by Hitler's annexation of Czechoslovakia. In Britain unemployment was rife; and so, among a certain brand of intellectuals, was discontent. In mid-January 1939 Auden and Isherwood left Britain for the United States with the firm intention of emigrating and becoming American citizens. Auden told MacNeice that in England then, 'the artist feels essentially lonely, twisted in dying roots, always in opposition to a group'. The homosexual, too, of course, and Auden's homosexuality must have been a major factor in his decision to 'find the complete anonymity' he needed in a foreign culture. He was also tired of his role as 'court poet to the Left'.

Britten decided to emulate his friend. He was 'a discouraged young composer – muddled, fed-up and looking for work, longing to be used'.[7] In one significant respect his disillusion differed from his friend's. Auden by 1939 had come round to the view that 'the political history of the world would have been the same if not a poem had been written, not a picture painted nor a bar of music composed'. Britten believed that the artist's duty was to create art in the hope, at any rate, that it might make a difference. At this time, though, it seemed that his native country, where he had no wish to be regarded as 'master of the Left's music', had little to offer him. The *Frank Bridge Variations* had shown him that he was better appreciated abroad: McNaught, in *The Musical Times* (November 1937), had paid glib compliments – 'virtuosity ... not a dull bar ... brilliant ingenuity of the scoring', but had blunted them by wishing that the music was as original as the 'strikingly original effects'. McNaught again, reviewing the piano concerto in *The Musical Times* (September 1938), had written that 'Mr Britten's cleverness, of which he has frequently been told, has got the better of him and led him into all sorts of errors, the worst of which are errors of taste... Mr Britten is exploiting a brilliant facility that ought to be kept in subservience.' The last work

Britten completed in England was his music for the BBC dramatization of T.H. White's Arthurian novel *The Sword in the Stone*. He was not present when it was recorded and left detailed instructions attached to the score.

Britten and Pears left England in May 1939, spent several weeks in Canada, became lovers in Grand Rapids in June and arrived in New York in late June. There, at Woodstock between 23 and 29 July, Britten wrote a work for piano, string quartet and string orchestra, *Young Apollo*, op. 16, for the Canadian Broadcasting Corporation. This was performed in Toronto in August and later withdrawn. (It was revived at the 1979 Aldeburgh Festival.) He also wrote his op. 17, choral settings of Gerard Manley Hopkins, but withdrew these before performance as below standard. A light-hearted product of the Canadian stay was the orchestral *Canadian Carnival* completed in December 1939 and broadcast by the BBC from Bristol on 6 June 1940, when most people's thoughts were on the fall of France. Britten also took with him the uncompleted score of some settings of Rimbaud dedicated to Sophie Wyss. Two of these songs – which eventually became *Les Illuminations* – were performed separately by Miss Wyss, first in Birmingham with Johann Hock and his string orchestra and again at the Proms on 17 August 1939 (the songs were 'Being Beauteous' and 'Marine', nos. 7 and 5 of the full cycle). Miss Wyss, in her 1977 broadcast talk, recalled how Britten first told her of his decision to set *Les Illuminations*: 'Coming back from a recital, Benjamin told me that he spent the weekend with W.H. Auden's parents, and he had read some most thrilling poems by Arthur Rimbaud and said "I must put them to music".'

On 21 August Britten and Pears attended the first New York Philharmonic performance of the *Frank Bridge Variations*. They were invited to Stanton Cottage, the home of Dr and Mrs William Mayer at Amityville, Long Island. Pears had met the Mayers eighteen months earlier when he toured America with the New English Singers. Dr Mayer, a psychiatrist, had left Munich for the United States in 1936. His wife Elizabeth was a devotee of the arts and made her home a meeting-place for many of the talented creative people living and working in the United States at this time. She was like a second mother to Britten, with unshakable faith in his genius and always trying to 'feed him up' because she thought he was frail. He was constantly ill in these years with streptococcal sore throats. (There was a remarkable parallel with Mahler's illness: in each case there was a medical history of a severe ailment – pneumonia or rheumatic fever – leading to heart-valve damage.) Mrs Mayer also knew how to cope with Britten's moods of black depression. He was homesick, and already by October 1939 was writing to friends in England saying that he would return home as soon as the war was over. Pears had planned to return to England at the end of August but the outbreak of war altered his plans, and Stanton Cottage became his and Britten's base. Driving to Amityville, Britten had been delighted to read the name 'Suffolk' on a signpost. One of the first works he completed in the New World was his Violin Concerto. This was finished at St Jovite, Quebec; at Amityville on 25 October he completed *Les Illuminations*, which had its first performance on 30 January 1940 in London from Sophie Wyss and the Boyd Neel Orchestra. Other performances followed, conducted by Reginald Goodall and Adrian Boult. Writing in the *New Statesman*, Edward Sackville-West redeemed much English critical writing about the young Britten: 'This is a truly remarkable composition and justifies the expectation of great things from Britten. I know of no modern composition by a British composer that has impressed me so favourably as this. What strikes one at once is his truly musical invention and its copiousness. Each piece is a gem perfectly finished and original in character.' Compare this with McNaught's response, in *The Musical Times*, to the first British performance of the Violin Concerto by Thomas Matthews and the London Philharmonic Orchestra conducted by Basil Cameron in the Queen's Hall on 6 April 1941: 'The concerto has all the marks of character and technique that win approval except one: it makes little direct appeal to one's sense of enjoyment. It illustrates what we mean nowadays by "composers' music", a term (curiously) of reproach that stands for too much preoccupation with originalities of craftsmanship. This is a game of which Britten is one of the cleverest of players ... All this wizardry goes a long way, but music goes further.' 'Clever', 'a game', these pejorative words are a *leitmotiv* in British criticism of Britten. Only 'facility' is missing from this choice example. The concerto had had its first performance over a year earlier, in New York on 28 March 1940, when it was enthusiastically received. Antonio Brosa, who had edited the solo part, was soloist with the Philharmonic-Symphony Orchestra of New York under its English conductor, John Barbirolli.

At the end of January 1940 Britten was the soloist in the first American performance of his Piano Concerto, in Chicago, conducted by Albert Goldberg. The work was well liked. At about this time he contracted a severe streptococcal infection which made him seriously ill in New York during February and continued to affect him for the rest of the year, but it did not affect his creative powers, which seemed to be stimulated by the friendliness of his welcome in America. During the summer he wrote the *Diversions*, op. 21, for Paul Wittgenstein, the Austrian pianist who lost his right hand in the First World War and had since then commissioned a series of works for the left hand and orchestra (from Ravel, Strauss and Prokofiev among others). This was the kind of problem which attracted Britten: 'in no place in the work', he said, 'did I attempt to imitate a two-handed piano technique but concentrated on exploiting and emphasizing the single line approach'.

He was also at work on a symphony, having been asked by the British Council if he would write a work for a festivity affecting 'the reigning dynasty of a foreign power'. Britten agreed provided that 'no form of musical jingoism' was required, for 1940 was not the time for such things. The foreign power was Japan, which was marking the 2,600th anniversary of the foundation of the Mikado's dynasty. Various other composers, including Strauss, had received commissions. Britten sketched his *Sinfonia da Requiem* and the Japanese approved the outline. But six months after the completed score had been sent to Tokyo, Britten received an outraged protest from the Japanese that the Christian dogma underlying the work – the three movements of which were entitled *Lacrymosa*, *Dies Irae* and *Requiem aeternam* – was an insult to the Mikado and the work was rejected. He felt free to arrange a performance not contingent on any Japanese rights in the work. A more fruitful contact with oriental customs had come about for Britten in the summer of 1939 when, at Stanton Cottage, he met the Canadian composer Colin McPhee, an authority on Balinese music. McPhee had transcribed some Balinese ceremonial music for two pianos which he and Britten recorded. The seed of interest planted then was to flower years later in *The Prince of the Pagodas* and *Curlew River*.

In August 1940 Britten and Pears spent some time in Maine, where the *Diversions* was finished, and went on to Williamsburg, Massachusetts. Auden was there and he and Britten worked on or planned several projects: for an American folk-opera to be called *Paul Bunyan* (the mythical lumberman of the Pioneer period), a *Hymn to St Cecilia*, and two songs for a monologue, *The Dark Valley*, which Auden had written for the actress Dame May Whitty. *Paul Bunyan* arose from a suggestion by Britten's American publisher that he and Auden should write something suitable for performance by an American high school. Returning to Amityville in October, Britten completed the first of his works specifically composed for Peter Pears's voice, the *Seven Sonnets of Michelangelo*, op. 22; this received a private performance at the Mayers' house. The following month he composed the *Introduction and Rondo alla Burlesca* for two pianos for the English piano duo, Ethel Bartlett and her husband Rae Robertson, who lived in the United States. They had drawn Britten's music to the attention of their old friend Barbirolli (Ethel Bartlett had begun her career as Barbirolli's partner in cello recitals) and this had led to the first performance of the Violin Concerto at the New York Philharmonic and was to lead to the first performance of the *Sinfonia da Requiem* under Barbirolli in New York on 29 March 1941. These two performances were important in giving prominence to Britten's progress and Barbirolli in later years was hurt that the composer never acknowledged the help he had been given at this point of his career.

Returning to New York in November 1940, Britten and Pears joined the household at 7 Middagh Street, Brooklyn Heights. This house was owned by George Davis, a journalist friend of Auden and Isherwood, who later married Kurt Weill's widow Lotte Lenya. Its residents, the equivalent of an exotic artistic commune, were presided over by Auden. They included, at various times, Carson McCullers, Gypsy Rose Lee, Salvador Dali, Louis MacNeice, Chester Kallman, and the scenic designer Oliver Smith. Work progressed on *Paul Bunyan*; and Britten also became involved with New York's ballet scene through his friendship with Lincoln Kirstein, director of American Ballet, whom he had met in Williamsburg. In 1936 and 1938 he had adapted and orchestrated several pieces by Rossini for the GPO Film Unit. These became the suite *Soirées Musicales* which had been used by Antony Tudor in 1938 for the ballet *Soirée Musicale*. Now, for Kirstein, Britten arranged another Rossini suite, *Matinées Musicales*, which was added to the earlier work. The result was the ballet *Divertimento*, with choreography by Balanchine. For another company Britten made a new orchestration of *Les Sylphides* in 1940.

Amid all this activity, Britten was increasingly aware that, even though he was a conscientious objector, there might be ways in which he could contribute to the war effort in his native land, apart from the recitals in aid of British War Relief which he and Pears gave. He had done nothing about American citizenship, even though Auden was by now naturalized, and items of news from home added to his mental struggle. On 10 January 1941, Frank Bridge died. Beth was living at The Old Mill while her husband was on active service and two of her three children were born there. Partly to keep some contact with the name Suffolk, Britten agreed in 1941 to be conductor of the Suffolk Friends of Music Orchestra, a venture comprising professionals, amateurs, and students which gave concerts in the Long Island area, where

Pears also conducted a choir. But Britten's main preoccupation in the early part of 1941 was *Paul Bunyan*. This had become a 'choral operetta' in two acts and a prologue. It was given a preview for the League of Composers on 4 May 1941 before a week's run from 5 May in the Brander Matthews Hall of Columbia University, New York. Pears did not sing in this work but helped in its copying. Britten had found that American composers tended to be too nationalist in their rejection of European tradition. 'Why not make the best of both worlds?' he wrote in *The New York Times* in 1940. 'With lessons learned from Europe, let an American style develop naturally ... which it will surely do, if the composer ... writes the best music he can for every occasion that offers itself.' And here he was, writing a work on an American folklore subject which an American critic, thirty-five years later when *Bunyan* was revived, was to describe as the most American opera yet written. But this was emphatically not the general opinion in 1941. 'Bewildering and irritating', said *Time*. 'Didn't jell', said *The New Yorker*. In the *Herald Tribune*, Virgil Thomson described Auden's contribution as a 'flop' and Britten's music as 'eclectic though not without savour ... modernistic and safe'. He made the astute diagnosis, as early as 1941, that Britten's model was Shostakovich. 'Mr Britten's work in *Paul Bunyan* is sort of witty at its best. Otherwise it is undistinguished.' On the other hand, Olin Downes in *The New York Times* predicted that Britten had shown that 'opera written for a small stage ... is not only a possibility but a development nearly upon us'.

For all the apparent confidence he showed in the art of composition, Britten suffered always from periods of unsureness when he felt he had dried up and was 'no good'. But the withdrawal of *Paul Bunyan* after its relative failure in 1941 was not the result of the hostile criticism it received. Both Auden and Britten were self-critical and felt that the operetta did not entirely 'work properly'. They began to revise it but both were busy with other projects and within a year Britten returned to England. Auden died in 1973 and it was not until 1974, when convalescing after a severe operation, that Britten eventually took up *Paul Bunyan* again, revised it, gave it the opus number 17 which had belonged to the withdrawn Hopkins settings, and released it for performance and publication.

At some point after the *Paul Bunyan* performance Britten and Pears decided that they had had enough of the kind of life afforded in Middagh Street. It was, to quote Donald Mitchell, 'altogether too Bohemian for the two English musicians, Puritans both'.[8] They went to Escondido, California, to stay with Ethel Bartlett and Rae Robertson. There and at Amityville, between July and October, Britten wrote two more two-piano works for them, the *Mazurka elegiaca*, in memory of Paderewski, and the *Scottish Ballad*, with orchestra. The former was first played, with its earlier companion piece in op. 23, the *Introduction and Rondo alla Burlesca*, by Bartlett and Robertson at a New York recital in the winter. They also gave the first performance of the *Scottish Ballad* on 28 November in Cincinnati, where the conductor was an Englishman, Eugène Goossens. During this summer, too, Britten composed the String Quartet No. 1, op. 25, which received its first performance in the Library of Congress, Washington D.C., on 30 October from the Coolidge Quartet. This had been commissioned by Elizabeth Sprague Coolidge, one of America's most beneficent musical patrons, and won for Britten that year's Elizabeth Sprague Coolidge Medal of the Library of Congress for services to chamber music.

While in California Britten picked up a back number of the BBC periodical *The Listener*, dated 29 May 1941. It contained the script of a broadcast talk by E.M. Forster about the poetry of the East Anglian George Crabbe (1755–1832) in which Forster described Crabbe's birthplace, Aldeburgh: 'A bleak little place; not beautiful... What a wallop the sea makes as it pounds at the shingle!... [Crabbe's] poems ... are easy to read. They are stories in rhymed couplets, and their subject is local scenes or people... A famous one is *Peter Grimes*: he was a savage fisherman who murdered his apprentices and was haunted by their ghosts; there was an actual original for Grimes...' The article profoundly affected the increasingly homesick Britten. Pears went into a bookshop and found a copy of Crabbe's poetry, which Britten had not known. Britten read *The Borough* and particularly the section about the fisherman Peter Grimes. 'I suddenly realised where I belonged and what I lacked', he said twenty-three years later.[9] 'I had become without roots.' He decided to return to England, but at that point in the war, with the Battle of the Atlantic approaching its height, it was next to impossible to obtain a passage.

The delay had happy consequences for Britten. He went to Boston for the performance there on 2 January 1942 of the *Sinfonia da Requiem* conducted by Serge Koussevitzky, who, impressed by the symphony's essentially dramatic nature, shrewdly asked him why he had not yet written a full-scale opera. Britten replied that he was thinking of making one out of Crabbe's *The Borough* but that the planning and composition of an opera 'demanded a freedom from other work which was an economic impossibility for most young composers'.[10] A few weeks later Koussevitzky told him he had arranged for the Koussevitzky Music Foundation to provide 1,000 dollars towards the opera (which he would like to be dedicated to the memory of his wife Natalie, who had died the previous year), and would produce it at the Berkshire Festival.

On 16 January Britten went to Philadelphia to hear Paul Wittgenstein give the first performance of *Diversions*, conducted by Eugene Ormandy. On 16 March he wrote in Mrs Mayer's visitors' book at Amityville 'The end of the week-end' (which had begun there on 21 August 1939), and that afternoon she drove him and Pears to the quay in New York harbour where they boarded the Swedish M.S. *Axel Johnson*. During the voyage Britten resumed work on the *Hymn to St Cecilia*, op. 27, another Auden setting, and also composed *A Ceremony of Carols*, op. 28. He arrived in Liverpool on 17 April 1942, having been away for a month short of three years.

It was symbolic that *Hymn to St Cecilia* should have been completed on the voyage home, for it was the end of the close collaboration with Auden which had lasted seven years and had yielded a substantial body of work: films, plays, radio features, two song-cycles, the *Ballad of Heroes*, and, perhaps the best of them all, *Paul Bunyan*, which began with modest aims and ended as a major operatic achievement. Yet, however little Britten recognized it at the time, it was in *Paul Bunyan* that the growing unsatisfactoriness of their artistic partnership came to a head. The verbal pyrotechnics of Auden's poetry had become increasingly difficult to set to music. Dazzled at first by Auden's extraordinary command of vocabulary, and as we have learned from his own words in his diary, conscious of a sense of inferiority to such brilliance, Britten was stimulated by the challenge of the texts Auden provided. Yet even in *On This Island* he had to struggle to translate Auden's imagery into music. By the time of *Paul Bunyan*, Auden's delight in conjuring tricks with words led him into the conceit of the 'Love Song':

> No animosity
> Only preciosity:
> Eyes' luminosity
> Ears' curiosity
> Nose's monstrosity
> Cheeks' adiposity
> And Life's verbosity
> All with velocity
>   Bear down on you.

In 1940–1, Britten devotedly set this to music, but when the operetta was revised in 1974 it was jettisoned, with other parts of the libretto which perhaps he regarded (and probably always had regarded) as

anti-musical. In an unpublished tribute to Britten on his fiftieth birthday, Auden in 1963 took the blame for the failure of *Paul Bunyan*,
saying: 'I knew nothing whatsoever about opera or what is required
of a librettist.' Auden's influence for good on the young and immature
Britten should never be under-estimated: he opened magic casements
for the composer. But as Britten matured he needed to disengage
himself from the coils of his friend's domineering personality. He came
to find Auden too dogmatic – intellectually 'bossy', as Donald Mitchell
has put it. To a man like Britten with a profound distrust of articulate
dexterity in conversation, it was not easy to shrug off some of Auden's
ideas as mere persiflage, not to be taken seriously. It was time, in
1942, for both men to develop as independent creative figures. Their
subsequent estrangement was a source of unhappiness to Auden, who
always expressed his admiration for Britten's music. In January 1942
he advised Britten on 'the dangers that beset you as a man and as an
artist', especially the choice between bohemianism and bourgeois
convention. 'Wherever you go you are and probably always will be
surrounded by people who adore you, nurse you, and praise everything
you do... You see, Bengy dear, you are always tempted to make
things too easy for yourself in this way ... by playing the lovable
talented little boy. If you are really to develop to your full stature,
you will have, I think, to suffer, and make others suffer, in ways which
are totally strange to you at present...'[12]

In his three years in America Britten's music had matured and
deepened. Already one could trace the pattern of his artistic creed,
expressed many years later, 'to be useful and to the living'. He believed
in 'occasional' music and, as he said in his Aspen Award speech,
'almost every piece I have ever written has been composed with a
certain occasion in mind, and usually for definite performers, and
certainly always *human* ones'.[11] The songs for his brother's schoolboys,
the *Te Deum* for a London church choir, the violin concerto for Brosa,
the piano concerto for himself, the settings for Sophie Wyss, the *Frank
Bridge Variations* for Boyd Neel, the *Diversions* for Wittgenstein, the
two-piano works for Ethel Bartlett and Rae Robertson, the *Michelangelo Sonnets* for Peter Pears – already he had been of considerable
use. There were sketches of a clarinet concerto for Benny Goodman,
which, alas, came to nothing. Now he was determined to put down
his roots.

6

The return

The picture of Ben Britten which those who saw him in 1942–3 retained as an unchanging image (until, with a shock in the late 1960s, we suddenly saw an ageing man) was of a boyish, wavy-haired youth, looking younger than his thirty years, with the figure of a tennis player or a centre-half, shy and diffident, serious, but with a half-smile playing round his mouth, neatly but casually dressed, and with lazy, slightly-closed eyes which looked as though they needed glasses. His eyelids were hooded, and if the hood came down that was the time to beware of raising subjects or making critical observations which might provoke a testy response. His manner appeared relaxed, but this concealed tensions. When he was composing, friends say, his expression changed to one of severe concentration, almost ruthless. Nobody then would interrupt him, and he would probably not have paid them any attention. But when scoring a work, he could carry on a conversation at the same time. He spoke in a pleasant deep baritone, without accent or affectation, and he sometimes still used schoolboy adjectives like 'ripping' and expletives like 'Cor'.

This was the composer who re-entered British musical life in the spring of 1942, a Britain battered by bombs at home and defeats abroad, but a Britain in which appreciation of the arts, and especially of music, was thriving as never before. This was a musical Britain still over a year away from the first performance of Vaughan Williams's Fifth Symphony but getting ready to celebrate his seventieth birthday in October, a musical Britain in which the unexpected alliance with Russia had stimulated the public appetite for an apparently limitless diet of Russian piano concertos, in which orchestras played in cinemas and factory canteens, Covent Garden was closed to opera, and Walton was regarded as the outstanding figure among the younger composers. The names of Britten and Tippett were known, but not yet widely.

The first necessity for Britten and Pears on their return was to appear before a conscientious objectors' tribunal. They were granted exemption from military service on condition that they gave recitals under the auspices of the Council for the Encouragement of Music and the Arts (founded in 1939 and the forerunner of the present Arts Council of Great Britain). This they did, performing in towns and villages throughout the country. The first major Britten event after his return was the first British performance of the *Sinfonia da Requiem* which Basil Cameron conducted at the Proms on 22 July 1942. McNaught, writing a week later in *The Listener*, at last felt that Britten had answered those critics like himself who wondered when the 'undergraduate cleverness' would be coupled 'with a graduate mind and purpose'. He found the 'flights of technique ... relevant to the mood and plan of the movement. It looks, then, as if Britten has found himself at last.' Three more first performances followed in the autumn. On 23 September, at the Wigmore Hall, Pears and Britten gave the first public performance of the *Seven Sonnets of Michelangelo* which Britten had composed two years earlier. '"Fine songs for singing"', wrote the critic (probably Frank Howes) of *The Times*, quoting Stevenson. 'Though they are big songs, they made a singularly direct appeal.' Writing a month later in *The Musical Times*, Ferruccio Bonavia, Italian by birth, found the poet's emotion enhanced by 'the unconventional but wholly attractive nature of the musical elements'. He recorded that the work was received enthusiastically. A second performance of the cycle was given on 22 October at one of the famous National Gallery lunchtime concerts which the pianist Myra Hess had founded as a major contribution to keeping up morale in wartime London. On 22 November, Britten's twenty-ninth birthday, the BBC Singers, conducted by Leslie Woodgate, showed the listening public for the first time the gentle and felicitous attractions of his latest choral piece, the *Hymn to St Cecilia*. The same happy inspiration and inventiveness are to be found in *A Ceremony of Carols*, for treble voices and harp, given its first performance at Norwich Castle on 5 December by the women's voices of T.B. Lawrence's Fleet Street Choir with Gwendolen Mason (harp). This had its first London performance at a National Gallery concert by the same artists on 21 December. On 28 April 1943, the Griller Quartet gave the first English performance of the first string quartet at the Wigmore Hall. The critic of *The Times* was slightly disconcerted by its 'sharply contrasted elements' but detected that Britten 'has begun to advance from his easy accomplishment into some new phase of development'. But Bonavia, in *The Musical Times* of June 1943, deplored that a composer of Britten's standing 'should be satisfied with the narrow outlook and range of this work ... Even Britten's slow movement bears the same stamp of restlessness and uneasiness as the others.'

None of the above works had been composed in Britain, but the feeling of being back where he belonged stimulated Britten's creative impulse and he was soon at work, inspired as always by fellow-musicians. In the summer of 1942 he met the horn-player Dennis Brain, then 21 years old. They became friends and Brain asked him for a work. So began the *Serenade*, op. 31, for tenor, horn and string orchestra which opens and closes with an evocative horn solo framing a highly imaginative selection of English poems about evening and darkness. This great work ('not important stuff, but quite pleasant,' Britten wrote) celebrates other friendships, that with Pears, of course, and with the dedicatee, Edward Sackville-West, poet and critic, with whom Britten collaborated in 1943 on a radio-drama, *The Rescue*, based on Homer's *Odyssey* and broadcast on 25 and 26 November of that year. The *Serenade* had its first performance in the Wigmore Hall, on 15 October, with Pears, Brain, and strings conducted by Walter Goehr. Britten paid tribute[1] to Brain's help in writing the work: 'He was always most cautious in advising any alterations. Passages which seemed impossible even for his prodigious gifts were practised over and over again before any modifications were suggested, such was his respect for a composer's ideas... For a period, it seemed that no one else would ever be able to play it adequately. But, as usually happens when there is a work to play and a master who can play it, others slowly develop the means of playing it too.' What must composer and executant have thought of the anonymous critic in *The Musical Times* who ruled out the prologue and epilogue as 'both unnecessary'? This writer spectacularly failed to spot a masterpiece: 'Were the composer unknown, one would hail it as a work of unusual promise.' It was 'an experiment that succeeds in parts'.

What was to be one of Britten's most touching and enchanting works, the festival cantata for chorus and organ, *Rejoice in the Lamb*, op. 30, arose from a commission from the Rev Walter Hussey, vicar of St Matthew's, Northampton, for a work to celebrate the fiftieth anniversary of the church's consecration. Mr Hussey had already shown enlightened patronage of the arts by commissioning a statue from Henry Moore and a mural by Graham Sutherland. Britten set passages from the poem 'Jubilate Agno' written by Christopher Smart (1722–71) when he was in a madhouse. It is a kind of Benedicite, its naively joyous simplicity and innocence finding an inspired response in Britten's music. Britten completed it in July 1943 and conducted the first performance in the church on 21 September. Nearly thirty-four years later, Walter Hussey, then Dean of Chichester, gave the address at the Westminster Abbey memorial service for Britten, and Peter Pears read some of the text of *Rejoice in the Lamb* during the service. A debt to another friendship was also paid on 23 June 1943, the tenth anniversary of the foundation of the Boyd Neel String Orchestra. The orchestra had 18 players, so Britten wrote a *Prelude and Fugue*, op. 29, for strings in 18 parts for the occasion. This is the point, too, at which another important friendship began. The composer Michael Tippett, eight years Britten's senior but a 'late developer', attended the first performance of the *Michelangelo Sonnets* and was overwhelmed. He was at this time director of music at Morley College and invited Pears to be soloist in a choral work, thereby also meeting Britten. Impressed by their intense musicality, he wrote his cantata *Boyhood's End* for them, the first work by another composer which their partnership inspired. They gave the first performance in June 1943. Tippett was also a conscientious objector and shortly after the performance was sentenced to three months in prison for failure to comply with a directive that he would better serve the war effort by working on a farm than by directing the music at Morley and organizing concerts. While he was in Wormwood Scrubs, Britten and Pears gave a concert there and he contrived to be on the platform with them – as assistant page-turner to John Amis! Later, Britten suggested some alterations in Tippett's oratorio *A Child of Our Time* and helped to promote its first performance in March 1944. Writing from prison to Evelyn Maude, Tippett described his affinity with Britten: 'Ben is v. near just because he is himself, I sense, so moved by my imprisonment'.

Meanwhile, a start had been made on the Crabbe-inspired opera which Koussevitzky had commissioned. While still in America, Britten had asked Christopher Isherwood to be his librettist, but this invitation was declined. So while they were waiting for a ship to take them home, Britten and Pears worked together on shaping something from Crabbe's *The Borough*, 'sketching out bits here and there'.[2] They decided that the central figure should be the fisherman Peter Grimes, but a different Grimes from Crabbe's. 'A central feeling for us', Britten said,[3] 'was that of the individual against the crowd, with ironic overtones for our own situation. As conscientious objectors we were out of it. We couldn't say we suffered physically, but naturally we experienced tremendous tension. I think it was partly this feeling which led us to make Grimes a character of vision and conflict, the tortured idealist he is, rather that the villain he was in Crabbe.' They had gone sufficiently far with the plot when they returned to England for Britten to be able to hand it over to his chosen librettist 'with clear ideas on how it was to run'. The librettist was Montagu Slater, with whom he had first worked in 1936 and for whose two one-act puppet plays, *The Seven Ages of Man* and *Spain*, he had composed incidental music in

1938. Work on the libretto lasted from about June 1942 to the end of 1943 and did not always run smoothly. Slater was working in the films unit of the Ministry of Information and could not devote all his time to the libretto. He proved to be a slow worker, not readily responsive to Britten's wishes. Eric Crozier, at that time stage director at Sadler's Wells, was called in as adviser on the technicalities involved in opera composing – on what was and what was not possible on the stage. Britten and he became friends and met each week to discuss the progress of the libretto, which Crozier candidly criticized. They then met Slater to try to persuade him to make alterations, especially of those lines which were written in a sub-Auden-ish style unsuitable to the opera house. Slater, reserved, pipe-smoking, small, with a deep sympathy for the underdog, would listen and sit silent.

Composition of the music began in January 1944. Most of it was written in The Old Mill at Snape, where Beth and her children were still living. It was completed in February 1945. He later told the author Ronald Blythe that 'however tidy he left his workroom in the evening, the next morning would find it pale and matt with dust. Flour from long-ago grindings filtered from the beams and walls in the darkness and powdered his furniture and score.'[4] Throughout those months Britten carried the sketches around with him in a large music case, being unwilling to let them out of his sight in case they were destroyed in a flying-bomb raid when he was in London. At Snape he worked to a strict routine (as he always did): from breakfast to 1 or 2 p.m. In the afternoon he walked down by the river Alde and round the Maltings, a collection of nineteenth-century industrial buildings by then showing signs of decline, and worked again from teatime until dinner. He never worked at night because he distrusted work done then, feeling that an artist might pass things he would not allow in the morning. (He would, on the other hand, orchestrate after dinner, regarding this as, in a sense, non-creative.) On one of his afternoon walks he confided to Crozier how much he missed having any musical tradition in which he could work – the cry of the English composer down the years, it seems. (Holst to Vaughan Williams in 1903: 'It is all that makes up an "atmosphere" that we lack in England.')

It is hardly surprising that, preoccupied with *Peter Grimes*, Britten wrote only three other very short works during 1944. Two Auden settings for unaccompanied chorus, *A Shepherd's Carol* and *Chorale* (later withdrawn), were included in a BBC feature *A Poet's Christmas*. The third was a *Festival Te Deum*, composed in November for the centenary of St Mark's Church, Swindon, where it was sung for the first time on 24 April 1945. Just before beginning *Peter Grimes*, Britten wrote *The Ballad of Little Musgrave and Lady Barnard* for male voices and piano. He had heard from Lieutenant Richard Wood, a prisoner-of-war friend in Oflag VIIb at Eichstätt, Germany, of the enthusiasm with which he and his fellow-prisoners had listened to the H.M.V. recording by Britten and Pears of the *Michelangelo Sonnets* (their first recording). Lieutenant Wood, whose sister Anne had sung with Pears in the BBC Singers, added that they were planning a musical festival, so Britten sent them the manuscript of *Musgrave*, a splendid and dramatic work. He completed it at Snape on 13 December 1943 and the prisoners gave the first performance towards the end of February 1944, repeating it three more times. Perhaps the only other work to have been rehearsed and performed (and composed) in comparable circumstances is Messiaen's *Quatuor pour la fin du temps* in Stalag VIIIa in Silesia in January 1941.

7

The Borough

'It is encouraging that you too sense that "something" in the air which heralds a renaissance. I feel terrifically conscious of it',[1] Britten wrote in a letter in 1943. It sometimes seems as if British music since 1880 has been in a continuous state of renaissance, according to which generation of composers is speaking. But anyone who lived through 1943–4 will understand what Britten meant. There was still a long way to go, but it was obvious that the Allies were bound to win the war. Hopes of a brave new world, or at least a different new world, filled the minds of servicemen and civilians alike. In the arts, the war had stimulated a public appetite such as had never existed before. The Olivier-Richardson-Thorndike seasons of plays in the West End, the ballet with Fonteyn and Helpmann, the re-creation of the Hallé by Barbirolli, the National Gallery concerts, the employment of composers such as Walton and Vaughan Williams for film music – these were but a few of the outward signs of this appetite. Another was the gallant survival, amid tremendous wartime difficulties, of the Sadler's Wells Opera Company. After spending most of its time in the provinces when Sadler's Wells Theatre was closed, the company had in 1942 returned to London under the artistic directorship of the soprano Joan Cross. On his return from America Peter Pears joined it and soon became one of its principal tenors. Interviewed at the end of 1943 by the music magazine *Tempo*[2] (house journal of Boosey and Hawkes), Britten expressed his passionate interest in the establishment of a 'successful permanent national opera'. It had to be 'vital and contemporary' and to 'depend less on imported "stars" than on a first-rate, young and fresh, permanent company. Sadler's Wells have made a good beginning.'

While he was composing *Peter Grimes*, Britten saw several of the Sadler's Wells productions, including *La Traviata*, *Così fan tutte*, *Rigoletto*, *La Bohème*, and *The Bartered Bride*. Joan Cross had scarcely heard of him before 1942, but was introduced to him by Pears and eventually went to stay at Snape where she learned about the projected opera. In 1944, while the company was in Liverpool, Britten played the

Prologue and Act I to her and to Tyrone Guthrie, general administrator, Lawrance Collingwood, musical director and chief conductor, and Crozier. They were all strongly impressed and decided that this was the work with which to re-open Sadler's Wells Theatre in Rosebery Avenue when the war was over. Guthrie, though not a musician, sensed the work's drama (telling Crozier that, if he were producing it, the brightest colour on the stage would be 'a shade of pale black') and was as enthusiastic as his colleagues. (There was no possibility of the opera having its *première* in America because the Berkshire Festival had been indefinitely postponed because of transport difficulties.) Miss Cross approached Boosey and Hawkes, who had bought an interest in the Royal Opera House, Covent Garden, and possibly had *Grimes* in mind for its re-opening. But, under pressure from Britten, they ceded it to Sadler's Wells.

Rehearsals began while the company was on tour and, distracted by wartime travel and the presentation of eight performances a week of other operas, they found the idiom of the new work difficult and challenging. Guthrie realized that it was an occasion for young men and appointed Crozier as producer and Reginald Goodall as conductor, though Collingwood took some rehearsals. (Goodall was later to be neglected by opera companies until his re-emergence in the 1960s as one of the most admired of Wagnerians.) They were convinced that *Grimes* was a major achievement, but this was by no means the general opinion. The singer originally cast and rehearsed for Balstrode, for example, gave up the part because he 'could not be bothered to learn such outlandish stuff'. Crozier has written[3] that the campaign against *Grimes* began in February 1945 when 'a group of principal singers came together to press their grievances against the director and management...' They complained bitterly because the composer, leading tenor and producer of *Grimes* were conscientious objectors and they declared that it 'was a waste of time and money to stage such "a piece of cacophony"'. Rehearsals, therefore, were conducted in an atmosphere of tension and conspiracy. Six days before the first performance a group of leading singers demanded that the governors should appoint them as an executive committee in charge of the company. They complained about the amount of publicity accorded to Britten and his opera. As Scott Goddard wrote at the time:

There had been much publicity over this production, valuable for the event itself, though it did no good to the work. Generous enthusiasm was immediately countered by spiteful antagonism, each answering each before the opera had even been seen. It became impossible to mention the work without discussion degenerating into argument. Nothing could be discovered of its artistic quality, so heavy was the cloud of sociological, political, even ethical bickering surrounding *Peter Grimes*. It may at least be granted that no English opera has ever had such a press.[4]

Nevertheless there were no delays and, thirty days after the end of the war in Europe, *Peter Grimes* had its first performance on 7 June 1945, as historic a day in the annals of English music as 19 June 1899, when Elgar's *Enigma Variations* was first played. Before the curtain rose, Guthrie visited Joan Cross in her dressing-room and said: 'Whatever happens, we were quite right to do this piece'. The sets and costumes were by Kenneth Green, a friend of Britten and Pears, who had painted portraits of them in 1943. The cast was headed by Pears as Grimes and Joan Cross as Ellen Orford, with such other singers as Edith Coates, Roderick Jones and Owen Brannigan. 'Expectations ran high and were not disappointed', *The Times* critic wrote in a remarkable notice worthy of extensive quotation:

> It is a good omen for English opera that this first-fruit of peace should declare decisively that opera on the grand scale and in the grand manner can still be written . . . *Peter Grimes*, making one or two feints at an episodic method, proceeds by sharp turns of the dramatic screw to situations of great power . . . intensified by orchestral music of diabolic cunning . . . The chief character is Public Opinion and the protagonist who plays it is the chorus. Everything, from the intonation of the General Confession to crowd scenes unparalleled outside the Russian operas . . . is provided in profusion by the composer. The name-part requires the interpretation of schizophrenia which makes Purcell's 'Mad Bess' look simple. Lyrical moments are rarer, but they are there for tenor and soprano, as is traditional and right . . . The opera is filled to the brim with . . . effortless originality and spills over with interest . . . [Goodall's] piloting of chorus and orchestra through a complex score was the chief factor in the opera's successful performance . . .

It was an exciting occasion; but, as John Amis recalled[5] over thirty years later, 'the orchestra had never been asked to play such things before' and the first and subsequent performances of the Passacaglia and other Interludes showed that 'they couldn't cope'. The chorus, who had been restive at rehearsals, struggled in places too, Mr Amis remembered, 'but the power and the glory of the work came across, fresh and invigorating like the storm that blew in when the pub door was opened'. The opera's impact, said Eric Walter White,[6] was such that 'all who were present realized that *Peter Grimes*, as well as being a masterpiece of its kind, marked the beginning of an operatic career of great promise and perhaps also the dawn of a new period when English opera would flourish in its own right'. Not quite all. Mr

McNaught was there for the *Manchester Guardian*. He gave Britten his due for an orchestral score 'full of vivid suggestion and action, sometimes rising to a kind of white-hot poetry', but doubted if the work was really operatic, and this was the fault of the libretto. He thought *Peter Grimes* failed 'in the important matter of getting itself across' but the company 'did nearly everything that could be done to help the work over its obstacles'. The Cambridge professor of music, E.J. Dent, is reported to have said that the music reminded him of 'the noise of a motor bike starting up' – an echo there, of course, of the schism within the company. After the last of the scheduled *Grimes* performances, when a wildly cheering audience was acclaiming cast and composer, the management ordered the sudden lowering of the iron safety curtain, presumably because it was feared that the excitement might lead to a demonstration.

McNaught and Dent were in a minority. Audiences and musicians flocked to Sadler's Wells to hear *Peter Grimes*. Its fame spread across the world. Britten was acclaimed as the first natural English composer of opera to arise since Purcell had written *Dido and Aeneas*. Within three years his opera was produced in Stockholm, Zürich, Basle, Tanglewood (conducted by the young Leonard Bernstein), Hamburg, Berlin (conducted by Robert Heger), Milan (conducted by Serafin), New York, and in several other opera houses, including Covent Garden on 6 November 1947, conducted by Karl Rankl. No one was more surprised by this success than Britten. 'It never occurred to me that the opera would work', he said a generation later.[7] '... I had no confidence about *Grimes*. Besides, at that time such an offbeat story was hardly thought right for an opera. This, and the quarrels going on in the company, were not very good auguries. At the dress rehearsal I thought the whole thing would be a disaster... Looking back, I think it broke the ice for British opera.'

How was the ice broken? This is not the place to go into the imbroglio of the re-opening of Covent Garden, except to note that the lease of the Royal Opera House was taken in 1945 by Boosey and Hawkes, Britten's publishers. The new administrator there was David Webster, a friend of Britten, and he set out to establish a national opera company based on singers of international stature. But this company did not give its first performance until January 1947 and meanwhile Britten had committed himself to a smaller form of opera production, knowing that the costs of mounting operas by young English composers at an international theatre such as Covent Garden would be prohibitive. Notwithstanding the success of *Peter Grimes*, which was a defeat for them, the management of Sadler's Wells were divided about the future. In March 1946, a change of policy occurred which led to the resignations of Crozier, Joan Cross and Pears, those 'who believed in the Wells as a progressive centre for British opera', to quote Crozier again. *Peter Grimes* was withdrawn from the company's repertory. This breakaway group determined to form a company, in Britten's words, 'dedicated to the creation of new works, performed with the least possible expense and capable of attracting new audiences by being toured all over the country'. Plans to form this group were already being made in the winter of 1945. Eric Crozier approached Rudolf Bing, general manager of the Glyndebourne Festival, in the November and a month later sent him plans for a new 'opera and play company'. Bing was enthusiastic and described the idea to Audrey Christie, wife of John Christie, founder and owner of Glyndebourne, as 'really constructive'. He thought that Glyndebourne should be associated with it: 'it centres round two creative artists of real importance: Benjamin Britten and Ronald Duncan (the poet whose latest work at the Mercury had an extraordinary success)'.[8] Britten had written some incidental music for Duncan's verse-play, *This Way to the Tomb*, produced at the Mercury Theatre on 11 October 1945. They were now collaborating on a chamber-opera on a subject suggested by Crozier, *The Rape of Lucretia*. It was completed in the Spring of 1946. Bing was present on 4 May when Britten finished the score and played it through. He wrote to Mrs Christie: 'I really was enormously impressed ... as far as I could judge from this very rough performance, [it] may be among the really important works of our time. It is brilliant, full of inspiration and, for John's [Christie] benefit, full of some lovely tunes.' In its brochure for the 1946 season, Glyndebourne announced that it had made itself responsible for 'a new operatic venture ... in process of formation... It is hoped and intended that one or two new English works will be produced every year by the new company in collaboration with Glyndebourne.' Eric Crozier, in an article in *Tempo* (March 1946), wrote that the Glyndebourne English Opera Company would 'provide a method by which singers of the first rank can devote five months of each year between June and October – slack months in the concert world – entirely to the rehearsal and performance of opera.'

Such were the high hopes and ideals of 1946. Fourteen performances of *Lucretia* were given at Glyndebourne between 12 and 27 July. Eric Crozier produced, John Piper designed the sets, and there were two casts. In the first, Lucretia was sung by Kathleen Ferrier, the young contralto whose tragically short career had begun, as far as the London musical scene was concerned, with her singing in *Messiah* in

Westminster Abbey in 1943. Britten had attended that performance and had been deeply impressed both by her voice and presence. She was his first choice for Lucretia, although she had never sung in opera, and she suggested Nancy Evans as the Lucretia for the second cast. Also in the first cast, which was conducted by Ernest Ansermet, were Pears, Joan Cross, Owen Brannigan and Anna Pollak. The second cast was conducted by Reginald Goodall and included Aksel Schiøtz, Flora Nielsen, Norman Walker and Catherine Lawson. The critic of *The Times* acclaimed the 'very sure touch' with which Britten made 'very bold experiments in operatic structure . . . a new form in which the age-old balance of music and drama is struck anew'. The libretto's anachronistic introduction of Christian moralizing into a classical tragedy was severely and often savagely criticized by many writers, and Duncan was hurt that Britten never acknowledged that he, the composer, had wanted this epilogue and continued to allow his librettist to take the blame. *The Times* carried easily the most favourable review; in a further article a few days later its critic referred to Britten's search for new forms 'that will lift opera out of the dead end in which it has been stuck since the death of Puccini'. Elsewhere the story was different: 'in a blind alley', said Ernest Newman; 'rotten with insincerity and pretentiousness . . . reluctant admiration for so much musical cleverness whose purpose remains neither intelligible nor sensible . . . I was bored', W.J. Turner in the *Spectator*; 'the pseudo-religious ending is appalling . . . Everywhere Mr Britten reminds us of his favourite composers – Purcell, Bach, Gluck, Verdi, Massenet, Puccini, Mahler . . .', William Glock. Even Desmond Shawe-Taylor found the epilogue 'an artistic error'. A few days after the first performance, Britten wrote to a friend: 'I used to think that the day when one could shock people was over – but now, I've discovered that being simple and considering things of spiritual importance produces violent reactions!'[9] After the Glyndebourne season, the opera was taken to Edinburgh, Glasgow, Manchester and Liverpool, ending at Sadler's Wells. The provincial tour was a box-office disaster, for it was too early to expect audiences at that time to appreciate this new genre. When *Lucretia* was then taken to Holland, Bing found himself the object of the 'incredibly unfriendly attitude of the Group', who blamed him for failing to publicize the tour sufficiently. Christie stood the large financial loss even though he disliked everything about the opera, from the sets to the singing and the music, but made it clear that he would not be financially responsible for the 1947 repetition of *The Rape of Lucretia* nor for the promised new opera, which materialized as *Albert Herring*. In the autumn of 1946, Britten and Crozier wrote to Christie telling him of their intention to found a non-profit-making company and offering to buy Glyndebourne's production of *Lucretia*. Early in 1947 the formation of the English Opera Group was made public. The chairman was Oliver Lyttelton, M.P. (later Lord Chandos); the directors were Sir Kenneth Clark, Tyrone Guthrie, Ralph Hawkes, Mervyn Horder, Denis Rickett, James Smith and Erwin Stein; and Britten, Crozier and John Piper were the artistic directors. The Group's manifesto stated: 'We believe the best way to achieve the beginnings of a repertory of English operas is through the creation of a form of opera requiring small resources of singers and players, but suitable for performance in large or small opera houses or theatres.'

This manifesto also stated that it was the Group's policy to encourage young composers to write operas and poets and playwrights 'to tackle the problem of writing libretti in collaboration with composers'. Britten's method of work with his librettists was first to discuss the shape of the whole drama. They would spend several days on this task, often working at the same desk. They would then break up the drama into appropriate musical forms. In an introduction to the published libretto of *The Rape of Lucretia*,[10] Britten said: 'The composer and poet should at all stages be working in the closest contact, from the most preliminary stages right up to the first night'. But, although Britten collaborated again with Duncan, they wrote no more operas. Plans for an opera about Abelard and Héloise, for one based on Jane Austen's *Mansfield Park*, to be called *Letters to William*, and for *The Canterbury Tales* came to naught.

To return to the summer of 1945, after the launching of *Peter Grimes*: Britten went to Germany in August as accompanist to Yehudi Menuhin on a tour of Belsen and other German concentration camps. The full horror of what had occurred in these places had been revealed by the liberating armies. No artist of Britten's sensitivity could be unaffected. On his return to England and while suffering from a high temperature, he wrote the *Holy Sonnets of John Donne*, nine poems in which death and repentance are recurring themes. He had previously contemplated setting them and now composed them literally at fever-pitch. Pears and he gave the first performance in the Wigmore Hall on 22 November 1945. A musical influence on these settings was Purcell, who was much in Britten's thoughts at this time through preparations for the commemoration on 21 November of the 250th anniversary of his death. Britten's principal contribution to this occasion was his Second String Quartet, first played at the Wigmore Hall on the anniversary by the Zorian Quartet. Its last movement is a magnificent Chacony, a twentieth-century re-creation of the very spirit of Purcell. Nor was this all. He and Pears began their performing edition of Purcell's songs (some of Britten's realizations having been performed while he and Pears were in America), and Britten also selected a Purcell theme as the basis of a set of variations which accompanied a Ministry of Education film, first shown on 29 November 1946, illustrating the instruments of the orchestra. The text for this documentary was written by Slater, but the work became better-known as a concert-piece, *The Young Person's Guide to the Orchestra*,[11] with a script by Crozier and was first performed in this form by the Liverpool Philharmonic, conducted by Malcolm Sargent, on 15 October 1946.

Other compositions of this period were the incidental music for Louis MacNeice's radio play, *The Dark Tower*, first broadcast on 21 January 1946, and Britten's only solo organ work, *Prelude and Fugue on a Theme of Vittoria*, written for St Matthew's Church, Northampton, on 18 September 1946. On 2 July the revised version of the Piano Concerto had its first performance at the Cheltenham Festival. Britten conducted and Noel Mewton-Wood was the soloist in place of Clifford Curzon, who had quarrelled with Britten over the composer's lateness in supplying the draft of the substitute slow movement.

In August 1946 Britten returned to the United States to attend the American première of *Peter Grimes* at Tanglewood. There he renewed his friendship with Auden and Copland and accompanied Koussevitzky, the opera's 'godfather', to the first performance. After a European tour as conductor of his own works and as accompanist to Pears, he settled down to composition of the new chamber opera promised for the 1947 Glyndebourne season. Working with Eric Crozier, they adapted Guy de Maupassant's short story *Le Rosier de Madame Husson*, giving it an East Anglian setting and converting it into the very English comedy of *Albert Herring*. The first performance was given at Glyndebourne on 20 June 1947 by the English Opera Group ('who come as visitors', the programme stated). Frederick Ashton produced, John Piper was designer, and Britten conducted. The cast was headed by Pears and Joan Cross and included Nancy Evans, Margaret Ritchie, Gladys Parr, Frederick Sharp and Norman Lumsden. On the first night John Christie's mournful greeting to his guests was 'This isn't *our* kind of thing, you know'.[12] Apparently the 'lower-class speech' of some of the characters gave offence. 'A diverting piece on the second plane', McNaught wrote in *The Manchester Guardian*, and the critic of *The Times*, who told Crozier it was 'a ghastly little work', complained that 'the music does not engage the heart. Mr Britten is still pursuing his old problem of seeing how much indigestible material he can dissolve in music'. *The Rape of Lucretia*, with a new aria for Collatinus in Act I and some other adjustments of text and music, was revived at Glyndebourne that summer. It was to be thirty-four years until a Britten opera was again performed there – *A Midsummer Night's Dream* in 1981. Since then three more of his operas have been performed there, including a memorable Peter Hall staging of *Albert Herring*. So the wheel came full circle.

8

Aldeburgh

The choice of *Albert Herring* for the 1947 Glyndebourne visit by the English Opera Group was symbolic of the beginning of an important change of direction in Britten's life. He had seemed, since 1938, to be a cosmopolitan figure in English music, linked to the European and American mainstreams rather than to the English main tradition. With the success of *Peter Grimes* he was acclaimed, almost overnight, as the first English composer for centuries to have a continental reputation (critical memories being notoriously short, Elgar's fame throughout Europe, Russia and the United States from 1900 to 1914 was forgotten). But *Albert Herring*, with its overtones of Gilbert and Sullivan,[1] was a comedy about Suffolk rural life, poking fun at committee meetings, Lady Bountiful, the village policeman and the corner-shop. After *The Rape of Lucretia*, it seemed to some to be a cosy choice of subject. Within a few months of its first performance, Britten was to plunge into an enterprise which would involve him, willy-nilly, in committee meetings, coffee mornings and collaboration with the likes of Lady Billows and Miss Wordsworth. His preliminary step was to move from Snape into Aldeburgh itself. For the next ten years, his and Pears's home was Crag House, 4 Crabbe Street, on the sea front.

Here, Britten continued the work-obsessed puritanical régime which he followed almost to the end of his life, a routine which included cold baths, long walks with the dogs, plain food and early bedtime. If he did not work every day he felt miserable. He was really only happy when composing. 'Ben lived and breathed music', Pears has said. Yet photographs of him taken in these years show very often a distressed countenance. He had realized since his student days in 1933 that his idyllic childhood was a lost Arcady. The realities of adult life did not match up to the hopes engendered in the weald of youth. Like Elgar, who had also regarded his childhood as a golden age, Britten increasingly began to search in his music for that lost childhood and to lament the end of innocence. Just as Elgar escaped into *The Wand of Youth* and *The Starlight Express*, so Britten escaped into *Saint Nicolas, Noye's Fludde* and a host of similar works.

After the 1947 Glyndebourne season, the English Opera Group toured Holland and Switzerland, a costly business. While Britten, Pears and Crozier were driving to Switzerland, Pears suggested that they should have their own festival at home, an Aldeburgh Festival. The inhabitants of the borough were enthusiastic, money was raised, the Arts Council offered financial aid, and the first festival was held from 5–13 June 1948. Britten's friend the Earl of Harewood, a passionate lover of opera, was president and the committee comprised local personalities chaired by the Countess of Cranbrook.

The festival opened with Purcell. The English Opera Group performed *Albert Herring* – there was no room in the pit for harp and percussion, so they were put in the auditorium, a screen round the harp and eiderdowns draped round the two drums – Britten and Pears gave a recital, and the music of Purcell and Lennox Berkeley was accorded special attention. On the opening night Leslie Woodgate conducted the first performance of a new Britten-Crozier cantata, *Saint Nicolas*, in Aldeburgh parish church. This was written during the previous winter and the full score was not finished until 31 May 1948. It was composed for first performance at the centenary celebrations at Lancing College (where Pears had gone to school) on 24 July 1948, but the college kindly allowed the cantata to be given two performances at Aldeburgh. It was especially suitable for Aldeburgh conditions, with its parts for solo tenor (Pears), small instrumental forces, boys' voices in addition to chorus, and with its inclusion of two hymns in which the congregation could join. The critics were asked not to comment on *Saint Nicolas* until the Lancing performance.

The opera and recital performances at Aldeburgh were given in the Jubilee Hall, which had a very small stage and held only about 300 people. This first festival was a success and it was decided that the event should become annual. Henceforward, the festival, its planning and execution, became increasingly the focal point of Britten's life. 'Ultimately, to me it is the local thing that matters most', he was to say some years later – and even favourite artists who were discovered to have accepted some other engagement in June were sometimes tardily forgiven. He saw the festival develop from the unpretentious music-making of the early years, run on a shoestring, to a major European event.

Festivals sprang up on every side in post-1945 Britain. From 1947 there was the three-week Edinburgh Festival, with hundreds of events and the expensive delights provided by visiting opera and ballet companies, orchestras and the world's leading soloists. From 1945 Cheltenham devoted itself to contemporary British music (the first concert performance of the Interludes from *Peter Grimes* was given at the first festival). But Aldeburgh, from its inception, had its own charm and attraction. The smallness of the seaside town, the participation of local people and children, the mixture of the makeshift and the highly professional, the golf, the sailing and the wildlife – these brought visitors back year after year as devotees. It could have seemed very parochial and inward-growing had it not been for its central figure and *raison d'être*, Britten himself. Not only was he the pivot of the festival as a composer, his gifts as a performer were phenomenal. As conductor, solo pianist in a concerto or accompanist unparalleled, or merely playing the one note on his viola in Purcell's *Fantasia on One Note*, he bestowed on the festival artistic genius of the highest order. Moreover he was a brilliant administrator and programme-planner. For his associates, the Aldeburgh days were a special delight. 'I can remember Ben saying he wished he had three lives, one for composing, another for becoming a fine pianist and the third for becoming a tennis champion!', Basil Coleman wrote in Covent Garden's programme for the memorial performance of *Peter Grimes* on 24 March 1977. 'They were the days when, as recreation from intensive work on his next opera, he loved to drive his car very fast down small Suffolk lanes, take three and four sea-bathes a day, discover new churches, play several sets of tennis or go for long country walks. The walks were particularly memorable, partly because of his knowledge of so many things, mainly for his marvellously fresh response to everything we saw or heard, bird flight and song, wind movement in reeds and on water, cloud formations and changing light.'

In addition to Britten's music, the festival programmes featured his enthusiasms. Thus, there were memorable performances of Purcell, Mozart and Schubert, of Byrd, Dowland and Holst, of J.S. Bach and Haydn, of Mahler, Berg and Bridge. Rarities such as Schumann's *Scenes from Faust* were revived. The international fame of Britten and Pears ensured that illustrious composers and performers visited and took part in the festival. Poulenc, Copland, Henze, Kodály, Walton, Berkeley, Arnold, Maxwell Davies, Oldham, Birtwistle, Tavener, Williamson, Rubbra, Crosse, Bliss, Bennett, Tippett, Gerhard, Musgrave, Goehr, Lutyens, Maw, Bedford, Fricker – these were among the composers. Where performers are concerned, the list would be enormous but, apart from Britten, Pears and Imogen Holst, some of the greatest Aldeburgh names are Julian Bream, George Malcolm, Dietrich Fischer-Dieskau, William Primrose, Yehudi Menuhin, Joy Boughton, Cecil Aronowitz, Osian Ellis, Janet Baker, Steuart Bedford, and Sviatoslav Richter. In a category of their own because of the close friendship which developed between them and Britten are the cellist Mstislav Rostropovich and his wife, the soprano Galina Vishnevskaya, for both of whom he composed fine works.

Unforgettable by those who attended the 1952 festival was the sole appearance by the contralto Kathleen Ferrier, the original Lucretia. Already dying of cancer – she had fifteen months of life left – she went to Aldeburgh at Britten's invitation as part of her convalescence after an operation. Towards the end of her stay she agreed to join Britten and Pears in a performance of Britten's second Canticle, *Abraham and Isaac*, written for the three of them to perform during a series of recitals given early in 1952 to raise funds for the English Opera Group. Writing after her death, Britten described[3] the poignancy of this last performance: 'the beautiful church, her beauty and incredible courage, and the wonderful characterisation'. Of course, there was another side to the festival, stories of a clique, of who was in favour with the directors and who had fallen from grace, of artists peremptorily told they would not be welcome there again because some act or word of *lèse-majesté* had been reported. Such tales are inseparable from a closely-knit circle, intent on the task in hand, and from the temperament of certain kinds of creative genius. They do not lessen, even if they tarnish, the immense contribution of the Aldeburgh Festival to British musical life.

Britten's first composition to be completed at Crag House was the first of the five vocal works to which he attached the description 'Canticle', implying a religious subject, though the texts are not those of the liturgical canticles. *Canticle I, My Beloved is Mine*, op. 40, is a setting for high voice and piano of a poem by Francis Quarles (1592– 1644) based on a verse from *The Song of Solomon*. It was written for the memorial concert, on 1 November 1947, for Dick Sheppard, former vicar of St Martin-in-the-Fields, and founder of the Peace Pledge Union in 1934, and was therefore a re-affirmation of Britten's pacifism. This was followed by a work written for Nancy Evans, Eric Crozier's wife, *A Charm of Lullabies*, completed in December 1947, and by the cantata *Saint Nicolas*. But Britten's major preoccupation at this time was his 'realization' of John Gay's ballad-opera *The Beggar's Opera*, which he made for the English Opera Group. The libretto was discreetly amended by Tyrone Guthrie, who had brilliantly produced the first Covent Garden *Peter Grimes* in November 1947; Britten included 66 of the 69 airs chosen by Pepusch for the original version in 1728. The first performance, conducted by Britten, was given at Cambridge on 24 May 1948, with Pears as Macheath and Nancy Evans as Polly. Performances followed in Holland, Cheltenham and London, Belgium,

Austria and Scandinavia. For some later revivals the part of Macheath was transposed for baritone.

During the winter of 1948–9 Britten worked on three new compositions: incidental music for Ronald Duncan's new play *Stratton*; a new piece for the second Aldeburgh Festival; and the *Spring Symphony*, which had been requested by Koussevitzky for the Boston Symphony Orchestra. The Aldeburgh work was the unusual and original *Let's Make an Opera!* devised by Eric Crozier. In the first part a group of children – named after the sons, daughters and nephews of the festival chairman, Lady Cranbrook – help the grown-ups to plan, write and rehearse an opera; the second part is the opera itself, *The Little Sweep*, scored for string quartet, piano (four hands) and percussion. Norman Del Mar conducted the first performance at Aldeburgh on 14 June 1949 in a production by Basil Coleman and Stuart Burge. Audiences then and since were captivated by this touching and effective work, which has probably had more performances than any other Britten opera. Britten's ability to write for children without patronizing them and by setting them a challenge not impossible to surmount was here powerfully demonstrated. Audiences had to sing four of the songs and Imogen Holst has recalled that 'they caused a hubbub of excitement' in 1949, with people exclaiming: 'What! In *five-four*?' and '*What*? Diminished octaves?'

The *Spring Symphony* was Britten's first large-scale choral work. He had planned since about 1947 to compose 'a symphony not only dealing with the Spring itself, but with the progress of Winter to Spring and the re-awakening of the earth and life which that means',[4] very much as Stravinsky had been stimulated over thirty years earlier by the end of the long Russian winter to write *The Rite of Spring*. The first plan was for a text in mediaeval Latin but this was fortunately abandoned: 'a re-reading of much English lyric verse and a particularly lovely Spring day in East Suffolk, the Suffolk of Constable and Gainsborough' were the factors which led to his choice of several English poems ranging from Anon. to Auden as the basis of this Mahlerian concept of song-symphony. Koussevitzky ceded the first performance to the Holland Festival (which, under Peter Diamand's direction, was something of a Britten stronghold). In Amsterdam on 9 July 1949 Eduard van Beinum conducted the Concertgebouw Orchestra, the Dutch Radio Chorus, a boys' choir and the three soloists, Jo Vincent (soprano), Kathleen Ferrier (contralto) and Peter Pears (tenor). Britten had attended all the rehearsals, showing special concern about the boys' articulation of their words. 'Bite your consonants as though they were an apple', he advised. Koussevitzky conducted the first American performance a month later at the Berkshire Festival, Tanglewood. Van Beinum conducted the first English performance in the Royal Albert Hall on 9 March 1950.

Staying with Britten in Amsterdam were his friend Marion Stein, daughter of Erwin Stein, and her fiancé, the Earl of Harewood. For their wedding at St Mark's, North Audley Street, London – the church for which Britten had written his *Te Deum* fifteen years earlier – Britten wrote *A Wedding Anthem (Amo ergo sum)* to a text by Duncan. This was performed at the ceremony by Joan Cross, Peter Pears, the choir and organist to the intense interest of the bridegroom and the intense boredom of his uncle, King George VI. Originally Duncan's text included a plea for the Virgin Mary to bless the couple, but Authority would not allow this in the presence of the Head of the Church of England, so her intercession was substituted. A manuscript copy of the anthem was one of three objects buried beneath the foundation stone of the Royal Festival Hall, London's new concert-hall on the South Bank of the Thames being built to be ready for the Festival of Britain 1951 which the Government had planned as a celebration of the country's emergence from the war and its aftermath. A vast musical programme, in several centres, was arranged. Knowing that a new opera was in progress, the Arts Council commissioned it from Britten; after he and Pears had returned from a tour of North America at the end of 1949, he settled down to work on it.

The subject was an adaptation of Herman Melville's posthumous novel *Billy Budd, Foretopman*, the story of a sailor hanged from the yardarm for striking his superior on an English man-o'-war shortly after the mutinies at Spithead and the Nore. His librettists were Eric Crozier and the novelist E.M. Forster, who not only had been the vicarious cause of Britten's setting *Peter Grimes* but had become a regular visitor to the Aldeburgh Festival. Composition began in February 1950 and the opera was finished in the autumn of 1951.

Crozier and Forster first discussed collaborating on an opera libretto in August 1948, but had no idea of a subject. A few months later Britten suggested *Billy Budd*. He had been so excited by the book that he had written about it to Forster, whose passage on the story in his *Aspects of the Novel* he had also read. Crozier, in a broadcast talk,[5] spoke of the genesis of the libretto, which exists in five manuscript versions, the first being merely notes of the first meeting in 1948. In January 1949 the three men had further talks at Britten's house in Aldeburgh. At this time Forster suddenly became very excited about the subject and impatient to proceed; he wrote the prologue ('I am an old man who has experienced much ...') which Britten, equally excited, set unaltered. The libretto is unusual in being almost entirely in prose, because Forster could not write poetry. Britten said in a broadcast in 1960 that the prose style influenced his music. When the music needed 'to flower', as Forster put it, small lyrical episodes were provided.

The librettists discussed each episode in detail. Sometimes both of them wrote a scene in draft; they then discussed it and often amalgamated the two versions. Crozier dealt with the more technical aspects, reading many books on the naval history of the period, visiting Nelson's *Victory* at Portsmouth and the National Maritime Museum at Greenwich, and wrote most of the dialogues. Forster did 'the big slabs of narrative'. The third version of the manuscript, dated March 1949, was the result of several weeks' work by the three collaborators at Aldeburgh. 'Britten was busy at the other end of the house scoring his *Spring Symphony*', Crozier said, 'but midway through the morning he would visit us to see how things were going and to read what we had written. Forster, whose age at that time [70] equalled mine and Britten's put together, was in tremendously high spirits... Before long, we had managed to draft all the main scenes.' Six months later, Britten's musical ideas were developing and he invited Forster and Crozier to Aldeburgh for a month to make revisions. 'At this stage he began to assume the dominance in our partnership and to lead the discussions. He wanted a big new chorus-scene as climax to the first act – one of the few occasions on which we added anything that was not directly suggested by Melville.' This scene, in which Captain Vere addressed the crew, was deleted in the 1960 revision of the opera. Originally the opera had been planned in two acts but, for reasons Britten could not remember, it was made into four. When opportunity arose he reverted to his first plan. Another divergence from Melville was the suppression of the Afterguardsman who tempts Billy with the guineas and the use in his place of the terrified little Novice. Revisions to the libretto were finished at the end of 1949 and, with this fourth draft, Britten began composing six months later.

Billy Budd used a large orchestra for the first time in a Britten opera since *Peter Grimes*. It was a 'big' opera because Forster had said that was the way he felt opera should be. The first plan was for the Sadler's Wells Opera to perform *Billy Budd* at the 1951 Edinburgh Festival but they decided it was beyond their resources and the first performance was given at the Royal Opera House, Covent Garden, on Saturday, 1 December 1951. Britten conducted, taking over at the eleventh hour when Josef Krips withdrew from the production. Basil Coleman produced, John Piper designed the sets, and the dedicatees were 'George and Marion' (Harewood). The title role was sung by an American baritone, Theodor Uppman, with Peter Pears as Captain Vere and Frederick Dalberg as the villainous master-at-arms, Claggart. Britten had wanted Geraint Evans to sing Billy but Evans felt the part was too high for his voice. David Webster discovered Uppman at auditions in America.

Philip Hope-Wallace, in the *Manchester Guardian* of 3 December, straightaway described *Billy Budd* as Britten's 'new and best opera'. He continued: 'Few operas can have been cradled with so much goodwill; few composers of Mr Britten's age have won such acclaim – but then few composers since the eighteenth century have done what he has done. This stern and beautiful opera enhances his reputation.' He wrote of 'an originality, effectiveness and fineness of musical creation altogether magnificent'. In a long and thoughtful notice he found much to criticize in the libretto, which he blamed for his saluting the work as 'a qualified success of esteem' instead of as a masterpiece. The critic of *The Times* thought that the opera 'just misses tragedy' but that it answered those Britten admirers who wondered 'when and whether he would sound the deeper music of humanity'. Some idea of the importance Britten had by now attained in British music can be gained by turning up the January 1952 issue of the magazine *Opera*, then edited by Lord Harewood. Three long critical appreciations of the first performance were included, one by the French critic F. Goldbeck, who ended: 'It has a perfection of its own, and there is about this music and this perfection a touch of precariousness that never impairs its quality – that touch of strangeness that Britten himself so rightly ascribes to his beloved Purcell.' In spite of this level of specialist appreciation, *Billy Budd* did not become a real success with the public until over twenty years after its first performances. Covent Garden toured the original production in the provinces in 1952 and took it to Paris, where it was disliked. The first German production, at Wiesbaden in March 1952, was a decided success, although the opera was severely cut. Scenes from the opera opened the N.B.C.'s televised opera season in New York on 19 October 1952, the first operatic music by Britten to be relayed by this medium.

Only two other original compositions date from 1951, the second canticle, *Abraham and Isaac* and the *Six Metamorphoses After Ovid* for oboe solo, written for the Aldeburgh Festival and first played by the dedicatee, Joy Boughton, from a punt on The Meare at Thorpeness. The manuscript copy, in the composer's hand, fell into the water and had to be retrieved, swiftly. Britten also worked on an edition, or 'realization', of Purcell's *Dido and Aeneas* as his contribution to the English Opera Group's Festival of Britain programme. In this he collaborated closely with Imogen Holst, daughter of the composer Gustav Holst. They provided other music by Purcell for the missing scene between the Sorceress and the Enchantress and the dance at the end of Act II. Britten conducted the first performance from the harpsichord at the Lyric Theatre, Hammersmith, on 1 May 1951.

On 28 July of this Festival summer, he was admitted as an honorary freeman of his birthplace, Lowestoft. He took the opportunity to state his artistic creed: 'It is not a bad thing for an artist to try to serve all sorts of different people, to have to work to order. Any artist worth his salt has ideas knocking about in his head, and an invitation to write something can often direct these ideas into a concrete form and shape'. Then he went deeper: 'Artists are artists because they have an extra sensitivity – a skin less, perhaps, than other people; and the great ones have an uncomfortable habit of being right about many things, long before their time... So when you hear of an artist saying or doing something strange or unpopular, think of that extra sensitivity, that skin less; consider a moment whether he may not after all be seeing a little more clearly than ourselves, whether he is really as irresponsible as he seems, before you condemn him... It is a proud privilege to be a creative artist, but it can also be painful.'

9

Gloriana

From 1952 dates a critical phase in Britten's life. In the nine years since he had returned from America he had gone from triumph to triumph. Each new work had been widely publicized, particularly since the success of *Peter Grimes*. While Vaughan Williams, approaching eighty, occupied a special position, Britten had eclipsed his contemporaries and most of his elders. Walton, for example, had been written off as an almost-extinct reactionary. But immense success and fame breed envy and malice, as Wagner and Richard Strauss had discovered in their time. Other English composers looked askance at the young Britten's progress along the Suffolk lanes in an old Rolls-Royce. They looked askance at the zealous promotion of his works by his publishers and at the formidable array of critical pens deployed in his favour. (A good-humoured example of their attitude, attributed to John Ireland, was the quip, 'If Britten can make it, Boosey can hawk it'.) His friends in aristocratic and influential places were duly noted. It was also noted that he was the favoured British composer where Covent Garden was concerned. Inevitably, some of the envy took an unpleasant form. His Left-wing tendencies before the war, his 'defection' to America, his wartime conscientious-objector status – these were black marks. Homosexuality was then still a criminal offence, so although no mention of Britten's homosexuality could have been made in public, there was no lack of innuendo, including much objectionable comment. Thus, a 'buggers' alliance' was supposed to 'run' British music. 'Homo sweet homo' was put forward as the name of Britten's house in Aldeburgh. Beecham made a joke about Covent Garden performing '*The Twilight of the Sods* – and about time!' and he disposed of Britten with the remark 'I never comment about the works of struggling young composers'.

This, it should be said, was the gossip and preoccupation of 'in' musical circles. Little of it mattered to the general public. Those who were young in the 1940s and 1950s recall how each new work by Britten was seized upon with delight. There was always some new and exciting turn of musical phrase, some divine simplicity, some memorable device, on which discussions could be held for hours – and as the recordings were issued, they were snapped up eagerly. Let there be no gainsaying that, whatever the future holds for Britten's reputation, he went straight to the hearts of thousands of his contemporaries. This is not to say that there was no criticism and no scepticism. We have already seen how unwilling the critical establishment was at first to concede anything more than cleverness to him when he was making his way. When he was on a pinnacle, those were not lacking who wanted to bring him down; and Britten's greatest admirers handed them the weapon they wanted when, in 1952, there was published, under the editorship of Donald Mitchell and Hans Keller, a 410-page symposium entitled *Benjamin Britten: a commentary on his works by a group of specialists*.[1]

Such a comprehensive survey of a living English composer under the age of forty (or one of any other nationality) had never appeared before. The contributions included a biographical sketch by Lord Harewood and chapters on the vocal music by Pears, the Purcell 'realizations' by George Malcolm, the choral works by Hans Redlich, the operas by Arthur Oldham, Erwin Stein and Norman Del Mar, the chamber music by Paul Hamburger, the string works by Boyd Neel, the piano music by Georges Auric and A.E.F. Dickinson, the works for children by Imogen Holst, the light music by Lennox Berkeley and the incidental music by William Mann. The editors contributed two general essays which stirred up most of the hostility directed towards the book. Ernest Newman, in *The Sunday Times*, however, directed most of his sallies against Britten's 'impatience of hostile criticism'. The real polemic came in the April 1953 issue of the quarterly *Music & Letters*[2] in an article, 'Britten and the Brittenites', by Peter Tranchell which devastatingly exposed some of the jargon used in certain of the essays, complained about the 'modishness' of much of the writing, and ended by offering condolences to 'the victim of so inopportune an outburst of noble intentions'. For those who wish to recapture the sound of that era's sharpening of feline claws, Peter Tranchell's brilliant article is required reading. It appeared two months before the most disastrous episode of Britten's career.

In February 1952 Queen Elizabeth II came to the throne. During March, Britten went ski-ing in Austria with George and Marion Harewood. Lord Harewood suggested to Britten that he should write a 'big national opera' to mark the Queen's Coronation in June 1953. They spent several days discussing the subject and, after Henry VIII had been abandoned, Harewood put forward Elizabeth I. According to Ronald Duncan, Harewood suggested him as librettist but Britten was prevailed upon to work with the poet and novelist William Plomer, with whom he had been planning a children's opera on the subject of space travel, now abandoned. Permission was obtained from the Queen and the project went ahead, based on Lytton Strachey's book *Elizabeth and Essex*. Britten had to work fast. He wrote nothing else in 1952, but had a busy schedule of festival recitals with Pears in Aldeburgh and abroad. However, he had recently engaged Imogen Holst as his 'music assistant', a post she occupied until 1964. She copied out his sketches for each scene as soon as they were written and made a piano arrangement for the singers to use at rehearsals. 'He was able to say', she wrote,[3] 'in the middle of October, when he was just beginning Act I, that he would have finished the second act before the end of January ... He managed to keep to his time-schedule in spite of the disastrous interruption of the East Coast floods in January, when the sea reached the windows on one side of his Crabbe Street house and the river came in at the doors on the other side. When he began work on the full score of the opera, he wrote at such a tremendous speed that I thought I should never keep pace with him. He managed to get through at least twenty vast pages a day, and it seemed as if he never had to stop and think.'

Plomer and Britten had selected the relationship between Elizabeth and the Earl of Essex as the basis of their plot. But whereas Strachey had concentrated on the protagonists' love-affair, the opera, which was named *Gloriana*, op. 53, was more concerned to present a character-study of the Queen against the background of her reign. Britten, adept as ever at providing the right work for a particular occasion, took advantage of the opportunities for an opulent and beautiful production by composing the Norwich masque scene and the courtly dances in the Palace of Whitehall. The opera was completed on 13 March 1953 and first performed on 8 June at a Royal Gala at Covent Garden in the presence of the Queen, who had been crowned six days earlier. The sets were by John Piper, the production by Basil Coleman, the choreography by John Cranko, and John Pritchard conducted. Joan Cross sang the part of Elizabeth, Pears was Essex and the cast also included Jennifer Vyvyan, Monica Sinclair, Adèle Leigh, Geraint Evans and Michael Langdon. A few days before the performance, Britten, not yet forty years of age, was appointed a Companion of Honour in the Coronation Honours List.

That first performance is already a legend. The audience, stiff with diplomats, civil servants, and others to whom *Merrie England* would have represented a musical experience of the most adventurous and intellectual kind, had no idea what to make of *Gloriana*. Many were bored, many openly showed their disrelish, and many regarded the choice of subject as an outrage against good taste. Stories spread far and wide of interval conversations about elephant-shooting in the days of the Raj; scatological versions of the opera's title were circulated in the clubs. The music critics' response was guarded but their voices in any case were drowned in the controversy over the opera. The correspondence columns of *The Times* resounded for days with criticisms of the choice of subject and the expense. It was left to Professor Anthony Lewis to express belief that 'English music has been splendidly represented by Mr Britten's *Gloriana*. Page after page of music of superb richness and invention testifies to the continued excellence of the composer's creative powers.' Caryl Brahms thought that 'English history has been slighted' by the choice of subject, so did Marie Stopes; Woodrow Wyatt M.P. asserted that if the first-night audience was frigid that was a reflection on them, not on *Gloriana*; it was money well spent. Vaughan Williams pointed out that 'the important thing ... is that, so far as I know, for the first time in history the Sovereign has commanded an opera by a composer from these islands for a great occasion. Those who cavil at the public expense involved should realise what such a gesture means to the prestige of our own music.'

A shrewd comment was made in *The Spectator* of 19 June by Martin Cooper, who ascribed criticism of the opera to 'an almost sadistic relish or glee that has little to do with the musical merit or demerit' and to jealousy over 'special patronage and special conditions of work and performance not accorded to other performers'. No doubt about it, this was the philistines' revenge on the Brittenites. But audiences in the 1953–4 Covent Garden season liked the work[4] and it was toured by Covent Garden to the Rhodes centennial exhibition in Bulawayo, Southern Rhodesia, in August and in the British provinces in 1954. It was then to wait another twelve years for its next staging. Realizing, perhaps, that the music's stage future was dim, Britten extracted a concert suite of four movements (with optional tenor solo), which was first performed in Birmingham in September 1954, and published the Choral Dances for unaccompanied chorus.

Gloriana remains, in 1992, the only Britten opera not to have been recorded complete, although a video exists of the English National Opera's staging. This opera also had a role in two significant events in Britten's personal life. In 1953, its failure encouraged Pears to persuade Britten to turn his back on metropolitan operatic life and to concentrate thenceforward on Aldeburgh; and, if Stephen Spender is to be believed, a letter from Auden to Britten containing criticisms of the word-setting in *Gloriana* led to the final rupture in their friendship.

Britten tore the letter into small pieces and sent it back to Auden. This break, Spender remarked, was one of the 'deepest griefs' in Auden's life, the thought of which reduced him to tears. In 1973, Britten's response to the news of the poet's death was, in Donald Mitchell's words, a storm of tears.

10

Gamelan

Whatever the personal distress caused him by the reception of *Gloriana*, it made little difference to Britten's creative powers. For the Leeds Festival in October 1953 he composed the song-cycle *Winter Words*, settings of eight poems by Thomas Hardy, which received its first performance at a morning concert in Harewood House given by Pears and Britten. It was dedicated 'to John and Myfanwy Piper', and it was Mrs Piper who was the librettist of Britten's next chamber-opera, an adaptation of Henry James's *The Turn of the Screw*. They had chosen this subject when Britten received a commission for an opera for the 1954 Venice Biennale. At an early stage it was planned to call it *The Tower and the Lake*, but James's title was kept. *The Turn of the Screw* is about the haunting of two children in a Victorian country house by the ghosts of a valet and the governess he has seduced. Its choice by Britten is usually interpreted as another example of his preoccupation with evil and corruption, and possibly it reflects a sexual episode from his schooldays. But, like many a good dramatic composer, he liked a ghost story, and his interest in them was fuelled by his own tendency to believe in the unexplained or inexplicable. He frequently claimed to have had 'premonitions' and could usually be drawn into conversation about 'curious happenings'. He had first heard James's story as a radio play in 1932.

Work on the libretto, much of it in telephone conversations, was not all smooth going and, as Mrs Piper has related,[1] 'there were bombshells'. One of these was Britten's decision, in April 1954, when the first scenes had been composed, that the opera needed a prologue. The marvellous scene of the Governess's letter was a late insertion. Another cause of problems was the churchyard scene. Britten wrote to Mrs Piper: 'I feel that one must for dramatic and musical reasons have a set piece for the kids at the beginning of it. What else can it be? I don't see how a gentle make-believe of a choir procession (unless done grotesquely) could offend anyone; and I don't see why the words should offend more than the music – most people would anyhow recognise the tune first especially if they start it off stage as I'd like'.

Which tune was to be parodied is not known but Mrs Piper could think of no way of parodying a hymn. A clergyman suggested to her that she should use the *Benedicite*.

Britten had begun to compose the music in February 1954, writing with his left hand because he was suffering from an acute attack of bursitis (inflammation of the capsule enclosing a joint) in his right shoulder. Time was short, and Britten wrote very fast. Imogen Holst copied the vocal score several pages at a time and posted them to the publisher. 'It seemed incredible', she wrote[2] 'that a composer could be so sure of what he wanted that he would risk parting with the beginning of a scene before he had written the end of it'. He composed the 13-part fugue in a train between Ipswich and Liverpool Street.

The opera received its first performance at the Teatro la Fenice on 14 September 1954. The English Opera Group was conducted by Britten, sets were by John Piper and the producer was Basil Coleman. During composition Britten had confided his misgivings to Coleman in a letter[3]: 'I have never felt so insecure about a work – now up, now down – and it helps a great deal to know that you, who know so instinctively what I'm aiming at, like it so much'. Britten conducted a rehearsal of the work, to a small audience of relatives and friends, in the Workmen's Hall, Thorpeness, before departing for Venice. There it took time for the Italian theatre staff to work the many scene changes and the complicated lighting cues, so necessary for the ghosts, and Britten became very nervous and was exceptionally upset when things went wrong. But the performance went well.

The Italian critics praised the music and had reservations about the libretto. Colin Mason's review in *The Manchester Guardian* of 15 September 1954 was both perceptive and amusing:

> What should an Italian audience make of a sung version in the original language of a story which English readers have been reading for years without ever really finding out what it means? Clearly their practice in Pirandello stood them in good stead and they fell outside into dozens of little groups gravely, ingeniously and obscurely explaining and counter-explaining and all ready to die rather than look blank... The book is made to yield very varied musical opportunities... Britten, as always, instantly seizes them and sets them so vividly to music that it seems absurd ever to have thought, as many of us did, that the story had not the makings of an opera in it... He has tackled yet another problem, brought off yet another *tour de force*, and, it seems likely, created yet another masterpiece.'

The opera had its first London performance at Sadler's Wells in October with the same cast, among whom Jennifer Vyvyan gave an incomparable performance as the Governess and Peter Pears sang the role of Quint. The important role of the boy Miles was sung superbly by David Hemmings, later to achieve fame as a film actor. In August of the following year, a recording of the opera by the original cast was issued by Decca, the first Britten opera to be recorded complete and surely the first British opera to be recorded within a year of its first performance. Decca's association with Britten's music had begun before 1939, with the recording of the *Variations on a Theme of Frank Bridge* by the Boyd Neel Orchestra. The *Serenade* was recorded shortly after its first performance, but whereas these earlier works were issued on 78 r.p.m. discs, from 1951 the long-playing record transformed the musical scene and full-length operas could be issued on five or six sides compared with over forty. Decca showed immense faith in Britten – to the chagrin of other composers – and recorded nearly all his major works almost as soon as they appeared. *Winter Words*, for example, was available early in 1956, with the *Michelangelo Sonnets*; the issue of *The Turn of the Screw*, followed by *The Little Sweep*, began the complete series of Britten operas (with the still dismaying exception of *Gloriana*), all conducted by the composer apart from *Noye's Fludde* (Norman Del Mar) and *Death in Venice* (Steuart Bedford). Thus, posterity has the benefit of practically the whole of a great composer's work in performances directed or supervised by him and with, in nearly every case, the original casts and performers. Pears's interpretations of the operatic and other vocal roles, Jennifer Vyvyan's Governess, Janet Baker's Phaedra, Rostropovich's cello works and, of course, Britten's own accompaniments both as pianist and conductor, are available to future interpreters as guide, challenge and touchstone.

The only other work composed in 1954 was the third canticle *Still Falls the Rain*, a setting for tenor, horn and piano of lines about the 1940 air raids on London taken from Edith Sitwell's poem *The Canticle of the Rose*. This was dedicated to the memory of a young and brilliant Australian pianist, Noel Mewton-Wood, who had committed suicide in December 1953 because of his grief over the death of a close friend. The first performance of the canticle was intended for a Mewton-Wood memorial concert in December 1954, but Pears's illness caused it to be postponed until 28 January 1955, along with works also written for the occasion by Bliss and Alan Bush. Afterwards Edith Sitwell wrote to Britten: 'I am so haunted and so alone with that wonderful music and its wonderful performance that I was incapable of writing before now [26 April 1955]. I had no sleep at all on the night of the performance. And I can think of nothing else. It was certainly one of the greatest experiences in all my life as an artist... I can never begin to thank you for the glory you have given my poem.'[4]

After the exertion of composing three major operas in three years, Britten relaxed in 1955. After recitals with Pears in Belgium and Switzerland, he went on a ski-ing holiday to Zermatt, in company with Pears, Ronald Duncan and his wife, his sister Beth and the artist Mary Potter, resident in Aldeburgh and former wife of the writer Stephen Potter. Mrs Potter injured her leg; to amuse her while she was laid up, Britten wrote his *Alpine Suite* for recorder trio. This led to a *Scherzo* for recorder quartet, written later in the year for Aldeburgh Music Club. Two works for choir and organ followed, the *Hymn to St Peter*, composed for the 500th anniversary of St Peter Mancroft, Norwich, and the *Antiphon*, completed in March 1956 for the centenary of St Michael's College, Tenbury.

In November 1955 Britten and Pears went on a world tour lasting four months. They visited Austria, Yugoslavia, Turkey, Singapore, Indonesia, Japan, Macau, Hongkong, Thailand, Bali, India and Ceylon. For much of the journey their companions were their close friends Prince Ludwig of Hesse and his wife Princess Margaret (a Scotswoman, the daughter of Lord Geddes). The Prince and Princess were generous patrons of the Aldeburgh Festival. Under the pseudonym Ludwig Landgraf, the Prince provided the German translation of several of Britten's works, including *The Turn of the Screw*. The visit to Bali in January 1956 was a reminder for Britten of the Balinese music to which he had been introduced by Colin McPhee sixteen years before. Now he heard the gamelan in its native surroundings and wrote to Imogen Holst: 'The music is *fantastically* rich – melodically, rhythmically, texture (such *orchestration*!) and above all *formally*. It's a remarkable culture... At last I'm beginning to catch on to the technique, but it's about as complicated as Schoenberg.'[5] Such *orchestration* – the first effects of that spellbinding impression were to be heard in Britten's next major composition, his full-length ballet *The Prince of the Pagodas*.

Britten's wish to write a large ballet arose from his admiration for the work of the choreographer John Cranko (1927–73). In January 1954 it was announced that there would be a Britten-Cranko ballet in the Sadler's Wells Theatre Ballet's 1954–5 season, but this was premature. Cranko wrote a draft scenario for a ballet which would be 'a vehicle for creative choreography rather than "classical" pastiche.'[6] He therefore chose a mythological fairy-tale as framework for 'a series of images from traditional fairy-tales' which would provide the various divertissements. This scenario was revised when Britten said he would introduce various themes on which he would 'make variations short enough to provide the episodic dances, but which would give the work as a whole a sense of continuity'. Britten completed the music in the autumn of 1956. Into Act II went the sounds of the Balinese gamelan, but the score is also evidence of the truth of his reported remark that he had the score of Tchaikovsky's *The Sleeping Beauty* beside his bed while he was working on his own ballet. The first performance was advertised for Covent Garden in September 1956, but for once Britten fell behind schedule with the scoring and it was postponed until 1 January 1957, with Svetlana Beriosova and David Blair in the principal roles. The sets were by Piper and the costumes by Desmond Heeley. The ballet was not a success despite an enthusiastic first-night reception. The *Manchester Guardian* critic complained of a 'wild and woolly' story, 'bitty and inconsequent' choreography, and that a work 'of great but intermittent interest' seemed 'forever to be stopping and starting again'. The music was 'rich, tuneful, various and strong' and would 'certainly stand up to the challenge of the concert-hall'. The ballet was later performed in New York, Milan, Stuttgart, Munich, Leningrad and even by the Hungarian State Puppet Theatre. But so far it has not maintained a regular hold on audiences and must be set alongside *Gloriana* as a major initial failure in Britten's career.

Undeterred, Britten worked in 1957 on two new works for the 1958 Aldeburgh Festival, the six *Songs from the Chinese* for high voice and guitar (his first tribute to the wonderful playing of Julian Bream) and a children's opera, *Noye's Fludde*. In April he was elected an honorary member of the American Academy of Arts and Letters and of the National Institute of Art and Letters; and in the late summer and early autumn he conducted several English Opera Group performances of *The Turn of the Screw* at Stratford, Ontario, and at the Berlin Festival. The *Songs from the Chinese*, settings of translations by Arthur Waley, was the last work Britten completed at Crag House. In November 1957 he moved into The Red House in a more secluded part of Aldeburgh; its previous occupier, Mary Potter, took over Crag House. (Later she moved back into a small studio house next to The Red House.) *Noye's Fludde*, op. 59, based on one of the Chester Miracle Plays, was begun at Crag House on 22 October and finished at The Red House on 15 December. For some years he had wanted to provide a successor to *The Little Sweep*; one plan was to make an opera from Beatrix Potter's *The Tale of Mr Tod* but copyright difficulties put paid to it (and was it, perhaps, too near in subject to Janáček's *The Cunning Little Vixen*?). Then there was his idea of an opera about cosmonauts which he and William Plomer began but abandoned. But whatever riches have been denied us by the non-fulfilment of these projects there is more than ample compensation in *Noye's Fludde*. As in *Saint Nicolas*, the audience participate by singing well-loved hymns, but the greatness of *Noye's Fludde* lies in its imaginative involvement of the children and in the invention of evocative sounds from such unusual instruments as sandpaper rubbed together and the famous 'slung mugs' – cups or mugs of differing sizes and thickness suspended by their handles from a string and struck by a wooden spoon to give a magical impression of raindrops.[7] The impact of this touching work on its first audience – and on all its subsequent audiences – in Orford Church on 18 June 1958 might have seemed out of all proportion to the musical substance and means employed to anyone not familiar with music's ability to attain emotional profundity by apparently the simplest or oddest methods. Sir Kenneth Clark (later Lord Clark) summed it up when he wrote: 'To sit in Orford Church, where I had spent so many hours of my childhood dutifully waiting some spark of divine fire, and then to receive it at last in the performance of *Noye's Fludde*, was an over-whelming experience'.[8] The production and set were by the young Colin Graham, costumes and masks by Ceri Richards, and the cast, which included Owen Brannigan and Gladys Parr as Noye and his wife and Michael Crawford (later to be well known as a television actor) as Jaffett, was conducted by Charles Mackerras.

11

War Requiem

'It does not matter what style a composer chooses to write in, as long as he has something definite to say, and says it clearly.' That sounds like Vaughan Williams, but it comes from *The Story of Music* by Britten and Imogen Holst, published in 1958. Serialism was much in the air at that date and it had been noted that he had used a 12-note theme as the basis of *The Turn of the Screw*. But this represented neither musically nor theoretically a move towards Schoenbergian principles, it was merely another facet of Britten's creative eclecticism. He told Murray Schafer that serialism had never attracted him as a method. He did not feel that tonality was outworn, and he found many serial rules arbitrary. 'For example', he said, 'my *Nocturne* opens with a long vocal melisma descending, and it closes with its inversion ascending, but I would consider it no great virtue to consciously know that.' The *Nocturne*, op. 60, was written in the summer in 1958 and is one of his 'anthology' works, like the *Serenade*. In this case, poems by eight poets were set for tenor and string orchestra, with seven *obbligato*[1] instruments added, each lending a particular colour to the movement in which it, or they, is used. The work was written for the centenary of the Leeds Festival and first performed there on 16 October 1958 by Pears and the BBC Symphony Orchestra, conducted by Rudolf Schwarz. It is dedicated, like Berg's *Wozzeck*, to Mahler's widow Alma.

The other 1958 work showed that he had lost none of his youthful skill in setting a foreign language, this time German. The *Sechs Hölderlin-Fragmente*, op. 61, dedicated to the Prince of Hesse, were sung by Pears, accompanied by Britten, at the Prince's home, the Schloss Wolfsgarten at Langen, near Darmstadt, on 20 November 1958, the Prince's fiftieth birthday. The first performance had been broadcast in Britain a few days earlier. In 1959 Britten composed two special commissions, the academically tongue-in-cheek *Cantata Academica*, op. 62, written for the 500th anniversary in 1960 of the foundation of Basle University and performed there on 1 July 1960, conducted by Paul Sacher, and the *Missa Brevis*, op. 63, for boys' voices and organ, which marked the retirement of George Malcolm as organist and choirmaster of Westminster Cathedral. It was first sung, in the cathedral, on 22 July 1959. But now, after five years, work began on a new opera to celebrate the enlargement of the stage and orchestral pit and other improvements at the Jubilee Hall, Aldeburgh, for the 1960 festival. With less than a year in which to work, there was no time to have a libretto written, so Britten 'took one that was ready to hand'.² He and Pears decided to adapt Shakespeare's *A Midsummer Night's Dream*, a play Britten had always loved. He was not at all daunted to tackle a masterpiece

which already had a strong verbal music of its own ... The first task was to get it into manageable shape, which basically entailed simplifying and cutting an extremely complex story ... I do not feel in the least guilty at having cut the play in half. The original Shakespeare will survive ... I actually started work on the opera in October and finished it on, I think, Good Friday [15 April 1960] – seven months for everything, including the score ... It is the fastest of any big opera I have written, though I wrote *Let's Make an Opera!* in a fortnight.³

This speed is the more remarkable in that Britten was ill during its composition. 'A lot of the third act was written when I was not at all well with flu. I find that one's inclination, whether one wants to work or not, does not in the least affect the quality of the work done.'

Britten's op. 64 was first performed in the Jubilee Hall by the English Opera Group on 11 June 1960, conducted by the composer. The producer was John Cranko and the designer John Piper, assisted by Carl Toms. Not everything went as planned in this production for, as Colin Graham has explained,³ at this time 'Cranko was beset by personal and professional problems that inhibited his work on the opera (particularly his own preparations) and that finally resulted in his leaving the country' (to take a post in Stuttgart). Jennifer Vyvyan created the role of Tytania, with Forbes Robinson, Owen Brannigan, Thomas Hemsley, Johanna Peters, April Cantelo and Marjorie Thomas in the cast, and Pears in the relatively minor role of Flute. The opera paid tribute to one remarkable voice the owner of which had impressed Britten by his artistry in Purcell – the counter-tenor Alfred Deller. As Oberon, the unearthly sounds of this great singer made the unforgettably right effect; so did the use of boys' voices for the fairies.

The veteran critic of *The Times*, Frank Howes, fell in love with the opera. He described it, on 17 June 1960, as 'a major opera of the size and quality to follow *Peter Grimes* around the world, for it contains music as imaginative as the text to which it is set ... The impression made by the performance ... was that of being gripped by a spell, of being subjected to a dose of Oberon's own medicine.' The imaginative quality of Britten's invention, Howes wrote, was 'comparable to Shakespeare's use of the common words of the language. No need of twelve little semitones all in a row, nor of any doctrinaire formulae, if a composer can invent as Britten does by merely contemplating his drama, his text and his orchestra. His invention in this opera is as fully saturated as Wagner's in the concentrated *leitmotiv* of *The Ring*.'

Later in June *A Midsummer Night's Dream* was taken to the Holland Festival and performances throughout the world soon followed, as Howes had foretold. On 2 February 1961 it was first performed at Covent Garden, with a larger body of strings. Georg Solti conducted and Sir John Gielgud was the producer, with new sets by Piper. Covent Garden had in that year taken over managerial and financial responsibility for the English Opera Group.

Britten's other principal task in 1960 was also operatic, a revision of *Billy Budd* from four acts to two. The title-role was taken by Joseph Ward, who was then singing as a baritone. Britten wrote to him[4]: 'I am sure you are going to be a terrific Billy Budd – you have all the gifts for it ... He is rather a wonderful character'. Ward had created the role of Starveling in *A Midsummer Night's Dream* and was dubbed by Britten and Pears 'Joe, the first excellent Moon (pp!)' because he devised a way of singing 'moon shine' which amused Britten. This new version was first heard on radio on 13 November 1960 in a BBC studio performance conducted by Britten. It did not reach the stage until 1964, at Covent Garden. Another event in 1960 was to have far-reaching effects, musical and personal. In September of that year Britten went to the Royal Festival Hall to hear the first performance outside Russia of Shostakovich's first Cello Concerto, with the dedicatee, Mstislav Rostropovich, as soloist. This was the period when the Soviet Union was ruled by Nikita Khruschev and a much more liberal attitude towards the arts prevailed. Soviet musicians travelled abroad more freely, and reciprocal visits were welcomed. The restrictive grip on Soviet composers which had led to the Zhdanov condemnations of Shostakovich and Prokofiev in 1948 had relaxed. Shostakovich went to London for this first performance and invited Britten to sit in his box. Afterwards, in the green-room, Shostakovich introduced the cellist to Britten and Rostropovich at once asked Britten to write a work for him. 'I'll come to your hotel to discuss it tomorrow morning', Britten replied.[5]

So began one of the warmest friendships in Britten's life. The two men were opposite in character, the Englishman shy and aloof, the

Russian open-hearted in his affection and admiration. Music bound them tightly together. They communicated in a form of German which they called 'Aldeburgh Deutsch', and soon Rostropovich became 'Slava' and Britten was nicknamed 'Beninka'. At the hotel meeting Britten agreed to write a cello sonata. This was completed in January 1961. Britten sent the manuscript to Russia, inviting Rostropovich to give the first performance at that year's Aldeburgh Festival. They first played it through together at Britten's flat in St John's Wood at a meeting at which they were both very nervous. 'Ben said, "Well, Slava, do you think we have time for a drink first?" I said, "Yes, yes", so we both drank a large whisky. Then Ben said: "Maybe we have time for another one?" "Yes, yes", I said. Another large whisky. After four or five very large whiskies we finally sat down and played through the sonata. We played like pigs, but we were so happy.'[6] When they gave the first performance in the Jubilee Hall on 7 July 1961, Rostropovich became passionately committed to the whole idea of the Aldeburgh Festival. With him, also staying at The Red House with Britten, was his wife, the soprano Galina Vishnevskaya, one of the Bolshoy's leading singers, and she, too, became one of Britten's most precious friends. The photographs taken of these three people at the 1961 festival radiate happiness.

Yet all this time Britten had another preoccupation. The one type of work missing from his output was a really large-scale choral piece, an oratorio. In the 1950s he asked Auden for a libretto and received one which was impossible to set because of its length. At Zermatt in 1955 he asked Ronald Duncan for a work suitable for York Minster. A text based on St Peter was sent but never used. The impetus Britten needed – some special occasion – was supplied with the building of the new Coventry Cathedral to a design by Basil Spence. Several artists – Sutherland, Epstein, Piper and Hutton – contributed work to the building, and for its dedication in the Spring of 1962 an arts festival was organized, with several commissioned works. Tippett's opera *King Priam*, for example, was a Coventry commission. Britten was asked for a big choral work. He readily agreed, stimulated by two factors. First, there was the challenge of the acoustics of the new building. 'The best music to listen to in a great Gothic church is the polyphony which was written for it, and was calculated for its resonance', he said in 1964.[7] 'This was my approach in the *War Requiem* – I calculated it for a big reverberant acoustic, and that is where it sounds best.' Secondly, as a lifelong pacifist he was deeply stirred by the thought of a new cathedral being erected near the ruins of the mediaeval cathedral destroyed by bombs in 1940. He saw the chance to make a public declaration of his hatred of war and the destruction it caused and to emphasize the importance of reconciliation.

He had the brilliant idea of a requiem on two planes: a traditional setting of the Latin Mass for the Dead for soprano solo, chorus and large orchestra, and, interpolated among its six main movements, settings for male soloists and chamber orchestra of nine poems by the First World War poet Wilfred Owen. In a selection of his favourite poems which he chose for a BBC programme in 1958, Britten had included Owen's 'Strange Meeting', and his 'The Kind Ghosts' is one of the movements of the *Nocturne*. Moreover, Owen's preface to his poems said everything Britten wanted his music to say: 'I am not concerned with Poetry. My subject is War, and the pity of War. The Poetry is in the pity. Yet these elegies are to this generation in no sense consolatory. They may be to the next. All a poet can do today is warn. That is why the true Poets must be truthful.'[8] The theme of reconciliation, epitomized in lines from 'Strange Meeting'

I am the enemy you killed, my friend...
Let us sleep now

was further emphasized by Britten in his wish that the soloists at the first performance should be English, German and Russian – Pears, Dietrich Fischer-Dieskau, and Galina Vishnevskaya – but this was frustrated in the event by the soprano's unavailability. Her place was taken, memorably, by Heather Harper. The work was dedicated to the memory of four of Britten's friends, three of whom had been killed in the Second World War. The fourth committed suicide in 1959.

Britten completed *War Requiem*, op. 66, on 20 December 1961. Five days before the first performance, William Mann, in *The Times* of 25 May 1962, wrote a preliminary article which ended thus: 'It is not a requiem to console the living; sometimes it does not even help the dead to sleep soundly. It can only disturb every living soul, for it denounces the barbarism more or less awake in mankind with all the authenticity that a great composer can muster. There is no doubt at all, even before next Wednesday's performance, that it is Britten's masterpiece.' No one who was in Coventry Cathedral on the evening of 30 May will ever forget the emotional effect of the first performance in which Meredith Davies conducted the large chorus and orchestra and Britten the chamber orchestra. Mann, in *The Times* next day, wrote of the work as 'so superbly proportioned and calculated, so humiliating and disturbing in effect, in fact so tremendous, that every performance it is given ought to be a momentous occasion ... the most masterly and nobly imagined work that Britten has ever given us'.

Not since Walton's *Belshazzar's Feast* in 1931 had a choral work so impressed the British public and critics. Over the next two or three years, performances were mounted by all the leading concert societies. London first heard it, in Westminster Abbey, on 6 December, a night of thick fog. It was performed in several foreign cities. Decca recorded it in January 1963 and when the recording was issued in May 1963 it sold over 200,000 sets in five months, an extraordinary figure for any work, let alone a contemporary one. With the use it makes of the Owen poems, the *War Requiem* was by chance perfectly timed for the commemoration in 1964 of the fiftieth anniversary of the outbreak of the First World War. Ten years earlier, with *Gloriana*, Britten had seemed to offend the nation[9]; now he had spoken for it. 'I hope some day to do a great work – a sort of national thing that my fellow Englishmen might take to themselves and love.' Elgar had said that in 1898; if Britten had ever felt likewise, he had certainly, in 1962, fulfilled the hope.

Or perhaps he echoed a composer nearer to his heart, Holst, in saying 'Every artist ought to pray that he may not be a "success". Woe to you when all men speak well of you.' At any rate the unprecedented success of the *War Requiem* marked a climacteric in Britten's career. Never again was he to deliver such a large-scale piece of oratory. Henceforward his style was to become more severe, his utterance more intimate. Even the next 'public' work, *Cantata Misericordium*, op. 69, composed in 1963 for the centenary of the Red Cross, was on a more restricted level. Writing[10] at the time of his fiftieth birthday in November 1963, Britten confessed to his misgivings. 'People sometimes seem to think that with a number of works now lying behind, one must be bursting with confidence. It is not so at all. I haven't yet achieved the simplicity I should like to in my music, and am enormously aware that I haven't yet come up to the technical standards Bridge set me.' He put it even more bluntly in a conversation when Nicholas Maw told him that work was going well on his own opera. 'Good!', Britten said, 'get as much done now as you can, because it gets more difficult as you grow older'.[11]

Inevitably, too, some of the critics, disconcerted perhaps by the unrestrained rapture with which the *War Requiem* had been acclaimed, even perhaps worried by its immediate appeal and popularity, began to search for, and find, flaws in it. But perhaps the most celebrated reaction to its success was that of Stravinsky, who had shown a too-coincidental penchant, after 1951, for following in Britten's footsteps.

He too set the *Lyke-Wake Dirge* in his *Cantata*; he too wrote a musical play about Noah (*The Flood*); and he too wrote a sacred ballad *Abraham and Isaac*. He was fully aware of this, and abandoned his original title – *Sinfonia da Requiem* – for the *Requiem Canticles*! Stravinsky had not been amused when Auden reported to him that Britten liked *The Rake's Progress* – 'everything but the music'. He was not uncomplimentary about the *War Requiem* itself but was irritated by the English critics' adulation, and particularly by the critic of *The Times* who asserted that 'practically everyone who has heard it has instantly acknowledged it as a masterpiece'. To this Stravinsky countered Craftily[12] that 'the Battle-of-Britten sentiment' was 'so thick and the tide of applause ... so loud that I, for one, was not always able to hear the music ... Kleenex at the ready, then, one goes from the critics to the music, knowing that if one should dare to disagree with "practically everyone", one will be made to feel as if one had failed to stand up for "God Save the Queen". The victim of all this, however, is the composer for, of course, nothing fails like success ...'

So sour a reaction was not the general response, however. At the end of the Coventry performance (unsatisfactory acoustically as it was), Fischer-Dieskau was so upset that Pears had difficulty persuading him to leave the choirstalls. 'I was completely undone,' the baritone wrote in his memoirs *Echoes of a Lifetime* (English edition 1989), 'I did not know where to hide my face. Dead friends and past suffering arose in my mind.'

12

Noh-play in Orford

Britten wrote only two small works during 1962. On 1 May he composed a setting of *Psalm 150* for children's voices and instruments. This was his offering for the centenary of his Lowestoft preparatory school, South Lodge, by then re-named Old Buckenham Hall School, and it was performed there in July. (The first public performance was a year later, at the Aldeburgh Festival on 24 June 1963.) In December he completed *A Hymn of St Columba* for chorus and organ to mark the 1,400th anniversary of Columba's missionary voyage from Ireland to Iona. This was sung at Gartan, Co. Donegal, the saint's birthplace, on 2 June 1963. On 22 October he was made an honorary freeman of Aldeburgh and in his speech of acceptance again stressed his belief that 'an artist should be part of his community'. Without direct contact with his public, he said, an artist's work lacked focus.

> This has made a great deal of modern work obscure and impracticable, only useable by highly skilled performers and only understandable by the most erudite ... I am against experiment for experiment's sake, originality at all costs. It's necessary to say this because there are audiences who are not discriminating about it. They think that everything new is good; that if it is shocking it must be important. There is all the difference in the world between Picasso, the great, humble artist, or Henry Moore, and the chap who slings paint on canvas; between Stravinsky, and electronic experimenters ...

Behind these words lay a rueful appreciation of the divisions which in 1963 were the subject of polemics among the musical intelligentsia of the time. This was the period when serialism, in its several forms, was regarded as the passport to musical salvation. The post-Schoenbergians in Britain, after years of neglect which they attributed partly to the dominance of such folk-song nationalists as Vaughan Williams, were now clamouring to be heard, and the BBC at any rate was striving to correct the imbalance of previous decades where they were concerned. A younger generation of British composers, not all of them by any means card-carrying serialists or atonalists, reacted against Britten's music, which they found 'irrelevant'; among them, for example, was the increasingly important figure of Peter Maxwell Davies, who later recanted and described Britten, in a memorial tribute, as 'our supreme creator of music'.[1] But the consensus of opinion in his native country was that Britten was the outstanding composer of his time, a 'modern' whose music was also accessible. To the avant-garde in Europe (and to its followers in Britain) he was, however, too accessible, this being regarded as a sign of superficiality. Composers such as Boulez in France and Nono in Italy had no time for Britten, nor had the influential musicologist Adorno. So that when Englishmen spoke or wrote proudly of Britten's high reputation abroad, certain reservations had to be made. However, the Austrian-born Hans Keller, bringing a cosmopolitan approach to his view of British musical life, roundly declared that Britten was 'the greatest composer alive',[2] a statement which apparently caused its author to be *persona non grata* with Stravinsky!

In March 1963 Britten and Pears visited the Soviet Union for a British Council festival of British music in Moscow and Leningrad, another sign of the lessening tension between Russia and the West during the Khruschev era. Among works by Britten performed were the *Interludes* from *Peter Grimes*, *Sinfonia da Requiem*, *Serenade*, *Winter Words*, *Sechs Hölderlin-Fragmente* and the Cello Sonata. He was warmly received and he told *Pravda* that the Soviet public 'showed an enviable breadth of artistic perception. It is a wonderful public'. While in Russia he worked on the *Symphony for Cello and Orchestra*, op. 68, which he was writing for Rostropovich, and completed it on 3 May on his return to Aldeburgh in the hope that the first performance would be given at that year's festival. However, Rostropovich was ill and the work was held back. Three weeks later he finished *Cantata Misericordium*, op. 69; Ansermet conducted the first performance in Geneva on 1 September, with Pears and Fischer-Dieskau as soloists. Two other 1963 works were *Nocturnal after John Dowland*, op. 70, for guitar, written for Julian Bream to play on 12 June at the 1964 Aldeburgh Festival, and another 'Night Piece', *Notturno* for piano solo, composed as a test piece for all competitors in the newly established Leeds International Piano Competition with which Marion Harewood was associated. An incident connected with this short piece illustrates Britten's continued touchiness where criticism was concerned. At a dinner to mark the inauguration of the competition in September 1963 to which Britten was invited, his neighbour innocently wondered aloud what the critics would say about the *Notturno* and was dumb-founded when Britten walked away. He was sometimes visited by the fear that his critics might be right; he tended to believe them. The perceptible change in his style after 1963, which began with the *Cello Symphony* and was to be even more marked in his next stage work, was a deliberate paring of his music to basics, perhaps caused by his suspicion that the public success of the *War Requiem* was attributable more to its theme than to the actual quality of the musical invention.

Assailed as he may have been by such doubts, he was left in no doubt of the place he occupied in his country's music as he approached his fiftieth birthday on 22 November 1963. Celebrations began on 12 September with an all-Britten Promenade Concert at which he conducted the first British performance of the *Cantata Misericordium*, with Pears and Thomas Hemsley. There was a new production of *Peter Grimes* at Sadler's Wells (16 October), and, under the editorship of Anthony Gishford (1908–75), a friend of long standing, Faber and Faber published a *Festschrift*³ comprising articles by about thirty-five of Britten's friends, including Forster, Plomer, Prince Ludwig and Edith Sitwell. The *Concerto for Orchestra* by Tippett was dedicated to Britten 'with affection and admiration'. A television profile, *Britten at Fifty*, was relayed on the night of the birthday itself and on radio there was a 'live' broadcast of the celebration in the Festival Hall, a concert performance by the Polyphonia Orchestra conducted by Bryan Fairfax of *Gloriana*, with Pears as Essex and Sylvia Fisher singing the role of Elizabeth 1. Nothing could have been chosen with more chance of pleasing the composer, but in the event he must have wondered whether there was not truly a curse on this opera for, just before the performance began, rumours began to circulate in the audience that President Kennedy had been wounded by an assassin's bullet and by the time of the first interval the President's death had been confirmed. As Deryck Cooke wrote in *The Listener* of 28 November, 'it seemed utterly intolerable to have to concentrate on music at such a moment'. Yet the occasion was not to prove sterile, for this timely revival led, as the BBC studio performance of *Billy Budd* had also led, to a stage revival within three years.

The performance provided the critics with the opportunity to reassess the opera in a more favourable light. 'Its three acts are a succession of magnificent and varied numbers ranging from almost *Aida*-like ceremonial pieces to some of the most moving operatic music Britten has ever written', Colin Mason wrote in *The Guardian* the next day. 'Dramatically it is tremendously taut and powerful.' Edmund Tracey, in *The Musical Times* of January 1964, declared that it was high time

Gloriana was staged again. 'We are not so well off for contemporary operas that we can afford to ignore *Gloriana*.'

For some time past, Britten had become a willing slave to the attractions of Venice and thither he went in February 1964 to concentrate on his next stage work, a new type of opera which he had invented and which he called 'parable for church performance'. This was to be *Curlew River*, op. 71; its origin was in the visit to Tokyo in February 1956. Britten, Pears and the Prince and Princess of Hesse went to see a fifteenth century Japanese Noh play, *Sumidagawa* (*The Sumida River*), about a mad woman who boards a ferry-boat while looking for her lost son. The ferryman tells her of a boy whom he had ferried across the river a year before. The child was exhausted after escaping from robbers and died on reaching the other side. The woman weeps, realizing it was her son, and the ferryman takes her to his grave. As the Prince has told us, the visitors were at first baffled by the language and the production –

> no scenery, except a stylised painting of a pine tree on the back wall of the stage. In the middle, against this back wall, two drummers sit. They let off sudden bursts of clacking and gonging drum-sounds with their hands. To these drummings they recite in strained voices, like people about to vomit ... Everything on the stage happens in retarded motion ... Most of the costumes are obviously historical, made of the most pleasant silks and brocades ... With the finest clothes go the wonderful masks which can change their expression by a tilt of the head ... We feel this is more than an interesting experience.[4]

Britten, too, recorded[5] the 'tremendous impression' the occasion made upon him:

> a totally new 'operatic' experience. There was no conductor – the instrumentalists sat on the stage as did the chorus, and the chief characters made their entrance down a long ramp. The lighting was strictly non-theatrical. The cast was all-male, the one female character wearing an exquisite mask which made no attempt to hide the male jowl beneath it. The memory of this play has seldom left my mind in the years since ... Was it not possible to use just such a story ... with an English background (for there was no question in any case of a pastiche from the ancient Japanese)? Surely the mediaeval religious drama in England would have had a comparable setting – an all-male cast of ecclesiastics – a simple austere staging in a church – a very limited instrumental accompaniment – a moral story?

He approached William Plomer, who had lived in Japan, for a libretto. 'And so', Britten said, 'we came from Sumidagawa to Curlew River and a church in the Fens, but with the same story and similar characters; and whereas in Tokyo the music was the ancient Japanese music jealously preserved by successive generations, here I have started the work with that wonderful plainsong hymn *Te lucis ante terminum*, and from it the whole piece may be said to have grown.' Plomer convincingly converted the work from its Buddhist philosophy to a Christian outlook, and Britten framed the work with the plainsong hymn sung by the Abbot and the monks as they enter and leave the church in procession. On reaching the acting area, the monks who are to play the parts of the Madwoman, the Ferryman and the Traveller are ceremonially robed and at the end resume their habits. There is no conductor and each performer must time his part. To ensure that the singers and players knew which part had precedence at particular moments, Britten invented a pause mark ⌒ which he called the 'curlew sign', to indicate that 'the performer must listen and wait till the other performers have reached the next barline, or meeting-point – i.e. the note or rest can be longer or shorter than its written value'. The instrumentation of the work reflects the Japanese original in its extra emphasis on percussion, with parts for five small untuned drums, five small bells and a large tuned gong. To these were added flute (doubling piccolo), horn, viola, double bass, harp and chamber organ.

The producer of the first performance, Colin Graham, had to invent 'a new convention of presentation and performance',[6] in no way theatrical:

> The simple setting – basically a raised and raked circle, some sixteen feet in diameter, approached from two directions by a spiralling ramp following the curve of the circle – is accordingly placed at one end of a church ... At the foot of the ramp, to one side of the stage, sit the instrumentalists – lay brothers ... The action of the story itself was as formalised as a ritual: the miming, an integral feature of the performance, was symbolic and reduced to its essentials. This kind of movement must of course be charged with intensity if it is not to become merely static, but unlike naturalistic acting, the emotion should never be expressed with the face or eyes but always by a rehearsed ritualistic movement of the hands, head or body ... The art of acting in masks is hard to assimilate, but with every tilt or angle of the head a well-designed mask can take on an almost magical life of its own ... Every movement of head or hand, like every note and word in the score, must be essential and, although formalised, must be designed and executed with intention and the utmost intensity. This requires enormous concentration on the part of the actor – an almost Yoga-like muscular and mental control.

Britten completed *Curlew River* in Aldeburgh on 2 April 1964. He dedicated it to Tippett 'in friendship and admiration', and the first performance was given in Orford Church on 12 June during the 1964 festival. Britten rewrote the climax of the work five times during rehearsals. The first performance began nearly an hour late because, during a severe thunderstorm, a generator was struck and the audience was left in darkness. 'I thought this would be disastrous', Britten recalled,[7] 'in fact, it allowed people time to meditate and get into the right frame of mind. I'm sure this contributed to the work's impact.' Colin Graham's production was enhanced by Annena Stubbs's striking costumes. The critics were respectful and faintly puzzled; for example, Jeremy Noble in *The Musical Times* of August 1964 found the work 'flawed by what seems to me a confusion as to its true aims ... Musically [it is] almost impossible to find fault with, as long as one can accept that, as in Noh, the music is the handmaid of the drama and at times a very submissive one.'

After Venice, Britten travelled to the Soviet Union to conduct the first performance of the *Cello Symphony*, with Rostropovich as soloist, in Moscow on 12 March. John Warrack, the English music critic, was present and reported in *The Musical Times* of June 1964 that the reception accorded to Britten was 'of the cordiality reserved for a friend, not an honoured stranger'. He ended his review by declaring the work to be 'one of Britten's major achievements, his greatest instrumental work to date. It is music so "right" that one cannot believe one has not known it half one's life'. When Britten was in Leningrad he attended a concert performance of *Peter Grimes*, its first in Russia. This led to stagings of the opera in Leningrad and Moscow later in the year. Nineteen sixty-four was a year of travelling for Britten. In Budapest in the Spring he met the twins Zoltán and Gabriel Jeney, aged twelve, sons of a distinguished flautist, and was impressed by their gifts:

> Each played the piano, one the flute and the other the violin: they sang, sight-read, and answered difficult musical questions ... At the end of the meeting they approached me and charmingly, if forcefully, asked me to write them a work. Though I claimed that I was too busy, my refusal was brushed aside; however, I insisted on one small bargaining point: I would do it only if they would write me a long letter telling me about themselves, their work and their play – in *English*. I felt safe. After a week or two, however, the letter arrived, in vivid and idiosyncratic English, and I felt I must honour my promise. *Gemini Variations* is the result.[8]

In May Britten was told that he was to be the recipient of the first Aspen Award in the humanities, established in 1963. (He had received the Hanseatic Goethe Prize of Hamburg in 1961.) This, a sum of 30,000 dollars, was the benefaction of Robert O. Anderson, chairman of the Institute of Humanistic Studies at Aspen, Colorado, to honour 'the individual anywhere in the world judged to have made the greatest contribution to the advancement of the humanities'. More than 100 artists, scholars, writers, poets, philosophers and statesmen were nominated by various international intellectual and cultural leaders; the citation of Britten's award described him as 'a brilliant composer, performer, and interpreter through music of human feelings, moods, and thoughts' who 'has truly inspired man to understand, clarify and appreciate more fully his own nature, purpose and destiny'. Britten travelled to Aspen to receive the award on 31 July before an assembly of about 1,500 people. At the ceremony he delivered his celebrated address, which has already been quoted several times in this book. It was a declaration of his belief in the value of 'occasional' music, written for particular people and places. 'It is the composer's duty, as a member of society, to speak to or for his fellow human beings ...'[9] The most controversial part of his address was the section in which he deplored that, through modern science, works like the *St Matthew Passion* were available to 'any loud roomful of cocktail drinkers at the turn of a switch ... Music ... demands some preparation, some effort, a journey to a special place, saving up for a ticket, some homework on the programme perhaps ... It demands as much effort on the listener's part as the other two corners of the triangle, this holy triangle of composer, performer and listener'. For many, of course, the homework is done most effectively by listening at the turn of a switch to their radio or gramophone, and one has not attended many cocktail parties at which the *St Matthew Passion* was deemed a suitable aural background, but Britten's plea for music not to be debased by its too-easy availability remains valid and important. Six years later, in the interview with Alan Blyth already quoted on page 44, he admitted he might have 'slightly' overstated the case. 'A record is wonderful to have as long as we realize it is a substitute, not the real thing ... A record *can* give the wrong impression of a piece of music. As long as we keep that in mind, we are free to enjoy them. Of course, they have another purpose in preserving a style of performance...'[10]

In October Britten travelled with the English Opera Group to Riga, Leningrad and Moscow, where performances were given of *Albert Herring*, *The Rape of Lucretia* and *The Turn of the Screw*. During these visits to Russia the friendship with Dmitri Shostakovich was cemented, and it was in Moscow on 14 October that Shostakovich gave to Britten a photograph inscribed 'to dear Benjamin Britten. One of my most beloved composers'. The English Opera Group had earlier taken *Curlew River* to the Holland Festival after its first performance at Aldeburgh. The 1964 Aldeburgh Festival was also notable for Rostropovich's performance of the cadenzas Britten wrote for him to play in Haydn's Cello Concerto in C and for the first British performance of the *Cello Symphony* on 18 June. Few of the critics were as positive about the *Cello Symphony* as John Warrack had been, although the critic of *The Times* wrote that 'it does not need our good wishes, for plainly it is a masterpiece and plainly, too, its deeper meaning will clarify in the course of future hearings'. The title of the work caused considerable argument. Was it a symphony or a concerto? Jeremy Noble, reviewing the first London performance on 15 July, declared it a 'hybrid' and 'neither the symphony its title claims it is, nor the concerto it implies it is not. Is this because Britten has attempted to use the duality inherent in the concerto medium (soloist and orchestra) as a substitute for the more profound duality of musical ideas inherent in the concept of the symphony?' (The critic of *The Times* had found 'the nature of the thought ... symphonic in the fullest sense of the term'.)

Britten's association with Boosey & Hawkes ended at this time after thirty years. The relationship had been deteriorating for some time and the last straw came with the termination of employment at Boosey's of Donald Mitchell, the music critic and co-editor with Hans Keller of the 1952 Britten symposium. He had been appointed, at Britten's insistence and suggestion, as a consultant on new composers, with a special responsibility for Britten's affairs. At the same time he was part-time adviser to Faber & Faber on building up their list of books on music. In a letter to Mitchell, Britten wrote something to the effect that he sometimes wished Faber might publish his music. Mitchell mentioned to Faber's that Britten was seeking another publisher – could they do anything about it? They immediately decided that somehow they would, and eventually Faber Music emerged as part of Faber & Faber. Henceforward Faber published all Britten's new works, beginning with the guitar *Nocturnal*, op. 70, and *Curlew River*, the scores of which appeared in 1965. In 1966 Faber Music became a subsidiary company with its own board, of which Britten was a member. From 1966 to 1971 Richard de la Mare was chairman. He was succeeded by Peter du Sautoy, who as vice-chairman of Faber & Faber in 1964 had first approached Britten. In 1977 Donald Mitchell became chairman of Faber Music, retiring in 1986. These events are a significant example of Britten's ability to perceive a pattern that might come about through certain friends, acquaintances and institutions being brought into a new conjunction. Not only did he see how it could help him, he also firmly believed that a new music publishing house in Britain was needed in any case.

13

Moscow and Maltings

In 1964 Britten was awarded the Gold Medal of the Royal Philharmonic Society and in 1965 was appointed a member of the Order of Merit, the honour he cherished most. Since the Order's institution in 1902 only two musicians had been members of this most exclusive body, limited to a maximum of twenty-four at a time, all appointed by the sovereign personally. They were Elgar (1911) and Vaughan Williams (1935). Now, at fifty-one, Britten followed them – indeed, he outstripped them, since he was also Companion of Honour.

On his return from Russia, he wrote the *First Cello Suite*, op. 72, in November and December 1974. He and Pears decided that 1965 should be a 'Sabbatical year' where conducting and recitals were concerned, and they gave no performances except at the Aldeburgh Festival. In the Spring they went to India, for a holiday. There, at Thekaddy, Britten began to keep his promise to the Hungarian twins and started *Gemini Variations*, op. 73, completing it in Aldeburgh in March. On 6 April he completed a new song-cycle for voice and piano, his first for eight years. This was *Songs and Proverbs of William Blake*, op. 74, composed for Dietrich Fischer-Dieskau and dedicated to him – 'For Dieter: the past and the future'. He and Britten gave the first performance at the Aldeburgh Festival on 24 June 1965, three days before Rostropovich played the *Cello Suite*. The *Gemini Variations* were also introduced at the festival, on 19 June, played by the twins and with Kodály in the audience – the theme of the work is taken from the fourth of his *Epigrams* (1954). The festival over, there was one more commission to fulfil in July, an anthem for chorus, *Voices for Today*, for the twentieth anniversary of the United Nations, which had a simultaneous triple first performance on 24 October in New York, Paris and London.

On 3 August 1965 Britten and Pears flew via Moscow to Yerevan in Armenia, where they had been invited to stay in the Composers' Home for Creative Work in Dilidjan, with Galina and Mstislav Rostropovich. At London Airport Britten bought the Penguin edition of Pushkin's poetry to read on the flight. Beguiled by the poems, he thought he might help his Russian if he set some of them and asked Rostropovich and his wife to read aloud to him those he had chosen and to teach him the correct pronunciation. He then worked out a transliteration and began to compose the cycle *The Poet's Echo*, op. 76. Four of the songs were composed by 16 August, the fifth a few days later after he had been ill with an upset stomach and the sixth a week later. Two of the songs were included in a Britten festival which began in Yerevan on 28 August. After leaving Armenia they all visited the house at Mikhailovskoe, near Pskov, in which Pushkin had been ordered to live from 1824 to 1826, after he had been dismissed from government service for supporting atheism. They were shown

the clock tower and its cracked clock which was there in Pushkin's time and still struck its old hours ... Our host begged to hear the Pushkin songs ... The last song of the set is the marvellous poem of insomnia, the ticking clock, persistent night-noises and the poet's cry for a meaning in them. Ben has started this with repeated staccato notes high-low high-low on the piano. Hardly had the little old piano begun its dry tick-tock tick-tock than clear and silvery outside the window, a yard from our heads, came ding, ding, ding, not loud but clear, Pushkin's clock joining in his song. It seemed to strike far more than midnight, to go on all through the song, and afterwards we sat spellbound...[1]

The Pushkin songs received their first complete public performance in Moscow Conservatory on 2 December 1965, with the dedicatees as performers, Vishnevskaya being accompanied by Rostropovich as pianist. A projected performance of the *Cello Symphony* with Rostropovich was forbidden by Britten because, to quote Pears's *Armenian Holiday*, a diary of this trip, the 'silly young conductor from Moscow' spent his four rehearsals on the *Grimes* Interludes and the *Young Person's Guide*, imagining the *Cello Symphony* to be a case of easy concerto accompaniment. Britten's *A Midsummer Night's Dream* had its first Russian performance on 28 October when Gennadi Rozhdestvensky conducted it at the Bolshoy Theatre, Moscow.

For the winter of 1965–6, Britten worked on his second church parable, *The Burning Fiery Furnace*, which he dedicated to Donald Mitchell and his wife Kathleen. The libretto was again by Plomer; as soon as *Curlew River* was produced, they had begun to plan a successor, 'something much less sombre, an altogether gayer affair', Britten said. While on holiday, Britten had been impressed by the colours in the windows of Chartres Cathedral and by a sculpture of Nebuchadnezzar and the Fiery Furnace. So the second parable began to stir. Work on it was delayed by Britten's illness, which culminated in an operation for diverticulitis. Nevertheless, it was completed on 5 April 1966, and the first performance was given in Orford Church on 9 June, again in a collaboration between Colin Graham and Annena Stubbs. Later the English Opera Group performed it in Holland and at various English festivals. The critics found it more human and colourful than *Curlew River*, and one of them had his ear to the ground for the beginnings of a rejection of Britten by the new generation. 'Britten', said Edward Greenfield in *The Guardian* of 10 June, 'has attempted a cross-fertilisation from Oriental music more striking than in *Curlew River*. No doubt the avant-garde will condemn the experiment for its "reactionary" qualities, but in some ways Britten is here as close as any of the avant-garde ... to achieving the new "complex of sounds" which is the confessed ideal of Pierre Boulez'.

Yet the most satisfaction Britten can have attained in 1966 came from the genuinely warm and appreciative critical reception of the revival of *Gloriana* by Sadler's Wells Opera on 21 October, with Sylvia Fisher as the Queen, John Wakefield as Essex and Jennifer Vyvyan, who had created the part, as Lady Rich. The producer was Colin Graham and the conductor Mario Bernardi. For this production, Britten revised the Queen's soliloquy in Act I and the opera's epilogue. '*Gloriana* may not be faultless', wrote Winton Dean in *The Musical Times* of October 1966, 'but it is marvellously rich in invention and technical skill. Dependence on set numbers and ensembles and interweaving of public and private conflicts ... recall Verdi.' 'This is no mere pageant opera', wrote Edward Greenfield in *The Guardian* of 22 October. 'Now we can see that the display passages – lute-songs, fanfares, a complete masque – are not just adornment but an essential part of a rich and moving entertainment.'

In December 1966 Britten and Pears again went to Moscow and Leningrad to give recitals, staying on to celebrate the Russian New Year with the Rostropoviches and Shostakovich. The Rostropoviches had spent Christmas at Aldeburgh the previous year and this was reciprocation. After dinner on 26 December they all played 'Happy Families'. 'Slava had been champion at Aldeburgh', Pears wrote,[2] 'but this time it was Dmitri who triumphed'. The talk spread to 'Stravinsky and the drivelling muck written about Dmitri by Nabokov, etc. Ben tells his recent dream of Stravinsky as a monumental hunchback pointing with quivering finger at a passage in the *Cello Symphony*: "How dare you write that bar?" Dmitri quickly excited and depressed.' On 30 December they visited the Hermitage art gallery in Leningrad to see the Rembrandts – 'surely greatest of all the Prodigal Son [*The Return of the Prodigal*] (of course, this is the subject for the next

Church Parable).' Pears relates that on 2 December they attended a rehearsal of Shostakovich's Thirteenth Symphony, his setting of poems by Yevgeny Yevtushenko which condemn anti-Semitism. Present at the lunch afterwards with Shostakovich and his wife were, to quote Pears again, 'Z and wife. This man has ... been the arch-enemy of liberal artistic musical thought for 20 years ... We have met him several times. This Gruyère-faced man is immensely dislikeable.'

Just before he left for Russia, Britten completed a setting of the folk-tune *Hankin Booby*, for wind and drums, which had been commissioned by the Greater London Council for the inauguration of the Queen Elizabeth Hall on the South Bank on 1 March 1967. (He conducted most of the opening concert.) The previous summer, on 26 August 1966, he had finished a work for the 1967 Aldeburgh Festival, a 'vaudeville' for boys' voices and piano based on the English ballad *The Golden Vanity*. This was the result of a request in 1964 from the Vienna Boys' Choir for a short (eighteen-minute) opera for their concert programmes. The boys particularly asked Britten – with some feeling, one suspects – that they should not have to play girls' parts. Colin Graham wrote the libretto and the choir sang it in English. The first performance was such a success that the whole eighteen-minute work was immediately repeated.

The 1967 festival, extended to three weeks, was 'special', because it marked the completion of the new concert hall and opera house, The Maltings, at Snape, so called because it was the conversion (at a cost of £476,000) of an old building where barley had been processed into malt for brewing beer. John Culshaw, who produced most of Britten's major Decca recordings, remembered[3] that

> it was in the summer of 1965 that Ben and Peter invited me to go and explore an old building at Snape which might, by a considerable stretch of the imagination and a lot of money, be converted into the kind of multi-purpose hall that was so urgently needed by the Aldeburgh Festival. We walked round The Maltings and then clambered inside. It was all but impossible to imagine what it would be like when gutted, because at that stage it consisted of floor upon floor, with no through sight-line. We kept on descending until we reached the ovens in the basement. And yet ... there was a feeling about the place, about its setting by the river with the view of Iken Church through the reeds and across the marshes, that made it *right*. If Ben was to have a concert-hall on his doorstep, this was it...

The Maltings, which seats 800, was opened on 2 June 1967 by the Queen, accompanied by the Duke of Edinburgh. Later she lunched at The Red House. The original plan was for a concert hall as the first stage, but a Gulbenkian Foundation grant of £25,000 enabled the provision of dressing-rooms, an orchestra pit and stage lighting and equipment for opera. Grants from the Arts Council, the Decca Record Company, the Pilgrim Trust and £40,000 in private subscription paid for the hall. At the first concert, by the English Chamber Orchestra, Britten conducted a short new work he had written during December 1966 and January 1967 and had finished scoring on 16 March. This was *The Building of the House*, op. 79, for orchestra with optional chorus (East Anglian choirs at the first performance). This, Britten said in his programme-note, 'was certainly inspired by the excitement of the planning and building – and the haste! I wanted to find a suitable text, and to fit it to music singable by an amateur chorus with a professional orchestra. Imogen Holst suggested the text from *The Scottish Psalter*, and the old chorale tune which Bach loved to use'. The warmth and richness of the hall's acoustics were immediately acclaimed and proved equally suitable for opera when Colin Graham's new production of *A Midsummer Night's Dream* was staged on 7 June. On 3 June the Vienna Boys' Choir, in costume but without scenery, gave the first performance of *The Golden Vanity*. As directed in the score, the action was mimed – only a few basic 'props' such as telescopes and a rope are needed. On 25 June Britten conducted Peter Pears's shortened version for concert performance of Purcell's masque *The Fairy Queen* in an edition by Britten and Imogen Holst.

During August 1967, Britten completed a second *Cello Suite*, op. 80, for Rostropovich; in September he conducted Bach's *Christmas Oratorio* for a BBC television recording in Long Melford Church and then travelled with the English Opera Group to Montreal where performances of the two church parables were given at Expo '67, the international exhibition. He and Pears went on to New York to give recitals, following this visit with a recital tour of South America. They were heard much together also during the 1968 Edinburgh Festival, at which the then artistic director, Peter Diamand, built the programmes round Schubert and Britten. Thus not only did the festival audiences enjoy Pears and Britten as performers of the works they had in the most profound sense created, they heard, too, their incomparable interpretation of *Winterreise*. During the festival the world was shocked by the Russian invasion of Czechoslovakia to crush the more liberal régime of Dubček, and extra poignancy was given to the performance on 1 September of the *War Requiem*, with the three singers for whom it was written, Vishnevskaya, Pears, and Fischer-Dieskau.

But, increasingly, it was the Aldeburgh Festival which dominated Britten's life; his retirement into the world of Suffolk was almost complete, and after 1964 most of his works were written for, and first performed at, the festival. For the performers it was always a happy time. John Shirley-Quirk, writing in 1977 in the Covent Garden *Peter Grimes* memorial programme, recalled afternoons at The Red House

> for the families of the whole cast and orchestra with Ben and Peter as perfect hosts: vicious games of croquet played to Red House rules, whirlwind table tennis which I was not quite quick enough to watch, Indian or China tea to choose from, and rich cakes for young and non-slimmers alike ... Visits to The Red House also meant wonderful rehearsals ... where one could glimpse and marvel at the sleight-of-hand transformations of notes into moving (in every sense) universes of music.

With the added stimulus of The Maltings, Britten was particularly prolific for the 1968 festival, going to the only rival to Aldeburgh in his affections, Venice, in the early part of the year to work on his third church parable, *The Prodigal Son*, op. 81, dedicated to Shostakovich. He returned home, to become seriously ill a few days later with an infection which led to sub-acute bacterial endocarditis, the affliction which killed Mahler but can now be treated with massive doses of antibiotic drugs. This was the first ominous clue to the existence of a valvular heart-lesion, probably the legacy of a childhood attack of rheumatic fever, undiagnosed at the time, rather than of any congenital fault. This illness distressed him because he feared he might not finish the new work in time. With his strong sense of responsibility to others, he was keenly aware of the people whose jobs for the summer depended on the piece. He finished it just in time, on 22 April.

It was during the preparation of *The Prodigal Son* that another fascinating Britten operatic project finally evaporated. On his visit to Russia in 1963 he had heard Vishnevskaya as Natasha in Prokofiev's *War and Peace*. He mentioned this to Colin Graham, who suggested an opera based on Tolstoy's *Anna Karenina* as a vehicle for Vishnevskaya. Encouraged by Britten, Graham worked on a libretto and by 1967 there were plans for a Bolshoy *première* with Vishnevskaya in the title-role and Rostropovich as conductor and translator. However, when the Russians invaded Czechoslovakia the next year, any such production became diplomatically impossible. So the idea of adapting it for Snape grew, but by now Graham was dissatisfied with his libretto and sought Plomer's advice. Unfortunately, news of the project leaked into the Press. Britten was hypersensitive to premature discussion of his work and the outburst of interest by journalists and impresarios was enough to inhibit him. A similar occurrence had killed off *King Lear*. 'Public interest in the idea (leaked to the press) inhibited and froze it: Britten didn't need advice from unknown Shakespearians', wrote Pears.[4] One may sympathize with Britten's reaction while at the same time wondering if the 'public interest' did not provide him with an excuse to abandon subjects with which he was not entirely happy. If a creator is determined to create, it needs more than press speculation to put him off, as Britten himself was to show when he wrote *Death in Venice* in spite of allegations that the Visconti film had given him the idea.

14

The fire

The Prodigal Son had its first performance in Orford Church on 10 June 1968, and Rostropovich played the new *Cello Suite* in The Maltings on 17 June. On 13 June, Sadler's Wells Opera performed *Gloriana* at The Maltings. Two other short works were re-introduced on 19 June at a concert by the Ambrosian Singers, conducted by Philip Ledger who was now an artistic director of the festival. Encouraged by his new publishers, Britten had looked again at some of his boyhood works. He re-wrote two carols, *The Sycamore Tree*, composed to a traditional text in 1930, and *A Wealden Trio: The Song of the Women*, a 1929 setting of Ford Madox Ford. The first was dedicated to Imogen Holst, the second to Rosamund Strode, a former pupil of Imogen Holst, who had succeeded her in 1964 as Britten's music assistant and was an important member of Britten's Aldeburgh staff. In the summer of 1968 he re-wrote the five settings of Walter de la Mare which he had composed between 1928 and 1931, publishing them as *Tit for Tat* and dedicating them to the poet's son Richard, chairman at this time of Faber Music. They were performed by John Shirley-Quirk, accompanied by Britten, at Aldeburgh on 23 June 1969. In the Spring of 1969 Britten also re-wrote the *Five Walztes* for piano (he retained the childhood misspelling) composed as his 'Opus 3' between 1923 and 1925 and dedicated to his father. And on 18 March 1969 he completed a *Suite for Harp*, op. 83, written for Osian Ellis, who played it first on 24 June 1969 in the Jubilee Hall, Aldeburgh. This particular festival programme provided fuel for those of Britten's critics who felt that he had retreated too far from reality into an almost domestic world of his own in which the idealized past was treated with nostalgia. *The Prodigal Son* seemed to them to symbolize this retreat.

If anyone in Suffolk had thought of The Maltings as a 'white elephant', erected in the countryside for the benefit and pleasure of an annual festival and its visitors and useful for only three weeks in a year, they were soon to be proved false prophets. It soon became internationally known. Band concerts were given there, the BBC recorded a jazz series, an antique dealers' fair was held, and it was hired for many recordings. In February 1969, the BBC filmed *Peter Grimes* there for television, with Pears as Grimes, Heather Harper as Ellen and Britten conducting. The producer was John Culshaw, a close friend of Britten who had made most of his Decca recordings and was now BBC Head of TV Music Programmes. For the 1969 festival Britten planned the achievement of an ambition, to conduct the English Opera Group in Mozart's *Idomeneo*. The festival opened on 7 June, with the announcement that, after four years of intensive fund-raising, the full £176,000 had been collected or promised for The Maltings. Valiant work had been done in this respect by Stephen Reiss, manager of the festival from 1956 to 1971, who had persuaded the United States Treasury to register Aldeburgh as a 'foreign charity' and thus to relieve Americans of paying income tax on their contributions. In addition to this good news, the building had won a Civic Trust award for design and this was to be presented on 19 June. The first concert, on the Saturday afternoon, ended with Britten joining members of the Amadeus Quartet and Adrian Beers in a performance of Schubert's 'Trout' piano quintet. Ticket sales for the three weeks were approaching 90 per cent. Euphoria.

At 10.30 on that Saturday night a customer leaving the Crown public house noticed flames on the wooden roof of The Maltings and raised the alarm. There had been no evening performance there and the building had been empty since about 6 p.m. Ten fire engines were soon fighting the fire but the roof was ablaze and there was no hope of saving the building. The composer Richard Rodney Bennett helped to rescue some of the *Idomeneo* costumes. Members of the English Opera Group who had been performing in the Jubilee Hall in Aldeburgh drove the six miles to Snape to help with salvage work. Britten's Steinway piano was destroyed, so was Adrian Beers's double bass. In the early hours of Sunday morning, Britten and the festival directors met for two hours, rearranging the festival. All Maltings events were transferred, including *Idomeneo*, to Blythburgh Church, with the ready co-operation of the church authorities. They also announced, with what Britten described as 'wild, hysterical courage', that the hall would be rebuilt and improved in time for the 1970 festival. The walls remained standing, the building was fully insured, and local tradesmen telephoned immediately to offer every possible help. There could have been no finer demonstration of what the festival meant to Suffolk. Donations flowed in throughout the next hectic three weeks. Britten and Pears had already planned a recital tour of America in the autumn to raise money for a reserve fund: this would now become a rebuilding fund. Within two months of the fire, Britten announced that improvements were to be made to the hall. 'Our first two seasons revealed serious limitations in the site's amenities, despite its tremendous virtues.' The project now was for extra rehearsal rooms, larger dressing-rooms, installation of a pit lift and a new lighting switchboard, better air-conditioning, a recording room, and other facilities.

In addition to the *Harp Suite* and *Tit for Tat*, the other Britten first performance at the 1969 festival was his arrangement, with English translations by Pears, of *Five Spiritual Songs* by J.S. Bach. In the summer he composed a new song-cycle for Pears, *Who are these children?* op. 84, twelve settings of English and Scottish poems by the Scottish socialist William Soutar (1898–1943). (They were not performed until 1971, when seven of them were sung by Pears, accompanied by Britten, on 7 March at the Cardiff Festival of Twentieth-Century Music.) Britten and Pears gave their Maltings fund recitals in New York and Boston in October: a photograph of them taken in New York startlingly shows the strain of the previous year on Britten's face. Gone is the boyish athlete and in his place is a haunted man. On his return to Suffolk Britten bought Chapel House, Horham, twenty-three miles from Aldeburgh. Low-flying aircraft over Aldeburgh and the many visitors to The Red House had impelled him to seek a quieter alternative where he could compose, and it was at Horham that most of his last works were to be written. He began concentrated work on the first of these in the Spring of 1970 after travelling to Australia with the English Opera Group, who performed at the Adelaide Festival, and giving recitals with Pears in New Zealand. The new work was an opera, commissioned for television by the BBC in 1966. (He gave the fee of £10,000 to the Maltings fund.) He returned to Henry James for his subject, *Owen Wingrave*, and, as in the case of *The Turn of the Screw*, chose Myfanwy Piper as librettist. He had wanted to set *Owen Wingrave* for years; he had discussed the project with Mrs Piper before he wrote the *War Requiem*. Now the Vietnam war, and in particular the shooting in May of American students demonstrating against it on the campus of Kent State University, Ohio, fired his determination to use the medium of television opera to deliver an anti-war message to a huge audience. The libretto was again the subject of much discussion, for the characters had to be 'filled out' from the story much more than in the earlier James opera. Britten's musical instincts prompted this process. In May 1969 he wrote to Mrs Piper:

I have been working a bit on the opera from a more musical point of view, and one thing does strike me. I think we need a sort of musical flowering bit for Coyle and Mrs C. in the first scenes and what has occurred to me could be a little number about *youth* for Coyle ... Something about rashness, madness, pomposity etc. of youth – a more general piece than we have now. And for Mrs Coyle (this is very tentative...) a rather lyrical bit about the attractiveness, excitement of youth.[1]

Both these suggestions were acted upon and are among the finest parts of the work.

Each part in the opera was written with a particular singer in mind: it was cast before a note was composed. 'I always think of the voice, personality, appearance, nature of the singer when I'm writing a part', Britten said,[2] adding the wonderfully telling phrase, 'You could say people are my note-rows'. He chose *Wingrave* for television because it was a 'very intimate, reasonable story. At first, I thought I would write it in a very conversational *Pelléas*-like way, but then I felt I must give the singers something really to sing.' The medium presented him with a set of new problems. 'You have to persuade viewers to take the occasion seriously. On the other hand, you can't really calculate for those who are bored, arrive late, or are interrupted by the telephone. You can't keep repeating the plot, like a cricket score or something. Then there's the whole problem of making singers seem credible on television.' Britten always had the stage in mind as the opera's ultimate home: he would never have wasted all the labour involved in writing an opera on a medium which offered only one or two showings.

By what must always seem like a miracle, Britten and his co-directors of the Aldeburgh Festival (and the building contractors) kept their promise. The Maltings was rebuilt in time for the 1970 festival. The Queen attended the first concert on 5 June. The hall was found to be even better than before. A vintage programme was provided for the three weeks, even though – for the first time since 1962, and scarcely surprisingly – there was no new work by Britten. But he conducted the English Chamber Orchestra in the first performance outside Russia of Shostakovich's Fourteenth Symphony (14 June, with Vishnevskaya as soprano soloist and Mark Rezhetin the bass). This song-cycle in the guise of symphony was dedicated to Britten and seems to have taken his *Nocturne* as a model. On 5 June, the opening day, Britten conducted the Festival Singers in extracts from *Gloriana* (with Essex's lute song sung by Pears), and on 22 June Henze's *El Cimmarón* had its first performance. *Idomeneo* was staged on the scale originally intended in 1969 before the necessary emergency readjustments. 'My approach to Mozart', Britten told Alan Blyth,

derives essentially from my tremendous sympathy with and passion for his music ... In *Idomeneo*, and all his mature operas, there is nothing that is merely illustrative; everything derives from situation and character. Then there's that essential in all music, the phrasing. But, I think, most important of all is a passionate involvement and a realisation, with *Idomeneo*, of how a man of 25 could understand so marvellously the father-son relationship or how he could have created a character so close to Euripides as Electra.

Britten's conducting of the opera drew a charming compliment from Peter Stadlen in *The Daily Telegraph*: 'His ease in achieving fluency and precision amounts to a vindication of the conductor's craft or, if you like, to an indictment of their guild.' Janet Baker sang the title-role in *The Rape of Lucretia*, Rostropovich played the *Cello Symphony*, and Walton's *Improvisations on an Impromptu of Benjamin Britten* had its first European performance on 27 June.

It is because of the existence of The Maltings that we are now fortunate in possessing recordings of Britten conducting important works by several other composers. (In 1970 he added *The Rape of Lucretia*, with Janet Baker, and *Owen Wingrave*, with the original cast, to his recorded interpretations of his own operas.) He would never in these later years have stayed in London for the periods necessary to make recordings; but with the facilities on his doorstep, in the atmosphere he liked and had created, it was a different matter. Between 1968 and 1973 he recorded J.S. Bach's six *Brandenburg Concertos* and the *St John Passion*, Mozart's Thirty-eighth and Fortieth Symphonies and *Serenata Notturna*, Purcell's *The Fairy Queen*, Schubert's *Unfinished* Symphony, Elgar's *Introduction and Allegro for Strings* and *The Dream of Gerontius*, several rare pieces by Percy Grainger, and Schumann's *Scenes from Goethe's Faust*. The unexpected name among these composers is that of Elgar, for certain of whose works Britten developed an admiration at this time. He conducted *Gerontius* in The Maltings at the 1971 Aldeburgh Festival, recording it later in the year with Pears as Gerontius, Yvonne Minton as the Angel, John Shirley-Quirk as the bass-baritone, and the London Symphony Orchestra and Chorus. Those present at the sessions recall that Britten was 'far fussier about *Gerontius* than he ever was about one of his own works' and made nine 'takes' of the Prelude to Part I (which he referred to as 'Act I'!) before he was satisfied. Certain remarks of his at the rehearsals have been preserved. Thus, in the Demons' Chorus: 'Make it sulky' and 'Laugh as if it were the oldest joke you've ever heard'; in the *stretto* in the chorus 'Praise to the Holiest': 'If you feel in your bones that you can't stop it getting faster, you know we're making the *accelerando* just right'; at 'Novissima hora est': 'Make it sound like a long-forgotten lullaby'; to the cellos during

'Sanctus fortis': 'Don't dig into the string; glide over it, it'll be too heavy otherwise'.[3]

That recording still lay in the future in November 1970 when the television version of *Owen Wingrave* was recorded at The Maltings, with Britten conducting. It was transmitted on 16 May 1971, after Britten had returned from a visit in April to Moscow and Leningrad to conduct the *Cello Symphony*, with Rostropovich and the London Symphony Orchestra, during a British music week. The great cellist's visits abroad at this date were restricted, for he was in disfavour with the authorities for his defence of the 'dissident' Russian novelist Alexander Solzhenitsyn. Britten wrote a third *Cello Suite*, op. 87, for him in late February 1971, intending that it should have its first performance four months later at Aldeburgh. But Rostropovich, Sviatoslav Richter and the Borodin Quartet were all forced to withdraw from the festival.

The publicity for *Owen Wingrave*, described by the television critic Sean Day-Lewis in *The Daily Telegraph* of 10 May 1971 as 'one of the most important artistic events yet managed by the medium', was widespread. Before the week is out, Mr Day-Lewis pointed out, 'the production will have been seen in the United States ... and on 12 European networks, extending from Iceland and Norway to Yugoslavia – achieving what will almost certainly be the largest and widest audience any opera has ever had for its *première*'. Having seen a preview, he warned his readers that 'the work is very much opera first and television second ... it often looks like a studio production of a stage work ... *Owen Wingrave* is likely to be received with enthusiasm by Britten addicts like me, and perhaps by some of those opera-goers who usually complain that it is impossible to convey the art on a small screen. But it is not calculated to convert those who find the broad and melodramatic strokes of an opera a ludicrous convention'. The cast included Pears, Shirley-Quirk, Benjamin Luxon (in the title-role), Jennifer Vyvyan, Janet Baker, Heather Harper and Sylvia Fisher. Martin Cooper, reviewing the opera in *The Daily Telegraph* of 17 May 1971, thought it 'unmistakably one of the composer's most powerful utterances'. Returning to it in a long article five days later, he showed himself much impressed by Britten's treatment of the theme of the young man who rebels against the military traditions of his family and dies in an attempt to prove that he is not a coward.

Britten himself, in an interview at the beginning of that year's Aldeburgh Festival, left no doubt that he had been scarred by the 'difficulties he had experienced in preparing *Owen Wingrave* ... Television was a very complicated and powerful medium, and recording for it involved a tremendous amount of intensity. He would not be producing another opera for television for a long time'.[4] He had been irritated by the long delays, by the demarcations between which of the technical staff could do what, and by the feeling that money was being wasted. Ill-health kept him from many important camera rehearsals and he was often presented with results he did not like but could not alter. In addition, Colin Graham, with whom he liked to work and who had become an artistic director of the Aldeburgh Festival in 1969, was supposed to be director of the production but was gradually pushed on one side by BBC officials who did not greatly care for 'outsiders'. Graham was made to feel that he was there only at Britten's request. (Despite these discouragements, in John Culshaw's time at the BBC television films were made not only of *Peter Grimes*, *Billy Budd*, *The Burning Fiery Furnace*, *Owen Wingrave*, *Noye's Fludde*, and the Canticle IV, *Journey of the Magi*, but also of the Britten-Pears *Winterreise* and the Aldeburgh *Idomeneo*.) No wonder Sean Day-Lewis, in the article already quoted, remarked that 'it does look as though a disproportionate amount of time and resources has gone to Benjamin Britten and his collaborators', diplomatically adding 'It may well be that posterity will bless Mr Culshaw for this bias'.

With the rebuilding of The Maltings, a kind of appendix to the festival was established in late September. In 1970, the three church parables were performed there and in 1971, on 26 September, Pears and Britten gave the first Aldeburgh performance of *Who are these children?* The new Britten work at the 1971 festival proper was the fourth canticle, *Journey of the Magi*, op. 86, composed in January of that year. It is a setting of a poem by T.S. Eliot for counter-tenor, tenor, baritone and piano and was sung by the three dedicatees, James Bowman, Pears and Shirley-Quirk, accompanied by Britten, on 26 June.

In the October of 1971 Britten went to his beloved Venice with John and Myfanwy Piper and Peter Pears. There, appropriately but, as it transpired, with tragic aptness, he began serious work towards completion of what was to be his last opera, *Death in Venice*, an adaptation by Mrs Piper of Thomas Mann's *novella* (1912) about the writer who, on a visit to Venice, falls unspokenly in love with the beauty of a young boy he sees there and dies of cholera. Britten had begun to sketch the music of the opera in the spring of 1971 and had 'got stuck' at the end of Act I. Earlier in 1971 Visconti's film of the book, using Mahler's music, had achieved considerable *réclame* and Britten was at pains, through his publishers, to point out that he had been considering this project for five or six years and had 'certainly not' been prompted by the film, which he never saw. But he had in fact encountered legal difficulties over copyright which had delayed matters.

Work on the opera continued in March 1972 at Schloss Wolfsgarten. Britten returned home for the twenty-fifth Aldeburgh Festival. With Rostropovich still not able to visit Britain, the *Third Cello Suite* continued to await performance. But Britten and Pears repeated the Soutar cycle, *Who are these children?* and Britten conducted an unforgettable performance of Schumann's *Scenes from Goethe's Faust*, imparting to the music a grandeur and vision which no other conductor has seemed able to discover (and which, perhaps, it does not really possess). He also conducted *The Turn of the Screw*, impelling Robert Henderson in *The Daily Telegraph* of 17 June to describe it as 'a performance of a gripping and apparently inexorable dramatic power' with a 'remorseless cumulative tension'. This was a particularly good time for Britten opera productions. Sadler's Wells Opera (it was not yet English National Opera) had kept *Gloriana* in its repertoire and gave two performances in Munich in 1972 as part of the Olympic Games celebrations. The Welsh National Opera staged what many considered to be the finest production to date of *Billy Budd*; and in the autumn of 1971 at Covent Garden there was high and general critical acclaim (not shared by Britten himself) for Jon Vickers's interpretation of the role of Peter Grimes.

In September 1972 Britten recorded the Schumann *Faust*, the solo singers including Jennifer Vyvyan, Elizabeth Harwood, Pears, Fischer-Dieskau and Shirley-Quirk. This was his last recording as a conductor. Within the next few weeks he recorded *Journey of the Magi*, and some Schubert songs with Pears, and supervised another Grainger recording which was conducted by Steuart Bedford. On 17 December he composed the last notes of *Death in Venice*.

1 Britten at the age of nine in 1923.
Courtesy of The Britten Estate

2 With Frank Bridge in 1930. *Courtesy of The Britten Estate*

3 With Sophie Wyss and her son in 1936. *Courtesy of Sophie Wyss*

4 The autograph score of the first page of 'Marine',
one of the songs in *Les Illuminations*, composed 1938–9.
©1940 Boosey & Hawkes and *The Britten Estate*.

5 With Auden in New York in 1941 while *Paul Bunyon* was in rehearsal.
Courtesy of The Britten Estate

6 With Peter Pears at the Mayers' house, Stanton Cottage,
Amityville, Long Island, on 29 December 1941.   © *Lotte Jacobi*

7 Discussing the score of *Peter Grimes* in 1945 with Eric Crozier, producer (left), Montagu Slater, librettist (standing) and Reginald Goodall, conductor (right).
BBC Hulton Picture Library

8 Interval refreshment with Tyrone Guthrie, the producer, while conducting the first performance of his realization of *The Beggar's Opera*, Cambridge, on 24 May 1948.
Courtesy of The Britten Estate

9 With Peter Pears and Kathleen Ferrier at Birmingham
22 January 1952, on tour in aid of the English Opera Group.
Courtesy of The Britten Estate

10 With E. M. Forster at
Aldeburgh in 1951
BBC Hulton Picture Library

11 Rehearsing *Albert Herring* in 1947,
watched by the producer, Frederick Ashton.
BBC Hulton Picture Library

12 With André Ravasio (Mr Squirrel) at rehearsal for *Noye's Fludde*, Orford Church, June 1958.
© *Peter Hutten*

13 With Imogen Holst and Peter Pears in the 1950s.
© *Peter Hutten*

14 Britten and Pears playing
recorders in the garden of Crag
House, Aldeburgh, *c.* 1955.
© *The Britten Estate*

15 First run-through of Britten's
Cello Sonata by Mstislav
Rostropovich and Britten in the
studio of The Red House, 1961.
© *Erich Auerbach*

16 With John Culshaw, the producer, and Pears as Peter Grimes during the television recording of the opera in The Maltings, Snape, in February 1969.
BBC copyright photograph

17 The Red House, Britten's Aldeburgh home from 1957, showing the croquet-lawn.
© *Jack Phipps*

18 The Maltings, Snape,
photographed in 1967.
© *John Donat*

19 A joke while rehearsing Bach's
Christmas Oratorio in Long
Melford church in September 1967.
© *Jack Phipps*

20 Discussing the score of *Phaedra* with its dedicatee, Dame Janet Baker, and the conductor, Steuart Bedford, for the first performance at Snape in June 1976.
© *Nigel Luckhurst*

21 The Last Spring . . . Britten at Chapel House, Horham, in April 1976.
© *Rita Thompson*

22 With Pears at The Red House on 20 May 1976 shortly before being created Lord Britten of Aldeburgh.
© *East Anglian Daily Times*

23 One of the last photographs, taken on 24 September 1976. The score is the Third String Quartet.
© *Bertl Gaye, Cambridge*

15

Death in Suffolk

In 1971 and 1972 it became obvious that Britten was far from well. Symptoms of a heart disease were increasingly prominent. For years he had complained that whenever he conducted he had a pain in his left arm. Was this an anginal pain, an unrecognized symptom of his heart lesion? Coronary insufficiency commonly manifests itself as pain in the left arm. Early in the autumn of 1972 his doctors diagnosed the need for an operation to replace a deficient valve. Britten made a pact with them: he was to be allowed to finish *Death in Venice* and then he would put himself in their hands. 'I was rather difficult to cope with then, I know', he told Alan Blyth in 1974.[1] 'I wanted passionately to finish the piece before anything happened. For one thing it is probably Peter's last major operatic part; for another, it was an opera I had been thinking about for a very long time as it had already been postponed once. I had to keep going.' His original calculation was that he would be ready for the doctors by October 1973, when he would have conducted the first performance of the opera and perhaps even recorded it. But work on the opera, his longest score in number of pages of manuscript, exhausted him. It became an obsession, a burden; whatever happened, he was determined to finish it. The importance of *Death in Venice* to Britten was explained by Pears[2] thus: 'For Ben, the opera was, in some sort of way, a summing-up of what he felt, inspired even by the memories of his own idyllic childhood ... At the end, Aschenbach asks what it is he has spent his life searching for. Knowledge? A lost innocence? And must the pursuit of beauty, of love, lead only to chaos? All questions Ben constantly asked himself'.

After the 1972 Aldeburgh Festival it was obvious that Britten's schedule was over-optimistic, and in September he conducted the recording of the Schumann *Faust* only by working for short periods. He realized, after completing the composition sketches of the opera in December, that he would not be able to conduct it and handed over all the preparations for the first performance to Steuart Bedford, a brilliant and painstaking young conductor who had practically grown up in the Aldeburgh scene (his mother was Lesley Duff, the original

Emmie in *Albert Herring*). From this time he could scarcely drag himself round the house; he could not go upstairs without stopping to rest on the way.

In March 1973 Britten went with Peter Pears to Germany, to the Schloss Wolfsgarten, in spite of the doctor's dismay, because he was determined to be there for the Princess of Hesse's birthday on the 18th. On that day he and Pears played Schubert piano duets. In April, having finished the full score of *Death in Venice* a couple of weeks earlier, he entered the London Clinic and on 8 May underwent an operation at the National Heart Hospital. Whether it was because his condition proved to be worse than had been thought, the operation lasted about six hours and, in the course of it, Britten had a slight stroke. This temporarily affected his speech and permanently affected his right hand. He never again played the piano and only by a dogged determination, refusing to use his left hand, could he write the notes of music on paper.

Two days after the operation, Steuart Bedford conducted the first stage performance of *Owen Wingrave* at Covent Garden. The division of critical opinion on whether the transfer from the television screen to the theatre was successful was nowhere more sharply demonstrated than in the columns of *The Daily Telegraph*. Martin Cooper, attending the first night, preferred the television version: 'For some reason the three-dimensional setting exaggerated the hysterical nature of the Wingrave family's obsession with war.' Eight days later, his colleague Peter Stadlen said that the opera had 'found its natural habitat' in the theatre and cited the dinner-table scene, which Cooper thought should have been 'wholly rethought', as a 'magic operatic moment.'

But all energies at this time were being directed towards the first performance of *Death in Venice*, op. 88, at the Aldeburgh Festival. Britten left the London Clinic on 1 June and went to Chapel House at Horham to convalesce. There was no possibility of his attending the opera's première on 16 June, though he listened to the first broadcast on 22 June. 'The score shows all Britten's accustomed aptitude, versatility and sense of atmosphere', Martin Cooper wrote in *The Daily Telegraph* of 18 June.

> ... the canonic textures accompanying Aschenbach's pursuit of Tadzio are true musical reflections in a Venice miraculously suggested by John Piper's spare but evocative scenery. The role of Aschenbach is one of Peter Pears's greatest triumphs, a huge undertaking carried out with all the range of expression and suggestion of a voice that seems here to have profited by the years rather than otherwise ... Colin Graham's production and Steuart

Bedford's conducting ... showed an understanding of the composer's intentions that must be all but unique.

Winton Dean, in *The Musical Times* of August 1973, found Myfanwy Piper's additions to Mann 'seldom felicitous' but Britten's score marked 'a partial and welcome return to those qualities of lyrical enchantment in which he is pre-eminent ... The thematic material is closely and convincingly worked, though not built up into substantial paragraphs as of yore.'

On 12 September Britten attended a semi-private performance of *Death in Venice* at The Maltings. This was specially mounted so that he could see his work for the first time. He was strong enough in October to travel by car to Wales with Pears and, on the 18th, to attend the final rehearsal and first London performance of the new opera at Covent Garden. How pleased he must have been by the critics' praise of Pears's performance – 'the greatest rôle of his career ... sang unforgettably', wrote Peter Stadlen, who also found that the Venice sets, with their Monteverdi associations, 'brought to mind the one composer who in the past has created a precedent to Britten's shifting tonalities and widely roaming recitative'. This perceptive comment was echoed in *The Musical Times* in December by Patricia Howard, who wrote of Britten's use of '300-year-old operatic conventions as if he had just invented them specifically to illuminate his interpretation' of Mann's book.

A brief holiday at Donald Mitchell's home at Barcombe Mills in Sussex was Britten's only other venture in 1973. Friends who visited him were shocked by his weakness and frail appearance. He could take no part in the widespread celebration of his sixtieth birthday on 22 November, heralded by the generous statement by Sir Arthur Bliss[3] that 'reviewing in my mind the history of British music through its 500 years, I cannot think of any composer who has been endowed with greater innate gifts'. There were, of course, many concerts, but perhaps the most remarkable tribute was on the following Sunday (25 November) when the BBC's Radio 3 devoted its whole daytime programme of broadcasting to Britten and in the evening BBC 2 television relayed a 105-minute anthology of extracts from those of his works which had been televised, introduced by John Culshaw.

Death in Venice was recorded at The Maltings over Easter 1974. Britten attended some of the sessions but was very ill. 'I couldn't really cope', he told Alan Blyth. Notwithstanding that, however, he was able still to solve an artist's problem with a few illuminating words which went to the heart of the matter. John Shirley-Quirk, for whom he had written seven parts in the opera, was troubled over some point of interpretation. He approached Britten, who immediately put him right. It was encouraging for Britten again to be involved in musical matters, but he had only one reason for living and that was to compose. His friends knew that unless he could create more music, he would lose the will to live. 'For a time after the operation', he said,[4] 'I couldn't compose because I had no confidence in my powers of selection. I was worried too about my ideas. Then I suddenly got my confidence back and composing has become a marvellous therapy ... I have the feeling of being of some use once more.' The first problem then was for him to be able to write the music down – he could not dictate it, as Delius had done to Eric Fenby. A start was made early in 1974 with revisions of a string quartet he had composed in 1931 while at the Royal College of Music and under the influence of madrigals. At the same time he was persuaded by Peter Pears to look again at the American operetta *Paul Bunyan* which he had 'written off' and suppressed after its 1941 failure. As a result, and as a trial run, the three ballads from the work were sung at an Aldeburgh Festival concert on 10 June. Britten was present (as he was later in the month at a concert by pupils from the Menuhin School) and when later in the summer he again went to the Mitchells at Barcombe, serious discussions were held about a full revival. Britten began work on revisions.

Meanwhile a more significant event occurred. In July Britten composed his first new work since *Death in Venice*, thereby removing his conviction that there would never be an op. 89. This was his fifth canticle, a short setting for tenor and harp of *The Death of St Narcissus*, a somewhat enigmatic early poem by T.S. Eliot. ('You don't *need* to know what a difficult poem means', Britten told a friend.) There is no doubt that this major step in his convalescence was the direct result of the advent in the Aldeburgh household of Rita Thomson. She had been a sister at the National Heart Hospital when Britten had his operation and she gave up her post in 1974 to act as his full-time private nurse. He had absolute confidence in her, and she inspired him to have confidence in himself. (He usually worked for an hour or so in a morning and again for a short time in the afternoon.) The Eliot canticle was significant also in the replacement of the piano accompaniment by harp. Britten realized that his illness deprived Peter Pears of an accompanist and he encouraged his friend to give recitals with the young American pianist Murray Perahia and with the virtuoso harpist Osian Ellis. The canticle had its first performance by Pears and Ellis on 15 January 1975 at Schloss Elmau in Bavaria. It was dedicated 'in loving memory of William Plomer', whose death in September 1973 had greatly upset Britten.

In October, while Peter Pears was in New York for the American première at the Metropolitan of *Death in Venice*, Britten went to Schloss Wolfsgarten to stay with Princess Margaret of Hesse. There he began work on his op. 90, the *Suite on English Folk Tunes* for chamber orchestra, sub-titled '*A time there was . . .*' (a quotation from Hardy's poem 'Before Life and After', which Britten had set as the last of *Winter Words*.) 'A time there was – as one may guess . . . before the birth of consciousness, when all went well.' This work incorporated, as its third movement, *Hankin Booby*, which Britten had written in 1967 and had long intended to provide with 'brothers and sisters', as he called the four new movements. It 'was quite a large undertaking', Britten said. 'I'm full of other ideas, just requiring the energy to get them on paper. Writing even a bar or two is quite a sweat. Physically I find it hard to get to the top of a large score, so the flutes and piccolos tend to get left out!' It was completed at Horham on 16 November. The year ended on a happy note with the French Government's award of the Ravel Prize (the citation mentioned 'scrupulous attention to detail, search for beauty of expression, sonority and invention') and a reunion with Rostropovich, who gave the long-delayed first performance of the *Third Cello Suite*, op. 87, at The Maltings on 21 December.

Britten's life was now organized solely so that he could direct what energy he could summon to composing the works which were crowding his mind. Few people outside Aldeburgh knew how ill he was. People soon become tired of other people's illness, and it seemed to outsiders that Britten had retired like a hermit into the seclusion of Suffolk. They could not know what a desperate, heroic struggle he was waging against debility and incapacity. All kinds of rumours were circulating – even that he was 'gaga', as he put it – and he was deeply concerned that people might misinterpret his refusals of their requests. 'It's simply because I'm not capable of fulfilling all the things I would like to do', he said to Alan Blyth. 'When I say "No" I'm not trying to get out of something. If people get upset that in turn hurts me. Then I'm depressed. What gets me back on the rails is working. Psychologically that's important. Whether it is musically, only time will tell.'

Time told very quickly, for in December 1974 and January 1975 he composed the masterly *Sacred and Profane*, op. 91, eight mediaeval lyrics for unaccompanied mixed chorus. It was written for the five highly skilled solo voices of Peter Pears's Wilbye Consort. This was followed in March by another work for voice and harp, *A Birthday*

Hansel, op. 92, seven poems by Burns set at the Queen's special wish for her mother's seventy-fifth birthday on 4 August 1975.

In May 1975, Britten greatly enjoyed a short holiday in the form of a trip along the canal in Oxfordshire in the Shirley-Quirks' narrow boat. His armchair from The Red House was placed at the prow. He returned refreshed for the 28th Aldeburgh Festival during which *Death in Venice* was revived. On 7 June the revised D major string quartet was given its first public performance (after forty-four years) by the Gabrieli Quartet and on 15 June *The Death of St Narcissus* had its second British performance in a programme in the Jubilee Hall designed as a tribute to Plomer. On 13 June, Steuart Bedford, who had been appointed a director of the festival the previous year, conducted the English Chamber Orchestra in the first performance of the *Suite on English Folk Tunes*, 'lovingly and reverently dedicated to the memory of Percy Grainger'. Thus old admirations were kept in trim. Queen Elizabeth the Queen Mother, patron of the festival, attended the concert and had lunch with Britten at The Red House.

After the festival Britten made what were to be his last visits to Covent Garden, on 7 July to see *Death in Venice* and on the 9th to see the new Elijah Moshinsky production of *Peter Grimes*. Back in Suffolk he worked on the cantata he was writing for Janet Baker. This was *Phaedra*, op. 93, scored for small orchestra and harpsichord. It was a setting of lines from the American poet Robert Lowell's translation of Racine's *Phèdre*. Unusually, he wrote out the full score from the start. In the preparation of a vocal score he was greatly assisted by the young composer Colin Matthews, who had worked with Deryck Cooke on his performing edition of Mahler's Tenth Symphony, and was now principal editor of Britten's music, preparing it for publication by Faber. *Phaedra* was finished on 12 August. On 14 September Peter Pears directed the Wilbye Consort at The Maltings in the first performance of *Sacred and Profane*. Britten's first unaccompanied vocal settings for many years were warmly received. 'Supreme confidence and dexterity' was but one critical accolade. It was almost like the harvest years. In October he began work on a third string quartet, his first work in the form since 1945. Many years before, he had promised the musicologist Hans Keller that he would 'write a quartet for him'. When he complained after his operation that he could not move his right arm sufficiently to cover a full score, Keller half-jocularly suggested to him that this was the time for four staves. The new quartet, written for his old friends of the Amadeus Quartet, was dedicated to Keller, and Britten continued to work on it when he went to Venice with William Servaes (General Manager of the Aldeburgh Festival from 1971) and his family in November. Rita Thomson accompanied them and Britten took his wheelchair, which enabled him to visit many of the buildings and galleries he loved so much. He completed the sketch of the quartet on 16 November, incorporating material from *Death in Venice* into the last movement.

On 1 February 1976 *Paul Bunyan* had its first European performance – on radio, in a Manchester studio production (recorded the previous spring) by Ernest Warburton and Charles Lefeaux, with Peter Pears singing for the first time the part of Johnny Inkslinger. Steuart Bedford conducted; four months later at the Aldeburgh Festival on 4 June he conducted the first British stage performance, produced by Colin Graham. The general reaction was astonishment that music so fresh, ingenious and apposite should have been withheld for so many years. Britten was genuinely surprised by the warmth with which certain 'forgotten' early works were being received on their revival. The Violin Concerto, for example, was enjoying a new springtime. At the 1976 festival *Our Hunting Fathers*, scarcely performed since 1936 – although a performance by Pears conducted by Britten was recorded by the BBC in 1961 – was sung by the Swedish soprano Elisabeth Söderström and conducted by André Previn. Britten told Donald Mitchell that he had grown so accustomed to being told how bad those early works were that he had come to believe it himself! *Paul Bunyan* was not even discussed in the Mitchell-Keller symposium, being unknown in Britain in 1952. By the 1970s he had almost forgotten it, or deliberately put it out of his mind. When he heard the BBC performance he was deeply moved, sometimes to tears, and said to Mitchell, 'You know, Donald, I simply hadn't remembered that it was such a strong piece.'

But the principal musical event of Aldeburgh 1976 was the first performance on 16 June of *Phaedra* by its dedicatee, Janet Baker, and the English Chamber Orchestra under Bedford. 'A stunning experiment in the field of dramatic music', Stadlen wrote in *The Daily Telegraph*. '... Not only does Britten demonstrate to what extent – unprecedented, I believe – a sacrifice in sheer length and explicitness is possible in the arts without loss of depth; the monumental stature of the play is mirrored, astonishingly so, in Britten's characteristic textures, as deceptively sketchy and spare as ever.' In *The Guardian*, Edward Greenfield called *Phaedra* 'an opera in microcosm' in 'four tautly-drawn sections ending in a powerfully Purcellian death scene ... moulded to the art of a great singing actress'. It was an emotional moment when Britten rose to acknowledge the applause after the first performance.

Part of that ovation was connected with news made public four days earlier. A very special garden party was held at The Red House on 12 June, the day of the announcement in the Queen's Birthday Honours that a life peerage had been conferred on Britten. He sat in his wheelchair surrounded by friends and associates. To some, of course, his acceptance of this honour caused dismay and surprise. Were not the O.M. and the C.H. enough? And presumably he had already refused a title in the form of a knighthood? But, though many British composers had been knighted, none had been raised to the peerage. It was a new tribute to the art of British music and for that reason Britten was delighted to accept it, although he knew he would never take his seat in the House of Lords.

He was becoming weaker. Though his condition would not allow them to stay for long, old friends were seen, rifts were healed. Basil Coleman remembers him at Horham 'sitting riveted to the view across the ploughed fields which surround his country retreat'. The walks they used to go in Suffolk were no longer possible, 'but his reactions to everything around him were as fresh and unjaded as I had ever known them'.[5] In February 1976 he fulfilled a promise to the violist Cecil Aronowitz by arranging *Lachrymae* (op. 48a, 1950) for viola and string orchestra. He arranged eight folksongs for voice and harp. After the festival he went with Peter Pears to stay at Bergen in Norway and there he began to set Edith Sitwell's poem 'Praise We Great Men', which she had dedicated to him in 1959, as a cantata for solo quartet, chorus and orchestra. He planned it for Rostropovich's first concert as conductor of the National Symphony Orchestra of Washington, D.C., in 1977. When he returned from Norway, during August he wrote the short *Welcome Ode*, op. 95, for children's chorus and orchestra, ready for the Queen's visit to Suffolk in her Silver Jubilee year 1977. In his businesslike way, he was making sure he left a tidy desk.

On 24 September the photographer Bertl Gaye went to The Red House. She had asked if she could photograph Britten's hands and he had agreed. He sat for her with his hands resting on a fair copy of the score of the Third String Quartet. When she left, she told Rosamund Strode that she feared the results would not be as good as she had hoped because she had been so distressed by Britten's frail appearance that her own hands shook. Four days later he sat in the library to hear the Amadeus Quartet play through the new quartet, written with their style and individual timbre in mind. 'People are my note-rows...'

He continued to work on the Sitwell cantata during November, but his grip on life was beginning to relax. There were three items of unfinished business to be completed. One was his sixty-third birthday.

Then, he wanted to know that the purchase of new premises as the festival offices in Aldeburgh High Street had been completed. Finally, on 30 November, there was a festival fund-raising occasion at Clarence House, with the Queen Mother present. Its success was reported to him by Pears. 'I don't need to fight any more', he said. 'I will just let it come.' He died in Pears's arms early in the morning of 4 December. Rita Thomson was with him, too, as she had promised him she would be.

He was buried in Aldeburgh Cemetery, close to the Parish Church, on 7 December. Lifeboatmen, of whom several were his friends, were included in the guard of honour. The grave was lined with rushes gathered from the marshes at Snape by Bob Ling, the caretaker of The Maltings, and his wife. The hearse drove through the town past closed shops on its way to the church. At the simple service his *Hymn to the Virgin*, written when he was sixteen, was sung and his only organ work, the *Prelude and Fugue on a Theme of Vittoria*, was played. The Bishop of St Edmundsbury and Ipswich, Dr Leslie Brown, said: 'Trying to describe his music is like trying to trap sunlight in a string bag ... Ben will like the sound of the trumpets, though he will find it difficult to believe they are sounding for him.'

The obituaries were long and comprehensive, but more constrained than they might have been if he had died ten years earlier – or twenty years later, when he would have been an octogenarian, full of years as well as honours. Hans Keller described them[6] as 'a macabre orgy of the bankruptcy of music criticism'. The British critics were obsessed, he decided, with Britten's 'ultimate standing', whereas in Germany H.H. Stuckenschmidt had told his readers forthrightly that one of the great composers, a genius, had died. Keller also detected signs of the attitude which had left even Lord Britten of Aldeburgh as an 'outsider'. He quoted the remark of a friend: 'To Oscar Wilde they did it while he was alive. To Britten they do it after he's died: that's progress.' It was another composer, Michael Tippett, who struck the right note: 'The most purely musical person I have ever met and I have ever known. It always seemed to me that music sprang out of his fingers when he played the piano, as it did out of his mind when he composed ... I think that all of us who were close to Ben had for him something dangerously near to love. And it gave us, perhaps, an anguished sensibility for what might happen to this figure.'[7]

The Third String Quartet received its first performance at The Maltings on 19 December. Its last movement has no finality, the last notes are strangely inconclusive. Donald Mitchell suggests that it is as if Britten were saying, 'I'm not dead yet.'

On 10 March 1977, a service of thanksgiving for his life and work was held in Westminster Abbey. Queen Elizabeth the Queen Mother attended, and the world of music was represented in all its aspects. Before the service, organ music by J.S. Bach, Purcell, Britten, Bridge and Malcolm Williamson was played by Stephen Cleobury. Croft's Sentences were sung. Among the hymns were the settings of 'God moves in a mysterious way' and 'The Old Hundredth' from *Saint Nicolas*. The anthem was Britten's *Antiphon*. Peter Pears read the lesson, the story of Abraham and Isaac which had been the subject of the second Canticle, and he read part of Christopher Smart's poem which Britten had set as *Rejoice in the Lamb* '...For M is musick and therefore he is God'. The address was given by the Very Rev. Walter Hussey, Dean of Chichester, who as Vicar of St Matthew's, Northampton, in 1943 had commissioned *Rejoice in the Lamb* from the young composer. The Gabrieli Quartet, with Olga Hegedus, played the Adagio of Schubert's String Quintet in C and the service ended with Purcell's *Hear my prayer, O Lord*. The congregation left the Abbey to the sound of Mozart.

In 1978, on the eve of the sixty-fifth anniversary of Britten's birth, his friend Lennox Berkeley unveiled a memorial stone in Westminster Abbey next to that for Elgar and near to the graves of Stanford, Vaughan Williams and Henry Purcell. The *Antiphon* and *Saint Nicolas* were performed, with young singers and instrumentalists from the Royal College of Music and the Snape Maltings Training Orchestra. So the English musical pantheon admitted Peter Grimes at the last; and at the Abbey memorial service the prayer had been uttered: 'O eternal Lord God, we give Thee thanks for Thy servant Ben...'

16

Pride and prejudice

Michael Tippett, in his inspired broadcast tribute on the day of Britten's death, said that the triumph of *Peter Grimes* meant for Britten that 'he was now willing in himself, and, indeed, determined to be, within the twentieth century, a professional opera composer. That in itself is an extraordinarily difficult thing to do; and one of the achievements for which he will always be remembered in musical history books is that, in fact, he actually *did* it.'

He did it by surrounding himself with a team of all the talents. Some of the personnel changed but the aim remained constant: a truly co-operative artistic venture, in the tradition of the Diaghilev ballet. His librettists (Crozier, Duncan, Forster, Myfanwy Piper, Plomer), his producers (Crozier, Coleman, Graham, Cranko), his designers (John Piper, above all, and Annena Stubbs), his singers (outstandingly Pears, Shirley-Quirk, Cross, Vyvyan, Brannigan) and his instrumentalists, whose individual characteristics were built into the music he wrote for them to play, all worked together, amid the stresses and strains inseparable from operatic production. But, with his experience and his total professionalism, there was no doubt, as Janet Baker has written, that 'Britten was a king'. His whole early career had been a preparation for his work with the English Opera Group: in his days with the GPO Film Unit and the Group Theatre he had learned how to work with other artists. 'He took a positive delight in meeting challenges and overcoming problems of all kinds', Eric Crozier wrote.[1] He also had the remarkable power of engaging a collaborator's interest whole-heartedly. He could persuade people that ideas which might at first have seemed to them odd or unsympathetic were convincingly right. This extended to the practicalities of festival planning. 'Ben would always know exactly how many strings you needed in a particular hall for a particular work', said Jenni Vaulkhard, who booked artists for Aldeburgh.[2] 'He also understood about the right order of things in a programme. When the Beaux Arts Trio came, they were going to play the Ravel Trio, Schubert's B flat Trio and Haydn's Scottish folk songs. Ben said: "They must play nothing after the Schubert". When they arrived they said they would prefer to start with the Schubert and would I ask Ben? He said: "Tell them to play the way I want it and something marvellous will happen". And even musical philistines were bowled over.'

The verdict, on all the evidence, is that he was wonderful to work with; he had the gift for the telling phrase which could solve a hitherto intractable problem, although he sometimes displayed a lack of humour when the problem affected one of his own works. Orchestral players thought the world of him. Janet Baker cites[3] 'the clarity of his beat and the sureness of his tempi' as outstanding attributes which gave artists working with him 'a rare security'. 'One was upheld by his marvellous shaping of the phrase but at the same time given room, a sort of freedom, to yield to the inspiration of the moment. Only the very greatest conductors have this ability ... When he was conducting and one gave him, heart and soul, of one's best in performance, the look in his eyes, the expression of gratitude on his face, made such moments memorable ...' He was angered only by unprofessionalism. Never 'cosy' to work with, he could make cutting remarks, although he was psychologist enough to know that these could sometimes, with the right person, act as a helpful spur. The tenor Robert Tear, for example, re-thought his approach to music after Britten had rebuked him, a few minutes before a performance of *Curlew River* in London, for 'using my music merely for vocal exercises'. He was exacting in his standards and if individuals were found wanting they were dropped, without much ceremony. Some of the victims, unwilling to concede their shortcomings, were doubtless among those who spread tales of the 'Aldeburgh Mafia', of the cliquishness of the festival administration. On the other hand, personal considerations did sometimes enter and Britten, who could charm and persuade and cajole, could also be cold, ruthless, cruel and unforgiving. Those on the receiving-end could not be expected to like it and found in this behaviour a personal sadism complementary to the sadism which some perceive in his musical treatment of operatic subjects. Even so sympathetic a friend as Hans Keller wrote in 1952[4] of Britten's musical personality being distinguished by 'the violent repressive counterforce against his sadism'. It is only fair also to remember that any successful creative figure, especially one who provides a good deal of employment, may be expected to have his sycophants, but he can hardly be blamed for their excesses and more foolish pronouncements.

Part of the professionalism was also reflected in good and smooth organization of his working routine so that he was free – when he was not giving recitals or conducting – to concentrate on his main purpose, writing music. In this he was aided by the fortunate circumstance that, after the success of *Peter Grimes*, he became, to his surprise, reasonably wealthy. He could live comfortably and employ staff; his only personal extravagance was his delight in always having a good car (beginning with a Rolls and ending with an Alvis). From the 1950s onwards he had musical assistants to whom he devolved the tasks of making the instrumental score from his detailed working sketch. He always worked with pencil, so that he could quickly rub out and make alterations, and he marked the instrumentation very clearly in his sketch. Thus, with a Britten opera, there would usually be three stages, the detailed pencil sketch, the vocal score, which was dye-lined and sent to the singers, and the full score, several of which are the copying-work of more than one hand (e.g., Britten himself, Imogen Holst, Rosamund Strode, Colin Matthews). This full score provided the basis of the published score.

He several times described his method of composition. He was not a man for jotting down rough sketches (although he usually kept a small MS notebook handy), but he did a lot of thinking, on walks or on car and train journeys. He said that he usually had the music complete in his mind before putting pencil to paper. That did not imply that every note had been composed, perhaps none had, but questions of form, texture, and character had been very precisely worked out. Eric Crozier confirmed this. In the years during which he worked with Britten, he gained the strong impression that Britten worked from forms towards detail, thinking first in terms of balancing sections – fast against slow, contemplative against dramatic – as if he was an architect. (Britten on one occasion drew this very analogy when Crozier insisted that an extra ninety seconds of music were needed in a *Grimes* interlude to cover the change between the scene on the beach and that in the pub. He resisted, then sourly said, 'You're like someone who goes to an architect when he has just finished building a cathedral and gives him a huge block of stone, saying "You must find room for this".') In one respect he changed in his methods in his later years. He told Murray Schafer in 1961 that he did not need physically to create an opera's production when he was working, though he made an exception of the children's game with the ball in *Albert Herring*. But John Piper has written[5] that Britten tended more and more to demand advance information and needed to visualize a scene before he could compose. Thus, the model for the church parables set was designed and made before a note of music was written.

Britten's almost morbid sensitivity to criticism has been mentioned in an earlier chapter. It attained such proportions that one may be tempted to deduce from it that he suffered from that deep inner insecurity which afflicted Elgar and other composers. Like most artists, he experienced days when he feared that his power of invention had deserted him. He is said to have remarked that if the critics said a piece was no good (and how rarely they did say that, anyway), he could not help believing them. He was worried, if a piece appealed too easily, that it was 'like Puccini', yet he was fundamentally a melodist and proud of it. He was genuinely modest – he would regularly deflect compliments on his piano-playing of Schubert and Mozart with 'Well, it's a glorious piece, isn't it?' – but he was not falsely modest. He knew, whatever fleeting doubts he may have had, that he was a very considerable composer, to put his own estimate no higher, although those who knew him well all his life believed that because of his inferiority complex he was never really convinced that he was as good as he wanted to be, despite his tremendous determination to succeed. Before a first performance of his music or before he gave a concert as a performer, he was a victim of nerves, and this often led, as it does with many people, to physical nausea: he had to go and be sick. This nerviness showed itself also in a quite extraordinary tension, as a friend discovered at Covent Garden in 1954 when, at the first night of an opera in which Peter Pears was singing, he removed a long white cotton thread which was clinging to Britten's dinner jacket. Britten turned on him, scarlet with anger, and snapped: 'Leave it! I *like* it.'

No one who knew Britten could have failed to be impressed by his tremendous willpower and determination to complete any task he set himself. One close associate saw in him the image of the six-year-old boy among a group of nine-year-olds, determined not to be left out of things, determined to keep up and to do as well as the older boys. In his association with Auden and his circle, he was very conscious that he was much the youngest. No doubt the pressure he put upon himself by this 'keeping up' was a partial cause of the nausea and of the severe depressive reaction he would undergo after completing a composition. But he also saw where the older boys made mistakes, and he did not join all their clubs. He refused to dissipate his energies by engaging in activities which were not directed towards the one thing which mattered most for him: music. He was convinced that he best served the causes in which he believed by devoting himself to his job, making music.

Like many composers, Britten had strong likes, dislikes and prejudices where other people's music was concerned (just as, among singers, he disliked a 'beautiful voice' for its own sake). Mozart, Purcell and

Schubert were his gods, Bach too. There was special admiration for Mahler, Berg, Shostakovich and Bridge. He thought Webern was 'very fresh and cleansing, but the baby seems to have gone out with the bath water.'[6] Brahms was a major passion' until he was seventeen, 'then I suddenly found that his music didn't contain what I needed at that moment. I love the early works still – the D minor concerto and the Piano Quintet – In striving for formal perfection, I feel that he somehow lost something, and that something is what I miss in his later music.' He told Murray Schafer he was 'galled' by the 'crudity of the sound' in Beethoven's *Coriolan* overture: 'the orchestral sounds seem so often haphazard. I certainly don't dislike all Beethoven, but sometimes I feel I have lost the point of what he's up to. I heard recently the piano sonata, Op. 111. The sound of the variations was so grotesque that I just couldn't see what they were all about.' He was 'disturbed' by the limitations of serialism: 'its methods make writing gratefully for voices or instruments an impossibility.' He disliked electronic music. He made no public comments about his English contemporaries except Bridge. About Vaughan Williams he seems to have been ambivalent, associating him with the repressions of the R.C.M. Generally he disliked most of his music – though Pears, he and the Zorian Quartet in 1945 made one of the greatest recordings of *On Wenlock Edge* – but his reference to Vaughan Williams as 'a tremendous figure to me' in his 1958 letter of condolence to Ursula Vaughan Williams was a genuine tribute.

How much does Britten's homosexuality matter? As earlier chapters have shown, it mattered a good deal in some areas of covert public response to his work, where unspoken and unwritten knowledge of, and prejudice against, his homosexuality and that of some of his circle was a dominating factor. There should perhaps be no more prejudice against homosexuality than against someone's being left-handed, but there is. Even in the freer atmosphere which has existed since the 1960s, the prejudice persists – listen to the conversation of almost any group of people from any class and it will be heard to declare itself. To most people it is still 'abnormal' to be homosexual; the term 'queer', even if sanctioned by homosexuals themselves, betrays the attitude. Britten's silence on the matter – in contrast to the 'overt' articulateness of Isherwood and others – seemed to indicate an unwillingness to allow himself to be regarded as any kind of standard-bearer for 'gay liberation'. As Pears has said,[7] 'the word "gay" was not in his vocabulary'. Britten's middle-class upbringing and outlook ensured that he was deeply shocked by the boasted promiscuity and bohemianism of Auden and others (the New York 'commune' had been altogether too much for him in 1941, and it smelt, too). 'Ben thought that decent behaviour, decent manners were part of a fine life', Pears said. 'Gracious living, if you like ... But the "gay life", he resented that. He was more interested in the beauty, and therefore the danger, that existed in any relationship between human beings – man and woman, man and man; the sex didn't really matter.'

It emerges from Britten's diaries and letters that he had considerable difficulty coming to terms with his sexuality, whether through guilt or reticence one cannot know. He had the good fortune to enjoy one abiding and artistically as well as personally satisfying relationship; like many a long and even happily married heterosexual, he also had several satisfactory affairs, some prolonged, some transitory. Britten had a highly developed persecution complex and he knew very well, as a famous public figure, that this unconventional aspect of his character made him an obvious target. To connive at even a thin veil of pretence, in view of his position and his friendships with the highest in the land, cannot have been other than a source to him of displeasure and even of strain. No doubt when this strain showed it led to conclusions epitomized by Raymond Leppard[8] in his statement that Britten 'was anguished, he had an enormous load of guilt, which he tried to hide. When Ben was at a party he would simply emanate distress, and soon everybody in the room would be aware of it ... Ben had demons in him.' (He could, of course, merely have been bored by the party.) That he was, like many a genius and certainly like any artist as sensitive and compassionate as he, deeply troubled – tortured, as some would say – by man's inhumanity to man, by the power of evil at loose in the world, is self-evident from his work. But to confuse this with guilt over his own nature is to reach a misleading diagnosis of his personality.

As for the effect of his homosexuality on his music, we have the reference[9] by so close a friend and colleague as Hans Keller to 'the enormous creative advantage of Britten's homosexuality: however little Britten may have been alive to the fact, his psychosexual organization placed him in the privileged position of discovering and musically defining new truths which, otherwise, might not have been accessible to him at all'. What were these 'new truths'? To take them first at a rather superficial level: some will say that they do not leave a performance of *Peter Grimes* or *The Turn of the Screw* with any impression that they have been the target of a homosexual 'message' or tract. In one sense this is true: these works can be experienced as a purely musical and operatic phenomenon, in terms only of composition, drama and stagecraft. Yet it would also be limiting that experience – not in any way diminishing it – if one was not aware, and not in any condemnatory manner, of why this particular composer chose to set these particular subjects. It is going to one extreme to interpret *Peter Grimes* solely as an allegory on the plight of the homosexual 'outsider' in the Britain of 1945; equally it is at another extreme to ignore any such consideration and to regard it as merely a sympathetic operatic re-interpretation of Crabbe's 'depraved' fisherman. There has to be receptivity based on an appreciation of all the work's facets. In that lies its greatness. Nor can one evade Britten's own words: 'A central feeling for us was that of the individual against the crowd, with ironic overtones for our [his and Pears's] own situation. As conscientious objectors we were out of it ... we experienced tremendous tension. I think it was partly this feeling which led us to make Grimes a character of vision and conflict, the tortured idealist he is ...'[10] Is it to be seriously doubted that 'and homosexuals' were unspoken but implied words in that statement?

Britten's homosexuality brought him a deep insight into areas of the human psyche which are denied to heterosexuals and enabled him, as Hans Keller pointed out, to explore the use of sound, such as the particular quality of boys' voices, which he might not have attempted if he had not been homosexual. Even so, it would be rash to assert that an imaginative heterosexual composer could not achieve comparable effects. Here, again, one must beware of a too naive response. It is only in the vocal music that one could dare to assert that such-and-such derives from Britten's homosexuality; to say it about any of the instrumental works would be foolish. In the long run, all that matters about Britten is the quality of his music. To ascribe 'emotional immaturity' to it on the grounds of his homosexuality is as impertinent as it would be to criticize Leonardo da Vinci's achievements by the same yardstick.

Music, whatever its structure and craftsmanship, is an expression of emotion. The emotion felt by the listener may be very different from that experienced by the composer while he created. No matter – emotion has generated an emotional response, and that emotional response can take many forms, joy in sensuality of sound, response to imagined shared feelings, delight in sheer skill. In this respect nothing more sensitive and memorable has been written about Britten than these words by Donald Mitchell:[11] 'At the centre of his music there is an intensely solitary and private spirit, a troubled, sometimes even despairing visionary, an artist much haunted by nocturnal imagery, by sleep, by presentiments of mortality, a creator preternaturally aware of the destructive appetite (the ever-hungry beast in the jungle) that feeds on innocence, virtue and grace.'

In Britten's works, the theme of innocence destroyed or betrayed, of evil triumphing over good, of purity besmirched, of grace and virtue defiled or derided, frequently recurs. But the innocence, purity and grace themselves are often triumphant and bewitchingly celebrated. His works could almost (but too literally) be divided into two groups, the works of light and the works of darkness, of day and of night. In some, the two commingle. As he grew older the darkness tended to predominate – perhaps it can be said that as his awareness of the devil increased, so some of the devilry went out of the music – but he never wholly lost that unsullied ability to rejoice with an open heart, to be, as suggested earlier, the six-year-old Benjamin gleefully showing his elders that he was more than their equal. With this in mind, it is time to look at his works not sectionally but (in the main) chronologically, for in most cases each major work of its period was closely related to several others, which were like tributaries to the broad river.

17

1923–35

A Hymn to the Virgin – Tit for Tat – Simple Symphony –
Sinfonietta – Oboe Quartet – Suite – *Friday Afternoons –*
Holiday Diary – A Boy Was Born – Te Deum – Russian Funeral

A composer who was writing prolifically at the age of eight obviously
provides a fascinating subject for a detailed study of how the innately
gifted child became the mature artist. Such a study must await
complete collation of all the sketches and manuscripts in the archives at
Aldeburgh. But it is evident that, from the start, he had a natural flair
for melodic invention, perhaps still the most precious gift the muses
can bestow on a composer. This can be heard in the Chopinesque *Five
Walztes* composed for piano between 1923 and 1925 and re-written
for publication in 1969, in which charm and surprisingly mature wit
give almost an air of sophistication to the music. The second waltz
was later converted into part of a violin sonata written for Britten's
brother. But the most remarkable of the boyhood works was the
Quatre chansons françaises, settings of Hugo and Verlaine composed in
1928. This was Britten's first song-cycle with orchestra: the assurance
with which the orchestra is handled, the expressive woodwind writing
and the sense of form of each poem are of an astonishing maturity. Of
course the music is eclectic – echoes of Berg in the opening 'Nuits de
Juin', of Debussy and Ravel throughout and of Wagner's *Tristan und
Isolde* in the coda of the final 'Chant d'automne' – but the invention and
imaginative insight are recognizably Britten's, nowhere more than in the
third song, 'L'Enfance', in which a mother lies dying while her child
plays, a Mahlerian concept most tellingly carried through.

Waltzes written in 1923 were some of the ingredients reprocessed
ten years later in *Simple Symphony*, op. 4, for strings, and perhaps
treated a little portentously by the twenty-year-old composer, whereas
he might have been more indulgent towards this boyhood eclecticism
had he waited until he was nearer sixty. Yet how remarkable are the
string textures in what is one of Britten's first works to lie within the
range and capability of amateurs as well as professionals. The climax

of the 'Sentimental Saraband' is an example of what Britten was so often to accomplish in later works – the ability to invest the commonplace with a touching freshness and spontaneity. In the 'Boisterous Bourrée' the ostinato patterned around the second subject is also prophetic. This is engaging music in every sense, and deeper than perhaps Britten himself admitted.

Nothing could be much more prophetic about Britten's personality as a composer than that, as a boy, he should have been beguiled by the poetry of Walter de la Mare. Not only did de la Mare, like the mature Britten, have a remarkable insight into a child's mind, he also conveyed the lurking, nameless terrors of childhood, the sinister magic, in addition to the innocent delights. There is darkness in his childhood fantasies, with shifting shadows. In 1969 Britten revised and published under the title *Tit for Tat* five de la Mare settings composed between 1928 and 1931 which, though he himself made no claims for their importance or originality, are both important and original, the former as pointers to the later Britten's felicity in word-setting and the latter as showing his instinctive sympathy for the objects of cruelty. The song *Tit for Tat* (1928), placed last in the published set, has a controlled savage irony expressed with economical clarity:

> Have you been catching of fish, Tom Noddy?
>   Have you snared a weeping hare?
> Have you whistled 'No Nunny', and gunned a poor bunny,
>   Or a blinded bird of the air?

This setting has the natural opera composer's sense of drama; and the skilled mood-painter is latent in 'Autumn', with its lyrical touch, and in 'Silver'. From the same period (1930) comes the anthem for mixed voices in eight parts, *A Hymn to the Virgin*, Britten's first surviving piece of church music, a gentle and fluent work belonging very strongly to the tradition of English religious art but with a freshness that has never faded and with that quality which, for want of a better word, can only be described as 'innocence'.

Sinfonietta, op. 1

Britten's first published work, for flute, oboe, clarinet, bassoon, horn and string quintet or small string orchestra, was written in the summer of 1932 while he was at the R.C.M. It is dedicated to Frank Bridge and is in three movements. Erwin Stein pointed out in the Mitchell-Keller symposium that Schoenberg's Chamber Symphony No. 1 was part of the background of this work, not that they sound alike. What seems to have appealed to Britten was the Schoenbergian method of giving unity to a composition through the intricately contrived relationships and derivations obtainable from thematic motifs or 'cells'. Professor Peter Evans, in his masterly analytical study,[1] has demonstrated how almost every work by Britten is skilfully constructed on a basis of thematic derivation, in other words that he was a very good craftsman. Yet such processes are the nuts and bolts of music of which Britten himself hoped the listener would be unaware while concentrating on the more poetic and visionary invention. He knew that, in another art, those who drew pleasure from a great painting were not much concerned to know which brushes or which type of paint the artist used.

Practically all the themes, or ideas, of the *Sinfonietta* may be traced to the opening of the first movement, but they are presented in an unbroken line and with an economical bareness of such detail as chromatic relationships. Absolute sevenths on the strings are a feature of the harmony, and the woodwind individually contribute to a first-subject melody from which later subjects grow. Of considerable importance is the pentatonic horn fanfare followed by a descending scale (Mixolydian). The construction of the movement is an early example of Britten's way with sonata-form, with a new development taking the place of the conventional recapitulation. The dramatic key conflicts of the exposition emphasize that, while departing from classical practice, Britten was committed to tonal procedures, however ambiguously he used them here. That this is music by an English composer in the 1930s is nowhere more evident than in the Variations slow movement, in which the first movement's second subject is treated in the rhapsodic-pastoral style all too familiar at that time; but not many English rhapsodies contain the elaborate section which follows, when the principal motifs are again transformed, with ninths now the sustaining interval. Britten's fondness for the interval of a second emerges when the variation theme, with typically twining counterpoint, is played by the violins:

Ex. 1

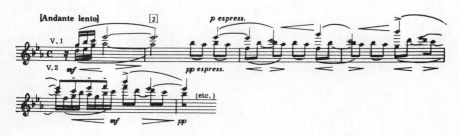

The Tarantella finale is in the *moto perpetuo* form which Britten was often to exploit with success and is again concerned with metamorphosis of first-movement motifs. Again, the recapitulation is treated in novel fashion. Back comes the first subject of the movement, but not as a grand peroration. Instead, it forms the background to a final *pizzicato fugato* section in which themes from all three movements are recalled, with the horn-call ascending in the closing chords and clinching D as the work's tonic key. In barely fifteen minutes much has happened. It is springy, agile music, with Britten's lyrical warmth suppressed and little sign as yet of his knack for instrumental characterization, a work to admire for all that it implies rather than to warm to. It would be difficult to deduce from it the direction the mature Britten was to take.

A trial-run for the *Sinfonietta* was composed a year earlier (1931), the String Quartet in D which Britten re-touched and allowed to be published in 1975. Bridge, he told us, said the counterpoint was 'too vocal', but John Ireland disagreed. The material of each movement is linked, and there is a *pizzicato fugato* in the finale which yields the best music. Rhapsodic touches in the first movement and the contemplative elegy which forms the Lento are reminders that the young composer could not entirely escape from his environment. What Bridge meant about the counterpoint was presumably the elaborate development section of the first movement, but that this is natural string-quartet music, its roots in the Mozart-Beethoven tradition, is everywhere apparent.

Phantasy Oboe Quartet, op. 2

The distinction of being the first musician whose individual artistry inspired a Britten work belongs to the oboist Leon Goossens, and it is as if the stimulus of a soloist had freed his imagination from some of the constraints which seemed to be operating in the *Sinfonietta*. The opening, with its ghostly march rhythm on the cello in conflict with the viola's drumming as a prelude to the oboe's gently insinuating entry, is dramatic and arresting:

Ex. 2.

Those for whom too much adherence to the despised so-called English pastoral school automatically ensures a black mark find this work 'self-indulgent' in its approach to the oboe's natural tendency to rhapsody, while the episode for strings alone in the slow section (dominated by Britten's own instrument, the viola) is for them uncomfortably near to an Ireland-Bax world in its sixths and sequences. Yet there is plenty of contrast and conflict in the key relationships – for instance, in the opening bars, the F sharp and A of the cello and the E and F natural of the viola – and Britten convincingly handles the one-movement Phantasy form specified by W.W. Cobbett who, in offering his chamber-music prizes, required that works should conform to a combination of the sixteenth-century fantasy with the cyclic form of the nineteenth century. Several Cobbett Phantasy works pay mere lip-service to this regulation and are four-movement pieces thinly disguised as a cyclic single movement through use of a motto-theme. Britten, again following Schoenberg's precept, constructs a work honeycombed with cross-referenced derivations, just as ingenious as the *Sinfonietta* but executed in a more leisurely, casual way. The *Sinfonietta* may earn more academic marks, but the Oboe Quartet is pleasanter listening.

Holiday Diary, op. 5, and Friday Afternoons, op. 7

Britten's personal voice can be identified for the first time in the de la Mare settings which became *Tit for Tat*. In the suite *Holiday Diary* (originally entitled *Holiday Tales*), his first published piano work, dedicated to Arthur Benjamin, Britten in three of the four movements – 'Early morning bathe', 'Funfair' and 'Night' – seems to be looking askance at the piano styles of, respectively, Benjamin himself, Stravinsky and Bartók. But the second movement, 'Sailing', has an importance far beyond the suite as a whole. Gone are the harmonic contortions of the *Sinfonietta* and Oboe Quartet. Over a lapping accompaniment of seconds, fourths, sevenths and ninths, a serene melody in D major, simple but deeply expressive (Ex. 3), sails unruffled into F major and back to D to be magnified in its visionary nature by a Lydian fourth, a Britten hallmark which will be heard again at high moments in the *Cello Symphony* and the operas.

Ex. 3

Friday Afternoons is the first of his works for children. These songs were composed 1933–5 for the boys at his schoolmaster brother's school in Prestatyn and remain among Britten's freshest melodic inventions, heightened by the wittily resourceful piano accompaniments. The setting of Udall's 'I mun be married on Sunday' suggests a folk-origin but is original; the 'New Year Carol' has that serene simplicity which makes 'Sailing' so memorable; and the sheer fun of 'Begone, dull care' and the canonic dirge 'Old Abram Brown' never stales, for listeners or performers.

Suite for Violin and Piano, op. 6

Britten began this *Suite* in Vienna in November 1934 and allowed three movements to be played in the following month. Six months later two more movements were added. (At the end of his life he authorized its republication in three movements, *March*, *Lullaby*, and *Waltz*.) It is based on a motto-phrase, E–F–B–C, which tempts thoughts of a Schoenbergian row, and makes frequent use of scales displaced by transposition of octaves: the Introduction opens with an octave-transposed whole-tone scale followed by a Lydian fanfare. The March movement, taut, restless, fragmented, is the young Britten in experimental form, perhaps delighting to show the R.C.M. what could have happened if he had been allowed to study with Berg; and the *moto perpetuo* continues the tonal ambiguity found in all these early instrumental works. The top is kept spinning with dexterity. In Lullaby, diatonic harmony reasserts itself, and Waltz is a spiky parody rounded off by the return of the motto-phrase and the introductory theme. This is the last of what one might call Britten's prentice instrumental works. They contain few glimpses of the mature artist: not many heavens are seen in these grains of sand. They are the products of an extremely talented young composer, not so much 'facile', the pejorative term favoured in first reviews, as fluent and intelligent – and capable, though still shy, of emotional warmth. To find the work of this period which proclaimed Britten as much more than a talent, something nearer to genius, we must go back to 1932–3 and his Opus 3.

A Boy Was Born, op. 3

The choral variations *A Boy Was Born*, for unaccompanied mixed chorus and boys' voices, may be heard, in retrospect, as Britten's first step on the road to opera (notice the many felicities of word-setting). The text is brilliantly chosen, a Christmas narrative which needs no narrator, and awoke in Britten his instinct for matching the verbal images with the appropriate musical images. It is music written by one to whom the Christian faith had real meaning, as we know it had for Britten, and it manages to illuminate the Christmas message in the English tradition of folk-song, mediaeval poetry and liturgical worship without resort to the archaizing of Holst or the luxurious chromaticism of Bax, Warlock and others. This is Christmas music entirely free of nostalgia and sentimentality; in their place are directness and joyful affirmation, expressed with a technical virtuosity which, in the work's original version, asked too much of the singers in the way of awkward intervals. Imogen Holst has suggested with good reason that Britten would have eliminated these at the time (instead of in the 1955 revision) if he had been enabled to rehearse and perform the work at the College.

A Boy Was Born is in the form of a Theme ('A Boy was born in Bethlehem; Rejoice for that, Jerusalem! Alleluia.') and six variations, No. 1 a setting of an anonymous sixteenth-century poem 'Lullay, Jesu', No. 2 'Herod', No. 3 'Jesu, as Thou art our Saviour', and No. 4 'The Three Kings' (all Anon., fifteenth century), No. 5 'In the bleak mid-winter', by Christina Rossetti, and No. 6 'Noël!', with text from Anon., fifteenth century, Thomas Tusser and Francis Quarles. The theme, itself a beautiful invention, is a chorale but it is from its first four notes ('A Boy Was Born') that the work was built. The statement of the theme has a modal flavour, but sounds leaner than Vaughan Williams; there is no reliance on the triad but sevenths abound, under strict control. Britten's vivid response to the text is illustrated in Variation 1, 'Lullay' being sung to the cradle-rocking falling fifths while the boys' voices entreat 'Mine own dear Mother, sing lullay' as a descant. The 'Herod' Variation is a type of scherzo, the male voices describing the Massacre of the Innocents in irregular rhythms and perfect fourths. With the entry of the women's voices, a brighter key is reached, prelude to the simple and simply beautiful Variation 3, 'Jesu, as Thou art our Saviour', a boy treble pentatonically rhapsodizing on the theme to the name 'Jesu' above the homophony of the chorus. The sopranos keep to a high B, against which the harmonies of fifths, minor thirds, fourths and sevenths create the tension at the heart of what, in other hands, might have become static.

In 'The Three Kings', the journey of the Magi is represented by legato quavers, vocalized by successive sections of the chorus. This forms a background against which the events of the journey are sung. The effect is 'orchestral' in its illustrativeness. The images of snow and winter taken from lines from Christina Rossetti's poem permeate Variation 5, the women's voices intoning the words (to an inversion of the four-note theme) and creating an effect of bleakness and frost against which the boys sing the ancient 'Corpus Christi Carol' in a 12/8 andante not far removed from folk-carol. This contrasting of two disparate and ostensibly alien images – the mediaeval and the Victorian – is an amazing achievement at any time, let alone in an Op. 3. As if to relish these creative powers, Britten makes the finale the biggest and most ambitious movement, and never outruns his powers. It is a rondo in form, the carols being the episodes and the coda recalling themes from other movements. The excitement of 'Wassail' gives way to the first episode, a joyous 'Good day, Sir Christëmass' with fourths and fifths in the harmony, and then to 'Give ivy and hull' and its muttered quasi-parlando. 'Hosanna' is sung by the boys in a bell-like canon before the angels' message of 'Glory to God' brings back the theme in overlapping choral parts. Above it, the boys quote from the previous variations and expand the theme into a final carol 'This night a child is born', one of those Britten endings where a broad melody cuts through a texture of subsidiary detail to achieve a culminating affirmation.

Te Deum in C and Jubilate Deo

Written in 1934 for choir and organ, and orchestrated in 1935, this setting of the *Te Deum* is, for Britten, strangely conventional, though it makes a change to hear a devotional rather than ceremonial treatment of the famous text. Constant Lambert, reviewing the first performance, called it 'drab and penitential', which seems unduly harsh. In 1961 Britten added the *Jubilate Deo*, more characteristic and inventive and with a piquant, almost playful organ accompaniment binding together the two contrasted vocal lines. This setting was composed for St George's Chapel, Windsor, at the request of the Duke of Edinburgh, but was first sung in Leeds Parish Church on 8 October 1961. The original 1934 *Jubilate Deo*, in E flat, was published in 1984.

Russian Funeral

Britten's only work for brass ensemble was begun in 1935 and completed in February 1936. Its original title was 'War and Death', and clearly the music reflects Britten's pacifist concerns when totalitarianism was rife in Europe. It opens with a funeral march, Mahler-influenced, the theme of which is a Russian proletarian song which was played at the funeral of the demonstrators massacred outside the Winter Palace in 1905. It was used by Shostakovich (another influence on his work) in 1957 as the principal theme of the third movement of his Eleventh Symphony. Britten's middle section, returning in the reprise of the march, is the 'War' episode, a grim scherzo. After its first performance in March 1936, *Russian Funeral* was not played again until 1980. It is a kind of symphonic-poem, deeply impressive.

18

1936–39

Our Hunting Fathers – Variations on a Theme of Frank Bridge – On This Island – Piano Concerto – *Ballad of Heroes* – *Les Illuminations*

The astonishing advance encountered in *Our Hunting Fathers*, Britten's next opus number after *Friday Afternoons*, is easily explained, so far as these things can be explained: in 1935 and 1936 Britten worked for the GPO Film Unit and began to write incidental music also for the theatre. The discipline of having to work fast, to order, to exact length and with limited resources might have deterred some young composers but was food and drink to Britten, who positively enjoyed providing music for a social purpose. The scores of *Night Mail* and *Coal Face* are deftly imaginative, but perhaps even more important than their musical achievement is that they brought Britten and Auden together, two young men with social and political consciences quivering to be directed into creative impulses. So when the Norwich Festival commissioned a work from Britten for the 1936 event, it was to Auden that Britten went for his 'symphonic cycle' for voice and orchestra.

Our Hunting Fathers, op. 8

Auden provided a libretto dealing with man's relations to animals – as pests, pets, and quarry. He selected three poems, an anonymous prayer for deliverance from a plague of rats, an anonymous lament by Messalina for her pet monkey[1] and Ravenscroft's 'Hawking for the Partridge'. He enclosed these between his own prologue and epilogue, the latter giving the work its title:

> Our hunting fathers told the story
> Of the sadness of the creatures...

Auden's lines have a certain detached irony, but Britten's music goes the whole hog – perhaps an apt phrase in this context – in emotional commitment. Savage parody and sensitive compassion in the music are more explicit than the words which give rise to them. The result is a large-scale work, its 'symphonic' epithet fully justified by the derivations and transformations of a motto-theme – a major arpeggio falling to the tonic and ascending to the minor third – which binds and unifies the cycle. More than that, it feels symphonic, quite apart from the nearness of its shape to the classical four-movement design. It is scarcely surprising that the London Philharmonic Orchestra of 1936 had to be told to behave at the rehearsals: they would have met few works at that date in which so much emphasis was placed on exposed solos, on a concertante-like style, on sudden switches into the chamber-music orchestral style of Mahler. To this day the 'fragmented' style of writing sounds new and up-to-date. Equally alarming (in 1936) was the vocal writing, veering from coloratura to a kind of *Sprechstimme* and employing shrieks, trills and the rolled 'r' to point up the message. Yet, song of protest though this is, it never ceases to be first and foremost a musical experience.

The cycle begins and ends in C minor, with the middle movements in D major, D minor and D major but there are passages where the tonal centre is ambiguous or overlapping: one hears this as unrest and conflict in the music no matter what the key signature says. The soprano's recitative introduction, immediately ear-catching in its sustained line, may have lulled the first audience into a false sense of security, to be abruptly shattered by the bizarre incantations of 'Rats away!' with its staccato texture vividly illustrative of the rats spreading into all parts of the orchestra, and the vocal gymnastics at 'Dominus Deus'. This is wild music, but the grip on form is never relaxed: Britten, as always, knew just where he was going and how to get there. In 'Messalina' the extravagance of the verbal expression of mourning is matched by an instrumental accompaniment to the voice's almost baroque lamentations which finds fullest expression in the subsequent orchestral interlude. Here there is no hint of satire as Britten expresses genuine pathos by a Mahlerian subtlety in obtaining the most transparent effects of shading and colour from the players. In the woodwind's rhapsodizing we can hear the same 'atmospheric' lyricism which, nearly twenty years later, evokes the summer evening at Bly in *The Turn of the Screw*. This expression of compassion is succeeded by the furious contempt for man's cruelty to animals in the 'Dance of Death', the movement which so upset the Norwich audience. A pity they were not more prescient in their musical taste or they would have realized that they were being privileged to hear one of the first of Britten's virtuoso pieces for voice and orchestra. The ferocious rolling of the 'r', the harsh chanting of the dog's names and the ugly whoopings of the brass (satirized hunting 'halloos') create a tense rhythmic scherzo, obviously anticipating the *Dies Irae* of the *Sinfonia da Requiem* and especially in the fully worked-out treatment of all the movement's motifs in the orchestral interlude which precedes the Epilogue and leads into it with an insistent xylophone figure to which the rest of the accompaniment is literally out of key:

Ex. 4

The Epilogue becomes a funeral march – in emulation, perhaps, of the huntsman's funeral in Mahler's First Symphony? Yet it is not Mahler who comes to mind in this section but, to a lesser extent, Bartók and, to a greater, Shostakovich. The naive futility of the xylophone figure is a typical Shostakovich device, but even more typically Britten's are the curlew cries on the woodwind, his symbols of pain, and the movingly compassionate arioso for solo violin. The structural device of the interludes has been likened to Berg, but I do not hear a Berg sound in the orchestral writing. If the use of these names suggests eclecticism, one need only quote some wise words written about this time by Britten. 'It is the composer's heritage to take what he wants from whom he wants – and to write music', the last four words being the whole point.

It is an indictment of British musical life that this brilliant and moving work should for so long have been little known (though performances are now more frequent). The initial *succès de scandale* effectively killed it for nearly forty years, not on musical grounds but because it was felt that Auden and Britten had brought a pamphleteering class-consciousness into the concert-hall. Britten was right in regarding it as his effective 'Opus 1' – the parallel is with Mahler's *Das klagende Lied* ('the first work in which I really came into my own as "Mahler"').

Variations on a Theme of Frank Bridge, op. 10

When one knows *Our Hunting Fathers*, the astonishing brilliance and assurance of the *Frank Bridge Variations* are easier to accept as a gradual rather than sudden development. Another work, the *Temporal Variations* for oboe and piano, composed in 1936, is also a strong pointer to the eventual emergence of the 'Frank Bridge' set. All the sentiment and satire of the latter are present in the former, pithily presented and neatly balanced in form and mood. Britten's uncanny understanding of the oboe, shown also in the delightful and witty *Two Insect Pieces* of 1935, ought to ensure a place in the repertoire for this important resurrected work. The *Frank Bridge Variations* was the result of the kind of commission to which Britten unfailingly responded with the best of his art and craft. It was to be a showpiece for the virtuosity of the then 'crack' English string orchestra, the Boyd Neel, at their Salzburg Festival concert in 1937. It made Britten's name in international musical circles and has remained one of his most popular works. It is, however, much more than a collection of parodistic genre-pieces and was also intended as a portrait of Bridge himself, his energy, gaiety, sympathy, etc. The theme itself, taken from the second of Bridge's *3 Idylls*, op. 6, for string quartet, is sadly-serious, its drooping wistfulness deriving from the falling fifth and falling semitone, harmonized with sevenths and thirteenths, from which it is constructed (Britten had already used it in March 1932 for an uncompleted set of variations for solo pianoforte). He found in it another source of tonal ambiguity and conflict, creating a sombre air of tension in his statement of the theme, after the bold chords and flourishes with which the work begins. This is followed by ten variations, the first an Adagio, the lower strings brooding in slow dark harmonies as climactic outbursts from the violins grow more impassioned. In the work's first five minutes, we hear the wonderful power and variety of tone which Britten draws from a comparatively small body of strings. Some years later he said[2] that he was particularly attracted to the medium of strings by 'the possibilities of elaborate *divisi* – the effect of many voices of the same kind. There is also the infinite variety of colour – the use of mutes, pizzicato, harmonics, and so forth. Generally speaking, I like to think of the smaller combinations of players ...'

In the next five variations, Britten the witty parodist takes over, showing the Salzburg audience his quizzical regard and affection for some aspects of European musical styles and fashions. Let us hope that any Germans present in 1937 felt uncomfortable when they heard the satirical goosestep of the 'March', its rhythm a derivation from the theme's falling intervals and its progress accompanied by the fanfare-like shakes which are a principal feature of Britten's writing for strings. The 'Romance' is gracefully French, the violins' *dolce* melody an extension of Bridge's descending sequence. A strumming accompaniment *alla guitara* launches the hilarious 'Aria Italiana', making free with both the Rossinian crescendo and the coloratura trills of his operatic heroines – a reminder that a year earlier Britten had made his first orchestration of Rossini piano pieces published as *Soirées Musicales*, op. 9. This is much more obvious humour than the 'Bourrée Classique', a deliciously eye-twinkling grin at Stravinsky's neo-classic works but nearer to genuine Vivaldi baroque in its open-string fifths. The nod in Stravinsky's direction, though, implies the important influence on Britten at this time of *Apollo Musagetes*, a masterpiece which the young Englishman appreciated and absorbed well ahead of most of his contemporaries. In 'Wiener Walzer', a rare example of Britten labouring the point long after he has made it, the approach to Vienna is made by way of Ravel's *La Valse*. Inevitably, a Moto Perpetuo is included, the only movement in the work where the connection with the theme is tenuous and where virtuosity for virtuosity's sake has determined the music's shape. Yet it fulfils a vital role in the structure of the work as a whole: its relentless impetus changes the music's mood and the smile fades from its face preparatory to the Funeral March, the theme's falling fifth converted into an ominous drum rhythm against which chords prophetic of Britten's style ten years later pull as if striving to rise above the mourning before sinking back disconsolate. The string sound is rich and imaginative in its range and blend of colour. In the 'Chant' which follows, the muted harmonies become bleak and chill, like the winter snow on Bredon Hill. This sombre mood affects the restrained start of the fugue. Gradually the music becomes more supple and I seem to detect here a further tribute to Bridge in a reminiscence of his 'Sir Roger de Coverley' setting. When the theme returns, it is *lento e solenne* in the deep and tender D major which Britten, like Richard Strauss, favours for his most rapt and ecstatic visions. But the sound here is Mahlerian (the Fifth Symphony *adagietto*), more than anywhere else in the piece. These other composers' names are mentioned as points of reference for the reader; they should not be construed as a condemnation of eclecticism, for by this time Britten had reached the stage where he could put his models through the crucible of his fertile imagination and bring forth his own astonishing declaration of independence.

On This Island, op. 11

These five songs for high voice and piano were Britten's second collaboration with Auden (excepting documentaries) and the first in which all the words were Auden's. The poems have a period flavour, but not so strong that it makes them unacceptable to a generation almost half a century later. These songs are also Britten's first group with piano, and are often wrongly called a song-cycle, implying a formal unity they do not possess. Another set of Auden songs under the same title was intended but never materialized. The influence of Stravinsky's *Apollo Musagetes* is again pronounced and has been admitted by Peter Pears in his essay on the vocal music in the Mitchell-Keller symposium, but Peter Evans has pointed out that Britten sticks closer to traditional harmonic procedures. As in the Bourrée Classique in the *Frank Bridge Variations*, the baroque elements of the first song, 'Let the florid music praise!' are emulation rather than pastiche, the model being Handelian. In the three central songs, 'Now the leaves are falling fast', 'Seascape' and 'Nocturne', the harmonic relationships are classical in essence. In 'Seascape' the free-ranging vocal imagery, an acute and lively response to the poem, is intensified by the strongly-braced framework of the masterly accompaniment. Economy of invention, as in the spellcasting 'Nocturne', is made into a positive virtue. The smart thirties jargon (verbal and musical) of the last song, 'As it is, plenty', has not worn well.

These songs were followed by completion of the suite of Catalan dances, *Mont Juic*, op. 12, written in collaboration with Lennox Berkeley in 1936. They heard the dances in Mont Juic Park, Barcelona, in 1936. The first two movements (Berkeley's) are a stately dance and a polka. Britten's are a deeply-felt lament inspired by the Spanish Civil War, and an animated waltz which gathers speed.

Piano Concerto, op. 13

This was published as 'Piano Concerto No. 1', but it remained the sole composition of the kind by Britain's finest composer-pianist. In giving its four movements titles – Toccata, Waltz, Recitative and Aria (later replaced by Impromptu) and March – rather than the usual classical headings, Britten seemed to be deliberately avoiding comparison with heavier models and supported this belief in his programme note, in which he claimed only – only! – to be 'exploiting the various important characteristics of the piano, such as its enormous compass, its percussive quality, and its suitability for figuration. It is not by any means a symphony with piano, but rather a bravura concerto with orchestral accompaniment'. In other words, don't take it too seriously, it's more of a suite than anything else. It certainly is a valuable compendium of the styles in music which attracted an ear as keen and progressive as the young Britten's. As it happens, the first movement, Toccata, is one of his most ambitious and lengthy instrumental essays in sonata form. It begins in the spirit of Ravel's G major concerto, all dash and vigour, the D major first subject containing a major seventh which remains a pervasive feature. When the orchestra takes it up, there is a brass fanfare of two alternating chords which also has structural importance in the subsequent three movements. Conflict between the piano's Lisztian bravura and the orchestra's tendency to lyricism comes to a head over the second subject, its smooth course being interrupted by the fanfare, by volleys of toccata lead-shot and by the pianist's insistence on his own shorter and irreverent version of the theme. This is resolved by the broad orchestral re-statement of the theme in E major, with augmented fragments of the first subject as bass, and by a continuation of the conflict throughout the development. For the recapitulation a truce is reached, with the piano quietly taking the first subject and the strings the second as a counterpoint. The cadenza is based on the two alternating chords; it is no empty display of virtuosity but a kind of *étude*, and it is followed by one of those surprises which are such an attractive feature of Britten. As if converted at last, the piano takes up the second subject, slowly and lyrically and with a gentle accompaniment of quavers, while the strings provide D major harmonies. The mastery with which Britten sustains this Toccata for over ten minutes owes much to the clarity of the writing for the piano, which never becomes merely percussive.

The Waltz has been called a parody, but there is nothing of the *Variations*' 'Wiener Walzer' about it. The opening solo for muted viola suggests nostalgic wistfulness and may well be a reference to the

Nazis' annexation of Austria. The piano's entry is a further version of the two-chord fanfare. Towards the close, the scoring becomes more biting, the mood more savage, but the original mood of anxious concern returns at the end. This movement is followed by the substituted (1945) Impromptu, constructed from material written in 1938 but still unmistakably handled by the more experienced composer of seven years later. It is a passacaglia and seven variations, each preceded by a cadenza-like passage for the soloist in justification of the movement's title. The theme itself is based on augmented seconds and minor thirds, and its variations cover a wide emotional range expressed within a harmonic idiom which is distinctly less 1930-ish than the first two movements. But it is back to 1938 with a bang in the final March. The fanfare chords recur, as they did in the 'impromptu' cadenza between the sixth and final variations of the third movement, as the basis of the subdued and disturbed quiet central episode (the trio) of this finale and there are shadowy references to the shapes and texture of the Toccata. The cadenza is in strict march-time, with accompaniment of cymbals and bass drum. Is this March a satire on militarism such as Shostakovich or Prokofiev might have written, or is it a warning of the horrors of impending war? Either way, the tune itself lacks the bite and the urgency to be wholly convincing and ends by sounding too trivial for the weight placed upon it, for all the glittering orchestration.

There is superb music in this concerto, but there must be some explanation of its failure to establish itself alongside, say, Prokofiev's third concerto. After all, it is rewardingly written for the soloist and it is a fine example of craftsmanship. It tends to be taken up by young pianists anxious to appear as champions of a not-too-advanced twentieth-century concerto and, when they have made their name, to be dropped from their repertoire. The public invariably enjoy it, but it does not exert a continuing hold on them. There seems to me to be little doubt that, for all their beauties, the second, third and fourth movements are not the equal of the first. After the Toccata the temperature drops; the musical interest, stimulated by an unusually compelling concerto first-movement, is dissipated by the suite-like sequence. This might not have mattered if the March had been a more clinching affair instead of so obviously returning us to the off-putting provenance of the Peace Pledge Union and its propaganda. For those who do not remember or know about the Union, the March is merely a weak musical finale. The original slow movement, Recitative and Aria, has been recorded on compact disc and is a tongue-in-cheek imitation of Lisztian or Tchaikovskyan romanticism – and extremely well done. Perhaps the Britten of 1945 felt uncomfortable about it, hence the substitution.

Ballad of Heroes, op. 14

Britten's pacifist feelings were always practical rather than theoretical. His humanitarian instincts were roused to fervour by cruelty, to men or animals, and it is therefore no surprise that the text of *Our Hunting Fathers* should have drawn inspired music from him. The British volunteers killed in the Spanish Civil War are commemorated in his music far more movingly in the passacaglia of the violin concerto and the *Dies Irae* of the *Sinfonia da Requiem* than in his too glib response to the even more glib text (by Swingler and Auden) of the *Ballad of Heroes* for tenor (or soprano), chorus and orchestra, written for a festival of 'Music for the People' in 1939. His expertise in 'writing to order' for the documentary films was more than sufficient to enable him to fulfil this commission in, one suspects, the minimum of time. If one listens hard, one can hear the measured recitative of the *War Requiem* in the Funeral March and, in the final hymn, the floating phrases of many an operatic scene to come. Even more expertise was needed to give any kind of musical credibility to a setting for unaccompanied chorus of Swingler's dreadful doggerel in *Advance Democracy*.

Despite the authentic bitterness which survives in the *Ballad*, a truer Britten-Auden evocation of the 1930s can be heard in the Cabaret Songs written for Hedli Anderson from 1937 to 1939. The 'Funeral Blues' sounds a deeper, more universal note than the *Ballad's* mechanistic, almost cliché-ridden 'Dance of Death'; and the Britten admirer who seeks the composer's response to Auden at a level above satire and political point-making need only recall the music for the BBC radio feature *Hadrian's Wall* (1937), where the Northumbrian landscape called forth music prophetic of the play of sunlight and wave in the *Peter Grimes* interludes.

The imaginative Britten was stimulated, too, by the Arthurian magic and fun of T.H. White's *The Sword in the Stone*, broadcast as a radio serial in the summer of 1939; and towards the end of 1938 his natural flair for the theatrically evocative was heard for the first time in the West End theatre in his incidental music to J.B. Priestley's modern morality play *Johnson Over Jordan*, produced at the New Theatre, London, in February 1939. The play was a failure, appearing at the wrong time when the public was in no mood for it, but many regard it as Priestley's finest. It owed much to the music which helped to create the atmosphere of the various stages of Johnson's journey through his past life in the moments between his death and his arrival at the brink of eternity. The use of a wordless soprano for the sense of timelessness is particularly poetic and the pastiche dance music of the night club scene is a fine example of Britten as musical journalist, reporting the small-change of his time and giving it permanence. 'Strange how potent cheap music is.' The end of the play, when Johnson steps out into the unknown, moved many who saw it, not least the playwright himself who ruefully remembered the last performance and his disappointment at the failure of his masterpiece: '...the last farewell, the last glimpse of Johnson against that starry sky, the last sound of Britten's triumphant crescendo – never, never again – and I might have been staring into a grave'.[3] Fortunately for the rest of us today, a suite has been recorded.

This fine music, with two more GPO film scores, was the last Britten was to write in England for three years. But when he sailed for the United States in May 1939 he took with him a major uncompleted score which became *Les Illuminations*. Almost immediately on arrival he wrote *Young Apollo*, for piano, string quartet and string orchestra, performed in Canada and withdrawn until its resuscitation in 1979. It gives every impression of being part of something larger, but its uneasy, rhetorical gestures have little significance as they stand and one cannot help feeling that the composer was wiser to suppress it than his executors were to exhume it.

Les Illuminations, op. 18

Les Illuminations, some settings of the French poet Arthur Rimbaud, was composed for high voice and strings and dedicated to its first singer, Sophie Wyss. It has been said many times that Britten found his way to his operatic manner by clarifying his own style through his settings of English, French and Italian poetry. It would be truer to say that the language and imagery of the foreign poetry, notably Rimbaud's prose-poetry with its hectic and fantastic pictures of life and vice in industrialized society, extended Britten's range by stimulating his expressive faculties to match new regions of the emotional map. He had to find the music for such exotic imagery as: 'Le paradis des orages s'effondre. Les sauvages dansent sans cesse la Fête de la Nuit.' (The paradise of the storms collapses. The savages dance unceasingly the Festival of Night) or 'Des sifflements de mort et des cercles de musique sourde font monter, s'élargir et trembler comme un spectre ce corps adoré, des blessures écarlates et noires éclatant dans les chairs superbes.' (Wheezings of death and circles of muffled music cause this worshipped body to rise up, grow larger and tremble like a spectre; scarlet and black wounds break out on the proud flesh.)

In *Les Illuminations* one can hear (almost see) Britten changing from the pamphleteering protester of 1938 into the more withdrawn, self-communing figure who exiled himself – perhaps, he thought then, for ever – to the New World. The dazzling extrovert of parts of the *Frank Bridge Variations* stands before us again at the start of this later work when violins and violas are used yet again to sound an extended series of arpeggio-fanfares, with an incisive brilliance which trumpeters might envy, as heralds to the singer's dramatic declaration, over heavy plucked chords, of the recurrent motto-phrase 'J'ai seul la clef de cette parade sauvage'. The clash of B flat and E triads establishes the work's tonal pattern and leads into the Mixolydian and Lydian modes which so many of Britten's most striking harmonic passages inhabit. There is (wisely) no detailed illustration of the procession of bizarre verbal images in 'Villes'; instead the accompaniment keeps up a busy momentum and the singer provides glissandi altogether more elegant than those in *Our Hunting Fathers*.

In 'Phrase', over harmonics reminiscent of the bleakness in 'Chant' in the *Frank Bridge Variations*, the voice climbs steadily higher, in arching phrases, to the moment of high ecstasy on the word 'danse':

Ex. 5

This exquisite short song is a prelude to 'Antique', a setting which serves as an illustration of all that is meant by Britten's magical ability to take the simplest means and transport the listener to a new musical world. This is the Britten gift which entranced his contemporaries – 'it's so simple, so beautiful, *why* hasn't anyone thought of it before?'

The accompaniment is merely strummed common chords, the vocal line sensuous arpeggios based on a B flat chord. A ceremonial excitement pervades 'Royauté', but the significant feature is the freedom and flexibility of the vocal flourishes, a strong pointer to operatic dec-lamations. A favourite ostinato device underpins 'Marine', the singer's virtuosity reaching a peak for the 'whirlpools of light'. An orchestral interlude ends with the return of the opening declamation, no longer aggressive and now with a cushion of decorative string harmonies. 'Being Beauteous', in ternary form, is the most erotically impassioned song of the cycle, restless trills in the accompaniment representing the poet's shudders and gasps. Scarcely less vivid is 'Parade', a march to which the percussive harmonics of the double basses contribute a special touch of dark colour. (This song, incidentally, is a revision of the *Alla marcia* intended as the first movement of the suite for string quartet *Go play, boy, play* of 1933–6 but discarded.) Here the poet's imagery finds a more literal musical response, culminating in the emphatic return of the motto ('J'ai seul la clef...'). Symbolically the last song is 'Départ', ending the cycle in E flat after the C major and C minor of the preceding two movements. It is a simple vocal line over the plainest of accompaniments, on paper nothing to excite anticipation but when heard ... the very poetry of sound. It is only after the first spell of this cycle has worn off that one reflects that much of the singer's part is a monotone, whereas the impression one receives is of a vocal line swooping and darting like the swallow's flight. Of monotony there is none, and each renewal of *Les Illumi-nations* unfailingly recharges the spark of genius which keeps this masterpiece timelessly fresh. Although Peter Pears's singing of it is so widely known and admired, it gains in brilliance and colour from the use of the soprano voice for which Britten conceived it.

19

1939–42

Violin Concerto – *Sinfonia da Requiem* – *Diversions* – *Seven Sonnets of Michelangelo* – String Quartet No. 1 – *Scottish Ballad* – *Paul Bunyan*

At this stage in his career Britten was already a 'conservative' composer. Not that he was ever conservative in his outlook, in his readiness to try something new. He was always visionary, always looking for ways of avoiding the obvious, the commonplace or the repetitious. But in his use of tonality, in his adherence to a key system, in his respect for the classical forms, in his dependence on melodic invention, he was divorced from the avant-garde. To large numbers of the public in Britain, of course, and to some critics, he was avant-garde, but it must be remembered that in 1939 Bartók was still regarded as the ace cacophonist of the age and Stravinsky as an anarchist, while Berg and Schoenberg were not mentioned in polite conversation. Nevertheless, forty years later, it is clear that on the day he sailed for America, Britten was already a very different composer from the one he might have become at the time of the *Sinfonietta*. The role of anglicized Schoenberg, implicit in some of that work, evidently did not appeal to him.

In the preceding chapter I wrote that he took a half-finished work with him to North America. Probably there was another, the Violin Concerto, completed in Quebec Province on 20 September 1939.

Violin Concerto, op. 15

There are curious similarities, entirely coincidental, between Britten's concerto for violin and Walton's, written for Heifetz in 1938–9 and first performed in Cincinnati in December 1939. They share virtuosic brilliance with a deep vein of melancholy lyricism. The public has preferred Walton's, which has attracted more solo violinists, perhaps because its melodic interest is slightly more conventional and obvious and perhaps because Walton, eleven years older than Britten, had developed an idiosyncratic style. Both are extremely beautiful and skilfully wrought, and it is good to see that Britten's, after a slow start, is being performed more often. Britten's is the more subtle work, and it leaves no doubt of its seriousness of purpose: no ambivalence here such as marred the piano concerto. Like the piano concerto it is in D major, but the Britten D major of 'Sailing', from *Holiday Diary*, and the thematic derivations and metamorphoses – his 'cellular' technique – are as intricately contrived as ever. But a new freedom inhabits the music, which makes its effects not through a stringing together of ironic or savage or poetic character-pieces but by its self-generating force of emotional and truly symphonic logic embodied in the sound of the solo instrument. Probably he was the first composer since Beethoven to begin a violin concerto with the motto-rhythm on the timpani, a daring challenge vindicated by the soaring lyricism of the soloist's first entry with the rhythm transferred to bassoon and horn (Ex. 6). Britten's command of form is well demonstrated in this first movement, which is a struggle for supremacy between the lyrical impulse of Ex. 6a and the rougher, more strident rhythmic second subject (6b). Sonata-form procedures are used until what would normally be called the recapitulation, which Britten again makes the climax of the movement by omitting the second-subject group and giving the first subject a new importance wherein the drum-motto's influence on all the thematic material in the concerto brooks no argument, except that in this case recapitulation becomes a new line of argument. To the uninstructed listener, however, the movement is a threnody in which the violin's capacity for singing, for sustained and rapturous cantabile, is exploited to the full. Its capacity for dancing is the main factor in the exciting scherzo, with its stamping cross-rhythms and its sudden Berliozian foray into the fantastic when the violin falls silent after reaching the stratosphere and the iridescent scherzo theme is transformed into a rumbling solo for tuba with two piccolos supplying a staccato ostinato supported by the strings' harmonic tremolo, a marvellous piece of imagination and a graphic use of the tuba's serious, as opposed to merely comic, potentiality. The cadenza is used as a bridge between scherzo and finale and to bring back the drum-motto and other first-movement material. While the violin is rhapsodizing on the music with which it was first heard, the three trombones make their first entry with the theme of the Passacaglia, Britten's first use of a form in which he was to write some of his most impressive music.

Ex. 6

(a)

This is a worthy début; the ground theme is not strictly repeated but is heard on different groups of instruments and is tonally unstable in its alternation of tone and semitone. At each entry it begins a semitone lower and the theme is altered in rhythm, broken up and shortened, as the violinist shows more of the implications. And as this Passacaglia takes a grip, the orchestration becomes more strikingly original in what we now call its Brittenish sonorities – as recognizably personal as is the Elgarian sound. The clear, shrill woodwind, the edgy but still fulsome brass, the high violin lament – these are now heard as mature Britten. He now emerges as one of the great orchestrators. From his Opus 1 he had made it very clear that he had a gift for orchestration, but in and after the Violin Concerto his music, whatever its variations in quality, is invariably clothed in apposite and exact instrumentation which is worn as naturally as skin. For the final pages of this concerto Britten moves into a D major coloured by Lydian-Mixolydian modality, that harmonic area in which he brings a rapt simplicity to the expression of passionately felt emotion. The solo violin's final repeated phrases almost speak their grief and longing, bringing the work to an end which is no end (tonally inconclusive, too, between D major and minor). Inevitably Britten's vocal music receives most attention, but the composer of the Violin Concerto, the *Cello Symphony* and the three string quartets has done enough to be regarded as a master in purely instrumental forms of expression. Britten revised the concerto in 1950, simplifying the solo part and removing Brosa's editorial elaborations, and again in 1958.

Sinfonia da Requiem, op. 20

Britten's only orchestral symphony was written 'in memory of my parents' and the personal inspiration behind the music is unquestionable. It was written in 1940, at the height of a crisis in the war affecting the native land which Britten had left and where his brother, sisters and friends faced the threat of invasion and it clearly also reflects his response to events in Europe. It is a short work, not much more than twenty minutes, but so concentrated and taut that it gives the impression of a vaster time-scale, so great is the ground covered. In design the work is almost monothematic, that is to say that each theme comes from a common source, and there is liberal use of ostinato. Britten's individual use of sonata form, already stressed, is here even more marked: not only is the recapitulation the section where dramas occur rather than are recounted, but the exposition and development merge into each other so that the development becomes almost a recapitulation. If the thematic contrasts of this *Lacrymosa* are few, the harmonic excursions and adventures are many and complicated, and the orchestration, from the violence of the initial drumbeats and the wail of the alto saxophone's sevenths to the sombre legato of the cellos and the brilliance of the brass, as noble a depiction of unassuagable grief as can be found. It is always a chilling as well as a thrilling moment when the second subject is brought back by the brass as a conflict of minor and major triads with the first subject's major and minor thirds which is incapable of resolution and filters to a sustained A on the woodwind that becomes the flutter-tonguing start of the *Dies Irae* scherzo. For this frenzied ternary movement Britten unleashes all the savagery of the modern orchestra. This is no Auden-inspired dance of death, but an elemental eruption. For the trio the saxophone, over an ostinato, gives its syrupy version of the *Lacrymosa* first subject. After the return of the scherzo, the movement disintegrates into the musical symbols of disorder. The theme is splintered into fragments, explosive, spitting, asymmetrical. Perhaps the passage is less alarming fifty years after it was written, but it is still an arresting device and one is never unmoved by the composer's genius in salvaging yet another ostinato from the wreckage and giving it to harp, bass clarinet, cello and double bass as the ground support for the flutes' *Requiem aeternam* theme in D major, itself derived from a motif first heard on savage muted brass in the trio of the *Dies Irae*. From this point to the end, the music grows and glows, luminous and compassionate, the flutes' theme as consolatory as a hymn, the principal theme from the first movement now in D major – Britten's 'Death and Transfiguration', as it were.

The names of Berg and Mahler are often invoked in relation to this last movement, and the string writing does suggest the example of the latter. The saxophone's rising and falling seventh in the first movement is perhaps a direct tribute to Berg's Violin Concerto, where the same interval is given to the same instrument.

Discovery of the autograph score in Tokyo in 1987 revealed that Britten had revised the work when he provided a new full score for the New York performance. The changes occur in the finale, from which 32 bars were cut in three places. The Mahlerian development of the main theme was reduced from 28 to four bars, an extra section in the build-up to the *largamente* climax was excised, and the coda was changed in several details, including orchestration (an effective cymbal-roll was removed).

Between the concerto and the symphony, Britten relaxed by writing the little-known but entertaining *Canadian Carnival* (*Kermesse Canadienne*), op. 19, a collection of Canadian folk songs and dances enclosed between trumpet fanfares which, if not for the common man, certainly sound for Copland.

Diversions, op. 21

In his foreword to this score Britten states that he was attracted

> by the problems involved in writing a work for this particular medium [piano, left hand, and orchestra], especially as I was well acquainted with and extremely enthusiastic about Mr. Wittgenstein's skill in overcoming what appear to be insuperable difficulties. In no place in the work did I attempt to imitate a two-handed piano technique, but concentrated on exploiting and emphasising the single-line approach. I have tried to treat the problem in every aspect, as a glance at the list of movements will show: special features are trills and scales in the Recitative, widespread arpeggios in the Nocturne, agility over the keyboard in the Badinerie and Toccata, and repeated notes in the final Tarantella.

To emphasize Wittgenstein's virtuosity, Britten cast the work in variation form, which enabled him to vary the emotional temperature and to live up to the work's title by maintaining a mood of elegant and objective musical commentary on the orchestra's *maestoso* theme which is based on an ascending series of fifths, covering more than five octaves, followed by fourths. Thus, the theme implies twelve tonal centres but there is no twelve-note procedure – an obvious anticipation of the method used for the theme in *The Turn of the Screw*. *Diversions* is the last of Britten's genre-piece works and, although it is pleasant to hear, it lacks the 'edge' of the *Frank Bridge Variations* and does not bear repeated hearing nearly as well. On the other hand, it wears better than the Piano Concerto and, after all, not every work has to be a masterpiece – *Diversions* is crammed with pointers to works that *are* masterpieces. The theme begins in the orchestral depths and rises up through the instrumental palette to the brilliance of the brass and woodwind before sinking back to allow the soloist to make a solo entry in the florid 'Recitative'. Here and elsewhere, the writing for the piano is so good that the one-hand limitation is barely distinguishable; it is not surprising that Wittgenstein said that of all the works he commissioned – from Ravel, Strauss, Prokofiev and Schmidt, among others – this best fulfilled his requirements. The rest of the variations cover the range of pastiche that Britten by now had outgrown but could still deliver with style. The graceful elegance of the 'Romance'; the satirical 'March', using material from *Johnson over Jordan*; the anticipations of Miles's piano-playing in *The Turn of the Screw* in the 'Arabesque'; the orchestral introduction to 'Chant' which foreshadows the 'Moonlight' interlude in *Peter Grimes*; the limpid arpeggios of the 'Nocturne' set against the strings' simple but gripping exploitation of the theme's intervals – these are musical epigrams of telling point. In 'Badinerie' and 'Burlesque', the wry homage to Ravel and Stravinsky respectively lowers the temperature of inventiveness. In 'Toccata I' the pianist is silent while the orchestra, with percussion prominent, is used to convey dramatic excitement with the economic strokes now familiar from *The Rape of Lucretia* and *The Turn of the Screw*. 'Toccata II' combines with a cadenza to give the pianist a final solo flourish before the impassioned but laboured dialogue of the 'Adagio' ('wrong-note' Rakhmaninov). There remains only the sprint to the tape in 'Tarantella'.

Seven Sonnets of Michelangelo, op. 22

In the autumn of 1940 Britten completed the first set of songs written exclusively for Peter Pears's voice, the beginning of a long and memorable series of works which have a special place in the history of music as the fruit of a remarkable collaboration between a singer and a composer who was also a marvellous accompanist. It is impossible to discuss Britten's vocal works without constant reference to Pears's voice, since they reflect the stages that voice passed through between 1937 and 1976. The Michelangelo songs, set in Italian, were written for a young but mature voice, lyrical in its melodic span, floating a steady, smooth legato, sensitive to the nuances of the text, not a passionate operatic sound but poetic and with a noble breadth. If therefore, in setting Italian, Britten was deliberately setting himself an exercise in European stylization, he was also celebrating his partner's powers by choosing texts which invited broad, arching melodies, uninhibited in their shameless lyricism. To highlight the vocal line, the piano accompaniments are incisive and economical but still harmonically subtle. It is almost unnecessary to state again that the different moods of the poems – all on aspects of love – are unified and made consistent by intricate variants of basic motifs.

For example, the first song, Sonnet XVI, *Si come nella penna e nell' inchiostro*, is sustained in its declamatory rhetoric by the accompaniment's manipulations of a *leitmotiv*. The urgency of the second sonnet (XXXI) ranges widely in the voice while the piano is less adventurous, the quiet C minor close being followed by the G major in which the beautiful setting of Sonnet XXX, *Veggio co' bei vostri occhi un dolce lume*, begins. This is another of those Britten settings, so simple as to appear naive – some would say platitudinous – which, by a twist of the melody, moves into the realm of the miraculously unexpected. The Lydian fourth is prominent in the vocal part, with triads a semitone apart in the piano, the harmonic groundswell intensifying the singer's increasing intensity. The restless Sonnet LV is a foil to the ambivalent XXXVIII, *Rendete a gli occhi miei*, a serenade with more than a hint of anguish. After the breathlessly ecstatic whisperings of XXXII, *S'un casto amor, s'una pietà superna*, the last song, Sonnet XXIV, *Spirto ben nato*, moves into D major for its solemn rite:

Ex. 7

[Largo]

146

The piano and voice here divide, the former having a solo introduction, which recurs like a refrain, and accompanying the voice lightly or not at all until their reunion just before the end. The Lydian fourth again colours the harmony of a song which is the most 'English' of the seven in its use of flattened sevenths and diatonic chords but is still in the Italianate *bel canto* style of the cycle. One cannot forget the impact of these songs when they were new in 1942: they confirmed that Britten's 'waywardness' was more apparent than real but was a significant modification of the English vocal tradition, moving it on at one stroke into new possibilities. The recording Pears and Britten made of these songs just after the 1942 London performances evokes with startling clarity and brilliance their initial excitement. It is possible, incidentally, that the cycle was begun as early as 1938 and stems from a relationship other than that with Pears.

String Quartet No. 1 in D, op. 25

Britten's first published string quartet, composed in 1941, has never attained the popularity of the second and seems likely to be over-shadowed by the third. This is a pity, for it is an attractive and well-constructed work. Suspicion of the 'cleverness' of Britten's early works expressed by the critics when they appeared seems to have clung to this work more than to others of its period. Its start is arresting: high, tremulous (*molto vibrato*) chords, triple piano, over the cello's pizzicato. This andante section is more than a classical slow intro-duction, it alternates with the allegro vivo. These tempo contrasts provide the drama, while the harmonic and structural interest are concentrated on the motivic relationships propounded in the allegro's rhythmic first subject. The scherzo, *allegretto con slancio*, straightway invokes the spirit of Shostakovich in its bizarre trills and triplets; the *andante calmo* slow movement, however, is Britten's sound-world its premonitions of the 'Moonlight' interlude in *Peter Grimes* stemming from the 5/4 hesitancy and the way the tonality moves from B flat to C, then into D major and so to a coda in which neither B flat nor D achieves supremacy until the last chord's reversion to the tonic. What a dry way, though, to describe the sombre twilight stillness of this movement, its dark atmosphere dispelled by the skittish finale, and the quasi-vocal rhapsodizing of the first violin.

Before considering the most ambitious of Britten's American works, brief mention should be made of the last piece he wrote there, the *Scottish Ballad*, op. 26, for two pianos and orchestra. This lives up to its name to the point of being more Scottish than any ballad, every aspect of popular Scottish music being remorselessly plagiarized, from the psalm-tune Dundee by way of the lament 'Turn ye to me' to the inevitable final Highland fling. Done with spiteful affection, the work evades the problems of balance between two pianos and orchestra by ignoring them in the enjoyment of the fun, and its *panache* is of the kind associated with the Last Night of the Proms. Altogether it is better Britten than the first of the op. 23 works for two pianos, also composed for Ethel Bartlett and Rae Robertson, the *Introduction and Rondo alla Burlesca*. This chattering frivol is eclipsed by its partner, the *Mazurka Elegiaca*, composed in memory of Paderewski and saluting him by means of shadowy reminiscences of the Chopin mazurkas he played so well. A touching epitaph.

Paul Bunyan, op. 17

Those two-piano pieces were written respectively in 1940 and 1941, a period in which Britten was preoccupied with *Paul Bunyan*, his largest, and sole operatic, collaboration with Auden. This work has a singular importance and fascination both as Britten's first stage work and as one which was recalled in 1974 from the limbo in which it had been left in 1941, revised and found to be original and delightful. It is, after all, no more a prentice work than Strauss's *Guntram*. Where the one had *Don Juan* and *Tod und Verklärung* behind him, the other had completed *Our Hunting Fathers*, the *Sinfonia da Requiem* and the *Michelangelo Sonnets*. They both went into the opera theatre fully arrayed in technical and inventive resource. *Paul Bunyan* was written for students and provided many small parts rather than a few leading roles. Described by its creators as a 'choral operetta', its choice of subject represented a brave, not to say rash, gesture on the part of two young Englishmen self-exiled to America. For they could scarcely have selected a more 'American' theme than the legend of the pioneer lumberjacks' giant chieftain. Auden, in articles in the original programme and in the *New York Times* of 4 May 1941, pitched their aims high: to present in a fairy-story form 'the development of the continent from a virgin forest before the birth of Paul Bunyan to settlement and cultivation when Paul Bunyan says goodbye because he is no longer needed, i.e. the human task is now a different one, of how to live well in a country that the pioneers have made it possible to live in'. Bunyan was reputed to stand as tall as the Empire State Building and to have a stride of 3.7 miles, so it is not surprising that no attempt was made to show him on stage. He is heard as a speaking voice, to differentiate him from the human characters. His exploits, too, defy staging, so they are related in three 'simple narrative ballads between the scenes, as it were, as solo Greek chorus'. These ballads Britten set to a guitar accompaniment, a more unusual innovation in 1941 than it sounds today, when 'country and western' music has become part of the common coinage. The principal role, 'the compositional centre', is allotted to Bunyan's book-keeper, Johnny Inkslinger, 'the man of speculative and critical intelligence', Auden wrote, 'whose temptation is to despise those who do the manual work'. He and the Swedish foreman, Hel Helson, 'the man of brawn but no brains', both learn a lesson from their relationship with Bunyan. Inkslinger, said Auden, was the only person capable of understanding who Paul Bunyan really is and the operetta is 'an account of his process of discovery'. Auden regarded the legend as 'a reflection of the cultural problems that occur during the first stage of every civilisation' and suggested that it was universal in its implications. Today Paul Bunyan would no doubt be described by that modish term 'music theatre'. It is a hybrid, with Gilbert and Sullivan, John Gay, and Kurt Weill among its ancestry, but it is essentially operatic.

If Auden's preparatory remarks sound slightly pompous, his libretto is racy and swift-moving. It is consciously 'literary' and there is a good deal of humour and repartee entirely suitable to the 'students' rag' atmosphere which surrounds the work as a whole. But the important factor is that it induced Britten to compose an exhilarating, witty and touching score, joyous and spring-like in its freshness. The reappearance of *Paul Bunyan* as late as 1976, after one had heard *Death in Venice*, caused one's whole perspective to change in regarding his operatic output. *Peter Grimes* seems now less remarkable as a first opera – though no less remarkable as a first 'grand opera' – because *Bunyan* belongs among Britten's operas and should not be regarded as in a category of its own. Britten, one now sees, sprang fully-armed into the operatic arena, equipped in the most formidable manner to tackle the problems of the genre. In some respects, indeed, *Paul Bunyan* is more remarkable than *Peter Grimes* because it is less conventional, it makes its own rules almost improvisationally, it creates musical drama out of the personalities of the characters and the vocal contrasts. And how sure, how mature, is the lightness of touch with which Britten treats what is basically a serious subject and thus makes it doubly effective. So much in *Paul Bunyan* foreshadows the later operas: not only obvious thematic pre-echoes such as that, by the Wild Geese in the Prologue, of the Nieces' cries of 'O-o-o' in the storm scene of *Peter Grimes*, but the evocative sonorities drawn from a chamber orchestra, the capacity to invent a simple, almost banal yet magical phrase which turns the heart over and opens new vistas – the opening chorus and, a little later in the Prologue, the spiritual-like setting of 'Once in a while the odd thing happens' – the use of oriental sounds to describe the exotic happening of the moon turning blue, and the menacing anger of a crowd (cf. the Helson fight in *Bunyan* and the Borough mob in *Grimes*). With the hindsight of knowing *Paul Bunyan*, the deft humour and parody displayed in *Albert Herring* could obviously have been expected from this composer. Here, too, in the cooks' duet, is the operatic-parody vein of *A Midsummer Night's Dream*. In *Paul Bunyan* is the forerunner of *Noye's Fludde* and *The Little Sweep*, the concentration of drama into a restricted realm of time and space; and in it is all that Britten had learned from his apprenticeship in the Group Theatre and with the GPO Film Unit. The forest music in Act I and the horn solo during Bunyan's farewell, like an idealized Last Post, are the products of his schooling in incidental music. (The marvellous night sounds at the end of Act I, with the howling of the prairie dogs (bassoon and bass clarinet), were added in 1974 as background to some lines of Auden's written after the 1941 performance because the original finale of this act had proved to be unsatisfactory.) The score is full of the subtle allusions which came so readily to the pen of Britten the musical journalist, reporting on the events of his day. For example, the memory of Norwich 1936 and Vaughan Williams's *Five Tudor Portraits* at 'Hey Nonny No' in the chorus during the Christmas party. (Inkslinger's main aria, the beautiful 'It was out in the sticks' also seems to me to owe something to Vaughan Williams's *On Wenlock Edge*.) For sheer loveliness of invention the score holds little to equal Slim's 'I come from open spaces', not even the tender, touching soprano aria given to Tiny, not even the brief and poignant 'Inkslinger's Regret'.

We again hear Britten the astute, retentive observer in the sheer 'American-ness' of the whole score – it is extraordinary that after so brief a time in the United States he had absorbed not merely the sound but the inflection, the nuances and the general 'feel' of their music. The guitar-accompanied narrations were a novelty in this kind of production in 1941; the Blues quartet, 'Gold in the North', is to the manner born; and in the verbal-rhythms and accentuations of such passages as 'A telegram' the style of Stephen Sondheim is anticipated by two decades. Anybody who knows the Rodgers and Hammerstein musical *Oklahoma!* (1943) with its mock-funeral dirge 'Pore Jud is dead' is entitled to note with surprise that two years earlier Auden and Britten had pioneered the ground with 'Take away the body' in the Helson episode. This whole section, with the love duet of Tiny and Slim sung against a background of the offstage fight, merging into the mock-funeral march and ending with the exaltation of 'Great day of discovery', is the part of *Paul Bunyan* which most clearly points the way to *Peter Grimes* and *Billy Budd*, whereas the Christmas party finale is the forerunner of the lighter works such as *Albert Herring*. A characteristic of the later Britten occurs in the Litany at the end of the opera, when some of Auden's most self-consciously slick lines for the three animal characters are set to music of probing intensity. This leads to Paul's Farewell, which the dying composer found so moving when he heard it again after thirty-five years.

Of course *Paul Bunyan* has its flaws and miscalculations, as its two young creators recognized from the start – there were many hasty revisions during the week's run in May 1941. But the fortunate survival of a primitive but revealing recording of one of those performances is documentary evidence of several factors: that it was, on the whole, very well sung and played; that the audience entered into its spirit and were amused and moved; and that the 1974 revision, while substantial, has preserved the youthful zest and spirit of the original. (Two numbers were totally excised by the mature Britten, a chorus of film stars and models and a parody love-song with lines like 'Psychokinesia never gets easier'. As stated in an earlier chapter, Auden's verses had tended to become increasingly unsuitable for musical setting and these were prime examples.) In the 1941 recorded performance the order of numbers is considerably different and the haunting opening chorus is cut. In 1974 Britten composed a new instrumental Introduction, based on the horn melody in Bunyan's Farewell; the original overture, which was never used, apparently survived only in the composition sketch (laid out for two pianos) and was published after Britten's death in an orchestration by Colin Matthews.

A final observation on this remarkable work. It has been customary to date the renovation of the idiomatic American musical from the production of *Oklahoma!* It seems that *Paul Bunyan* has a strong claim to be this historical watershed.

The American venture concluded the evolution of Britten from *enfant terrible* (and not so *terrible* as all that) into mature master. As will be seen, the works which he offered on his return to England sound almost as if he were saying to his critics: 'There, you see now, I'm an English composer after all'. But to become one, he had had deliberately to forge his style by conscious assumption of foreign models. Was this what frightened McNaught and others, especially as the models were thoroughly suspect in England in the 1930s – Mahler, Berg, Stravinsky? Yet why could they not also have seen that every

English composer of any note has achieved his independence through contact with continental imports? It is the English tradition, stretching back to the spread of the madrigal from Italy, to Dunstable's wanderings on the continent, to Purcell's absorption of an Italian style, to Elgar's fertilization by the European mainstream, and to the nationalist Vaughan Williams's eventual 'liberation' from the Teutonic leanings of Parry and Stanford by means, ultimately, of a crammer's course with Ravel.

20

1942–45

Hymn to St Cecilia – A Ceremony of Carols – Rejoice in the
Lamb – Prelude and Fugue – Serenade – Peter Grimes

When Britten sailed for home in the spring of 1942, he had already
begun a setting of Auden's *Hymn to St Cecilia* and got 'stuck'. During
the voyage he unpicked the knot and completed the work. On board
he also wrote *A Ceremony of Carols*. These two compositions and the
Michelangelo Sonnets were performed in England before 1942 was
over: thus the composer who had left Britain three years earlier with
a reputation as a smart and facile sophisticate reintroduced himself
with three of his sweetest and most lyrical works. In retrospect one
can see that Britten's works hitherto were the music of an exile or of
a man contemplating exile. In that exile, through a chance reading, he
suddenly discovered his roots and the works he wrote from May 1942
until 1945 were a celebration of that discovery.

Hymn to Saint Cecilia, op. 27

Composed for five-part chorus with solos unaccompanied, this *Hymn*
is a setting of three Auden poems (dedicated to Britten and published
together as 'Song for St. Cecilia's Day') in which Britten creates an
extraordinary sense of spaciousness. The high and low registers are
widely separated and in the middle areas the voices seem full of air
and light; there is none of that compressed density which mars so
much unaccompanied vocal part-writing. Moreover, by his use of
simple unadorned triads, he brings grace into the music which is not
only apt to the celebration of music's patron saint but reflects Britten's
own relief at having found his way home. The work's three sections
comprise an opening in which 'Blessed Cecilia' is invoked in relaxed
and sweeping melodic phrases which lead to the first of three gentle
choral unisons ending 'come down and startle Composing mortals
with immortal fire'. C major and E major are the constituent strands

here, with E major emerging as the key for the swift and enchanting scherzo section, with its fast reiterated five-bar theme sung over a ground for altos and basses. The basses provide a ground, too, in the final (A minor) section over which the sopranos' (or trebles') Lydian 'O dear white children, casual as birds' floats with a rapturous innocence. In the lines where Auden refers to violin, flute, drum and trumpet, Britten inserts imitative vocal cadenzas. But the whole exquisite setting is a hymn not so much to the sounds as to the soul of music.

A Ceremony of Carols, op. 28

Britten's predilection in several of his religious works, especially in the church parables, for a processional based on plainsong, perhaps derives from Holst's example in *The Hymn of Jesus*. The *Hodie* Antiphon from the Nativity Vespers opens and closes this most popular and appealing of Britten's carol sequences, a work in which he again seems deliberately to be holding out an olive-branch to the English tradition without sacrificing his individuality. Harmonically and melodically the *Ceremony* is simple if not circumscribed, but the colour transformations and the easeful aptness of the vocal writing, together with the poetic harp part, explain why the public has preferred it, on the whole, to the more intricate and challenging *A Boy Was Born*. Who could fail to be charmed and delighted by the joyfulness of the 'Spring Carol', by the stillness of 'In freezing winter night', the music shivering with cold as the Phrygian intervals collide canonically, and by the blithe serenity of 'As dew in Aprille'?

Prelude and Fugue, op. 29

The first work Britten composed on his return to England was this short piece for 18-part strings, the exact constitution of the Boyd Neel Orchestra whose tenth anniversary it saluted. A broad *Grave* melody, returning as the coda, forms the Prelude (in E major), but Britten is principally concerned with the A minor fugal section, strenuously and, for once it must be said, rather turgidly worked out as a showpiece for each and all concerned. The tonal ambiguity of the work's opening – D–G sharp – and the richness of the initial statement are more characteristic of the 1943 Britten.

Rejoice in the Lamb, op. 30

This 'festival cantata' for chorus, with treble, alto, tenor and bass solos, and organ, was commissioned for the fiftieth anniversary of St

Matthew's Church, Northampton. The text is taken from *Jubilate Agno*, written by the eighteenth-century poet Christopher Smart when he was in the madhouse. It is a kind of naive Benedicite, with Smart finding divinity not only in man, but in his cat Jeoffrey, in a mouse ('a creature of great personal valour'), in his own madness even ('Silly fellow! Silly fellow!'), in the letters of the alphabet ('for H is a spirit and therefore he is God'), in poetry, and in what he calls 'the rhimes' of musical instruments – 'for the clarinet rhimes are clean seen and the like'. Such a text requires musical diversity, but it is also made-to-measure for Britten's acute sensitivity to verbal imagery. The cantata is even more luminously radiant in spirit and (relatively) simple in resource than the two previous works. It is possible to divide it into ten sections, an extraordinary reflection (in fifteen minutes) of Britten's fidelity to Smart's magpie-mind poem. But far from sounding diffuse and episodic, the cantata sounds tautly constructed, as indeed it is, through the unifying interval of a fourth and other cell-like relationships. But, listening to this seraphic music, with its dotted-note Hallelujahs (a borrowing from Purcell), its vocal fanfare-arpeggios, the organ's brilliant metamorphosis into both cat and mouse, and the marvellously tender triadic harmony in which Smart's 'mad' visions are clothed with the sanity of the pure in heart, there is no need to concern oneself with the 'how', only with the 'wherefore'.

Serenade for Tenor, Horn and Strings, op. 31

In the series of wonderfully beguiling works Britten wrote in his thirties, he demonstrated again and again that his enviable ability to win his audience at a first hearing was because he could convey the originality of what he was saying in a way that his listeners could relate to their traditional musical experience. Lambert's statement that Elgar was the last great composer to be in touch with his audience was shown by Britten to be a premature obituary for creative communication. As I write, I can still be moved by the recollection of the impact the *Serenade* made on its first appearance; much as one admired the song-settings of Vaughan Williams, Parry, Finzi, and others, it seemed that English poetry had never before been set to music like this, with such intensity, such musical penetration and saturation of the text, and with such unity of atmosphere as Mahler obtained in his cycles.

Britten's choice of poems about evening and moonlight, nocturnal fancies and fears, is marvellously skilful, as is the soloistic use of the horn throughout and especially in its prologue and epilogue (the latter off-stage), played on natural harmonics. The first song, from Cotton's 'Pastoral' ('The day's grown old'), begins with a 3/8 rhythmic figure for strings against which the tenor's dolcissimo entry suggests not only a contrast of basic tempo but implies harmonic ambiguity. Or one could simply describe it as unforgettable magic – as picturesque a description of sunset as has been achieved in music – and leading, by a transformation of the horn's cadence, into the richly baroque setting of Tennyson's 'The splendour falls on castle walls', baroque in its fanfares but truly Romantic in its ivy-covered musical imagery. 'Set the wild echoes flying ... The wild cataract leaps in glory ... The horns of Elfland faintly blowing ... Blow, bugle, blow' – Tennyson's verbal music, so eloquent in its own behalf, is now indissolubly enmeshed with Britten's expansive leaps and arpeggiated chains of thirds. Yet perhaps the greatest song in the cycle is that in which, paradoxically, the horn is the protagonist, Blake's 'Elegy' ('O rose, thou are sick'). Basically a diatonic setting, the chromatic worm which eats away the heart of the rose slides by semitonal stealth into the horn's solo. When the voice enters, it tells us only what we already know, emphasized by the horn's slithering portamenti.

The subsequent setting of the anonymous 'Lyke-Wake Dirge' has an operatic vividness, its obsessive nature conveyed by Britten's favourite use of a ground bass, in this case a descending G minor arpeggio. The basses initiate a fugue which sounds as if harrowed by hell and strikes terror into the heart when, at the seventh repetition of the ground, the horn blasts in with this subject. All this time, the tenor's sustained wail has been growing steadily more minatory. In the words of the work's dedicatee, Edward Sackville-West, 'the cloak of evil ... the sense of sin in the heart of man' are here articulated in musical terms. Tension is relieved by the work's only quick movement, the quicksilver setting of Jonson's 'Hymn to Diana', voice and horn overlapping in a display of agility which precedes the calm beauty of the final Keats Sonnet to sleep. Here, too, the sleeper's troubled conscience is chromatically depicted and motifs from the earlier songs are embedded in the texture. One may regret the over-explicit settings of the words 'lulling' and 'burrowing' as representing a Britten mannerism, the too-easy scoring of a textual point, but this is a small price to pay for gems of such worth.

The *Serenade* is, for many listeners, inextricably associated with the lyrical flexibility and monastic ecstasy of Pears's voice in 1943 and with the miraculous horn-playing of Dennis Brain. Fortunately, their authentic performance is preserved in more than one recording. But the music is capable of more than one interpretation, and the original performers' first word on the subject is not necessarily the last, though no others have fully supplied it yet.

Sackville-West, who had written so perceptively in 1940 about *Les Illuminations*, had practical experience of working with Britten in 1943 when they collaborated on the radio-drama *The Rescue*, based on Homer's *Odyssey*. The composer's 'unerring instinct' for finding the right musical accompaniment to the text and for inventing imaginative transitions won his deep admiration. Here, the music moves near to the realm of opera in a rich and rewarding vein. *The Rescue* was broadcast on 25 and 26 November 1943, about a fortnight before Britten completed *The Ballad of Little Musgrave and Lady Barnard*, his gift to his prisoner-of-war friend Richard Wood. Because it is short (about eight minutes) and modest in means (male voices and piano), this little masterpiece of choral writing should not be overlooked. The famous ballad – of Lord Barnard's bloody vengeance on his wife's adultery with Musgrave – is made the occasion for strophic treatment within a cyclic framework. The tolling piano accompaniment for the opening stanzas as the scene is set is a side-shoot of the sacred works' processional; it gives way to the graphic representation of the tiny page running alongside the coach to tell Barnard of his wife's secret. An even more remarkable use of the modest means is in the distant horn-calls on the piano which reach the guilty pair as Barnard approaches – 'Away, Musgrave, away'. The work is swift-moving and highly dramatic.

Written at about the same time was *A Shepherd's Carol*, for unaccompanied chorus, an Auden setting for a BBC documentary, *Poet's Christmas*. It is a further example of Britten's capacity for producing a rich and often touching response to words which could have suggested music to no other composer. It and its companion, *Chorale*, after an old French carol (which the composer later withdrew) were broadcast as Britten was putting the finishing touches to the work which more than any other signalized his homecoming for good, the opera *Peter Grimes*.

Peter Grimes, op. 33

Peter Grimes has passed into history. It was the first opera by an English composer to enter the international repertoire and to hold its place there; it was the opera with which Britten began his self-appointed task of forging and establishing an English operatic idiom. He succeeded, but two ingredients were indispensable to that success:

technique and the discovery of a spiritual *leitmotiv*. We have seen in the preceding pages how Britten forged his technique to be ready for the challenge of by far the longest span of music he had tackled. His 1946 broadcast *The Composer and the Listener* betrays how he still smarted from the disparagement by his elders of his 'cleverness'. 'There is', he said, 'unfortunately a tendency in many quarters today to believe that brilliance of technique is a danger rather than a help. This is sheer nonsense. There has never been a composer worth his salt who has not had supreme technique ... I'd like anyone to tell me where Mozart's inspiration ends and technique begins.' This was the legacy of Bridge's teaching.

The discovery of a spiritual *leitmotiv* could not be taught. It exists in most of the work of the great opera composers: redemption through love and corruption through power in Wagner; the conflict of love and duty in Verdi; the force of the human spirit despite the stifling of individuals by society in Janáček; the continuance of the Ancient Greek ideal in Strauss. For Britten the *leitmotiv* took the form of a parable, a word which may be applied with accuracy to very many of his works, how innocence can be tainted and corrupted by the world, how the ability to create depends upon a renewal of innocence. Britten's Peter Grimes is not Crabbe's; instead of 'the mind untouched by pity, unstung by remorse and uncorrected by shame', Grimes is represented as the introvert outsider – psychopathic, to be sure – at war both with his nature and his fellow-beings. The essence of Britten's Grimes is in Christopher Smart's *Rejoice in the Lamb*: 'For they said, he is besides himself ... For Silly Fellow! Silly Fellow! is against me and belongeth neither to me nor to my family.' Though it has been criticized, and though there are still passages which stick in the gullet, Montagu Slater's libretto deserves high praise for its swift action, its immediate establishment of the characters of each of the Borough's inhabitants, and its transference of the action from the eighteenth century to 1830, when the 'modern world' may be said to have begun. But we may surely detect the composer's guiding hand in the extremely artful and sure way in which the text is laid out as the basis for music – and, of course, in the use of Grimes himself as an instrument for the deployment of compassion.

There is no escaping the fact – why should we, anyway? – that *Peter Grimes* is an old-fashioned 'numbers' opera, constructed from set-pieces (arias, choruses, quartets, etc.) linked by recitative. Nor, though the revelation of *Paul Bunyan* makes it less surprising, can one forget the amazement in 1945 that the composer in his first 'grand opera' should show such mastery of well-tried ingredients – the big choruses, a storm, an aria against the background of a church service (as in Massenet's *Werther* and many another opera), a dance, and a mad scene. These were indeed old bottles into which to pour new wine, but it was the wine that (rightly) everyone noticed. How productively, too, Britten's creative eclecticism had learned the lessons of its models for this opera. The knowing ones in the 1940s pointed excitedly to Berg's *Wozzeck*, but the more one hears both works the less tenable this comparison becomes. Verdi, of course, is one obvious and potent model, Puccini another; not only in this opera but in its successors, modifications of Wagner's system of *leitmotiv* are employed. But the obvious 'prototype', even to its organic use of orchestral interludes, was Shostakovich's *Lady Macbeth of the Mtsensk District* (an opera, written fifteen years earlier than *Peter Grimes* and by a composer in his mid-twenties, which is strikingly more 'modern' than the British masterpiece); and Bayan Northcott has shrewdly pointed out the debts in structure and recitative which Britten owes not so much to Purcell as to Gershwin's *Porgy and Bess*. There is also a remarkable similarity of 'atmosphere' and realism, as well as in the force of compassion, to the operas of Janáček, though one must presume that these were then unknown to Britten.

Perhaps the most impressive feature of *Peter Grimes* is that Britten, while avowedly following 'the classical practice of separate numbers that crystallize and hold the emotion of a dramatic situation at chosen moments',[1] maintains an uninterrupted flow between the various numbers and ensembles in all but a few places. The cumulative growth of the drama and the mounting tension as a tragic outcome becomes inevitable are handled with unerring skill. Scarcely less remarkable is the sureness of the vocal writing combined with the sharpness of the characterization. In the prologue, a fine example of Slater's crafts-manship, the main outlines of the story and the personalities of the main and subsidiary characters are swiftly and pointedly revealed to the audience. The conversational recitative of the inquest sounded a new note in English music and etches itself on the memory for a lifetime. The pomposities of the municipal bigwig are immortalized in Swallow's 'We are here to investigate the cause of death ... on the 26th ultimo ... Will you step into the box'. The sustained chords – like the halo of string sound surrounding Christ's part in the *St Matthew Passion* – which accompany Grimes's replies are the first strong clue that Britten wants our sympathy for him, and it is significant that as soon as the emotions are engaged Britten abandons dry recitative for *arioso*. Mrs Sedley, Hobson the carrier and the widowed schoolmistress Ellen Orford are all delineated in this scene; and in the duet between Peter and Ellen which closes it, the whole futile relationship between these two, abortive from the start, is summed up in a few minutes' memorable music.

Ellen makes her impact with three arias, one in each act. We know her mainly through her sympathetic role in ensembles. 'Let her among you without fault/Cast the first stone' in Act I is her most convincing apologia for Grimes; after that, events force her further back on to the defensive and in Act II her 'We planned that their lives should have a new start' never flowers into an extended piece because the inhabitants of the Borough have so much to say in commentary upon it. Her Embroidery Song in Act III, beautiful in itself, seems a rather mechanical and not entirely convincing response to the discovery of the embroidered jersey which means that the second apprentice is dead; here one suspects that Britten felt he owed the 'heroine' a big moment before the end (too close a parallel, perhaps, to Clara's 'Summertime' in *Porgy and Bess*.)

Grimes's music is a consistent and always convincing representation of the composer's interpretation. The mixture of superb practical fisherman and haunted dreamer is conveyed in the long scene with Balstrode in Act I in the aria 'We strained into the wind'. In this A minor section, he looks back upon a devastating experience. Egged on by Balstrode he discloses his ambitions – 'I'll fish the sea dry' – in what amounts to the middle section of a *da capo* aria before, left alone, he sings, in A major, of his vision of a future with Ellen, 'What harbour shelters peace'. This is interrupted by the Storm Interlude and we do not hear Grimes again until his dramatic entry into The Boar when he continues his soliloquy in the aria 'Now the Great Bear and Pleiades'. The apparent operatic inconsistency of this rough fisherman singing such sentiments in a pub at the height of a storm and singing them amid an almost tangible stillness is yet one more tribute to the power of music – this is one of opera's great moments, haunting, cathartic, unforgettable. Another use of stillness at a supreme emotional and dramatic juncture is the demented Grimes's final entrance. He is preceded by the music of the last and most fanciful Interlude, a cadenza for several instruments constructed around the muted horn's chord of the dominant which represents the foghorn. This is the focal-point for a review of the opera's chief motifs. As it ends we hear only the foghorn and the chorus's distant cries of 'Grimes!' Thenceforward Britten turns the emotional screw until the final tragic stroke, the use of natural speech – further developed eight years later in *Gloriana* – as Balstrode tells Peter to drown himself out at sea.

The chorus is used both as a massed entity and as a collection of individuals. The opening chorus, partly in unison, partly in parallel thirds, is dramatically apt to the tedious work of the port and musically memorable so that its return at the end, as if the tragedy we have witnessed had never happened, is a perfect rounding-off. The imploring 'O tide that waits for no man, Spare our coasts' is a more obvious gesture, but the true climax of the opera is given to the chorus, the cries of 'Peter Grimes' which fill the theatre at the end of Act III scene 1 as the Borough bays for blood, the culmination of the music in Act II when, led by Hobson's drum, the crowd march to Grimes's hut to a passage of bare unison writing which chills the blood. This is followed by one of the smaller ensembles which are a distinctive feature of the score, in this case the most beautiful of all, a quartet for Auntie, Ellen and the Nieces ('From the gutter, why should we Trouble at their ribaldries'). The piercing beauty of the sound here, the voices trailed by a ritornello of falling thirds and seconds, owes much to the use of women's voices only. The Straussian sound of this quartet may be traced to the unexpected fact, revealed in Britten's letters, that he sent for and studied the score of *Der Rosenkavalier* while composing *Peter Grimes*. The rich entwining of the voices is a calculated contrast to the use of male voices in the scene at the hut, a scene which ends orchestrally as Balstrode searches the room. A solo viola sings an elegy for the dead boy and an eerie celesta whispers awareness of the fateful event which, we know, the mob would have liked to shout aloud.

These moments, so economically presented, are perhaps the most impressive proof of Britten's natural ability as an opera-composer. So, too, is the way in which he reconciles the conflict between the character of Grimes as presented by the librettist and as interpreted by himself – a conflict at the root of the character's difficulty for a singer-actor and which makes it such a fascinating challenge at each renewal, the stuff of exciting theatre. Grimes's 'outsider' element, both within himself and with the Borough, are represented by key-schemes, sometimes as a conflict between A and E flat, though this is by no means clear-cut, and by a network of thematic allusions and cross-references. Bitonality is another means of showing Grimes's instability; in the first duet with Ellen he sings in F minor and she in E major, but by the end both are singing in unison in E major through the reconciling enharmonic mediation of A flat and G sharp (Ex. 8). A similar enharmonic mediation occurs in the beautiful churchyard scene of Act II; and study of the score will reveal new and subtle examples of the prodigal technical skill which has gone into it.

The best-known parts of *Peter Grimes* are the six Interludes, four of which are a popular concert-work. Three are tone-pictures, two are commentaries on Grimes's mental state, and one is both. They are a magnificent and integral part of the opera's structure. While there is no doubt that the voice is supreme in *Peter Grimes*, the orchestra creates the atmosphere and it is frequently an instrumental inspiration which makes the most telling point (as in the case of the celesta, cited above). It was a major inspiration to place the first interlude, effectively the opera's prelude, after the prologue and before the main action begins. Whatever echoes of Bartók, Shostakovich and even of Sibelius the ear may detect in these interludes, there is no denying the originality of their very characteristic scoring, spare, graceful and by no means lacking in richness. The 'Dawn' Interlude perhaps owes something to Debussy's *La Mer*, but to English ears this is incontrovertibly the North Sea painted by Britten: violins in unison supported by flutes suggest (in A minor) the huge high sky above the sea and the cries of the gulls, the harp and clarinet arpeggios the wind rippling the surface of the waves, and beneath it all the swell of the ocean in A major chords from the brass. The 'Storm' (a rondo) is in three episodes, with fugal and bitonal passages. Its syncopated ferocity and chromatic blasts from trumpets and trombones are powerful enough, yet the originality lies in the stillness at the heart of the tempest, the unison strings' impassioned melody and that extraordinary passage where the full orchestra engages in an agitated ostinato but *ppp* – this is genius. The 'Sunday Morning' Interlude is the prelude to Act II. Here the originality is that Britten eschews the obvious use of real bells but instead has two horns tolling minor thirds against major thirds on the other two horns; above them syncopated woodwind chime in high octaves, suggesting smaller bells or, perhaps, the 'glitter of waves and glitter of sunlight' of which Ellen – whose sympathetic nature is suggested by the legato melody for lower strings – sings when the curtain rises and we hear the clangour of the real church bell (so prescribed in the score). It is a perfect introduction to the brilliantly constructed scene which follows. The central (fourth) Interlude is a passacaglia founded upon the augmented form of the crucial Grimes motif which occurs when he has struck Ellen in the church scene and cries out 'And God have mercy upon me':

Ex. 8

Ex. 9

This becomes the theme of the subsequent chorus 'Grimes is at his exercise!' In the Passacaglia it becomes the ground-bass over which the solo viola, representing the apprentice, poignantly gives articulation to this otherwise silent character. Ten variations follow, but the Passacaglia's end does not really come until the end of Act II, scene

2 when the boy is dead and the viola repeats the Grimes theme in an inversion.

The fifth Interlude, which introduces Act III, depicts the moonlight over the Borough and the sea. The 'added-note' chords for bassoons, horns and lower strings are the ocean-swell; the moonlight comes through the clouds on little shafts of light from flutes and harp, gradually filling the sky with its cold light until the strains of the Barn Dance and the shrieks of the revellers in the Moot Hall bring us down to earth. The last Interlude, the cadenza before Grimes's Mad Scene, has already been described. Thus, in this opera, Britten emerged as a consummate master of orchestral colour, but those who deplored his abandonment of the symphony orchestra for the chamber ensemble overlooked that several of the outstanding moments in *Peter Grimes* are those of orchestral chamber-music, something he learned from his love of Mahler, just as he learned from radio-drama how to handle the scene in the pub, with the storm raging outside and the customers' repartee set to a form of stylized recitative (for instance, Auntie's 'That is the sort of weak politeness').

When Nicholas Maw in 1963 complimented Britten on *Peter Grimes* he received the reply: 'But Nicholas, it's full of howlers!'[2] Even allowing for Britten's natural modesty, one need not regard this answer as wholly facetious. There are parts of *Grimes* where one is aware that it is Britten's first large-scale opera. It suffers – if that is the right word, for many a composer would like the disease to be contagious – from almost an excess of invention, as if there were so many plums they had to be put into the pudding somehow. Reducing this to musical terms, Act I is a case where the flow of action and music which I praised earlier is achieved in spite of the obstacles Britten places in his own path. Here his fondness for the short vignette such as we found in the orchestral works, the *Frank Bridge Variations* and *Diversions*, invades the opera. Hobson's 'I have to go from pub to pub'; Balstrode's 'Pub conversation should depend', with its refrain 'We live and let live'; the round 'Old Joe has gone fishing' and, in Act III, Swallow's 'Assign your prettiness to me' and the Rector's 'I'll water my roses', effective in their various individual ways, come perilously near to deflecting the opera from its main course and creating a patchwork effect – points of relief which nearly become relaxation – while Balstrode's Act I 'I'll give a hand' is the least competently 'stitched-in' seam in the opera.

That said, *Peter Grimes* remains a masterpiece. I have never known it fail to grip and hold an audience. A succession of fine singers has found a challenge in the roles of Grimes and Ellen, roles in which the personal qualities of the original artists, Peter Pears and Joan Cross, have entered the music which was imagined specifically for them, the tenor with his gift for agonized introspection, the soprano with a maternal sympathy, and both devoid of erotic or romantic connotations. It is a priceless gift to posterity that the whole of Pears's performance and some of Miss Cross's is preserved: what would we not give to hear, for example, a recording of the original Fiordiligi? *Peter Grimes* is a great piece of theatre, and it is one of a handful of works, along with examples by Purcell, Elgar, Vaughan Williams and Delius, in which the English spirit and the English scene are captured in music. Yet, because of its treatment of a theme which is universal in its appeal to humanity, it will hold its place in the admiration and affection of opera-goers who have never set eyes on the real Moot Hall nor heard the wallop of the sea on the shingle at Aldeburgh.

21

1945–48

The Holy Sonnets of John Donne – String Quartet No.2 – *The Young Person's Guide to the Orchestra* – *The Rape of Lucretia* – *Albert Herring* – Canticle I – *A Charm of Lullabies* – *St. Nicolas*

After the success of *Peter Grimes*, Britten reverted to the line of works in which he had made his name, producing in quick succession in 1945–6 a song-cycle, a string quartet and a set of orchestral variations. The other principal composition was his first chamber-opera, *The Rape of Lucretia*. The three concert-hall works, and in a sense the opera, too, were linked by the commemoration of the 250th anniversary of Purcell's death.

The Holy Sonnets of John Donne, op. 35

This was Britten's first song-cycle with piano for five years and it has remained one of his least performed works, partly because it makes immense demands on stamina from the singer and partly, perhaps, because audiences find its high-pitched emotional intensity, allied to a particularly intricate thematic scheme, exhausting in comparison to the more lyrical Michelangelo and Hardy cycles. It was written at speed while Britten was running a high temperature and there is something feverish about it. Yet it should be better known, for these are nine powerful songs, beautiful settings of the English language.

There seems little doubt that Purcell's *Divine Hymns* are one source of inspiration, but the close relationship of voice and accompaniment suggests Wolf. Donne's declamatory poetry has its own rhythmic music to which Britten in the first two songs responds with a relentless hammering rhythm in the piano, the vocal line in the first ('O my blacke Soule!') deriving from two rhythmic shapes. In the second ('Batter my heart') the piano reiterates a restless pattern of notes, a Britten mannerism which is Schubertian in origin. Contrast comes with 'Oh might those sighes and teares', indecision replacing assertiveness.

The fourth song, 'Oh, to vex me' is a *moto perpetuo*, its quicksilver succeeded by the complex detail of 'What of this present' and its vision of the last day. At last, in 'Since she whom I loved', the lyrical Britten reappears with one of those floating tunes which are economical in actual notes but almost profligate in the impression they give of 'endless melody'; for the well-known words of 'At the round earth's imagined corners', Britten returns to the florid Handelian fanfares of the first song in *On This Island*. The penultimate 'Thou hast made me' is another *moto perpetuo*, the voice uncoiling in an urgency that matches the text's headlong flight from the devil's wiles. A five-bar ground bass on the Purcellian model is the fundamental material of the last song, 'Death, be not proud'. The piano has the dominant role, as in the last Michelangelo Sonnet, for much of the song until, with a return to the opening theme and the tonic B, the singer steadily builds up to the noble and confident proclamation that 'death shall be no more', its unequivocal faith all the more remarkable when one considers that it was written after that visit to Belsen.

String Quartet No. 2 in C, op. 36

Although this marvellous work was first performed on the actual Purcell anniversary (21 November 1945) and has a finale entitled Chacony, the Donne songs are closer to Purcell. There is much argument among scholars over the effectiveness, in this quartet's first movement, of Britten's always original use of sonata-form principles. There seems to be more of free fantasia about it than adherence to the classical precepts. The exposition takes up nearly half the movement, measured by the number of bars, and opens with one of Britten's most memorable ideas, or, rather, with three of them, each in a different key and each introduced by the interval of a tenth. All three deserve illustration (Ex. 10). Each of these themes undergoes metamorphosis, either in counterpoint with one another or as an inversion, until the tenths are heard as glissandi in a Bartókian passage of harmonics. There is, in fact, so much development in the exposition that the formal development section does little except reiterate; and the abbreviated recapitulation itself shows every inclination to take on the role of additional development as the violins and viola, over cello arpeggios, combine the three themes into one contrapuntal web. It remains for the coda to insist upon the primacy of C major and the rhythm of the first subject. After such enthralling music, written with a natural flair for the medium, the scherzo is the strangest of *vivace* movements, muted throughout in C minor, with a trio in F based on an augmentation of the scherzo theme. It is often described as 'eerie', but this is not precisely the mood. Panic-stricken is nearer. The Chacony finale is longer than the two preceding movements combined and has a compelling design: the ground, a noble theme, is given out in unison. Six variations which explore the theme's harmonic implications are followed by a recitative-like cadenza for cello. Then come six rhythmic variations ending in a viola cadenza through which the second violin plays a sustained C. This is the opening of the next set of six variations, based on a new melodic counterpoint of the ground. Each of the four players has this new theme as a solo, for until the polyphony of the eighteenth variation the melodic strands are paramount and there is a striking anticipation of the Governess's final aria in *The Turn of the Screw*. It is now the first violin's turn for a cadenza and this leads into the last three of the 21 variations. These are concerned with further aspects of the original ground and with re-establishing C major in a final series of emphatic chords. So ends a most original and beautiful composition, one of the quartet masterpieces of the century which amazingly was to have no successor for thirty years.

Ex. 10

The Young Person's Guide to the Orchestra (Variations and Fugue on a Theme of Purcell), op. 34

Although this orchestral showpiece bears an earlier opus number, it was composed after the *Donne Sonnets* and the string quartet and after *The Rape of Lucretia*, op. 37; it will be discussed here as one of the 'Purcell works' of the time, although the homage is merely the use of a splendid hornpipe Rondeau theme from the music to *Abdelazer*. Britten wrote the work for a documentary film, *Instruments of the Orchestra*, with commentary written by Montagu Slater, but the concert-version (with commentary by Crozier) was performed (in Liverpool) before the film was shown. It has become very popular, some finding it an example merely of the 'facility' which Britten's critics attribute to him. It is difficult to subscribe to this view, for the music inventively serves its purpose: to show off the characteristics of individual instruments and sections. To do this, it has been said, Britten relaxed into orchestral clichés and platitudes. If this means that he showed the instruments in traditional guises, I suppose the criticism has some validity, but it ignores the fact that in each variation the colour of the instrument is peculiarly Brittenish; for example, the typical violin fanfares in their polonaise variation, with chains of thirds and arpeggiated triads. The double-basses are given an impassioned melody, anything but a cliché, as well as a lighter-hearted fanfare, and the bassoons' variation has that sinister flavour which was to recur some years later in the *Nocturne*. The horns are heard as huntsmen rather than as romantics. The woodwind chirp, lament and gyrate in a standard manner, but to children who might find their timbres difficult to differentiate Britten makes each explicit. The fugue, in which the instruments join in the same order as they have been introduced in the variations, is cogently and brilliantly presented, and the grandiose return of the theme is always a thrill. Too many professorial noses in the air over this unpretentious but polished piece!

The Rape of Lucretia, op. 37

Britten's first chamber-opera for the newly formed English Opera Group required a new theatrical style of presentation in which not only the singers but each member of the orchestra was a soloist. With the use of Male and Female Chorus to narrate and comment upon the action, the singers had to pass naturally from acting to mime. Britten's instrumentation, not much different from that of his *Sinfonietta*, is flute (doubling piccolo and bass flute), oboe (doubling cor anglais), clarinet (doubling bass clarinet), bassoon, horn, percussion, harp, piano and solo string quintet. His use of this force, drawing from it extraordinary sonority and an incredibly wide range of colour, has occasioned much praise, and no wonder. Each of Britten's operas is dominated by the distinctive timbre of one or two instruments, and in *The Rape of Lucretia* it is the harp more than any other which is used to create a particular atmosphere. Like so many Britten works, this opera is haunted by nocturnal images, and the first stroke of genius is the depiction of the sultry night outside Rome where the generals are in camp. The harp's tinkle and the double-bass glissandi not only have a pictorial role in representing the noise of crickets and bullfrogs, but also suggest the tension underlying the men's discussion of their women's chastity; Lucretia's sleep is illustrated by bass flute, bass clarinet and muted horn, evoking all the sinister mystery of night, of the worm in the rose, and suggesting with equal clarity the guttering of a candle; the harp's delicate arpeggios as Lucretia and her women work at their spinning-wheels is obvious enough, but not the tense punctuations of fourths on the double bass with the gong (which give rise at 'endless, so endless' to an anticipation of a passage in the *War Requiem*); the effectiveness of the full chamber-orchestra, its capacity for sharply-etched sound, is deployed in the accompaniment to the Male Chorus's account of Tarquinius's ride to Rome.

Scarcely less impressive are the beauty and contrast of the vocal writing, in the Choruses' mixture of cadenza and arioso (the Male Chorus is another part tailored for the Pears of the *Serenade*); in the exchanges between the men in the first scene, talking of sex, as soldiers not infrequently do; in the sensuous quartet for the women in Act I, scene 2 as they talk of love and fold the linen. The Male Chorus's description of Tarquinius creeping towards Lucretia's room owes everything to the English *Sprechgesang* of Walton's *Façade*; Tarquinius's 'Within this frail crucible of light' is the operatic extension of the lyrical melodic line of the Donne Sonnet 'Since she whom I loved'. The opera is an advance on *Peter Grimes* in its seamless transitions. Its only really weak passage is the confrontation between Lucretia and Tarquinius, where Britten falls back on humdrum operatic conventions, both vocally and in the scalic accompaniment. Ronald Duncan's libretto, so often unjustly maligned, is here at its most self-consciously 'poetic'. The rape scene is followed by the controversial interlude in which the Male and Female Chorus spell out the central theme of the opera – 'virtue assailed by sin' – and then step far beyond the Roman era and introduce Christ and Mary as elements of forgiveness. It has been strongly argued that Lucretia does not need forgiving for she could not have sinned in a Christian sense. But Britten is surely justified in extending his compassion to all generations of men and women; moreover, Lucretia is a subtly drawn character. She is repelled in one sense by Tarquinius but she tells him 'In the forest of my dreams you have always been the Tiger'. Her self-accusations in her final scene betray a clear recognition that one can be attracted with half of one's nature to what disgusts the other half. The critics of the first performance fussed too much about this point. They might have pointed out that, after the big passacaglia, the Male Chorus's final recitative, offering hope in Christ, has all the operatic justification it needs – it is lovely music, the crown of the work. Britten rises to the heights when dealing with remorse and shame leading to hope of redemption. The opera moves to the plane of high tragedy from Lucretia's Flower Song onwards, and its culmination begins with the wonderful passage for cor anglais and strings which precedes her reunion with Collatinus (for whom a new aria was provided in the 1947 revision).

The music of *The Rape of Lucretia* has all the motivic inter-relationships which are the basis of Britten's compositions, and it is not too much to say that in this opera the Wagnerian *leitmotiv* system is the fundamental starting-point for its thematic symbols: the scale passage which is associated with the men, especially Tarquinius, and the sequence of thirds which is Lucretia's and the other women's motif. The contrast and interaction of these *leitmotive* pervade the score. They are combined in the prologue when the Male and Female Chorus sing together. The women's motif underlies – an apt word, given the dialogue – the scene in the generals' tent. Three notes of Tarquinius's motif are the harp's cricket sounds in the same scene, symbolic of night desires. The same notes dominate the ride to Rome, but Lucretia's motif returns as Tarquinius and his horse reach their destination. And so on. Note how the rising thirds of the Lucretia motif at 'O what a lovely day', music of sunlight and Roman heat, become the lugubrious oboe and bassoon accompaniment to Lucretia's weaving of a wreath from the orchids, her husband's favourite flowers. No opera by Britten ends more magically: the tragedy and the compassion are over and it is as if the whole scene fades from our sight while the orchestra repeats a demi-semiquaver figure and the major and minor thirds of the Lucretia theme flicker across the accompaniment like fireflies.

For some listeners, this is Britten's greatest work, but its flaw, it seems to me, is the comparative failure to involve the audience in Lucretia's tragedy. Except at the very end, she is an unapproachable symbol rather than a creature of flesh and blood, and this in spite of having been sung by contraltos as expert in conveying human emotion as Kathleen Ferrier, Nancy Evans and Janet Baker. One observes her fate with a detachment unthinkable in the case of Grimes. It is as an essay in evocative sonorities rather than as a stage drama that *The Rape of Lucretia* commands profound admiration.

Albert Herring, op. 39

Britten's first comic opera, composed for the same instrumental forces as *The Rape of Lucretia*, is, like *Peter Grimes*, about the inhabitants of a Suffolk town (disguised as 'Loxford'). Their comic or ludicrous characteristics, rather than their sinister contribution to a human tragedy, engage the composer here. Eric Crozier's cunning libretto, based on Guy de Maupassant's short story 'Le Rosier de Madame Husson', serves the gift for parody which Britten had exhibited from his earliest days and at the same time allows for the serious, moralizing note and the moment of pathos without which comic opera degenerates into farce. Those who saw in *Albert Herring* only proof that Britten had abandoned his role as pioneer and become the willing prisoner of the Suffolk society he satirizes have overlooked the poignant vein running through the score.

The plot is simple. The local (and teetotal) Lady Bountiful, Lady Billows, has offered £25 for the May Queen as an encouragement to virtue. The difficulty is that none of the village girls is wholly virtuous. Candidates offered by the mayor, the vicar and the police super-intendent (prophetically named Budd!) are rejected because of some reported or known moral misdemeanour. Instead a May King is chosen, Albert Herring, who works in his mother's greengrocer's shop. Albert, as he tells his friend Sid, has never been allowed near the risk of any kind of danger. On May Day, when Albert is to be crowned, Sid laces his lemonade with rum. Lady Billows and others extol Albert's virtue. Embarrassed, Albert stammers a reply, empties his glass, calls for more and gets hiccoughs. (No doubt Britten remembered how brilliantly Peter Pears sang Vašek in Smetana's *The Bartered Bride* at Sadler's Wells). That night, in the shop, Albert overhears Sid and his girl friend Nancy sympathizing over his domination by his mother. He decides to break away. Act III opens with the distress and rumours which Albert's disappearance have generated. Mrs Herring is sure her son is dead. Albert's May 'crown', an orange-blossom wreath, is brought in, muddy and squashed by a cart. In the midst of general mourning, Albert slips in unnoticed. He explains that he has spent £3 of his prize on a pub crawl. Reproached by his mother, he tells her

172

it's her fault for bringing him up so puritanically. All depart self-righteously, except Sid, Nancy and the village children who wish Albert good luck. Albert throws away his orange-blossom wreath, saying 'Jolly good riddance'.

Even from such a brief synopsis, the opera's weak point is obvious. Is it really likely that Albert will have gained his freedom by a night on the tiles in which he has done nothing more than get drunk and be thrown out of two pubs? 'Never mind, Albert', one can imagine his mother saying, once she has regained her composure, 'you weren't yourself. It won't happen again.' And I bet it never did. So the anti-climax of the final scene is almost inescapable. Fortunately the fun up till then has been musically witty and, thanks to the effervescence of the orchestration, the opera makes delightful entertainment. Its popularity abroad is sufficient proof that it is no mere parochial 'charade' for English eyes and ears alone. This is, of course, because the musical jokes are good and universal – and small towns alike the world over.

In his affectionate parodies of his characters, Britten gives a virtuoso display of his awareness of the salient characteristics of an enormous range of music – no surprise, after *Paul Bunyan*. The vicar, for example, is given a mixture compounded of Victorian hymn-tune and of folk-song as it might be arranged by Vaughan Williams (in his introduction of Lady Billows at the May Day ceremony). The mayor has strong Italianate tendencies, Supt. Budd is pomp and splutter, Miss Words-worth turns naturally to the worst kind of drawing-room ballad. Lady Billows ranges from Baroque aria to Barnby anthem and on to a *Merrie England* jingoism which also casts, one suspects, a sly glance at the final scene of *Die Meistersinger*. (There is a direct Wagner quotation in the May Day scene – the Love Potion motif from *Tristan* accompanies the lacing of Albert's lemonade with rum and reappears when he drinks it.) Mrs Herring, the villain of the piece, is the only character whose music is derived from one motif, a scalic passage which serves her for scolding Albert, for lachrymose grief and for her final humiliated rage. Sid and Nancy are uncomplicated, their love music as warm and touching as any Britten wrote. The music for the three children, whether they are teasing Albert in the shop, doing their 'party piece' at the May Day ceremony, or joining in Albert's final fling, is neither patronizing nor embarrassing. This side of Britten's art was barely known in 1947 but was to earn wider acclaim two years later with *The Little Sweep*.

Albert himself is presented to us mainly in three soliloquies, two of them in Act II scene 2 on either side of the love-making between Sid and Nancy which provokes his rebellion. As he examines his wretched life, his growing frustration is depicted by a network of thematic allusions, a similar scheme to Grimes's soliloquy but in a different context. (Earlier, as he looks for matches with which to light the gas in the shop, the idea of darkness is evoked by bass flute and bass clarinet in a motif very similar to that which accompanied Lucretia's sleeping. It returns at the end of the act when Mrs Herring goes to bed.) This aria – the voice of Pears in its *Serenade* prime is its obvious inspiration – is a fine feat of organization. Albert, in struggling to find his own personality, has to do so through assuming characteristics of the vocal style of Sid, whose freedom (and Nancy) he envies. Whether he convinces us, in his Act III aria after his return, that he is changed forever is debatable, but his description of his night out is certainly not the musical climax it should be, small change rather than pay-off. This last scene is unforgettable for a nine-part threnody, in which all the characters, individually and together, mourn for Albert. 'Why was he born who had to run so short a race and die so young?' This is yet another Passacaglia. Beginning as a parody of a psalm-chant, it becomes an impassioned lament, with the individuals in turn singing their solo elegies. We have come to know these people as parodies, but here, though still in character, they are intensely serious, the vicar *espressivo*, the mayor *eroico*, Lady Billows *brillante*, Budd *pesante*, Sid *con gravità* and Mrs Herring *appassionato*. The total effect is more moving than the *Lucretia* passacaglia. Those who are disconcerted by such music in this context are urged to listen to *Così fan tutte*, where a similar ambivalence is sustained for a whole opera.

Britten's dexterity in producing such a different sound-world from the instrumentation he used in *The Rape of Lucretia* is another remarkable aspect of *Albert Herring*. Where the scoring in the Roman work was claustrophobically hypnotic, here it is fuller, freer, no less apposite and no less virtuosic. The work as a whole succeeds as comedy because, for all the broadness of the events depicted, the music – even when the inspiration is thin – is extraordinarily subtle and does not pall.

Just before beginning work on the first chamber-opera, Britten composed incidental music for Duncan's *This Way to the Tomb* (1945) and for Louis MacNeice's radio play *The Dark Tower*, the latter a masterpiece of the medium, to which the atmospheric music made a powerful contribution. The 'hypnotic' quality I have mentioned in *The Rape of Lucretia* is present here too. An *Occasional Overture* in C, given the opus number 38 and played by the BBC Symphony Orchestra, conducted by Sir Adrian Boult, on 29 September 1946, the opening night of the BBC Third Programme (for which occasion it was commissioned), was later withdrawn. Another occasional piece dating from September 1946 is the *Prelude and Fugue on a Theme of Vittoria*, Britten's only solo organ work (apart from his music for the play *They Walk Alone*), composed for St. Matthew's Church, Northampton. It is not characteristic, but the contrapuntal skill of the fugue and its closing diatonic *ppp* are noteworthy.

Canticle I, op. 40

Of more significance is the first of the five canticles which span Britten's music at intervals between 1947 and 1974 (there was a gap of seventeen years between III and IV). These are extended settings of poems which have religious or at any rate spiritual significance. Their mood is usually intense and obviously requires a more complex design than, say, a Donne sonnet, something nearer to a miniature cantata or to vocal chamber music. The first was composed for the memorial concert for the Rev. Dick Sheppard, founder of the Peace Pledge Union, on 1 November 1947. It is a setting for tenor and piano of a poem by Frances Quarles (1592–1644) which itself is a paraphrase of the *Song of Solomon*: 'My beloved is mine, and I am his'. Britten himself said that it was modelled on Purcell's *Divine Hymns*, but claimed it as 'a new invention in a sense'. The canticle is in three sections, and its novelty in 1947 lay in the melismatic vocal line which, while strictly controlled, gives an impression of freedom and throughout is independent of the piano part, which makes much use of two- and three-part counterpoint. The flowing two-part writing for the piano at the opening depicts the 'two little bank-divided brooks' of the text but it is kept up long after the verbal image has passed until, when the singer reaches 'we joined, we both became entire', it yields to a richer harmonic texture. A scherzo section precedes the ecstatic lento of the last two stanzas which moves from B flat to G major and to a consummatory peace of the kind which Britten's music always understands, when the voice floats free from any restraints and the accompaniment beneath seems like the everlasting arms.

A Charm of Lullabies, op. 41

Britten's next song-cycle was composed in December 1947 for Eric Crozier's wife, Nancy Evans, who was the second-cast Lucretia at Glyndebourne in 1946. Five poets are drawn on for the five songs but, lacking a central theme such as unified the *Serenade*, the cycle, for all the charm punningly implied in the title, makes a patchwork effect.

175

There is no denying the sleepy atmosphere induced by the opening Blake *Cradle Song*, but to sustain this for four more numbers, even if it were desirable, is to court monotony and Britten's evasions seem contrived until the happy inventions of the closing 'The Nurse's Song'. A better example of the 'sophisticated-naive' Britten is the first of his large-scale compositions written for performance mainly by young people, the cantata *Saint Nicolas*.

Saint Nicolas, op. 42

Written for the centenary celebrations at Peter Pears's old school, Lancing College, but first performed a few weeks earlier at the first Aldeburgh Festival in June 1948, *Saint Nicolas* is scored for solo tenor, mixed chorus including boys, semi-chorus of girls' voices, strings, piano duet, organ and percussion. Though composed for semi-amateur performance (the tenor, the strings' leaders, and the first percussionist should be professionals), the work is usually now performed by fully professional forces and to classify it as 'music for children' is only partially accurate. It tells in nine sections (to an excellent libretto by Eric Crozier) the life of Saint Nicolas, fourth-century Bishop of Myra. The lively differentiations in mood between each movement derive ultimately from the genre-piece style of the *Frank Bridge Variations*. It is the sound-world of this work which is recalled by the cantata's opening, when the strings play a long undulating melody in perfect fourths over an E pedal. This pedal, with its accompanying harmonic progression, is neatly transposed up a fourth at the end of the movement to take the tonality towards A, emphasizing that Britten's harmonic scheme is to be as flexible as usual. Nicolas's birth is a movement cast in that vein of blithe and knowingly innocent melody which either enchants or exasperates the listener, depending how responsive one is to this 'simplicity' in Britten. Strings and piano accompany the catchy melody which is punctuated by a monotone chant of 'God be glorified', to organ accompaniment. No doubt it was this kind of music which led Adorno to write of the 'triumphant meagreness' of Britten and his 'simplicity resulting from ignorance, an immaturity which masks as enlightenment, and a dearth of technical means'. The point has been missed, of course, that the simplicity is achieved only by technical means and these are worn so lightly that they may prove deceptive. Professor Evans's detailed examination of Britten's structural and harmonic technique answers these critics for ever.

There is little need to examine this cantata in detail; it is best experienced whole and without analytical preparation. The 'Storm' movement derives from the swift-moving narrative style developed in *The Ballad of Little Musgrave and Lady Barnard*. Nicolas's prayer in this episode beautifully exploits Pears's incomparable legato when a visionary quality is required. The other big set-piece is the miracle of the pickled boys, called back to life by Nicolas with similar incantatory power. Perhaps the invention fails in the mundane fugal section of the fifth movement, and there are conventional modulations in the choral writing of the penultimate section – 'His piety and marvellous works' – when the ghosts of Elgar and Fauré stand uncomfortably near for the good name of originality, but only Britten could have devised the 'Death of Nicolas', in which the tenor vanquishes fear of death in fluent thirds and the chorus chant 'Nunc dimittis' – a kind of miniature *Gerontius* but with no overtones of *Parsifal*.

At the end of Part 1 and at the end of the cantata, Britten borrows from Bach, Tippett and other composers the unfailing emotional device of using a well-known melody in which the audience can join. He chose the hymns 'All people that on earth do dwell' (*Old Hundredth*) and 'God moves in a mysterious way' (*London New*), the first with a descant, the second with a counter-melody for male voices in the second verse. In the latter setting, too, Britten does not spurn repeated cymbal clashes as a clinching means of grappling his music to the heart of English life in company with comparable works by Handel, Parry, Elgar and Vaughan Williams. At thirty-five, Britten in *Saint Nicolas* found himself master of a variety of musical styles, with his options open for development in any of several ways. E.M. Forster's description of the cantata as 'one of those triumphs outside the rules of art' says it all.

22

1949–54

Spring Symphony – The Little Sweep – Billy Budd – Canticle II –
Gloriana – The Turn of the Screw – Winter Words – Songs from
the Chinese

The *Spring Symphony*, op. 44, completed in June 1949, was Britten's
first large-scale choral work. It is scored for soprano, alto and tenor
soloists, mixed chorus, boys' choir and symphony orchestra. The
orchestra is used with the economy and mastery of tone-colour
developed in the first two chamber operas, the constituents of the
accompaniment varying for each piece. The work is divided into four
movements, roughly following the traditional symphony structure.
Each movement is 'divided into shorter sections bound together by a
similar mood or point of view'.[1] The text is an anthology of poems
relating to spring, ranging from sixteenth-century Anon. to Spenser,
Nashe, Peele, Clare, Milton, Herrick, Vaughan, Barnefield, Blake,
Beaumont and Fletcher, and Auden, as much a tribute to Britten's
literary taste as to their suitability for music. There was some discussion
in 1949 on whether it was a true symphony, but the term has been
stretched in the twentieth century, not to mention Beethoven's example
in his Ninth. The *Spring Symphony* was the model for Shostakovich's
Fourteenth, a work which also takes a single theme (death) and treats
it, in anthology form, with symphonic weight.

   Like Stravinsky with *The Rite of Spring*, Britten's initial inspiration
was 'the progress of Winter to Spring and the reawakening of the
earth and life which that means'. So the work opens with 'a prayer in
Winter, for Spring to come', a setting of the anonymous 'Shine out,
fair sun' in which the deadness of 'black winter' is projected as much
by the vibraphone's icicle tone as by the string harmonies. This section
is long and complex. The unaccompanied chorus is thrice interrupted
by an orchestral episode, each of which begins with the percussion
ritornello which opened the symphony and each being a slow fugue.
Music has to move, but this conveys a sense of frozen movement, with

nothing to disturb the air except the grey wolf's howl. Use of semitonal intervals, as in Ex. 11 (two bars after Fig. 5), and of the tritone underpin the whole structure:

Ex. 11

Spring comes with 'The merry cuckoo', a tenor solo accompanied by three trumpets, relying heavily on obvious imagery and lacking that special Britten magic which enters the work with the third poem's opening phrase 'Spring, the sweet spring' – impossible to read the words after one knows this music without hearing Britten's simple but perfect setting of them and its falling fifth D–G. Here the full orchestra is used, with a solo string quartet supporting the four soloists. Flutes, clarinets and trumpets are reserved for the inventive bird-calls. The invention is happy, too, in the boys' choir's introduction to 'The Driving Boy', where the falling fifth becomes part of the blithe accompaniment for woodwind, tambourine and tuba. The boys whistle and sing a poem by Peele; Clare's 'Driving Boy' itself is given to the soprano soloist, with high violins, a contemplative change of mood (based on the Peele setting) until soprano and boys combine in a merry coda.

Britten mixes the light and the dark; and Part 2 is concerned with 'the darker side of spring – the fading violets, rain and night'. For the first time we hear the contralto soloist, with dark harmonies from woodwind, harp and strings (excluding violins) in Herrick's 'Welcome, maids of honour'. The violins return as sole accompaniment to the tenor in Vaughan's 'Waters above', their *sul ponticello* triplets a deservedly famous representation of rain surfaces lit by watery sunlight. The section (the slow movement) ends with Auden's 'Out on the lawn I lie in bed', for contralto and the mixed chorus (singing 'Ah' as a ritornello). The poem's wry, rather than bitter, comment on the unreality of English country-house life where the dwellers 'do not care to know, Where Poland draws her Eastern bow, What violence is done', is set with a very precise response – the *Lucretia*-like alto flute

179

and bass clarinet suggesting 'the windless night of June', the flute depicting the nocturnal sounds of the roosting birds and the insects. When the brass erupt in the last verse, the effect is brutal. The strings are silent throughout this last and deeply disturbing final Britten-Auden union.

It is perhaps because the finale is constructed mainly as a setting of one long extract from *The Knight of the Burning Pestle* that it is the most satisfying musical entity in the work. The key progress is from A minor to a *Meistersinger*-like C major. The principal theme is an infectious waltz, as delightfully anachronistic in the context of six-teenth-century London as it is in the Rosenkavalier's Vienna and scarcely less enticing. Britten's use of the crude blare of the cow-horn as a punctuation of the Maylord's speech ('London, to thee I do present the merry month of May') is a memorable example of his oft-praised flair for the apt image – the sound, the smell, the cruelty, the rumbustiousness of Tudor England are conveyed by that one note, but don't ask me why or how! An allegro section is brilliantly studded with inventive imagery – the little fish and the creeping snails obvious examples – and the symphony's climax, before its sudden and poetic end, is an exciting combination of the waltz with the boys' unison descant of 'Sumer is icumen in' (sung in 2/4 against the prevailing 3/4, the rhythmical difference throwing the irruption into stronger relief).

It is impossible not to delight in the many happy and graceful touches in the *Spring Symphony*, not least in Britten's unflagging manipulation of so many disparate elements into an ordered whole. But there are passages – especially in the contrived canonic and arpeggio mannerisms of the three scherzo settings – where one is made uncomfortably aware of faltering invention, of the jam being spread very thin, of reliance on artifice. That said, it is also true that, while no occasional piece, it is very much a piece for an occasion, and if one is fortunate enough to hear a performance which unaffectedly captures the sheer enjoyment and poetry of the music, then one's doubts may be banished, at any rate for its duration.

The Little Sweep, op. 45

This adorable example of Britten's 'useful' music began as the second part of Eric Crozier's 'entertainment for young people', first performed at Aldeburgh in June 1949, under the title 'Let's Make an Opera!'. The first part showed, as a play, the writing and rehearsal of the opera. Part 2 was the opera itself, *The Little Sweep*. Nowadays the first part is usually dispensed with or replaced by producers' own material. The scoring of the opera is for string quartet, piano duet and percussion. In this work is crystallized all that we understand by Britten's capacity for writing for children without patronizing them. Nothing exemplifies this understanding more than his decision to involve the children in the audience in the opera: they have important parts to sing at four junctures, beginning with the overture, which therefore departs from custom by being choral. Two of the remaining three choruses take the place of what, in his adult operas, would have been instrumental interludes. By this device, practical Britten eliminated the danger of a talkative audience obbligato. The Bath Song is an ingratiating waltz and the Night Song a subtle introduction to the mysteries of Britten's nocturnal music while at the same time giving opportunity for bird-call imitations (owls, herons, doves and chaffinches. Imogen Holst, in her book on Britten, tells a delightful story of the consternation caused at the first rehearsals by the divisions into groups of birds: 'a tall, thin music critic rose to the occasion by waving his tightly-rolled umbrella and calling out to the conductor: "Excuse me, but where did you say the *herons* should be?"'). Crozier's libretto is a Dickensian tale (set in a Suffolk country house in 1810) about how the family children and their friends, aided by a sympathetic housemaid (Rowan), outwit the housekeeper Miss Baggott and the Sweep by rescuing Sammy, the nine-year-old sweep-apprentice, from his cruel trade. It is, of course, another Britten parable about cruelty and compassion, good and evil, with its origin in the Blake poem he was to set some years later, but one need not become too portentous in this context. Britten relies on children's natural perception to draw the moral; he does not labour it, nor need we. The music makes the point infallibly; at the same time, it is fun.

The composition is based on simple and easily memorable formulae and uses spoken dialogue instead of recitative. But sophisticated means are needed to obtain simple effects, as we can tell from the overture, in 5/4 time, where the tune's triplet quavers hurry along against the unchanging progression in the accompaniment. Each verse is preceded by a cry of 'Sweep!'; this has a different harmonization each time it occurs, so that the song passes in five verses to and from D minor by way of B flat major, G minor and E flat major. This formula of shifting harmony in a constant melody is used elsewhere also, and Britten makes much use of ostinato and ground bass. The elaborate ensemble when the child Juliet feigns a fainting-fit to prevent the hidden Sammy being found is a passacaglia so that the characters' reactions can be individually charted. The most profound music is given to Rowan in her 'Far along the frozen river', an aria which epitomizes the compassion inherent in the whole concept. One wonders, too, how many children's ears have been opened to orchestral music's illustrative powers by the bustling Pantomime to which the nursery is tidied.

The musical achievement of *The Little Sweep* is high enough to ensure that it should be judged by artistic criteria alone. Nevertheless it was this kind of Aldeburgh Festival work which helped to alienate Britten from a new generation of composers and commentators. The reason, given the emerging political climate of the second half of the twentieth-century, is not hard to discover. It was galling for some to find the 'master of the Left's music' of 1937–9 no longer composing ballads for revolutionary heroes but writing wedding anthems for, and dedicating operas to, friends in the Royal Family, to find him in the comfortable – they would have said cosy – surroundings of Suffolk with a countess as chairman of his festival committee. Where was the angry satirist of *Our Hunting Fathers* now? What was its acerbic composer doing, writing operas for twentieth-century children in which he held up to them, without social comment, the admirable deeds of children who regarded it as natural and inevitable to accept superiority to housekeepers and housemaids?

Such an approach is as ludicrous as if Wodehouse were to be blacklisted because Bertie Wooster had a 'gentleman's gentleman'. Yet it was at the root of the savage attack on Britten and the whole Aldeburgh operation as 'irrelevant' and a cultural 'conspiracy' based on the abhorred public-school system. Fatuities apart, it was overlooked that Britten's sympathies, which were never blunted, were for the individual rather than for a group or for a segment of society or that amorphous entity 'the people'. The titles of his works did not happen by chance – *Peter Grimes, Billy Budd, The Little Sweep, Saint Nicolas, Owen Wingrave, Death in Venice* (of one individual), *Albert Herring, Abraham and Isaac*. Britten probably felt that there would always be those to champion the aspirations of the crowd (not least the crowd itself), but fewer to worry about the solitary tortured soul. In any case, he remained committed to the belief that his job was to let his music be his message; and that message is as strong in *The Little Sweep* as it is in *Peter Grimes* or in the next major work, the opera *Billy Budd*. But before that sombre masterpiece is reached some shorter works should detain us.

Between September 1946, when he finished his organ piece, and 1955, when he composed the suite for recorders, Britten wrote only two works which did not involve words. Both were for individual virtuosi to play at the Aldeburgh Festival. For the violist William

Primrose in 1950 he composed *Lachrymae*, op. 48, subtitled 'Reflections on a song of John Dowland', the song being 'If my complaints could passions move'. This poetic piece comprises ten variations on the first eight-bar strain of a beautiful song which epitomizes Dowland's melancholy, each manifestation of hope being followed by depression. The key is C minor, with bitonal innuendoes; the sixth variation quotes Dowland's *Lachrymae* song 'Flow my tears', a touching anticipation of the ending, in which the final strain of the work's basic song, with Dowland's harmonies, is haloed by Britten's most expressive eloquence. In 1976 Britten provided an accompaniment for small string orchestra instead of piano, and thus added another work to the viola's small repertoire of concert-pieces.

Typical of Britten that in devising a work for solo oboe for Joy Boughton to play *al fresco*, he treated the instrument, without flinching, in its role of pastoral pan-pipe and even related it to six figures from classical mythology. Hence the *Six Metamorphoses after Ovid*, op. 49, the movements being Pan, Phaeton, Niobe, Bacchus, Narcissus and Arethusa. Each of these characters underwent metamorphosis, so each piece is a miniature variation on its characteristic opening figure. The obvious is not evaded – a mirror-image for Narcissus, hiccups for Bacchus, the cascading fountain for Arethusa – but the combination of a fine player's technique with this composer's inventive simplicity results in a work of much wider scope than its restricted nature might seem to suggest.

Britten summoned his most lyrical fancies for *A Wedding Anthem (Amo ergo sum)*, op. 46 (text by Ronald Duncan), written for Lord Harewood's marriage to Erwin Stein's daughter Marion in 1949. The soprano and tenor soloists are given fresh and imaginative arias, suitable for the union of two opera-lovers, and the writing for choir and organ is far from conventional. But the piece was perhaps too closely linked to its occasion and is rarely heard. The *Five Flower Songs*, op. 47, were a twenty-fifth wedding anniversary present for friends, Leonard and Dorothy Elmhirst of Dartington Hall. They are settings of Herrick, Crabbe, Clare and Anon. for unaccompanied chorus, Britten's first work in this genre since the *Hymn to St Cecilia*. These break no new ground, indeed they are very much in the English part-song tradition of Stanford and early Elgar, the best being the last, 'The Ballad of Green Broom', in which Britten reverts to his earlier penchant for imitative accompaniment, in this case a strummed lute.

Billy Budd, op. 50

In this opera based on Melville, with a marvellous libretto by E.M. Forster and Eric Crozier, Britten returned to the orchestra appropriate to a large opera-house but used it with the experience gained in the chamber operas. Only male voices are used, but there is no suggestion of monotony and this is in large measure due to the supremely apposite orchestral texture. Orchestral interludes are used, as in *Peter Grimes*, but here they are so integral a part of the score that any attempt to separate them from its tissue and perform them in the concert-hall would be disastrous. In every respect, *Billy Budd* is an advance on *Peter Grimes*, especially in the relentless growth and pressure of tension. So painful is this opera in its almost pitiless exposure of evil that some who acknowledge it to be a masterpiece cannot bear to hear it. For those who can overcome a squeamish response, the gain in acquaintance with a music-drama of shattering power is more than ample compensation.

Melville's novel, his last (1891), originated in a real-life event in the U.S. Navy in 1842 but he transferred the action to the Royal Navy in 1797 at the time of extreme tension after the Mutinies at Spithead and the Nore. In every ship any 'progressive' sentiments which might lead to mutinous thoughts or deeds such as had precipitated the French Revolution were regarded with fear and suspicion by officers who knew that most of the crew were serving against their will, having been seized by Press Gangs. This, then, is one level of the action aboard H.M.S. *Indomitable* commanded by Captain Edward Fairfax Vere. She is below complement, and when she sights a merchantman named *Rights o' Man* a boarding-party is sent to impress three of the crew, among them Billy Budd, a good and efficient seaman and a pleasant man but with the defect of an occasional stammer – 'it comes and it goes'. He is liked by all except the master-at-arms, Claggart, who determines to destroy him and falsely accuses him of inciting mutiny. Billy, shaken by the enormity of this villainy, is unable to answer the accusation because of his stammer and in frustration strikes out blindly, killing Claggart. There is no alternative for Vere but to sentence Billy to death. He is hanged from the yard-arm, calling out 'Starry Vere, God bless you' before he dies.

That is a strong plot, but its deeper meanings, its unspoken counterpoints, its theme of the corruption of good by evil, were bound to make a profound appeal to Britten. Idle to speculate on the private states of mind of this opera's creators, but that they sublimated them in a great work of art seems to me to be incontrovertible. No need here, as in *The Rape of Lucretia*, for the Christian values to be underlined by a Chorus: Billy is sentenced by a man who does not believe him guilty, a sentence legally just but morally unjust; his vigil before execution suggests Gethsemane; his cry to Vere from the scaffold is the equivalent of 'Father, forgive them'. Vere himself is the most fascinating character in the work. We see him first as an old man, looking back over his life and finding 'the good has never been perfect ... always some flaw ... some stammer in the divine speech. So that the Devil still has something to do with every human consignment to this planet... Who has blessed me? Who has saved me?' When he sentences Billy, he says, 'I am the messenger of death', and at the end 'I could have saved him'. He is a man of action and a disciplinarian, but an intellectual also. It is unfortunate that in the revision of the opera into two acts the one major excision removed his original first appearance in the main part of the action, when he was acclaimed by the crew for his qualities as a captain. In the revised version[2] he is first seen in his cabin, reading Plutarch. Because of the librettists' device of the framing prologue and epilogue, we see and interpret the tragedy through Vere's eyes.

Even more complex is Claggart, the incarnation of evil, but no melodramatic villain. He wants to destroy Billy because Billy represents all that he can never be, handsome, popular, loved. He, 'a depravity according to nature' (Melville's words) knows he cannot achieve Billy's virtue. But, underlying this, there is also the attraction of opposites and a powerful whiff of homo-eroticism, of repressed desire for the object of hatred. Claggart's hunting-down of Billy is depicted by Britten with a remorselessness which justifies Keller's use of the word sadistic in relation to one side of the composer's musical nature, a sadism comparable with Puccini's. Yet, even in its destruction, innocence triumphs in Britten: in the epilogue, Vere realizes that Billy was his life's salvation and as he sings 'I've sighted a sail in the storm, the far-shining sail', not only are the words Billy's, it is the music of Billy's last tender, serene, forgiving and accepting aria.

For this magnificent drama, Britten commanded psychological reserves of inspiration available to no other operatic composer of our day. If there are, as so often, acts of homage to Shostakovich and if Verdi's *Otello* is omnipresent as prime model and exemplar, the work is nevertheless Britten at his most idiosyncratic. Although the life and ritual of the *Indomitable*, the flogging, the shanties, the chase of the French ship, the officers' conference with the captain, are shown to us, these never take the attention from the central human crisis. The Borough in *Peter Grimes* may have inspired a more exuberant manner, but the concentration in *Billy Budd* is riveting in its single-minded exploration of the darker places of the human soul. The manhunt in *Grimes* is chilling, but the crew's inarticulate sounds of incipient rage and protest after the execution are even more terrifying as a (fugal) expression of pent-up fury in a claustrophobic society such as the world of a man-of-war of Nelson's day. It is like the sounds of animals in pain.

The librettists may take credit for one particular master-stroke. Claggart's ascent to the quarterdeck to lay his charges against Billy to Vere is interrupted by the sighting of the French ship. Then follows the excitement of the frustrated chase, after which Claggart returns to his mission, to Vere's obvious irritation. (Ernest Newman described this interruption as 'amateurishly inept', one further example of that over-rated critic's insensitivity.)

Structurally the opera is among Britten's greatest and most intricate achievements. Again, one can do no better than recommend Peter Evans's masterly analysis. There is space here only to call attention to the work's *Urmotiv*, a minor-within-major third heard in the opening bars:

Ex. 12

Most of the opera's thematic shapes can be related to this. In addition there is a crucial musical image, the opposition of the chords of B flat major and B minor, the harmonically remote semitonal interval symbolizing the irreconcilability of opposites and also providing a unifying thread of disunity for the whole score:

Ex. 13

In several scenes the dramatic tension is created by this undermining of one key by its neighbouring semitone: the Novice tries to bribe Billy in music hovering between F and F sharp minor; the sailors' roar of protest after Billy's death is in B and is silenced by the officers' B flat orders. Claggart's power for evil is represented by this bitonal clash, and other themes derive from it. The harmonic idiom is dominated to an extraordinary degree by the triad and the conflicts of major and minor triads, resolved only in the epilogue when B flat triads symbolize the love that passes understanding which has come to Vere. The motivic transformations and juxtapositions are so vividly presented that they strike home even to listeners who do not realize their existence. The power of the music comes from this coiled mass of theme-cells, sometimes giving rise to ambivalence between music and action. But when Professor Evans wonders why Claggart, in the Iago-like (or even Pizarro-like) credo in which he analyses his strange feelings for Billy, sings 'Having seen you, what choice remains to me?' to a reference to the 'Starry Vere' motif, the answer surely is that Claggart equates Billy with Vere, for no listener to this opera can be unaware that, in spite of his obsequious deference, Claggart hates Vere – and Vere ill-disguises his dislike of Claggart.

But so we could go on, for the opera yields new fields for speculation at each hearing. Some have found a fatal flaw in the work through the apparent implausibility of the officers' suspicions of Billy because of his shout of 'Farewell, Rights o' Man'. How, when they must have seen the name of the ship they raided for crew, could they think he was referring to Tom Paine's seditious book? The answer can only be that in 1797 the words were like a knell in any context – and Billy's 'Rights o' Man' phrase remains a *leitmotiv* for mutiny in the rest of the opera.

If one stresses here the structure of the score, that is only because its external beauties are more obvious. For all its sombre plot, it is an exciting, colourful work. The rich and varied scoring is dominated by brass, percussion and woodwind used with unerring skill and diversity – and, in the fugal assembly of the ship's company before the execution, with macabre deliberation. All the usual Britten flashes of brilliant, quickly memorable invention are there: the muted trumpet, side-drum roll and woodwind gulps for Billy's stammer; the trombones which stalk around with Claggart; the saxophone which plays its plangent lament after the Novice's flogging; the solo horn which accompanies Vere's conversation with Billy seems like a distant echo from the Tennyson bugle of the *Serenade* but for Britten now this image is turning, by way of *Billy Budd*, into the military signals of *War Requiem*.

There is no more atmospheric section of this score than the crew's singing below decks while Vere listens, ethereal beauty strongly contrasted with the rollicking shanties and the war-cries of 'This is the moment'.

But the whole point of opera, it must never be forgotten, is its voices and singing. Unquestionably, three superb arias crown the work: Vere's anguish after he has sentenced Billy; Claggart's 'O beauty, handsomeness, goodness!', its black and nihilistic rising and falling fourths not excluding, even from this evil being, an element of suffering; and Billy's sleepy, drowsy dream-aria which recurs when he awaits execution and symbolizes his innate goodness without a trace of sanctimoniousness. Britten's choice of a baritone for this role is here abundantly justified. Even so, the work's most unusual stroke is orchestral. This is the celebrated passage of thirty-four slow chords, played while the stage is empty after Vere has gone to tell Billy of the sentence of death. They are scored for the full orchestra, and individually for strings, woodwind, horns, and brass; they vary in dynamics and colouring and they form a vast harmonized F major arpeggio. But how can analysis define them and their effect? Melville, in the book, does not describe the scene between Vere and Billy but suggests that the captain 'may have caught Billy to his heart even as Abraham may have caught young Isaac on the brink of resolutely offering him up in obedience to the exacting behest.' Britten takes the amazing risk for an opera composer of eschewing words at this moment, and his instinct was right. It is not without significance that his next work was the canticle *Abraham and Isaac*, a second epilogue to the greatest of his secular parables.

Canticle II, op. 51

The second canticle, *Abraham and Isaac*, to a text from a Chester Miracle Play, was written for Pears, Kathleen Ferrier and the composer to perform during a fund-raising tour on behalf of the English Opera Group. In some later performances the contralto part (Isaac) has been sung by a counter-tenor and, even more aptly, by a boy near to Isaac in age. The work, in which can be detected the seeds of the church parables, opens with the voice of God represented by the two soloists singing in unison to the plainchant-like melody, another instance of a simple device put to telling, and in this case awe-creating, effect. God's command to Abraham is punctuated by a piano arpeggio-figure; this prologue is in E flat and the scene of Abraham's determination to obey is in A major, its opposite extreme, with a darkly menacing piano part. The folk-song lilt of the dialogue between father and son becomes more agitated as Isaac is told that he must be sacrificed, and it is into E flat that the music returns as God stays Abraham's hand. The work ends with a serene E flat epilogue which is a modified development of the earlier A major section but now with an accompaniment suggesting the gentle ringing of bells. The voices, no longer representing the characters, sing in canon, the piano's opening arpeggio now like a benediction. Even in so comparatively brief a work, the sense of drama is intense, albeit conveyed without the histrionic resource of *Billy Budd*.

Gloriana, op. 53

Britten's Coronation opera, in spite of the success of its 1966 Sadler's Wells revival for which it was slightly revised, remains the least-known of his stage works. It is a notable example of ceremonial music and it did not deserve its initial snubs. With the craftsmanship and sense of musical fitness which never deserted him whatever the context, Britten (and his librettist William Plomer) devised a work fitting to the occasion. The central figure is Elizabeth I, Gloriana herself, and no other character is allowed to challenge her supremacy. Although her love for Essex is a theme in the drama, Essex himself has a relatively small role and does not emerge with much credit. We see the queen in public, in council chamber, and in her private apartments, always as a human being. We see the conflicts between duty and love, and we see that never for a second did she consider anything but her duty to the realm as paramount. It is difficult to see how any tribute more apt to the crowning of the second Elizabeth could have been paid – or one more apt to the artistry of the first singer of the role, Joan Cross, to whom Britten owed so much.

As in *Billy Budd*, Britten placed the private drama within the framework of public ritual, in this case the life of the court in London and on a 'progress' in Norwich. Unlike the preceding opera, *Gloriana* deliberately is not given the motivic tensions and unity of that great work's relentless unfolding, for it is, quite rightly, a 'numbers' opera, almost a succession of tableaux, with little attempt to iron out any roughnesses in transition from one to the next. But it is still gripping drama, and one must salute Britten's refusal to be untrue to his poetic nature and to the nature of the libretto by courting easily-won applause at the close with some quasi-Elgarian or *Meistersinger* choral apotheosis. Instead, the queen is seen alone on a dark stage, and she *speaks* words associated with six episodes in her life which occurred after Essex's execution. These are accompanied by tremolo strings, wind or percussion. Between them the orchestra plays the lute-song, 'Happy were he', which Essex sang to the queen in Act I. Only three phrases, two of them quotations from the lute song, are sung by Elizabeth here. The opera ends with the off-stage chorus singing the noble 'Green leaves' chorus which has run through the opera. It was wise of librettist and composer to omit a scene for the condemned Essex. It is on the queen that the audience should concentrate, and by interpolation of a scene in which Essex's wife and sister plead vainly with Elizabeth for his life, the portrayal of the agonizing decisions confronting such a monarch is strengthened.

Britten reverted to the method of the *Grimes* prologue for his first scene, in which Essex fights with Mountjoy, his rival for the queen's favour, after Mountjoy has won a joust before the queen. Essex's impetuous and sulky character is quickly established, the chorus act as commentators and, like a coroner at an inquest, Raleigh delivers a 'plague on both their houses' verdict for the queen. Raleigh's aria sounds like an aristocratic promotion of Supt. Budd from *Albert Herring* and there are moments in this scene when Gloriana reveals herself as kith and kin of Lady Billows. However, the reconciliation ensemble returns the opera to its stately provenance in splendid fashion. In the second scene of Act I we are shown first the shrewd statesman-queen in council with Cecil, who warns her of Essex's lack of restraint, and then the woman in love when Essex comes to her. His motif:

Ex. 14

is to recur at tragic moments but here it leaps forth with a confidence which borders on *lèse-majesté*. Elizabeth commands two lute-songs from him; the first, 'Quick music is best', she rejects as 'too light, a song of careless hearts', and Britten has undermined its attempt at gaiety by accompanying it in the bass with the motif of the queen's 'cares of state'. The second song, of haunting beauty, begins with a quotation from Wilbye's madrigal 'Happy were he', but continues in Britten's most limpid vein. It is in C minor; later in the scene, during the duet, Essex's jealousy of other courtiers erupts in the same key in staccato rhythmic phrases which prefigure some of Quint's music in *The Turn of the Screw* and ultimately derive from Peter Grimes's 'These Borough gossips listen to money, only to money'. In her Soliloquy and Prayer at the end of this scene, the queen leaves no doubt that she sees no future in her relationship with Essex. As surely as the Marschallin, at the end of Act I of *Der Rosenkavalier*, foreshadows her renunciation of Oktavian, Elizabeth here stresses her allegiance to her divine mission beside which Essex counts for little.

In Act II Britten shows another side of the queen. Her appreciation of the masque at Norwich (scene 1) is regally gracious and her music appropriately flowing. But in scene 3, in the Palace of Whitehall, when, by a trick, she spitefully acquires Lady Essex's striking dress and dances a lavolta. While wearing it (it is a bad fit), the musical distortions of the lavolta (which Lady Essex has danced earlier) have the triple task of symbolizing the gown's unsuitability, the contrast with the dance when it was last heard, and the unpredictable aspect of her nature which results in her sudden return later in the scene to grant Essex his fatal wish to be Lord Deputy in Ireland. She makes the appointment in E flat minor, and it is in that key that, in Act III, scene 1, she signs his death warrant after an episode in which the B minor/B flat semitonal conflicts of *Billy Budd* are again called upon.

Gloriana, for all its pageantry, is not short of musical and dramatic subtleties. Some of the best music is in Act II, scene 2 when Essex and his wife, with Mountjoy and his mistress Lady Rich (Essex's sister), talk sedition in a quartet to which Britten's Lydian C major lends its flavours. Both in the Choral Dances in the Act II masque and in the court dances at Whitehall, Britten avoids any suggestion of pastiche but re-creates the Elizabethan age in his own idiom, in just the way the gittern-accompanied ballad-singer of Act III, telling of Essex's ill-fated rebellion, steers well clear of any distracting suggestions, to the practised Britten-listener, of *Paul Bunyan*.

The Turn of the Screw, op. 54

One of the essentials of composition, Britten said, was 'a firm and secure musical structure which can safely hold together and make sense of one's wildest fantasies'. In none of his works was it more necessary to hold the wild fantasies together than in his version of

Henry James's ghost story *The Turn of the Screw*. Here was a subject which, like *Billy Budd*, presented repressed emotions fanned, or brought into the open, in an isolated setting (in a ship – 'a tiny floating fragment' – in *Billy Budd*; in the early nineteenth-century Essex country house, Bly, in the James opera). Here, too, one of the chief characters unwittingly becomes 'the messenger of death'. In *Billy Budd*, Vere takes refuge in the strict letter of the law to avoid his moral dilemma; in *The Turn of the Screw* the Governess knows herself to be corrupted by the same evils which afflict the brother and sister, Miles and Flora, in her charge and, in thinking she has saved them, brings about the boy's death. The tension in *Billy Budd* was sustained in spite of the big set-piece interruptions, but in *The Turn of the Screw* there could be no kind of respite. Britten, whose handling of variations and of the passacaglia had given him some of his finest artistic triumphs, instinctively, it would seem, knew that the tension of this ghost-story would not only be sustained but magnified in the theatre by use of elaborate variation-form. To tell the story, the librettist, Myfanwy Piper, and composer selected fifteen scenes and a prologue linked by sixteen orchestral interludes in the shape of a theme and fifteen variations. The theme is based on a row of twelve notes, but there is nothing Schoenbergian or serial in its application (Ex. 15).

The six intervals may be interpreted as ascending fourths or descending fifths. In each case the first note is a tonic and the second a subdominant. The tonal plan of the first seven scenes up to the penultimate scene of Part 1 is in white-note keys; the first black-note key, A flat, comes in scene 8 (the end of Part 1) when the ghosts are first heard. Four of the eight scenes of Part 2 are in black-note keys, identified with the ghosts. The basic tonal conflict of the opera is A minor/A flat major.

Ex. 15

James's story, published in 1898, has an ambiguity which he resolutely refused to dispel when questioned: did the ghosts 'really exist'

or were they figments of the Governess's neurotic imagination? Nor did he define good and evil in the story. He does not tell us outright what the 'evil' is with which Peter Quint, ghost of the valet of the boy Miles's uncle and guardian, may corrupt Miles, though the assumption that it is homosexual may be justified from James's words: 'There had been matters in his [Quint's] life – strange passages and perils, secret disorders, vices more than suspected.' And is not Myfanwy Piper thoroughly explicit when she puts into Quint's mouth: 'I seek a friend ... he shall feed my mounting power. Then to his bright subservience I'll expound the desperate passions of a haunted heart...', especially as a variant of the theme principally associated with Miles, his 'Malo' song, is played by the horn as accompaniment to these words. Yet Quint's sexual tastes may be presumed to be impartial as to gender, since the other ghost, Miss Jessel, the Governess's predecessor, has also been his victim.

In the book neither of the ghosts speaks. How were Britten and Mrs Piper to retain the ambiguity and at the same time write an opera for singers? To have the ghosts silent and yet seen would have been ridiculous. So they are given words to sing in which Mrs Piper, by a skilful use of vague and baroque verbal imagery, retains much of the mystery. Britten specifically demanded *words*, 'no nice, anonymous, supernatural humming or groaning'. It is sometimes said that what the ghosts say would not corrupt or tempt anybody but she has justifiably defended herself by writing:[3] 'The child would not necessarily be attracted by evil, though evil might come out of it'. So, although in the opera the ghosts exist as far as seeing and hearing them is concerned, this miraculously does not diminish the work's power, for several producers have still contrived to convey that they could still be 'all in the mind' of the Governess. After all, Mrs Grose, the housekeeper who has hinted at their existence, does not see them, or says she does not.

Britten and Mrs Piper gave this theme the extra dimension he required by use of a line from Yeats which she inserted into the ghosts' colloquy in Act II: 'the ceremony of innocence is drowned'. This applies, of course, to the Governess as well as to the children. She is one of Britten's greatest roles for a singer-actress, for nothing less will do. Her character is developed musically by the various turns of the screw given to the variation-motif which is associated with her plight and also by subtle changes in the vocal style demanded of her, ranging from the confident, lyrical innocence with which she sings of the children and of their guardian, with whom at their interview (shown in mime in the prologue in some excellent productions) she has fallen in love. (Her love for Miles is a projection of this love.) As she becomes aware of the ghosts' hold on the children, hysteria enters and from then to the end of the work she is required to encompass the whole spectrum of musico-dramatic expressiveness, exemplified in its diversity by the twisting chromatic lines of 'Lost in my labyrinth' (an extension of Mrs Sedley's 'Murder most foul it is' in *Peter Grimes*, but how much more sophisticated) and the lovelorn triadic lyricism of her reading aloud of her letter to the guardian ('Sir, dear sir, my dear sir') all the more marvellous following the hurried orchestral description of her writing (Ex. 16).

To designate a work as 'Britten's greatest opera' is a risky business, but if one's choice were to fall upon *The Turn of the Screw* it would be because – notwithstanding the immense scale and terrifying power of *Billy Budd* – the musical realization of the drama is infallible and is untrammelled by any extraneous emotional counterpoints such as the 'Christ' motifs in *The Rape of Lucretia* and *Billy Budd*. The short-scene, variation-form design of the work seems to have fired Britten's imagination to produce his most beautiful sonorities from the thirteen instrumentalists. The opera is in the strictest form, but the music is the freest, the most sensual, the most haunting he ever wrote. The piano in the prologue; the entry of the chamber orchestra to depict the coach-journey; the treble voice of Miles, vulnerable yet guileful; the woodwind tendrils which curl round the Governess's rapturous invocation to the summer evening, an idyll to be shattered by Quint's appearance on the Tower to the celesta's hollowest chimes; the bass woodwind in Miles's bedroom; the side-drum echoes of Quint's 'What has she written?'; the use throughout of harp and bells – all this and much, much more is specific to the dramatic situation.

Quint's first vocal entry, the melismatic cadenza on the word 'Miles', suggested to Britten by hearing Peter Pears sing an unaccompanied Pérotin motet in a Suffolk church, is the personification of seduction and sweet corruption, irresistible yet repellent, a theatrical *coup* of the utmost memorability – dare one say Quintessential? The use of nursery-rhymes in the children's games, especially Miles's 'Malo' tune which is to return as the climax of the tragedy when the Governess sings it as a requiem after his death (this was the librettist's idea), and the virtuoso brilliance of the word-setting are other strong points of the opera. For example, no one of any responsiveness who has once heard this work could forget the music to which are set such lines as 'I'm just sitting, sitting and thinking', or 'Here my tragedy began', or 'Who is it? Who?' or 'Do you like the bells, I do', or 'What has she written?... Take it, take it' or 'I am bad' or 'the Dead Sea' or 'So, my dear, we are alone'. Words and music seem to have been imagined together, and it is no surprise to learn that Britten wrote this work at great speed. Every inflection in this opera, every sound, every note, matters and contributes towards the drama.

Ex. 16 (a)

(b)

In an absorbing essay,[4] Donald Mitchell has revealed how the climax of the work, the final struggle between the Governess, Quint and Miles, was strengthened by a last-minute revision in which the music of the ghosts' alluring duet is recalled at the very moment Quint is striving to gain – and does gain – the boy's soul for ever, like Goethe's Erlking. The return of this magical music heightens the tension immeasurably. This is merely one more creative miracle to add to the multiplicity which comprise this devastating work. 'I am all things strange and bold', Quint sings. It could be the opera's motto.

Winter Words, op. 52, and Songs from the Chinese, op. 58

Winter Words, eight settings of Thomas Hardy, were completed in September 1953, between *Gloriana* and *The Turn of the Screw*, for performance a month later at the Leeds Festival. They are not described as a song-cycle, merely as 'lyrics and ballads', but Britten's insight into Hardy's melancholy fatalism and naive imagery gives an overall unity to one of his most satisfying works for voice and piano. Gone is the florid ornamentation suitable to Michelangelo; in its place is an economical, epigrammatic austerity. Hardy's use of the humdrum as a launching-point for the philosophical is well matched by Britten's ability to invent a simple imitative figure which achieves deeper significance; for instance the C minor triads that depict the engine-whistle in 'Midnight on the Great Western' become the symbol of the 'world unknown' towards which the train is taking the boy. The convict's violin cadenzas in 'At the Railway Station, Upway', magically suggested by the piano, are converted into the 'life so free' for which the convict wistfully yearns. Similarly, the 'creak, creak' of 'The Little Old Table', the bird-song in 'Proud Songsters', and the flutterings of 'Wagtail and Baby' are elements of the musical structure in addition to illustration. The finest songs are the ballad, 'The Choirmaster's Burial', one of the great songs of English music – in which savage characterization of the insensitive vicar and the transformation of the choirmaster's favourite hymn, denied him by the church, into an angelic anthem are outstanding musical responses to Hardy's irony – and the final 'Before Life and After', repeated triads again the foundation of its texture. In this song, the closing heart-cries, 'How long, how long', suggest anticipation of the Governess's despair when she believes she has 'lost' Miles, but echo also many a similar passage in Britten's journeys into darkness, expressed in plain and simple musical terms.

The *Songs from the Chinese* belong to 1957 but may be considered here for they are comparable in stature to the Hardy songs. They differ in being written for Julian Bream's guitar accompaniment. Britten's ability to draw from an instrument even more than a virtuoso performer imagined possible was never more strongly displayed than in these six Arthur Waley translations. Neither the sound of the guitar nor its use here is specifically oriental, but the challenge of finding new sound-symbols to match his chosen text evidently stimulated Britten to write some of his best songs – still, alas, little known. A song like 'The Autumn Wind' goes, in its restrained and spare style, to the heart of the season's bitter-sweet unrest and may justly be compared with Mahler's richer Chinese-inspired settings. In 'The Old Lute', Britten asks for 'remoteness' and obtains it by strictly circumscribed variants of a chord-progression. More obviously pictorial is the guitar's plodding ox which accompanies the lyrical 'Herd-Boy'; here the guitar's single notes sound as if they were part of a much more complex harmonic texture such as we find in the glissandi of single notes and six-part chords in the desperate 'Depression', a lament for age of body and spirit. In the closing 'Dance Song', what starts as a triumphal rite ends as a cry of despair on which the guitar's climactic arpeggio is ironic comment. Both these cycles, musically self-sufficient though they are, are further manifestations of Britten's understanding of Peter Pears's voice in every phase of its development. Only a singer of rare technical skill combined with even rarer interpretative intelligence can hope to penetrate the subtle secrets of these songs.

23

1955–60

Canticle III – *The Prince of the Pagodas – Noye's Fludde – Nocturne – Sechs Hölderlin-Fragmente – Cantata Academica – Missa Brevis – A Midsummer Night's Dream*

For his third Canticle, Britten went to the poetry of Edith Sitwell and set lines from her *The Canticle of the Rose* beginning *Still falls the rain*. The poem is sub-titled 'The Raids 1940. Night and Dawn', and the wartime agonies of the bombed are allegorized in the imagery of Christ's Passion. It is a sombre poem and Britten responded to it with some of his starkest music. The soloists, with piano, are tenor and horn, but any resemblance to the romantic poetry of the *Serenade* lies only in the terror of that masterpiece's 'Lyke-Wake Dirge'. In the canticle the horn, for most of the work, is heard as a sinister agent and the voice part eschews lyrical lines, being mainly a declamatory recitative and even – where the poet quotes Marlowe at the height of her religious symbolism – *Sprechgesang*. The form of the work is a theme, heard at the outset on the horn and which draws on all twelve pitches but is not a serial row, with six variations for horn and piano presented as interludes between the recitatives. Each recitative is preceded – and therefore unified – by the refrain 'Still falls the rain', one of Britten's most haunting and memorable inventions. The tonality is mainly B flat, nearly every verse being heralded by an open fifth B flat chord. At the end of the work, as in the reconciliatory music of Canticle II, Dawn breaks with a merging of the work's two opposing keys, B flat and E flat, until the former is left for voice and horn. The music, unequivocal in its Donne-like exaltation, is Britten in a hair-shirt, flagellating his soul on behalf of suffering humanity. The result is uncomfortable, but a powerful work of art.

The Prince of the Pagodas, op. 57

After completing the Canticle in November 1954, Britten concentrated on his three-act ballet for Covent Garden and the choreography of John Cranko. It is a long work, playing for 125 minutes (the composer's recording makes some cuts) and its fairy-tale eastern setting is given aural authenticity and local colour by Britten's reference to the gamelan sounds (produced by normal instrumentation) which had made such an impression on him in Bali during his visit to the Far East in 1955–6 (see Chapter 10). The plot is a flimsy excuse for the set dances, of which there are almost too many. The old emperor of the Middle Kingdom has two daughters, Belle Rose who is nice and Belle Epine who is nasty, and a court Fool. (There the *King Lear* resemblance stops.) He humiliates Belle Rose and hands over his kingdom to Belle Epine. She is wooed by four kings and rejects them. The prince of the title appears to Belle Rose in a vision and transports her to Pagoda Land by way of moon, stars and sea. There she dances, blindfolded, with a salamander (the prince in disguise, of course). Meanwhile, as they say, back in the Middle Kingdom Belle Epine is empress and has imprisoned her old father in a cage (no, the *Lear* parallel persists). Belle Rose arrives with the salamander which turns back into the prince, who causes the palace and Epine to disappear. The last act is in Pagoda Land whose inhabitants have been 'liberated' (we have not been told who had enslaved them). A series of *divertissements* ends with the court Fool, still faithful to the old emperor, joining the hands of the prince and Belle Rose.

Even in such an inescapably episodic structure as a ballet score, Britten does not desert the close-knit thematic organization which is to be found in his operas and other major works. The score is so easy to listen to that one can easily overlook, as no doubt Britten hoped one would, the complexities of rhythmical and motivic transformation which he has effected. The principal characters are sharply defined, the emperor by his alto saxophone, the Fool by triplets which tumble through several keys, Belle Epine by a spiky string theme, Belle Rose by a wistful, wayward Tchaikovskyan oboe solo which is capable of many transformations of shape and mood. Heroic trumpet arpeggios are the prince's hallmark, and this theme also occurs in several guises.

With the exception of the gamelan music, which occurs in Act II, scene 2 when Belle Rose touches the pagodas, the score pays unaffected homage to its nineteenth-century models, particularly Tchaikovsky and

Delibes, and in this century to Prokofiev and Stravinsky (whose *Apollo Musagetes* is as potent an influence here as it was on the *Frank Bridge Variations* twenty years earlier). Some of the dances are of entrancing piquancy and originality, with the scoring the dominant feature. Those for the four kings are neatly characterized, North by a Gopak, East by oriental pipes and cymbals, South by drums and 'blues', West by what Peter Evans amusingly suggests may be a deliberate and unflattering parody of the embrace of Schoenbergian methods by that other King of the West, Stravinsky. However, the really memorable scoring is the pentatonic gamelan music, which is purveyed melodically by glockenspiel, celesta, piano and cello harmonics accompanied by flutes, xylophone, vibraphone and a second piano, the rhythm being provided by gong and double bass (in the first beat) and pizzicato cellos.

My difficulty in coming to terms with *Pagodas*, which I had always felt to be too much of a pastiche, was almost wholly solved when the complete score, which had never been heard before, was recorded in 1990. For his own recording, Britten had made over 40 cuts, entirely omitting four dances (one of them, for the Sea Horses, a memorably witty piece). The restoration of twenty minutes of music altered the perspective unbelievably.

Noye's Fludde, op. 59

Britten's principal composition in 1957 was a setting of the Chester Miracle Play about Noah's Ark, using the mediaeval language of the original text. It was written for performance mainly by children, of varying degrees of skill, and like *Saint Nicolas*, it involves the audience in hymn-singing. The parts of Noye, Mrs Noye and the Voice of God are taken by adults, with the children singing the parts of Noye's sons and daughter-in-law, Mrs Noye's Gossips (cronies) and all the animals. The orchestra is made up of a solo string quintet, recorder, percussion and organ and a large body of tutti strings and recorders. There are also bugles, handbells and percussion including the celebrated 'slung mugs' described in an earlier chapter. (In the first production the orchestra numbered some 150 players.) The form of the work – which is neither opera nor pageant, and might be better described as 'a parable for church performance', for it is the obvious precursor of those three masterpieces of the 1960s – is of spoken and sung dialogue interspersed with instrumental and choral interludes. It was written for Orford Church, and makes use of the whole area so that the audience see the Ark built and the animals march in procession up the aisle.

Whereas in *The Prince of the Pagodas* the quality of Britten's material flickered and faltered, here it never falls below the highest level and the work is a masterpiece by any standard. Great as is the complex and hypnotic Britten of *The Turn of the Screw*, the *Cello Symphony* and *Billy Budd*, to take three at random, in *Noye's Fludde*, which is easily his most lovable work, he makes an assault on the listener's emotions by inspired inventive imagery of the simplest kind, by the integration into the score of three of the finest and most evocative hymns of the Anglican tradition, and by the disarmingly touching blend of amateur and professional. Strong men have been known to weep unashamedly at the sound of the bugles which precede the animals' march and at the appearance of the rainbow, but let it not be thought that this is in any way a sentimental work. If our response tends to be sentimental, that is not Britten's fault.

Such an achievement requires superb professional artifice and, as scarcely needs reiterating, this is again a cunningly woven and inter-related musical structure, governed by tonal contrasts and tensions. Yet the listeners will leave the church remembering the realization in sounds of the composer's thought-processes. For example, they will think not so much of the instrumental 'prelude' in which the first hymn, 'Lord Jesus, think on me', is expounded as the carrier of the work's principal thematic conflict, as of the animals' entry into the Ark, chanting their excited *Kyrie* over an urgent bass accompaniment. (Each verse announcing the arrival of a different collection of species is in a different key, giving room for more and delightful charac-terization, the squeaking mice inevitably if incessantly calling to mind the powder-monkeys' chattering as they run to action stations in *Billy Budd*.) Comedy is provided by Mrs Noye's drunken refusal, until the last moment, to leave her Gossips and enter the Ark. The storm is a passacaglia, its bars rising in minor thirds by whole-tone steps, but the listener is conscious only of the magical sound of the first drops of rain (the mugs) and the fury of the storm, with the animals panicking, the rigging flapping, the Ark rocking, until out of the heart of the instrumental tempest as a choral counterpoint comes Dykes's 'Eternal Father, strong to save'. This great tune, with a fragment of the first hymn, passes to solo strings as the storm subsides and Noye sends out first a raven (chromatic cello solo) and then a dove (a cooing and flutter-tonguing waltz from recorder, with piano and strings). The rainbow appears to the sound of handbells – how explain in words their profound emotional effect? Better not to try. Noye, the animals and the congregation give thanks in Addison's 'The spacious firmament on high' sung to Tallis's Canon; moving as this is, it is the sound of the handbells, symbolizing the blessing of God, which gives the closing pages their poignant intimations of immortality. Undoubtedly we owe the particular organization of these thoroughly English chimings to Bali, but Britten has transplanted them with the sureness of touch which guided his hand at every note of a work which may unhesitatingly be called sublime.

Nocturne, op. 60

The *Nocturne*, composed in the summer of the 1958, for Tenor Solo, Seven Obbligato Instruments and String Orchestra, is dedicated to Alma Mahler, widow of the composer from whom Britten inherited the expressive possibilities of the genre. The choice of eight poems associated with a nocturnal theme may suggest that Britten was setting out to repeat, with the added experience and expertise of fifteen years, the *Serenade*. But the *Nocturne* is different in two major respects: the music is continuous and linked by an orchestral ritornello, and the poems are not selected for their varied poetic imagery so much as for their treatment of a common theme, dreams. Britten, after all, was advancing towards his operatic treatment of a dream, Shakespeare's *A Midsummer Night's Dream*. This dream world invades the music of the *Nocturne*. The tenor's part is a free-ranging arioso, ornate and asymmetrical, while the orchestral scoring is geared to a vivid representation of the text. For this purpose, Britten assigns an obbligato instrument (in one case, instruments) to impart its individual colour to six of the settings. Only in the first and last is the orchestra without a solo instrument. Where for most composers C major would be the key of daylight, Britten uses it here, as he does frequently, for the darker world he chose so often to inhabit.

The first song, from Shelley's *Prometheus Unbound*, is scored for strings only. Muted and divided, they introduce the rocking, lulling figure which suggests the untroubled sleeper before his dreams begin. Their entries overlap and blur, the tonic C occurring in the bass. The setting is in A B A form, the central section in G minor, and C major is regained for the last line 'Nurslings of immortality' until the voice's last D flat over C major strings – a prophecy of the work's final resolution. From this writhes the bassoon obbligato which is the representation of Tennyson's monster, the Kraken, sleeping until the heat of the Last Day shall dry up the sea. The poet's marvellous picture of a submarine world – 'huge sponges ... enormous polypi ... huge seaworms' – is matched by Britten's virtuoso figuration for the bassoon. The song is a ground bass, the form disintegrating as 'the latter fire' is mentioned, the singer's A on 'die' followed by the bassoon in its high register as a striking image of the dead monster on the surface.

Coleridge's mysterious moonlit vision of 'a lovely boy, that beauteous boy' in *The Wanderings of Cain* is a slow waltz in A major, with the harp the obbligato instrument adding its *Lucretia* delicacies to the voice's staccato patterning. Middleton's 'Midnight's bell' has the horn's onomatopoeic repertoire of bell, howling dog, owl, cat and mouse supported by the ritornello. There is no link to the next song, an extract from Wordsworth's *The Prelude*, since the literal-minded composer does not preface a poem about a sleepless night with his sleep motif. Timpani beatings disrupt this meditation on the September Massacres of the French Revolution, but tonal instability contributes equally to the sense of menace. (At the line 'The horse is taught his manage' the distorted harmonies of the heavily accented rhythmic accompaniment recall Tarquinius's ride.) There is no ritornello after this waking nightmare: straightway the cor anglais begins its chromatic undulations above an unvarying pizzicato tread of triads as Wilfred Owen's 'The Kind Ghosts' surveys in petrified calm the 'wall of boys on boys and dooms on dooms'. The ritornello leads into the graceful lines of flute and clarinet, together and in alternation, as obbligati in the airy fancies of Keats's 'Sleep and Poetry'. At the very word Sleep, the strings play a C major chord, soft and cushioning, and the rocking figure returns. The setting ends on D flat, and the full instrumental forces swell the major third of that key to launch the extremely beautiful setting of Shakespeare's Sonnet 43. The richly scored and impassioned texture becomes avowedly Mahlerian, the harmony coloured by doubling of instruments and with a Lydian D flat pulling with, not against, C minor. As the sleeper sinks deeper into untroubled slumber, C major is reached, but the last sound is a faint D flat.

There is much that is very fine in the *Nocturne*, notably the Shakespeare, the Tennyson and the Wordsworth. But there are also alarming variations in imaginative quality. Britten here offers hostages to those who find in his later works a too glib and mechanical response to word-setting, a brilliant manipulation of formulae. The neo-baroque figurations of the Coleridge and the Owen, the conscious conceits of the Keats, spring (it seems to me) less from the urgent promptings of the text than from its invitation to mannerisms.

Cantata Academica, op. 62

It is disappointing to find Britten below his best in as serious and important a work as the *Nocturne*; it matters less, perhaps, in an occasional cantata. In fact, though, the familiar gestures on which he sometimes relies in this work for S.A.T.B. soloists, chorus and orchestra, composed in March 1959 for the 500th anniversary of the foundation of Basle University, are delivered in such a light-hearted, tongue-in-the-cheek fashion that no one need frown on them. 'Academic' in the title is not to be taken at its face value even if the cantata does begin with a succession of twelve notes (13, with the return to the initial G), each of which either melodically or harmonically dominates each of the first twelve movements. The text is in Latin, for which heaven be thanked, since its orotund praises of Basle are worthy but dull, and Britten uses it merely as a pretext for a disarming display of florid, lyrical and charming elaborations. One feels he could have written the tenor recitatives standing on his head; they are necessary links between more entertaining sections. The theme appears as a continuous melody in the eighth movement and sounds like a Hymn Ancient. On the whole, the soprano soloist has the best of it all, with her widely spaced arioso above the chorus's hummed student song. The work is the typical small change of a great composer; comparable examples galore may be found among Vaughan Williams's choral output. They are shavings from larger and more significant works, and, in Parry's words, they usually contain 'something characteristic'. They also usually suffer from that heartiness endemic to English music of a celebratory nature.

Sechs Hölderlin-Fragmente, op. 61

Between the *Nocturne* and the cantata Britten reverted to setting a 'live' foreign language. To his French and Italian song-cycles he now added one in German with these settings of a poet who was by-passed by most of his compatriot Lieder composers. These songs have not achieved much favour with audiences, possibly because some of them are formidably bare, even ascetic in their music, not, however, the Romantic drooping sixths and canonic accompaniment of *Die Heimat*. Triads as symbols of beauty lend depth to *Sokrates und Alcibiades*, while the sixth song, *Die Linien des Lebens*, is structurally complex, with piano and voice in criss-crossing counterpoint, yet the most direct in its effect on the listener, perhaps one of its composer's best.

Before considering Britten's Shakespeare opera, three short choral works of this period should not be overlooked. The *Missa Brevis* in D, op. 63, was written in 1959 for George Malcolm's Westminster Cathedral Choir. This organ-accompanied setting of the Ordinary excludes the Creed. It is a little masterpiece of tonal relationships and fluctuations. Professor Evans's analysis nearly takes longer to read than the work does to be performed, which gives some idea of the concentrated nature of Britten's invention. The listener's chief impression will be of the splendid exploitation of the raw tone which George Malcolm encouraged in music which mingles uncloying sweetness with hieratic dissonance.

The two works for choir and organ which share opus 56 were written in 1955 and 1956, the *Hymn to Saint Peter* (a) for St Peter Mancroft, Norwich, the *Antiphon* (b) for St Michael's College, Tenbury. They are examples of the craftsmanship Britten invariably expended on even the smallest tasks. In both, the text has prompted literal imagery, and in both a treble soloist is used with that bright and focal effect of which Britten held the uncloying secret. The *Antiphon* is a setting of Herbert's 'Praised be the God of Love'. Its last line 'Who hath made of two folds one' is realized in antiphony between the 'one' of the soloist and the 'two' of the choir, repeated until both reach the tonic and so are 'one'. Herbert would have approved such a literal setting, done like this.

A Midsummer Night's Dream, op. 64

In their masterly adaptation of Shakespeare's play as an opera libretto, Britten and Pears needed only to invent one line and to omit about half the text! As Boito did with *Othello*, they have concentrated the essentials of the action into a superb framework for music. Britten used a larger chamber orchestra than in *The Rape of Lucretia* and *Albert Herring* (two flutes, doubling piccolos; oboe, doubling cor anglais; two clarinets; bassoon; two horns; trumpet; trombone; percussion – two players; two harps; celesta; harpsichord; and strings).

This truly bewitching opera is the high point of Britten's pre-occupation with the twin themes of night and sleep, which reaches back to 1937 and the setting in *On This Island* of Auden's 'Nocturne' ('May sleep's healing power extend'). He had been preparing himself for the task for several years – in the juxtaposition of natural and supernatural worlds in the sinister context of *The Turn of the Screw*, in the musical interpretation of one poet's variety of moods and styles (Hardy in *Winter Words*, Hölderlin in the *Fragmente*), and in the treatment of the subject in the *Nocturne*. For Shakespeare's *Dream* he had to invent convincingly evocative and different musical idioms for three strata, the fairies, the lovers and the rustics. That he did so, and triumphantly, is the key to the opera's hold on its audiences. It inhabits a sound-world quite distinct and apart from any other of his works, entirely a Britten sound-world but lit by an inner enchantment which seeps through the score like a potion.

As in the *Nocturne*, there is an opening orchestral motif which recurs as a ritornello, separating the five sections of Act I. This famous passage has more than one purpose. Its slow portamenti sighs at one level depict the wood at night, the creaking of branches and rustling of leaves; at another they represent the spell which is upon the wood and all who enter it, and this supernatural state is caused by the fairies. The slide from G–F sharp which creates the 'sigh' is found in the fairies' music throughout the opera. This prelude is a series of common chords for tremolo strings, with the 'sighs' between the chords. The roots of the chords cover the twelve notes of the chromatic scale, but the row is treated less structurally than in *The Turn of the Screw*. Almost of equal importance with thematic material here are the different instrumental colourings of the three strata of characters: harps, harpsichord, celesta and percussion for the fairies, strings and woodwind for the humans, bassoon and deeper brass for the rustics. The other-worldly nature of the fairies is enhanced by the use of boys' voices,[1] by the trumpet-cadenzas and drum taps which punctuate Puck's speech and acrobatics, by Tytania's coloratura, and most of all by the inspired and risky use of a counter-tenor for Oberon, a sound which manages to be both 'magical' and as terrifyingly sinister as Quint's temptings. The hypnotic setting of 'I know a bank' owes much to its Purcellian models and coldly glittering scoring but even more to the peculiar timelessness of the counter-tenor voice (in this case, inseparable from the artistry of the role's first singer, Alfred Deller).

The vocal writing for the lovers avoids the tedium inherent in their constant quarrelling by being in a fluent *recitativo accompagnato*, but they are awarded two of the great moments of the opera as ensembles. In Act I the antiphonal duet 'I swear to thee' between Lysander and Hermia mounts ecstatically through twelve major triads to a radiant C major. In Act III, when the four are reconciled, after distant horns have poetically accompanied their awakening, their quartet, starting at 'And I have found Demetrius like a jewel', also uses a variety of major triads in the orchestra to give it a sense of time standing still.

Enchantment can be for good or evil and part of the flavour of this score is the menace which lurks behind the exchanges between Oberon and Tytania, not entirely exorcised by their rapt slow saraband when

Tytania is reunited with him in Act III after her nightmare experience with Bottom. Yet it is for this 'nightmare' in Act II, when Tytania, under Oberon's spell, falls in love with Bottom in his ass-head disguise, that Britten composed the most seductive, passionate and lyrical music of the opera – of any of his operas. The coiling woodwind, the harps' ostinato, all so clearly defined in Britten's most elegant, graceful manner, hold the listener lulled in a trance as deep as the orchestral bed of chords into which Bottom and Tytania sink – the chords, *leitmotiv* for Oberon's spell, which had drowsily opened the act. They too contain the twelve notes of the chromatic scale, presented as four chords, and scored for muted strings (first chord), muted brass (second), woodwind (third) and harps and percussion. Britten follows this wonderful scene with the mounting tension and complexity of the lovers' quarrel, an ensemble marked by inventive fertility and economy of means. The agitated mood the foursome have created is dispelled when Puck lures them to sleep to the sound of the fairies' lullaby – music where the semitonal inflexions of D flat recall both harmonically and melodically the coda of the violin concerto.

Britten's treatment of the rustics has met with less than unanimous approval, but I find in it no falling-away from the prevailing high level. Their rehearsal of their ridiculous play in Act I is a point, for this listener, where the opera improves upon the play in humour; I do not find the performance itself in Act III tedious and banal, as some have done. Not at all, in fact. Nowhere else does Britten's gift for parody reach such creative heights as in this extended, affectionate and musically very witty commentary on the conventions of the Donizetti type of Italian opera (all tempo indications for this section of the score are in Italian; in the rest of the opera English is used). Provided the singers do not over-play it, it is a scene which yields fresh delights at each renewal.

Not least of the precisely delineated atmospheric achievements of the opera is the manner in which, when the action leaves the enchanted wood for the final scene, the magic sonorities depart from the score. It is thus that the rustics' play, in addition to being funny for its own sake, is a palpable re-assertion of 'normality', following on the splendidly down-to-earth ceremonial march for the scene-change to Theseus's court which takes us back into the 'ordinary' world. The rustics' Bergomask ends as midnight strikes. Suddenly we are back into the fairies' world for their mesmeric, irregular metred last song 'Now, the hungry lion roars'. Oberon and Tytania, after a duet, lead the fairies' blessing on the lovers' nuptials, 'Now until the break of day', set to a simple but incredibly touching melody based on a Scotch snap and accompanied by the rhythmical lilt of harpsichord alternating with harps. So this, one feels, is Arcady; but Britten brings us back to our senses with Puck's last gyrations (to music which is the English equivalent of the little page's final entry at the close of Strauss's *Der Rosenkavalier*), and a bright chord ends a work which ranks with Verdi's final masterpieces as a transference of Shakespeare to the opera stage wholly in the spirit and on the artistic plane of the original play.

24

1961–71

(A) Choral: *War Requiem – Cantata Misericordium – Psalm 150 – Voices for Today – The Golden Vanity – Children's Crusade*

With the *War Requiem*, completed in 1961 and first performed on 30 May 1962 during the festival marking the opening of the new Coventry Cathedral, which replaced the mediaeval building destroyed by bombs in the Second World War, Britten reached his widest public since the initial success of *Peter Grimes*. The occasion appealed to Britten the pacifist and hater of cruelty and violence. He determined, it would seem, to make a powerful public protest, in a world still ravaged by wars and terrorism, against the obscenity of mass slaughter. He drew upon all the resources of his art: the *War Requiem* is both an emotional and an artistic landmark in his development.

He took enormous risks. Rather than write a conventional choral work or find one suitable text, he set the Latin Mass for the Dead and interpolated settings of poems written during the 1914–18 war by Wilfred Owen, a victim of that war seven days before the armistice. Thus, he combined oratorio and song-cycle into two planes of emotion, the ritualistic Latin and the deeply personal English words, and realized this musically by employing three levels of sound, three sound-worlds, as he had done in *A Midsummer Night's Dream*. Here, the boys' voices and organ represent a distant, almost de-personalized, mystic world, far above the battlefields; the soprano soloist, choir and symphony orchestra are mourning humanity; and the tenor and baritone soloists, with the chamber orchestra, the voices of the victims.

The work begins with an orchestral passage of minor thirds which heave and strain in D minor, as if lugging some heavy piece of martial equipment through the mud. On the bells is heard the tritone, F sharp-C, which is to be the requiem's unifying motif appearing frequently but not pervasively. The choir's muttered 'Requiem aeternam' is the voice of mourning; the boys' entry with 'Te decet hymnus' altogether more controlled and priestly. Their unison melody contains the tritone and is accompanied by triads containing all twelve notes. With the return of the mourning procession, the mood of unrest returns, its quietness broken by an agitated harp tremolando which introduces the first (and most famous) Owen poem, 'Anthem for Doomed Youth', sung by the tenor. Throughout the work Britten's inspired gifts of musical onomatopoeia are put to the grisly service of imitating the sounds of war, and the 'rifles' rapid rattle' and 'wailing shells' present him with no problems. The choice of a boys' choir is reinforced when the singer reaches the lines

Not in the hands of boys, but in their eyes
Shall shine the holy glimmer of goodbyes

and the 'Te decet' theme is recalled by the oboe accompanied by a broad ascending scale of triads. Finally the tenor takes up the boys' theme with its twelve-note accompaniment.

In the *Dies Irae*, the 'doom impending' is not only that of the Last Judgment, it is the battlefield, as Britten implies by the bugles which sound last posts rather than last trumps. Four Owen poems punctuate this sequence, the baritone's 'Bugles sang', with its poignant muted-horn echoes of the bugle-calls in the evening air, the jauntily ironic duet 'Out there, we've walked quite friendly up to death', bizarre in its music-hall evocation – 'old chum' – the baritone's apostrophe to a piece of artillery. 'Be slowly lifted up, thou long black arm', a magnificent and overpowering song, indignant with barely suppressed rage and requiring the main orchestra's trumpets for explosive emphasis, and the tenor's 'Move him into the sun' (the poem's title is 'Futility'), blessed by Britten's most affecting arioso line over tremolando chords (Ex. 17). The poem is split up as four interjections into the *Lacrymosa*. In the *Lacrymosa* the soprano soloist is heard as a symbol of tender grief, singing to a rocking accompaniment of woodwind unisons, pizzicato strings, percussion and silences. She has first entered in the dramatic, leaping fanfare rhythms to which 'Liber scriptus' is set.

The archaic style of the *Missa Brevis* is recalled by the boys' singing of 'Domine Jesu Christe' in the Offertorium, to an organ arpeggio accompaniment. At 'Quam olim Abrahae', the main chorus's fugal entry is to a theme from the Canticle II, *Abraham and Isaac*. This is no convenient textual gloss, for the next Owen setting is his grim use of the Bible story as an allegory for war, with its twist at the end when Abraham refuses to kill the ram 'but slew his son – and half the

seed of Europe, one by one...' The quotations from the canticle are
not literal, but the baritone joins the tenor to retain the two-part
texture for the voice of God. Memories of the battle music from the
Dies Irae accompany the preparations for the sacrifice; Britten repeats
the poem's punch-line, but the second time the boys' voices return
with their 'Hostias'.

From the *Sanctus* the clangour of war and the stench of death are
excluded – but not at first the tritone – while the soprano soars
operatically above the shimmer of percussion, the bells being a further
example of the gamelan influence. At 'Pleni sunt coeli' Britten remembers an effect in Holst's *The Hymn of Jesus* and asks the choir to
chant the text freely, like a rising murmur from a great crowd; for the
Benedictus the soprano floats her swaying 3/4 phrases above pro-
gressions of fifths. The *Hosanna* is a jubilant D major of trumpet
fanfares and it returns after the *Benedictus*. Its final shout of joy fades,
leaving behind the gentle F natural of the strings and horn of the
chamber orchestra as prelude to another superb baritone song 'After
the blast of lightning from the East', a desperate questioning of life
after death.

Ex. 17

The *Agnus Dei* is the emotional and musical climax of the work.
The Owen poem ('At a Calvary near the Ancre') and the liturgy are
closely interwoven, and move towards the analogy between the poet's
'They who love the greater love lay down their life' and 'Dona eis
requiem sempiternam' ('Give them eternal rest'):

Ex. 18.

The tritonal relationship F sharp-C and C-F sharp governs the movement's structure, which is basically an ostinato of the descending scale
of B minor and its inversion (from tonic to dominant) on C. Any
rigidity which such a pattern might imply is dispelled by the fluctuating
5/16 metre. By such dry words one can convey nothing of the profound
sorrow, bitterness and weary resignation expressed in this wonderful
music. The work's large-scale finale, *Libera me*, recalls earlier themes,
its solo bass drums preceding a new version of the halting march
which opened the *Requiem*. As the tempo quickens, at 'Dum veneris',

the 'Te decet hymnus' and 'What passing bells', sections of the first movement return. A kind of frenzied panic fills the soprano's 'Tremens factus', which leads back to the bugle fanfares of the *Dies Irae*. The orchestra, at its loudest, has the major role here, the chorus and soprano desperately repeating 'Libera me' as the sound diminishes.

This disturbing vision of supplicant humanity in its death throes fades, and the chill of the tomb is on the chamber orchestra's strings as they sustain the G minor chord which precedes the supreme Owen setting, 'Strange meeting', that compelling poem in which a soldier has a vision of escaping 'down some profound dull tunnel' where a dead soldier addresses him – 'I am the enemy you killed, my friend'. This is set for tenor and baritone, the latter's slow and mainly diatonic recitative as the dead man in contrast to the more anguished vocal line given to the tenor in which the tritone recurs. In the orchestra we still hear echoes of war but they seem a long way off – Britten, by an alchemy which on paper seems too simple to convey such profundity, sets this music in some timeless realm of feeling, beyond hurt but not beyond pity. As the two voices blend for 'Let us sleep now', the boys' 'In paradisum' is joined by the main choir (in eight parts) and orchestra, with the soprano descanting above the rich swell of sound. So, for the first time, all the performers are heard together. The work closes with the chiming of the bells and the unaccompanied choir's resolution of the tritone with their 'Requiescant in pace'. This coda is a repetition of the music with which the first and second movements ended; its final chord of F seems in this context as inconclusive as an armistice.

The direct appeal of this music to the listener, eloquent tribute to Britten's mastery of the complications inherent in that bold and marvellously right decision to combine the liturgy and Owen, was immediately recognized. No one who was in Coventry Cathedral at the first performance will ever hear it with that 'objectivity' available to a later generation. But if the *War Requiem* was praised extravagantly at first, the reaction which set in later went too far the other way. If one looks at it dispassionately – which is how one could never *listen* to it – there is a disparity in invention between the large-scale liturgical sections and the Owen settings. The resemblances, extending even to use of the same key, to Verdi's *Requiem* (and also, I think, to Mahler's *Resurrection* Symphony) in the *Dies Irae* are disturbing, the orchestral writing much more obvious and conventional. Yet it seems likely that this was deliberate on Britten's part in order to highlight the instrumental detail in the Owen poems (and his scoring of these for the chamber orchestra is at his highest level). It is not surprising that the Owen settings are the finest and most characteristic music, for Britten is at his best in dealing with the dark and secret places of the heart, with the private rather than the public – the same dichotomy is discernible in *Gloriana*. The success of *Noye's Fludde*, which in many ways is a 'public' work, lies in its consistency within a context of innocence, emotional territory where Britten's guidelines were never deflected. Nevertheless, the *War Requiem* remains a memorable achievement. The sureness with which Britten handles its large-scale architectural design alone ensures it a high and permanent place within the English choral tradition, liberal in outlook, essentially conservative in practice. As much as any of the operas, it creates its distinctive world of sonority.

That it was written and performed as Britten approached his fiftieth birthday was fortuitous, but the *War Requiem* sums up the Britten who had increasingly dominated the English musical scene since 1943. For whatever reasons, he was a different composer afterwards. His music, as we shall see, grew sparer, was pared down to the bone, became generally more sombre in tone, and while still remaining eminently accessible was less frontal in its impact, tending to an oblique emotional approach. Britten from 1963 retired gradually into a more private music, very much as Elgar, after his last 'public' choral masterpiece *The Spirit of England*, to which the *War Requiem* bears some resemblance,[1] retreated into the intimate musing of the chamber works and the cello concerto.

A year after the first performance of the *War Requiem*, Britten added a postlude in *Cantata Misericordium*, op. 69, for tenor and baritone soloists, small chorus, string quartet, strings, piano, harp and timpani. This was composed for the centenary of the Red Cross and is far removed from the *Requiem* in its generally subdued tone. The text, by Patrick Wilkinson, has as its central theme the parable of the Good Samaritan and is in Latin. Violence (the attack on the traveller) is played down and the emphasis is on compassion, in Britten's most tender style. As in the *Nocturne*, the short sections are linked by a polyphonic ritornello, heard at the outset in F sharp minor from the string quartet and later accompanying the choir's first singing of the word 'misericordes' (merciful). It contrasts with the more robust and declamatory 'Beati' with which the choir make their entry. Alternation of these two motifs continues throughout the prologue until the parable begins. The baritone sings the traveller. After he has been left wounded by the wayside, the 'passing by' of the priest and the Levite are recounted by the chorus. The string quartet ritornello separates each encounter; before the third its rhythm is broken up to symbolize abandonment of hope and the baritone's cry for help is now short and feeble, to be answered by string tremolandi and the tenor's merciful arioso as the Samaritan succours the traveller and takes him to the inn – *War Requiem* is inescapably brought to mind as the tenor sings 'Dormi nunc amice' ('Sleep now, my friend') over a gentle accompaniment in which the harp is prominent. The chorus's moral-drawing epilogue recalls the opening chorus and fades as a D major ostinato ending on F sharp. All points, moral and musical, have been made with a concentrated lyricism.

Britten's op. 67 is a five-minute setting of *Psalm 150* for two-part children's voices and an accompaniment of any available treble instruments, bass instruments, percussion, keyboard and optional parts, transposed as necessary for clarinets, trumpet, horn, trombone and viola. It was written on 1 May 1962 for the centenary of his Lowestoft preparatory school and is in four brief sections, march, trio, round and return of the march. The trio, in F major and 7/8, happily lists the instruments of praise, from trumpet to loud cymbals (loud shout for them), to music that one dares to assert could have been written by no composer other than Britten. From the end of 1962 comes *A Hymn of St Columba*, for chorus and organ, a simple gesture, immaculate in craftsmanship, sensitive to the text. Its chance of outliving the friendly occasion which engendered it seems a good deal stronger than that of *Voices for Today*, op. 75, an anthem for adult and children's chorus with optional organ. This was commissioned for the twentieth anniversary of the United Nations in 1965 and is a mechanical, though obviously sincere, response to a text of highminded sentiments culled from fourteen sages as disparate as Sophocles, Christ, Camus, Shelley and Yevtushenko.

The Golden Vanity, op. 78, was written in 1966 for the Vienna Boys' Choir to sing at the 1967 Aldeburgh Festival. It is a vaudeville for double boys' chorus and piano to a libretto by Colin Graham based on the English ballad about a treacherous sea-captain who lets a cabin-boy drown rather than let him marry his daughter as reward for sinking a Turkish pirate vessel. Of all Britten's works for children, I find this the second least appealing. There is no denying the skill with which it is written, but the music sounds to me to be disconcertingly uncommitted. However, the original performers relished it, and so did audiences. It has now been dropped from the Vienna Boys' repertoire, and one fears that perhaps someone has decided that it did not suit their more genteel image. The least appealing – a personal opinion, I stress again – is the *Children's Crusade*, op. 82, another ballad for children's voices and orchestra of percussion, two pianos and chamber or electric organ. The libretto is Hans Keller's English translation of

Bertolt Brecht, and the work was written in 1968 for the Wandsworth School Choir and Orchestra under Russell Burgess to perform on the fiftieth anniversary of the Save the Children Fund in St Paul's Cathedral, London, on 19 May 1969. The staccato recitative, matching Brecht's unadorned narrative of the wanderings of a group of Polish children in 1939, and the aggressively harsh percussive accompaniment are a new sound in Britten. The trial which condemns the judge, the 'little socialist' who talks with 'confidence of mankind's rebirth', and the death from hunger of the dog (his elegy the work's coda) all evoke music more personal in tone and style than anything in *The Golden Vanity*, but the work is a taste more easily acquired by some than others. This is not to overlook the ironic symbolism of the use of drums – children's playthings and an appurtenance of militarism.

Four carols date from 1966 and 1967, though only one, a setting for women's voices and piano of Hardy's 'The Oxen', was truly written then. 'The Sycamore Tree', for unaccompanied chorus, was a re-writing from August 1930; 'A Wealden Trio: The Song of the Women', for unaccompanied women's voices, a re-writing from April 1929; and 'Sweet was the Song', also for unaccompanied women's voices, a re-writing in 1966 from 1931. The 'Wealden Trio' is a setting of wry verses by Ford Madox Ford which softens its initial asperities as the spirit of Christmas overcomes the pangs of hunger and cold; 'Sweet was the Song' is an unsentimental treatment, chaste in its overlapping lines; in 'The Sycamore Tree', the jubilant naiveties of the traditional text receive a more complex metrical scheme.

(B) The Church Parables: *Curlew River – The Burning Fiery Furnace – The Prodigal Son*

Britten's retreat from the oratory of the *War Requiem* is no more strikingly illustrated than by the three 'parables for church performance' which were his principal 'operatic' preoccupation in the decade after the completion of *A Midsummer Night's Dream*. It is described in Chapter 12 how the visit to a Japanese Noh-play in 1956 impressed Britten so deeply and led to his devising, with his librettist William Plomer, a means of transplanting the oriental play *Sumidagawa*, about a mad woman seeking her son, to an English medieval setting. The result was the highly stylized acting and production needed for *Curlew River*, as it became, also described in Chapter 12. The conductorless orchestra comprises flute, viola, horn, double bass, harp, percussion and organ, and a marvellous spectrum of colour Britten draws from it. Contrapuntal textures are very free, and make careful use of the avant-garde's 'random' non-alignment practices; the singers' recitative follows an independent metrical course, untrammelled by traditional bar-line divisions, and it is this, combined with the subtle colourings of the score, which gives *Curlew River* its overpowering sense of existing within an enclosed world, like an obsessive dream. So clear and stark is the sound that it was said Britten had evolved a new language, whereas the parables are merely the development of a thread which can be traced in other and earlier works and which the cathartic experience in Japan crystallized for him. They are another fruitful manifestation of his eclecticism. He was always ready to make use for his own purposes of whatever useful tools lay to hand. The twelve notes of the chromatic scale in *The Turn of the Screw* and other works did not mean that he had embraced pitch serialism; they were a Schoenbergian practice which he found interesting, as he had found Schoenbergian practices interesting since the *Sinfonietta* without particularly liking them. The colours and clusters in *Curlew River* betray an ear cocked towards Boulez for whatever might be converted to Britten practices.

Perpetually fascinating in a study of Britten's music is the way apparently 'new' developments (such as the church parables) evolve not as a continuous, logical development but from hints and fore-shadowings from years before which were left, to use Elgar's vivid verb, 'to incubate' until they found their context. The 'oriental' sound was further precipitated by Tokyo 1956, but it had begun with the friendship with McPhee in 1941 and had first invaded a Britten score in the 'moon turning blue' section of *Paul Bunyan*. The episode in *Saint Nicolas* when the pickled boys are revived and walk through the church was Britten's first use in a church work (not performed in costume) of an acted illustration of the text. A big step further on the road towards a kind of church opera was the great *Noye's Fludde*. None of this should be regarded as an attempt to decry the originality of the church parables, nor their unusual idiom, but merely as a further illustration of the strong thread of consistency binding Britten the young composer to the mature genius now under consideration.

The parables are a major stage in Britten's concern with clarifying and sensitizing his textures. One sees him, in imagination, as a stable hub surrounded by all kinds of influences, technical developments and emotional causes. Clinging firmly to the need to give his work a direct appeal, he achieved this not by indulgence in forays into exotic excess but by sensitizing (his word) each note so that it seemed to be both a crucial element in a musical pattern and to absorb the extra-musical nuances he wished to convey. *Curlew River* is perhaps his masterpiece in this process.

The musical starting-point for all the parables is plainchant, with which Britten found an English equivalent to the ancient Japanese music 'jealously preserved by successive generations'. In *Curlew River*, 'Te lucis ante terminum' is sung as the monks enter the church in procession (this, too, foreshadowed in *A Ceremony of Carols* and by the hymns which open and close *Saint Nicolas* and *Noye's Fludde*). Although it is not again heard in this form until the recession, its influence is rarely absent from the contours of the music, most obviously at references to God, more subtly in the horn motif for the river which accompanies the Ferryman's first entry (Ex. 19).

If anyone might think from their restricted format that drama and characterization are lacking in the parables, they will find that the restrictions he placed on himself stimulated Britten to astonishing imaginative feats. The character of the Madwoman (sung by a tenor) is one of his finest creations. The agony of a disordered mind has rarely been so poignantly and so powerfully put into music as in the unequal fourths of her opening cries 'You mock me! ... Let me in, let me out. Tell me the way', preceded by a flutter-tonguing flute. (It is the mad Peter Grimes, of course, who comes to mind as the forerunner of this scene.) This fearsome cry becomes the curlew-cry as she sings, in music of daring simplicity, of the 'Birds of the Fenland', a tranquil solo from which a memorable ensemble, with flute solo as descant, is built by multiplication of the minor sixth. (The flute almost assumes the significance of another vocal character.) Later, when she is taken to her son's grave, the madness of this cry is exorcized by the perfect fourths in the hymn which accompanies her pilgrimage. The score is a honeycomb of such allusive melodic and motivic manipulation, sealed into a single broad musical and emotional span.

Scalic themes, ostinato, major triads – we meet these in every Britten work. Here their tight organization is the cause of the obsessive atmosphere which somehow never becomes monotonous. The intensity is sustained by a drama inherent in each melodic progression. The Madwoman's duet with the flute 'Hoping, I wandered on' is perhaps the most inspired example of the creative impulse from plainchant; it is also one more astonishing act of homage to Peter Pears's vocal powers, an element of almost structural significance which should not be overlooked in any assessment of the effectiveness of this compelling work.

Ex. 19

The second parable, *The Burning Fiery Furnace*, op. 77, was completed in 1966. It follows the format of *Curlew River*, but has more direct action, more humour and a score in which the distinctive voice of the alto trombone plays a role as significant as that of the flute in the first parable. Plainchant, in this case *Salus aeterna*, is the melodic fount of the work's thematic material, and the interval of a fourth which occurs in it becomes the work's principal unifying factor. The contrast between the Israelites and the Babylonians amounts – with some divergences – to diatonic modes for the first and chromatic for the second (the Babylon music makes great play with the D major/E flat minor relationship). When the three Israelites refuse to eat at the feast they answer Nebuchadnezzar's contorted vocal line with courteous homophony. (A delightful interlude in this scene is the boys' – acolytes' – entertainment with its raw 'Do you know why? ... And so do I', irreverently suggesting that they may have been banished to Babylon from Oberon's kingdom, or even from Paul Bunyan's camp.)

Part 2 concerns the erection of the golden image of Merodak which

219

must be worshipped at the sound of 'cornet, flute, harp, sackbut, psaltery, dulcimer and all kinds of music' (set to a syncopated motif of instant and unforgettable aptness). The players try out their instruments before they march in procession round the church, during which each of the eight tried-out phrases is lengthened to five bars in 4/4 and for each of the different episodes an instrumental combination is used. Each group contains at least one instrument from the immediately preceding combination, and the groups become cumulative. The resulting sonorities are more oriental, appropriately enough, than any in *Curlew River*. The march (another conflation of D major and E flat minor) is followed by a pagan chorus dominated by the brazen barbarism of the alto trombone. By the simple device of the angel's perfect fourths sounding from the furnace, Britten also works a miracle other than that we are beholding by transferring the plainchant-inspired idiom to Nebuchadnezzar, whose conversion from paganism needs no further illustration. The role of Nebuchadnezzar is richly drawn, arrogant, humorous, dangerous, petulant, and at the end penitent. If *The Burning Fiery Furnace* touches susceptibilities on the raw less than *Curlew River*, its sounds are even more beautiful. To hear the final Benedicite in the gathering darkness of a noble church or cathedral is to participate in a musical experience of rare spiritual force. And although the audience has no role in the performance, in a sense it has – for, as Donald Mitchell has said, 'we become the very congregation before which a Mystery is to be enacted, a decisive change in status'.

The third Britten-Plomer parable – *The Prodigal Son*, op. 81 – was composed in 1968 and is based on the New Testament parable. Although within the same format, it widens its expressive dramatic capability still further and at its end we feel that Britten must inevitably return to the secular stage with an enhanced technical vocabulary, tempered in the fiery furnace of self-imposed limitations. In *The Prodigal Son* the governing instrumental colour is provided by the D trumpet and the alto flute. The chief difference is that the processional is not led by the abbot. He plays the Tempter and it is his voice that is first heard as a soloist as he enters through the congregation, telling of his intention to disrupt the harmony of the family scene we are about to witness – 'See, how I break it up'. The parallel with Quint is obvious.

In what amounts to the first scene, the pious Father is seen with his sons and servants, not unlike Job at the beginning of a similar soon-to-be-shattered pastoral idyll, Vaughan Williams's masque. A rich B flat chord spreads the comforts of this home life before us, but it is an uneventful life: the over-familiarity to his sons of the Father's homily is symbolized by the permutations it contains on its initial four notes (Ex. 20).

When the Tempter appears to the Younger Son, it is to a deliciously tempting bitonal harp figure which contrasts tellingly with the sober sound of the viola, chosen by Britten (autobiographically?) to depict the son's uncorrupted and earnest nature. 'I am your inner voice, your very self', the Tempter tells him; henceforward one may therefore associate the trumpet not so much with the Tempter as with the Younger Son's imaginings of the pleasures of yielding to temptation – 'Imagine, imagine', the Tempter insinuates, and the trumpet takes over at the climax. As the Tempter travels with the Younger Son to the city, the man's walk is a steady viola gait while the evil spirit prances and cavorts to harp arabesques. (The effect of trudging through the sands of the desert is conveyed by the shaking of a conical gourd, suggested to Britten by James Blades.) In the city Britten encountered the difficulty which had stymied other English composers (Elgar in *The Apostles*, Vaughan Williams in his Vanity Fair scene, Delius in *A Mass of Life*), namely to find convincingly lurid music for the evils of a rake's progress. It cannot be said that he succeeds any better than his predecessors. The pleasures of gambling, whoring and drinking sound all too decorous and are not helped by the Tempter's *Sprechgesang* invitations to vice – more than faintly risible in my experiences of the work. The off-stage siren voices (boys) are melancholy rather than inviting. Significantly, the trumpet's jazzy rasp paints a more garish picture.

Ex. 20

Britten is back on surer ground with the Younger Son's decision to return home (the moment of decision being reached when the viola reaches B flat, the Father's tonality). In the moving soliloquy 'I will arise and go', the two sides of this immature character now coalesce into a whole man, symbolized in an instrumental interlude in which the flowing counterpoint is not only a representation of the journey but also of the reconciliation of his two natures, the lion lying down with the lamb, the trumpet blending with the viola, and the flute (indicative of the Father and the pastoral life) rhapsodizing on the plainchant. There is no miracle in this parable, but this development of a human personality becomes an equally dramatic climacteric.

If *The Prodigal Son* is the most uneven of the church parables, in spite of ravishingly lovely sonorities, and tempts the thought that it might have been wiser not to add a third to the well-contrasted two, it points the way most clearly to *Death in Venice*.

In 1971 Britten returned to the canticle form he had not used since *Still Falls the Rain* in 1954. *Journey of the Magi*, op. 86, is a setting of the Eliot poem for – naturally – three voices, countertenor, tenor, baritone, with piano accompaniment. It is a concentrated work, the voices often singing as one in the manner of the poem's single narrator. Britten uses a modified rondo form, the first episode a typically graphic description of the journey by camel. The unmistakable 'Britten sound' derives from the alternation of minor third and major third and a chord which comprises a tone and a major third. Clusters in the accompaniment and the plainsong-like vocal writing show the continuing influence of the church parables; in addition, Britten emulates Eliot's mannerism of repeating a significant phrase ('but set down this, set down this') by extending it – rather irritatingly – to other parts of the poem. Thus the poem opens, in Britten, 'A cold coming, coming, we had of it'. The word 'satisfactory' which ends the first stanza is repeated by Britten eight times and from it, on the piano, comes the plainsong melody, *Magi videntes stellam*, which is the basis of the middle episode. The final section, when the Magi look back on their experience and ponder its central significance, returns to the refrain material. In the piano postlude, plainsong and triadic equivocation are reconciled. It is an impressive work, but somehow distant and less compelling than its predecessors.

(C) The Rostropovich Cello Works: Sonata – Suites 1, 2 and 3 – *Cello Symphony*

The stimulus to Britten's creativity of the executive gifts of a musician he admired has been repeatedly mentioned in connection with Peter Pears's voice, and with the voices of certain other singers. Would *The Prince of the Pagodas*, I wonder, have been more satisfactory if he had conceived an admiration for a particular dancer, for Nureyev perhaps? At any rate, the musicianship, virtuosity and friendship of the Russian cellist Mstislav Rostropovich led Britten to resume instrumental composition on a scale he had seemed to have abandoned and to five works for cello within the space of ten years.

The first of them was the Sonata in C, op. 65, composed in January 1961. Its five short movements and epigrammatic style anticipate the sparer style which followed the *War Requiem*. If outwardly the work resembles a suite, the key scheme produces the unity of a sonata and the first movement, *Dialogo*, makes a sonata structure from its wistful, oddly Brahmsian discussion of a rising or falling second, a nervous rhythmic tension being imparted by the piano's scalic thirds:

Ex. 21

The 'second subject', which sounds like a new theme, is merely this theme lengthened. Bartók's haunted nocturnal music is suggested by the scherzo, the cello playing pizzicato throughout. The slow *Elegia* is an impassioned song for the cello, rising to a climax and falling away again, a beautiful movement. A bizarre *Marcia* and a concluding *Moto perpetuo* emphasize the similarity of this work to the pre-1940 instrumental works, but the occasional callowness of those days gone by is replaced by subordination of both compositional and instrumental virtuosity to deeper musical considerations.

Rostropovich's playing of unaccompanied Bach was the inspiration of the three unaccompanied Suites Britten wrote for him. The First, op. 72, was completed in 1964. Its six movements are enclosed and divided by a *Canto* (*sostenuto e largamente*). This is not only a fine melody but the source of the work's cell-shapes, for instance the humorous dialogue of two staccato notes in the *Fuga*, the conflict within an expressive lyrical context of E and E flat in the *Lamento*, the unsettled modality of the pizzicato *Serenata* (the homage here being to Debussy), the ostinato of 'natural' open strings and upper partials in the *Marcia* (figures suggesting military fanfare and drum over a strict rhythm), the drone in the *Bordone* which underlies two themes, one a pizzicato reincarnation of a theme from the violin concerto, the other a gentle undulating phrase not unlike the first subject of Elgar's cello concerto, and the brilliant semitonal semiquaver elaborations of the *Moto perpetuo* from which the *Canto* emerges for its restatement.

The Second Suite, op. 80, followed three years later (1967). Its five movements in no respect suggest going over the ground tilled in the first suite. Britten finds exciting new ways of exploiting his soloist's mastery and of avoiding any suggestion of monotony in the use of one instrument. The subdued but witty *Fuga* which follows the weighty opening *Declamato* is ingenious in its working-out and generates its fascinating rhythmical attraction from the placing of the rests in the subject:

Ex. 22

The slow movement has the unusual tempo marking, *Andante lento*, the pizzicato being in 6/8 andante and the bowed melody in slower dotted quavers. Its alternation of major and minor thirds suggests that the inspiration Britten drew from this conflict was limitless. Nor are we surprised when the finale is a noble *Ciaconna* on a five-bar ground, endlessly resourceful.

The Third Suite, op. 87, completed in 1971, is the most personal of the trio and contains the most emotional music. Many will therefore find it the most attractive. Its nine movements never sound episodic and are unlike their equivalents in the earlier suites. They are unified by being based on four Russian themes, three being Tchaikovsky folk-song arrangements ('The grey eagle', 'Autumn' and 'Under the little apple tree') and the *Kontakion* (Hymn for the Dead). The variations of these themes are heard first; the tunes themselves do not occur in their original form until played in succession at the end of the last movement. Britten disperses the pre-echoes of these sources throughout the Suite. The opening *Lento* has a chant-like solemnity which derives from the *Kontakion* and ranges through several keys. The tonally disoriented *Marcia* is constructed from 'The grey eagle' and 'Autumn' and the *Canto* from 'Under the little apple tree'. The full melody of 'Autumn' may be found in the arpeggion figurations of the *Barcarolla* and elements of two other themes contribute to this elaborate movement. The *Fuga* is on a grander scale than either of those in the other suites; it is linked to the *Recitativo*, which turns itself into the *Moto perpetuo*, both acting as preludes to the *Passacaglia*, its ground in the shape of the *Kontakion*. It is an intricate structure, but the dark undercurrents of the music are what impress the listener. Are they merely a reflection of that sombre element in the Russian nature or do they reflect anxiety on Britten's part for the safety of his friend? The music certainly springs from deep wells of feeling.

Preceding the Suites, in 1963 Britten composed the *Symphony in D for Cello and Orchestra*, op. 68, his first major orchestral work on sonata principles since the *Sinfonia da Requiem* of 1940. This is not a concerto, since it is not a struggle between soloist and orchestra nor does it rely on bravura display. Equally it is not a symphony with cello obbligato as Berlioz's *Harold in Italy* is with viola. Cello and orchestra are equal partners in the Britten and a title such as *Cello Sonata for Orchestra* might more accurately convey its structural argument. The first movement (*Allegro maestoso*) is Britten's most regular sonata-form essay, the exposition and development of equal size (in number of bars), a re-statement less telescoped than is usual with this composer, and a coda. Like the Cello Sonata, the opening is concerned with an intervallic motif, here a falling semitone played by the cello over scales in the orchestral brass. When the full orchestra is heard, the characteristically transparent Britten sound is skilfully adapted to the needs of a cello work – double bassoon and tuba and high woodwind at the extremities, with the middle register diaphanous in texture. If the example is Bergian, the ear is also carried back to the Storm Interlude of *Peter Grimes*. The second subject's rocking sevenths, the orchestra's wild pizzicato counterpoint, and the reversal of roles in the recapitulation, when the woodwind (another curlew-cry) have the theme and the soloist the scales, are signposts to the listener in a movement which is as absorbing as any Britten wrote in its sense of drama and tragedy.

A nightmare scherzo (*Presto inquieto*) follows, obsessed with a scalic pattern of three notes, and exploiting *sul ponticello* for macabre and chilling effects. The nocturnal mood persists into the grave beauty of the adagio's main theme, punctuated by timpani outbursts (Ex. 23).

Ex. 23

Taking the thirds and the halting rhythms from this theme as his cue, Britten builds an elegy to which the funeral drums create a persistently disruptive element. The parallel with the disruption of the larghetto theme in Elgar's Second Symphony will not escape English listeners. As in his violin concerto, Britten precedes his passacaglia-finale with a cadenza which sums up all that has gone before. In the *Cello Symphony* the cadenza forms a link between Adagio and Passacaglia which, if one regards it as structurally a second development section, binds them into one movement, making a three-movement work of what is nominally in four. From the cello's musings suddenly erupts the bright sound of the trumpet with a diatonic D major theme based on a phrase from the Adagio. The contrast is almost a physical shock. To this theme the cello provides the ground bass of the six variations that follow. With increasing brilliance in the orchestral writing, the music emerges into the light, as it were, the cello's passionate peroration (reminiscent melodically of Billy Budd's 'far-

226

shining sail') based on the Adagio's main theme and the scales of the first movement accompaniment suggested in the rich polyphony. In terms of novel instrumental colouring, absorbing interplay of motifs and the emotional eloquence of the spiritual drama being enacted, this is Britten's orchestral apogee.

(D) Three Song-cycles: *Songs and Proverbs of William Blake – The Poet's Echo – Who are these children?*

The first two of these cycles date from 1965, the third from 1969. The *Songs and Proverbs of William Blake*, op. 74, was written for and dedicated to the great German baritone Dietrich Fischer-Dieskau, one of the original soloists in the *War Requiem*. Like Pears, he is a singer of high musical intelligence in the use to which he puts his immediately identifiable voice, its dark, grainy quality well suited to works in which tragic melancholy is a dominating factor. In addition, he sings English almost like a native (with clearer diction than many a native!). Britten had set Blake poems before: the Elegy in the *Serenade* is among his finest songs, with a searing intensity, a harrowing of heaven and hell. This intensity, at an even greater pitch of morose disillusion, is sustained throughout the cycle, which is performed without a break so that it forms one huge Blake vision. The text of the cycle was arranged by Peter Pears, who alternates six extracts from the *Proverbs of Hell* with six *Songs of Experience* and a final poem from *Auguries of Innocence*. The proverbs form links and cross-references with the songs. There is nothing here of the *vignette*-song to be found in *Winter Words*; not since the *Donne Sonnets* had Britten songs projected so remorselessly so consistent an emotional mood, but whereas religious ecstasy was at the root of the 1945 cycle, twenty years later gloom is the keynote. This is probably a reason why this song-cycle has remained relatively unknown; it is, in my opinion, the finest and most moving of them all.

The ritornello of the proverbs has all twelve notes arranged into three four-note shapes, the order of notes varying within these shapes (E, D sharp, D, G; C sharp, C, B, F sharp; B flat, A, G sharp, F). They are heard at first only in the piano (incidentally one of the most beautiful accompaniments that Britten wrote for himself) while the voice ranges in the free 'non-aligned' tempo which was the primary vocal innovation in *Curlew River*, but as the work progresses, the vocal line in the proverbs gradually takes more of the shapes of the note-row. From the start Britten's manipulation of his musical images to gain a direct impact from the text is at its most forcefully inventive –

'London' has an agitated, vagrant ostinato in the piano over which the voices' woebegone recital of horrors is declaimed in a stricter metrical scheme. In 'The Chimney Sweeper', high and clear sonorities on the piano paint a desolate winter-scene. At the words 'to pray', the major second in the accompaniment tries to support the boy's declaration of happiness, but the rests in the halting voice-part betray his real feelings and the last line's satirical reference to 'the heaven of our misery' descends to a low note (nearer to the region of hell). 'A Poison Tree' is wholly dark and convoluted in its powerful narrative, its twelve-note melody directly formed from the ritornello:

Ex. 24

Any composer might flinch from setting 'Tyger, Tyger'. Britten makes it the scherzo of the cycle, but a scherzo in keeping with the general mood: it is sung with barely restrained fury, its reined-in energy conveyed by the taut rhythms and the piano's scales. Blake's questions tumble over each other in frenzy. 'The Fly' is a gentle contrast, the insect's erratic flight beautifully limned in the high piano part. 'Ah, Sunflower' struggles hard against the piano bass line to achieve its aspiration – the opening of the *War Requiem* comes to mind. Its last chord is an image of eternity and this is the theme of the seventh proverb, 'To see a world in a grain of sand', where the voice at last makes use of all the twelve notes and embarks on the last song, 'Ev'ry night and ev'ry morn', a moving study in resignation born of experience. In this cycle, Britten sometimes repeats words in the way he was to do in the Eliot canticle some years later, but here this device seems unmannered and spontaneous, heightening the emotional effect. It will be remembered that, in the last year of his life (1958) when he was 85, Vaughan Williams composed some of his finest and most original songs (for voice and oboe) to poems by Blake, three of them being poems here set by Britten.[2] Thus two great English composers, in their different but equally valid ways, were moved to splendid feats of invention by this seer.

The Poet's Echo, op. 76, is the last cycle in which Britten set a foreign language (I am charitably not counting the Scottish poems in the Soutar cycle as 'foreign'!). These six Pushkin settings were written for Galina Vishnevskaya, like Fischer-Dieskau one of the singers for whom the *War Requiem* was written (although she did not sing at the Coventry première). There is no linking ritornello, nor are the poems a narrative, but the unifying theme (and again, it is morose) is the 'echo' – the poet, however passionate his utterance, receives no reply, just as the echo in the woods receives no reply, just as the rose ignores the nightingale's outpouring, just as the noises heard in a sleepless night have no defined meaning. There is a poignant contrast here between Britten's gloomy artistic 'message' in this song, and the ninth song in Shostakovich's Fourteenth Symphony (1969 and dedicated to Britten) in which the beleaguered composer addressed Britten personally under the guise of 'Delvig' and asked: 'O Delvig! What reward for lofty deeds and poetry? For talent, what comfort amid villains and fools?' He gave this answer: 'Immortality is equally the lot of bold, inspired deeds and sweet songs! Thus will not die our bond.'

The echo theme is musically represented as a major seventh, and the opening of the cycle, also dependent upon the elaboration of vocal line in *Curlew River*, is the 'key' to the cycle as a whole (Ex. 25).

Ex. 25

In spite of the promptings in the text ('savage howl', 'thunder's roll', 'shepherd's cries'), Britten eschews such detail in this first song, preferring to concentrate on echo canons which prolong the singer's phrases until, at the end, silence is used as the answer to the poet. 'My Heart', the second song, is the nearest in style to the Tchaikovsky songs Britten admired. 'The Angel' quotes the desolate triad figure from 'Midnight on the Great Western' in *Winter Words*, another poem about a vision of heaven. 'The Nightingale and the Rose' is unsurpassed for lyrical beauty in the music of Britten's last twenty-five years, the seconds in the piano supporting the singer's wide-ranging line and eventually taking over that line. 'Epigram' does not fit into the cycle and seems to be an attempt to emulate the type of savagely satirical song in which Shostakovich excelled. For the final 'Lines written during a sleepless night', the major seventh becomes the ticking clock's ostinato and fragments of the first ('Echo') song and the lyrical fourth song are heard in the singer's part.

Eight of the twelve 'lyrics, rhymes and riddles' which comprise *Who are these children?*, op. 84, are settings of Scottish dialect poems by William Soutar (1898–1943). Soutar was a socialist and an admirer of Owen, Lawrence and McDiarmid. Discovery of his poems seems to have re-awakened in Britten the 'protest' element which characterized his early works. It is not surprising that the composer of *Our Hunting Fathers* should have been struck by the Soutar poem which gives this cycle its title and was occasioned by a photograph, published in 1941, of a hunt going through a bomb-damaged village, watched by children. Similarly, lines from 'Nightmare' illustrate a perennial Britten theme:

The branches flowered with children's eyes
And the dark murderer was a man

The four sombre poems of protest, which have astutely been likened to Blake, were written in English. They are interspersed in this cycle among the eight dialect settings, most of them very short and composed to formulae as simple as the poems. The most attractive of them, 'A Laddie's Sang', could have been written by the Britten of 1937, risking use of the obvious to attain a direct and touching result. But it is the English songs which give this cycle its importance. 'Slaughter' has an obsessive and ferocious canonic accompaniment to its chromatic vocal line. 'Who are these children?' takes its symbols of war from the hunt's horn-calls and 'The Children' summons the melancholy intensity of the Blake cycle to its horrifying contemplation of children killed by bombing, its climax almost sadistic in its imagery. After this, the calm, almost dispassionate elegy of 'The auld aik' ('The old oak's down') seems apt commentary and finds Britten once again taking the simplest of musical symbols to express profound truths, as epilogue to a work which continued his journey through a dark night of the soul. 'It really *is* down,' he said, 'it's the end of everything'.

(E) Miscellaneous Instrumental Works

Of the five works from the decade of the 1960s which fit into no special category except that of Britten's 'useful' music, the two finest were written for admired virtuosi. Writing for Julian Bream, guitarist and lutenist whose artistry had revived the music of Dowland (and others) for audiences which might otherwise have never believed they could like it, Britten returned to Dowland and, as he had done in *Lachrymae*, gave this *Nocturnal after John Dowland*, op. 70, the subtitle 'reflections'. It is written not for lute but for guitar and superbly written, too: in writing for a solo instrument, as Rostropovich acknowledged, Britten always stretched it to its limit and beyond. There are several anecdotes about players such as Bream telling Britten that a passage was unplayable, only to receive the reply, 'Try it as I have written it', and then to discover that he was right. Like all Britten works on the subject of sleep, *Nocturnal* is a poetic, moving and hypnotic work, challenging but rewarding to the player. The subject of the reflections is Dowland's song 'Come, heavy sleep' (1597). Again, as with *Lachrymae*, the Dowland is not heard in full until the end, when it is given its original accompaniment. Before that the eight movements, in which harmony is elusive, make use of variants of a line of the song or its accompaniment as though it was being tentatively composed in our presence. The second strain should be repeated but is left unfinished in each variation and is not heard complete until the end. The finale is a passacaglia based on Dowland's accompaniment. At its stormy climax E major emerges to guide the music to the Dowland original.

The *Suite for Harp*, op. 83, written in 1969, is also a satisfying solution of problems inherent in writing for an instrument with a limited modal range. This has not prevented Britten from extending the soloist without asking him to employ freakish extra-musical devices. The instrument is treated traditionally and, since it was written for a Welshman, Osian Ellis, its final movement is a set of variations on the hymn-tune 'St Denio'.

In 1963 Britten wrote one of his few works for solo piano. This was *Night Piece (Notturno)*, a test-piece for the 1963 (and subsequent) Leeds International Piano Competition. Typically, it is no blueprint for a display of bravura but a test of musicianship, requiring control of dynamics and application of varied tone-colour rather than dazzling fingerwork. There are forty-four changes of time-signature in its seventy-seven bars. Two years later came the *Gemini Variations*, op. 73, for violin, flute and piano duet, written for twelve-year-old Hungarian twins as a 'quartet for two players' (both boys played the piano, one the violin and the other the flute). The twelve variations and fugue on a theme by Kodály are entertaining and, in the 'mirror movements', rather more than that. There is a version for four players.

The overture *The Building of the House*, op. 79, was composed for the opening of The Maltings in 1967 and has an optional part for chorus, who sing a version of the metrical psalm 'Except the Lord the house doth make' to the tune *Vater Unser*. This *jeu d'esprit* reflects the excitement and haste of the building operation at Snape. It is unpretentious, but its orchestration has an unusual texture which probably is the aftermath of the church parables. If the chorus is not used, extra brass or an organ take their place.

25

1970–73

Owen Wingrave – Death in Venice

Britten completed his first opera since *A Midsummer Night's Dream* in 1970, a gap of ten years during which he had undergone the nutritious experience of composing the church parables. *Owen Wingrave*, op. 85, is an adaptation by Myfanwy Piper of Henry James's story about the scion of an English family who rebels against its military tradition. Disinherited by his relations and rejected by his fiancée, Owen, in order to answer the taunt of being a coward, sleeps in the haunted room at the gaunt family mansion, Paramore. There he is found dead. This subject obviously appealed to Britten the lifelong pacifist, who knew from personal experience what it was to object through conscience to a military order, but its specific inspiration in the late 1960s was the wave of anti-war feeling which swept through the intellectuals of the United States and Britain during the Vietnam war and the refusal of many young Americans to obey the draft laws to fight in it. *Owen Wingrave*, therefore, is just as much a 'protest song' of that era as anything by Bob Dylan or Joan Baez.

Also, it was first performed on television (though transference to the stage was always in Britten's mind) and certain interludes were cues for use of flashback techniques or the superimposing of scenes such as the Horse Guards galloping past and encountering disaster.[1] Such vividly descriptive passages had always been a feature of Britten's music and he had long been asking his listeners to provide visual images in their minds, so the television screen was merely a mirror of the imagination. Although once again Mrs Piper wrote an extremely skilful libretto. *Owen Wingrave* does not have the chilling and gripping impact of *The Turn of the Screw*, their other James adaptation. There are similarities: both involve the supernatural and both are brooded over by a country-house, but *Owen Wingrave* is not as good a story. Owen himself does not engage our sympathy as the Governess does, for all that we may sympathize with his actions; his dreadful family are almost caricatures, not so much military as militant, and it would surely have been easier to share the enormity of Owen's action if more than one of them had been presented in a believable light (yes, I know there were, and are, people like them, but they usually have some redeeming charm); the sense of the supernatural depends on the family legend of a boy who rebelled as Owen does and was killed by his father in a room at Paramore, the father then dying in the same room on the day of the funeral – this is related by a ballad singer (the *Paul Bunyan* device again) at the beginning of Act II, but though we are told about the ghosts and briefly see them, they do not haunt us as they do in *The Turn of the Screw* perhaps because – and this is further justification of Britten's 1954 decision – they do not sing.

Another obstacle to credibility is the character of Kate, the girl Owen is to marry and has known since childhood. Her father has died in battle and she foresees that Owen will meet the same fate. Her reaction to Owen's renunciation is that he has abandoned the dreams of their childhood – 'I'll not allow him his treacherous thoughts' – and she rejects him as a 'poor creature'. She flirts with the empty, uncomplicated Lechmere, Owen's colleague at Coyle's military cramming academy, and issues the catastrophic challenge to Owen – a manifestation of her childish immaturity. It is no surprise to learn from Mrs Piper's essay, already quoted, that Britten regarded her as impossible, arrogant and unworthy of Owen, while his librettist felt that she must have had a gentler side for Owen to have loved her. Britten attempted to inject some tenderness into the part, which he wrote for Janet Baker, whose voice can convey subtleties of mood. But she disliked the character, too, and although she has written[2] sympathetically about Kate ('full of fear ... of insecurity and the vulnerability of youth'), the role still awaits its ideal interpreter, if such there be.

A charge of lack of originality which can be levelled against some of the music of this opera for its frequent reliance on memories of Britten's earlier operas may perhaps be the consequence of its having been cast vocally before it was composed. The staccato, shrill, agitated music for Miss Wingrave inevitably recalls Sylvia Fisher's portrayals of Gloriana and Lady Billows; Mrs Julian's labyrinthine anguish and excitability reflect too closely Jennifer Vyvyan's Tytania and Governess; the maternal, spinster-like Mrs Coyle is a further projection of Heather Harper's Ellen Orford. Later singers may eradicate these reminiscences, but the music is imagined almost too accurately for the roles' creators.

In Act I Britten displays the 'public' aspect of his argument: we see Owen's decision against the background of his academy in London, whereas all Act II occurs at Paramore in the private surroundings of home and family. Thus a familiar Britten scheme is repeated. That it does not succeed as well as before can be attributed to a major flaw: the opera is blatant propaganda. The 'message', heavily underscored, takes precedence. Scene 5, for example, when the Paramore brigade sing a quartet of hate against Owen, is embarrassingly feeble. All very well to say that this is deliberate parody comparable with *Albert Herring*, but in that comedy the parody, while sharply observed, had some alleviating affection. Here there is none; nor in words and music is there the savagery of *Our Hunting Fathers* which alone would have carried conviction, for all Britten's ability to make moral issues the stuff of opera-drama.

Which said, there is much fine music in *Owen Wingrave* and it is lamentable that it is in danger of being severely underrated as a Britten score. It contains some of his most subtle and original orchestral colouring, much of it the result of the refining process of the church parables. The use of brass and drums for the recurring military symbolism is imaginative and evocative, the woodwind writing recalls the textural clarity of the *Cello Symphony*, and while Owen reads Shelley in the park the harp arabesques take us back to Lucretia's Rome and a similar atmosphere of pending tragedy.

The score's harmonic basis is in the three twelve-note chords heard at the beginning on piano, harp and percussion which symbolize militarism. This motif recurs in its original form at several important junctures in the plot, at other points its rhythm is dominant. It is followed by a cadenza for solo instruments or groups of instruments which accompanies our sight of the portraits of Wingrave ancestors. This passage, is, as Donald Mitchell has brilliantly suggested, 'the audible archives of the Wingrave family' and it is used by Britten as source-material for the opera. All these cadenza passages are in some way grotesque and are played over a string chord which resolves on to a warm D for the eleventh cadenza, a noble horn solo representing Owen. Numerous subtle text-references are illustrated and illumined by use of the portraits-cadenza material, the basis of which is diminished triads. Once again, Britten defines his characters by allotting them distinctive and individually coloured accompanying motifs, but the amazing structural feature of this score is that such a wide emotional span is covered from an especially economical use of intervals.

In one very effective scene the portraits-cadenza is used vocally, when Sir Philip Wingrave, Owen's grandfather, disinherits the renegade. This outburst of fioritura is largely based on the ancestors' themes and

accompanied by horn and trumpets. It is sung off-stage while on the
stage the other characters comment upon the scene. Equally inventive
is the dinner-party, with its contrast of strained conversation and inner
musing. The Ballad sung at the beginning of Act II is foreshadowed
earlier in the memorable orchestral interlude which precedes the first
scene at Paramore. Here the strings' arching phrases, above the muted
brass's militaristic nagging, are based on the ballad's opening motif
(Ex. 26).

The Ballad is one of several melodic themes which represent the
opposing thread of the argument, the 'peace' music. It tells of the
murdered Wingrave boy and henceforward it is to pervade the score,
but it is not as memorable a tune as Miles's 'Malo', which has a
similar function, and Britten's invention failed him here, as it does at
the end, when Kate's elegy over Owen's body falls short of the
heartrending memorability of the Governess's final aria in a comparable
situation.

Ex. 26

In the music for Coyle, the sympathetic military tutor, and for Owen
we hear resonances from *Billy Budd*. The tutor's role and his melodic
line remind us of Captain Vere; and Owen's soliloquy about peace,
though it lacks the sheer radiance of Billy Budd's aria, prompts that
deep compassion at the heart of Britten's inspiration.

Death in Venice, op. 88

In any consideration of Britten's operas, Peter Pears's voice is a governing factor. Britten wrote for it with understanding, skill and sympathy. Vere in *Billy Budd* was the last 'heroic' operatic part he composed for him, although even there the introspective element is to the fore. Essex in *Gloriana* is a subsidiary role, with the emphasis on lyricism. Quint in *The Turn of the Screw* demands incisive and unearthly vocal characterization, Flute in *A Midsummer Night's Dream* is a character part, capturing Pears's sense of humour and timing, so apparent in his singing of folk-songs; the three magnificent roles of the Madwoman, Nebuchadnezzar and the Tempter in the parables exploit to the full his superbly controlled high tessitura and the range of dramatic colour he extracted from a voice which was never rich in the 'primary colours' of the natural operatic tenor; Sir Philip in *Owen Wingrave* is another character-part, relatively short, but although it is a role inviting caricature, Pears gave it a truth which lesser singers may find elusive.

With the role of Thomas Mann's ageing famous novelist Aschenbach in *Death in Venice*, Britten wrote his last, greatest, most testing and most moving tribute to the vocal, interpretative and intellectual qualities of his friend. In 1965 Pears, then aged fifty-five, had had the courage and wisdom to re-study his voice production with a teacher and thus to embark upon a further fifteen years of superb artistry. The role of Aschenbach crowned his career. It is long – the opera is almost like a *scena* for him – and histrionically demanding, yet how sensitively Britten ensured that, even in a large theatre, the voice, which is often soliloquizing in recitative, should always be clearly audible. These recitatives, likened to Monteverdi, originated in Britten's admiration for Pears's singing of the Evangelist in Passions by Schütz. They are also a masterly solution by Mrs Piper and Britten of the problem of conveying to the audience that Aschenbach is a writer and that this self-communing is his only articulate means of communication. (His tragedy is that he is emotionally isolated, and, as it were, tongue-tied at crucial moments.) These piano-accompanied recitatives fulfil a function similar to the ritornello in the *Nocturne* and provide continuity between the many short scenes of the opera, yet another illustration of Britten's genius flowering at its most profuse in a succession of vignettes (going back to the *Frank Bridge Variations* and *Diversions*). They are principally written in the unmeasured notation which he had developed in the church parables and which he handles here with consummate ease. But at the beginning of the opera, in the first soliloquy when Aschenbach tells of his creative impasse – 'My mind beats on and no words come' – the notation is measured, the accompaniment orchestral, and the voice, symbolizing the writer's struggle, ascends a twelve-note row which is followed by its inversion. Here we encounter the Apollonian side of Aschenbach, the servant of a chaste ideal beauty sought through his work, which is to be destroyed by its sensual, Dionysian opposite – the parallel with Billy Budd and Claggart is too obvious to need stressing.

To project this action-interrupted soliloquy or monodrama, Myfanwy Piper produced a libretto which, whatever small criticisms one may make of it, translated Mann's third-person narrative into vivid and generally faithful conversational scenes by use of a cinematic technique of quick 'fades' from one to the next. This in turn needed imaginative and unconventional staging. In his operas since *Gloriana*, Britten had opened up a whole new method of stage presentation by means of close collaboration with the English Opera Group in the Diaghilev-inspired manner which he had first encountered in the Mercury Theatre of the 1930s. For *Death in Venice*, he had Colin Graham as producer, John Piper as designer and Frederick Ashton, with whom he had wanted to work again since *Albert Herring*, as choreographer, a trio who understood his ways, both easy and difficult, and whom he trusted implicitly. The opera's arresting power and aromatic atmosphere owe much to its unheard but strongly sensed counterpoint of personal friendships and artistic relationships.

Other emotional aspects of *Death in Venice* claim attention. Like *The Turn of the Screw*, it was a subject ready-made for Britten, the words on the page waiting, like *The Dream of Gerontius*, for music to give them the extra dimension they seemed to have been created to inhabit. Like Mann, Britten loved and was fascinated by Venice's mixture of the grand and the shabby, and he brings it before our eyes with some of his most picturesque, evocative and haunting music. The republic's title ('La Serenissima') haunts the opera as a *leitmotiv* (Ex. 27b). It is first heard in an ironically brash version sung by youths who, with an elderly fop who disgusts the puritanical Aschenbach, are the writer's companions on the voyage to Venice, and it is meta-morphosed into the wonderful barcarolle which accompanies his jour-neys by gondola. It is the basis, too, of the opera's overture (not heard till after the prologue), an orchestral sound-picture of Venice into which the chanting in the city's churches and the sound of their bells are interpolated – one more marvellously poetic use of bells in a Britten opera. While Aschenbach travels by gondola the gondoliers' cries break into his musings, disembodied and wordless.

Britten had experienced Aschenbach's fear that inspiration had dried up; he knew, when he was writing the opera, that he faced an operation which could cost him his life, or shorten it, and the second part of the opera, describing Aschenbach's emotional and physical destruction, was therefore written with extra urgency and intensity. Its potent atmosphere, something between dream and nightmare, every nerve-end tingling, is the reflection not only of the plot of the work but of Britten's predicament. Then, there is the homoeroticism which is the crux of the opera. Aschenbach, at his hotel in Venice, sees three Polish children with their governess. The twelve-year-old boy, Tadzio, is of exceptional beauty and Aschenbach becomes obsessed with him, to the extent that he shadows the boy everywhere, even to his bedroom door, and remains in Venice, despite the incidence of plague, to be near him. In a terrible moment of self-realization he admits to himself that he loves the boy, but sings that his ' "I love you" must be accepted; ridiculous but sacred too and no, not dishonourable even in these circumstances'. He never speaks to the boy, who is perhaps only self-consciously aware of the writer's admiration. While plague is slowly destroying Aschenbach's body, the Dionysian sensuality of his love for Tadzio gradually corrupts his soul, leading him even to cast restraint aside and to rejuvenate himself at the hotel barber's into the kind of elderly fop he had despised earlier – to an ironic recall of the music of that scene. The undercurrents of this theme flow deep through the strata of Britten's psyche and they occur, in various guises, in at least a dozen of his works. That here, in his last operatic testament, the protagonist is a creative artist who admits to his obsession but has no language in which to express it to the boy is perhaps most significant of all. Britten here was writing out his soul, in anguish.

The practical musical problem of how to convey the beauty and fascination of a character who never speaks is solved by making the Polish family into dancers, whose natural musical means of communication is without speech. The boy's fascination for Aschenbach is conveyed by the use, whenever he appears, of a percussion band (again, the influences of *The Prince of the Pagodas* and the church parables) which produces sounds at once remote and obsessing – rarely can the vibraphone have been used more tellingly. Thus, as in the Shakespeare opera and the *War Requiem*, there are three sound-levels, the children's percussion gamelan, Aschenbach's bare recitative, and the richer orchestral sonorities of Venice and the other characters.

In the novella, Aschenbach is led (or impelled) towards his fate by four characters whom Mann links together by giving each of them the 'grin of Death' and the broad-brimmed hat of Hermes who conducts the dead across the Styx. Mrs Piper extends these to six by adding the Hotel Manager and the Hotel Barber, and also the voice of Dionysus 'the stranger god'. These roles Britten gave to one baritone, who thus complements Aschenbach dramatically and musically (and in doing so he wrote with searching eloquence for the vocal gifts of John Shirley-Quirk). The first of these Hermes figures is the Traveller who seductively persuades Aschenbach in Munich to journey to the South, to the 'steaming marsh', to see the 'sudden predatory gleam, the crouching tiger's eyes'. This aria 'Marvels unfold!' has as its opening (Ex. 27a) the motivic cell constructed from Britten's characteristic fondness for semitonal intervals and adjacent major and minor thirds. It is later to become associated with the plague (usually on the tuba at its most sinister), it insinuates itself into the music for Aschenbach's favourite view of Venice, and it is in the shape of his great outburst of 'I love you':

Ex. 27

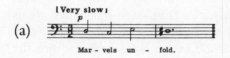

Thus the two agents of his destruction, the plague and the boy, flow from this source. Towards the end, when the clerk in a travel bureau tells Aschenbach the history of the cholera, from its origin in the Ganges delta to its devastation in Venice, his long narrative is accompanied in the orchestral bass by the music of the Traveller's aria. There is further subtlety here – the aria is written in the vocal technique and with the orchestral accompaniment which Britten developed in the church parables. Like the plague, the parable style originated in the East.

The lattice-work of motivic inter-relationships and cross-references in *Death in Venice* is highly complex, a source of pleasurable discovery as one knows the work more closely. At the outset we know (hear) the two sides of Aschenbach (whose characteristic key is E major) in the formal trumpet rhythms which signify his public fame and the flowing, overlapping string scales which accompany his capitulation to the Traveller's suggestion and imply the suppressed inner sensuousness which is to destroy him by undermining his lifelong adherence to a classical beauty unsullied by excess. The music which illustrates his pursuit of inquiries about the cholera and that which depicts his guilty longing for Tadzio becomes obsessive in its creation of a growing feverishness throughout Act II; the motifs which have represented Aschenbach's view of the world around him in Act I are altered, diminished, distorted. Only Tadzio's music (until a vital juncture) remains unaltered, curiously bright in sound and emotionally detached from the rest of the action, ritualistic (as in the scene of the games on the beach in Act I, when Britten writes another and very different set of choral dances from those in *Gloriana*) and with the boy's name called by his companions as if from the world of ancient Greece in which Aschenbach dwells spiritually. It is only when Aschenbach dreams of the rival claims in his own nature by Apollo (counter-tenor) and Dionysus (the Traveller-baritone) and sees that the latter has won that we hear Tadzio's music violently distorted and penetrated by the plague motif.

Ex. 28

The extraordinary atmosphere of the opera is heightened also in the ensembles: in the banality of the youths and the elderly fop, in Aschenbach's encounters with the street-vendors (the strawberry-seller singing a melodic phrase which – surely deliberately – recalls the poignant 'Tre lilii' sung by the soprano in the fourth song, 'The Suicide',

of Shostakovich's Fourteenth Symphony) and in the entertainment of
the guests by the Strolling Players whose leader is the most sinister of
the Hermes figures. Remorselessly, unwaveringly, Britten draws the
opera towards its end, summoning all the resources of his art for this
climactic effort. When Aschenbach relaxes the tension to sing the
Hymn to Beauty (based on Socrates' dialogue with Phaedrus, a passage
which Mann dwells upon in the novella) – 'This is beauty, Phaedrus,
discovered through the senses, and senses lead to passion, Phaedrus,
and passion to the abyss' – it is not an operatic aria we hear but the
most wonderful of the line of lyrical ariosos which Britten had written
for Pears from the *Michelangelo Sonnets* to this last epitome of a glory
of twentieth-century English music. And as Aschenbach dies on the
beach, having seen Tadzio humiliated in a game and seen the boy
beckon to him, the opera ends with an orchestral epilogue in which
the boy's theme and Aschenbach's, while still separated as they always
have been, shimmer into silence together. There are no words to
describe the sound of this music, which glows with rare and unearthly
and unforgettable colours comparable only with those we see in the
late paintings of Turner.

26

1973–76

Canticle V – *Suite on English Folk Tunes – Sacred and Profane –
A Birthday Hansel – Phaedra* – String Quartet No. 3 – *Welcome
Ode.*

The shadow of death falls across the music Britten wrote while he
was awaiting and after he had undergone his heart operation. This
stark fact should not be exaggerated in his case any more than in
Mahler's and Shostakovich's: there is no 'death-wish' or obsession.
Even in those earlier works where death might seem to be a preoccupation, Britten is inspired deeply not by death itself but by the
darkness which stains the souls of the living. When he had to live day
by day with imminent death, he faced the situation with courage and
drew upon it for his art. The first work newly composed after his
operation was Canticle V, a setting of T.S. Eliot's short poem *The
Death of Saint Narcissus*, op. 89. It was completed in July 1974.
Recognizing that his illness deprived Peter Pears of a recital partner,
he wrote the accompaniment to the voice for the harp of Osian Ellis.
This short setting showed that Britten had lost none of his power to
enter wholly (and autobiographically) into a poet's world and to find
the musical symbolism and structure to match it. Writing for the harp
seems to have spurred his imagination to new but economical effects,
yet there is nothing ungenerous about the musical span, and the writing
for the voice continues the broad but subtle expressiveness which
distinguished Aschenbach's part in *Death in Venice*.

Suite on English Folk Tunes, op. 90

Britten's last orchestral work, completed in November 1974, is the
Suite on English Folk Tunes, op. 90, subtitled *A Time There Was ...*
a quotation from Hardy's poem 'Before Life and After' which had
formed the last song in the cycle *Winter Words* – 'A time there was
... before the birth of consciousness when all went well'. The Suite is

undeniably poignant, its sound irradiated by those strange luminosities which, like the light of the dying sun, reflected from the score of *Death in Venice*. Sorrow for what can never be, love for all that has been, are in this music. The five movements, dedicated to the memory of Percy Grainger, comprise ten tunes, three of them rural folk-songs and seven dance tunes taken from Playford's 'The English Dancing Master' (1650). Each movement is based on two tunes. The first, 'Cakes and Ale', is a lively, clear-sounding scherzo marked 'fast and rough' – there is no sentimental 'folksiness' in this realistic treatment of 'We'll Wed' and 'Stepney Cakes and Ale', the strings and drums earthy and raw, the woodwind with that curious hollowness one finds so often in Britten. The movement peters out, giving way to the homophonic glitter of the harp and the rich string octaves of 'The Bitter Withy', with 'The Mermaid' as the centre of the ternary scheme. The third movement, 'Hankin Booby', dates from December 1966 and is scored for double woodwind, two trumpets and a drum. The drum (tamburo) provides a military background to the slightly strident two-part counterpoint contrived from the dotted rhythms of 'Hankin Booby' (or 'Half Hannikin') and the smoother lines of 'Mage on a Cree'. Something of the flavour of an American barn-dance comes from the sprightly open strings of the violins in four parts which open 'Hunt the Squirrel' and its companion 'The Tuneful Nightingale', but the string writing gradually becomes more sophisticated and ends with a flash of brilliance which might have found a place in the *Frank Bridge Variations*. The finale, 'Lord Melbourne', is the longest movement, 'slow and languid', in which fragments of the dance 'Epping Forest' enclose the beautiful eponymous melody and the solo cor anglais holds the tune (exactly as it was noted by Percy Grainger when he collected it) in delicate balance above an ostinato of strings and a funeral drum. It is as if Mahler had harmonized an English folk-tune, yet perhaps we are meant to infer a fleeting reference to the nostalgia and haze of 'Brigg Fair', another folk-tune which Grainger collected and on which Delius based his orchestral rhapsody. The music tells of the bloom that was on the hour; its piquant echoes linger, vibrating in the memory like the Hardy lines which give this work its point of reference to our human lot.

Sacred and Profane, op. 91

The Eight Mediaeval Lyrics, *Sacred and Profane*, op. 91, for unaccompanied five-part chorus (or solo voices) (S.S.A.T.B) was composed in December 1974 and January 1975. The poems are from the mid-twelfth to the mid-fourteenth century and are set in the original mediaeval English (the modern English 'translation' is an essential in a programme-book if audiences are to know that 'This fowles singeth ferly fele, And wliteth on huere wynne wele' means 'These birds sing, wonderfully merry, And warble in their abounding joy'). There is no central theme to the cycle, except that of the unaffected mediaeval juxtaposition of sacred and secular imagery, but there are motivic links between the third and fourth songs and the limpid G minor melody of the most appealing setting, the 'Carol', with its unfinished line in each stanza, is heard again in the succeeding 'Ye that pasen by', a stark Passion song. The settings are a conspectus of Britten's vocal styles, from the simple madrigalian lilt of the third lyric, 'Lenten is come' to the late, epigrammatic concentration of 'Yif ic of luve can' ('If I know of Love'). The cycle opens with a fervent prayer, 'St Godric's Hymn', its Britten fingerprint of a flat seventh on a C major triad pervading the texture, and ends with 'A Death', a catalogue of the physical manifestations of mortality which Britten sets with grisly relish. A great cry of 'All too late! all too late! when the bier is at the gate' momentarily wipes the wry smile from our lips, but Britten does not want our sympathy – the last line is a defiant 'For the whole world I don't care a jot!'

These madrigals, written for virtuosi, were followed by *A Birthday Hansel*, op. 92, seven songs by Burns set for voice and harp for Queen Elizabeth the Queen Mother's seventy-fifth birthday (4 August 1975). No agonies or profundities here, though 'My Hoggie' and 'The Winter' are in serious mood, the latter being especially memorable. Britten did not flinch from setting 'Afton Water', so familiar in another setting, and lets loose his harpist with a lochful of arpeggios. The inflexions of Scottish music are paid homage rather than parodied – 'My early walk' delightful in this respect – and the songs are performed without breaks, the harp leading from one into the next.

Phaedra, op. 93

The vocal artistry of Janet Baker, ill suited (many thought) to the thankless role of Kate Julian in *Owen Wingrave*, was celebrated by Britten in a more fitting manner in his only solo cantata *Phaedra*, op. 93, a setting for mezzo-soprano and chamber orchestra of strings, timpani, other percussion and harpsichord, of lines from Robert Lowell's translation of Racine's *Phèdre*. This work is written on a baroque model such as Haydn's *Arianna a Naxos*, where a single character encompasses a wide dramatic and emotional range. With the enormous labour of an opera score beyond his physical powers in 1975, Britten concentrated almost the time-span and scenario of an opera into these 15 minutes. Inevitably, in view of Dame Janet's success in the role of Lucretia, there were comparisons with that other tragic classical heroine. But the contrast is immense between the flower-strewn music of Lucretia and the spare, direct, angular music given to Phaedra thirty years and several operas later. Lucretia dies trailing wreaths of lyric melody; Phaedra's way to the tomb is along bare corridors of perfect fifths.

The ripples from the 'steaming marsh' of *Death in Venice* have not reached to *Phaedra*. The opera's web of motivic allusions and rich contrapuntal textures is replaced by direct, simple gestures – key associations and conflicts, the use of minor ninths to give variety to degrees of dissonance. Although Aschenbach's key of E major is reached in the rising scale to which Phaedra sings 'Death to the unhappy's no catastrophe!'

Ex. 29

and the cantata opens in the diatonic air of an Athenian spring, there is none of the obsessive frenzy of the opera in Phaedra's attitude to death. When she sings 'A cold composure I have never known gives me a moment's poise', it is difficult not to hear the composer's voice behind his singer.

Britten's hand had lost none of its cunning, though one may feel that the recitatives are rather dry in their effect and that the cello-harpsichord continuo is an acknowledgment of the fashion for the Baroque rather than a living presence in this score. It is for the nobility of Phaedra's apostrophe to death, its sculpted marble turned to music, that one most cherishes this powerful and dramatic opera-in-miniature.

Welcome Ode, op. 95

There was one more original composition involving the human voice. On 19 August 1976, Britten completed his last work, a short piece for young people's chorus and orchestra – the *Welcome Ode*, op. 95 – ready for Suffolk school children to sing to the Queen on her Silver Jubilee visit to the county. (The first performance was in the Corn Exchange, Ipswich, on 11 July 1977.) It is in five continuous movements. The second and fourth movements (*Jig* and *Modulation*) are for orchestra alone, the remainder use texts by Dekker, Ford, Anon. and Fielding. The delightful work is unpretentious, unpatronizing – and unpompous, as befitted the unofficial master of his Queen's music. So, posthumously, did Lord Britten of Aldeburgh welcome Gloriana's descendant on her progress through the Eastern Counties.

String Quartet No. 3, op. 94

After thirty years, Britten returned to the medium of the string quartet and in October and November 1975 composed his third, op. 94. The work is in five movements – as are some of the string quartets of Beethoven, Bartók and Shostakovich – and the titles of these movements are significant: *Duets*; *Ostinato*; *Solo*; *Burlesque*; *Recitative and Passacaglia (La Serenissima)*. The simplicity and tranquillity of much of the music of this quartet represent the essence of Britten's musical achievement over a creative span of fifty years. He looks back, yet this string quartet, like the end of *Death in Venice*, suggests a new beginning, the start of another phase in his development. His aim was always to simplify and to clarify and sometimes, in that process, there was a loss in some of the later works of that spontaneous lyrical inspiration which marked out the young Britten from his contemporaries. Here he achieved the clarity and the succinctness and recaptured the imaginative poetry. It is no exaggeration to compare the place of this composition in his life's work with that of the late string quartets in Beethoven's. Nor is there sacrilege in Hans Keller's statement that, in this string quartet, Britten ventured 'into the Mozartian realm of the instrumental purification of opera'.[1]

It is, I think, true, as Keller also says, that the operatically entitled first movement, *Duets*, is the most symphonically developed in the quartet. As the swaying seconds of the principal theme are heard on second violin and viola, the ambiguous tonality gives out resonances of such strange radiance and luminosity that the words of Stefan George which Schoenberg gives to the soprano in his Second String

Quartet are equally apposite here: 'I feel the air of other planets'. Other duet pairings interweave the material developed from the seminal influence of these seconds.

Ex. 30

In the highly original development, the gentle dialogues extend, by use of triple stopping, to an excited conversation with the sonorities of the *Sinfonietta*. But the term 'development' has few of its conventional implications here, for when the opening material of this ternary movement returns it is in a constant and subtle state of development, culminating in the quiet and profoundly beautiful coda. *Ostinato*, marked 'very fast', is also brief, but in its rapid passage it generates a hectic excitement. The ground of the ostinato is a series of sevenths, and the syncopation of their rhythms is one cause of the music's driving-force. *Solo*, the central slow movement, is a tribute to the special qualities of Norbert Brainin, leader of the Amadeus Quartet. The melodic line, high, calm and ethereal, is carried by the first violin, supported by triad arpeggios from the three other players, until it finds further sublimation in the concentrated rapture of a cadenza for the quartet in the central episode. When the serenity of the opening returns, the solo is accompanied by harmonics of rarified clarity. For *Burlesque*, Britten combines the sardonic vein of Shostakovich with the rhythmic fieriness of Bartók, and superimposes upon them a swift and ghostly review of the bizarre parodies of his youthful music and of the enthusiasms of his youth which persisted for a lifetime – Mahler, for example, for surely the Viennese waltz in the trio of this movement is a spectral reminiscence of the *Rondo Burleske* of the Ninth Symphony?

In both *Solo* and *Burlesque*, the spirit of Shostakovich is invoked, as if Britten was deliberately mourning his friend.

The finale's sub-title, *La Serenissima*, indicates that its music will have links with Venice (where this movement was written) and Britten's last opera; indeed its key of E major is Aschenbach's. In the opening *Recitative*, not only are there references to themes from earlier in the quartet – the ground of the *Passacaglia* was foreshadowed in the work's first theme – but the cello also recalls the barcarolle from *Death in Venice*, and other motifs from the opera are heard in solo passages from the other instruments. When the *Passacaglia* theme is heard, it is the transfiguration of all the similar themes which have wound through Britten's musical life. Using, in the string quartet, the purest, most intimate and most personal of musical forms, the composer's traditional confessional, Britten now unfolds this sublime movement, the apotheosis of his precious gift for imparting the deepest truths with the simplest, the most innocent means. As its semiquaver thirds coil and weave, as tender wisps of counterpoint and descant attend upon the theme's unhurried progress, the listener can scarcely doubt that he is hearing the greatest of all Britten's works and one of the greatest string quartets of a century which has produced many masterpieces of the genre. The coda hovers between this world and the next and seems to be drifting to a gentle finality, truly the still, sad music of humanity. But the sound fades on a G sharp and a long D in the bass; this last chord suggests no end, for who can say if death is end or beginning? Nothing is here for tears, only for thankfulness that from such springs could flow Britten's most profound musical thinking, his most delicate sonorities, and his most direct emotional appeal, 'a remarkable stillness and serenity of soul.'

27

Epilogue

In the catalogue of Britten's works there are many arrangements of works by other composers. Of these the most substantial are the versions he made of Purcell's *Dido and Aeneas* with Imogen Holst and of *The Beggar's Opera*. The Purcell, planned and advertised as early as 1946, was an offering for the 1951 Festival of Britain and was first performed, in a double bill with Monteverdi's *Il Combattimento di Tancredi e Clorinda*, at the Lyric, Hammersmith, on 1 May 1951, with Nancy Evans as Dido. Britten conducted. The significant features are Britten's realization of the harpsichord's figured bass and his provision of other music of Purcell's to fit six lines of libretto after the present end of Act II, for a scene between the Sorceress and her Enchantress, and a dance to end the act. He believed that the original music had been lost, not only because the act ends weakly as drama but because the opera's key scheme, closely adhered to elsewhere, demands a return to D minor (or F major).

His adaptation of *The Beggar's Opera* (1728) was made in 1948 for the English Opera Group in collaboration with Tyrone Guthrie. Britten found the tunes in this concoction by Gay and Pepusch to be 'the most characteristically *English* of any of our folk-songs ... They have strong leaping intervals, sometimes in peculiar modes, and are often strange and severe in mood'. For his version he returned to an edition of Pepusch's original arrangements in order to restore the 'toughness and strangeness' which he felt had given way to 'lyrical prettiness'. He used sixty-six of the sixty-nine original airs (the famous Frederic Austin version used only forty-five). Thirty-six were presented in their original keys and the rest were transposed to fit in with a tonal conflict between the Macheath-Polly love affair and the grimness of Newgate. Although the Britten version has been strongly criticized for 'cleverness', it will be found that his treatment of the tunes restores their freshness, enhanced by the piquancy of his orchestration. Britten also wrote an overture, to be played after the Beggar's spoken introduction. This is a *pot-pourri* of tunes associated with the principal characters. In 1963, when this Britten version was revived, he wrote a new prelude to Act

III based on Lucy's air at the beginning of the act but orchestrated to give another Britten impression of bells – in this case the alarm-bell announcing Macheath's escape from Newgate.

Other Britten 'realizations' reflect his love of Purcell. There is a concert version of *The Fairy Queen*, with Imogen Holst as co-editor, devised by Peter Pears for performance at Aldeburgh, and there are many of songs and duets. His edition of the G minor *Chacony* for strings is frequently played. In addition there are numerous arrangements of English, Irish and French folk-songs for voice and piano or harp or orchestra. In the last summer of his life he made a further eight of these settings, which had always been a popular and eagerly awaited 'lollipop', to borrow Beecham's term, at the end of his recitals with Pears. Every arranger of folk-songs brings to them the harmonic quirks and idiom of his generation and aspects of his own musical personality. Britten was no exception. A generation of concert-goers grew up with his engaging whistling 'Ploughboy', with the sly humour of 'The Foggy Foggy Dew', and with the poignancy of 'O Waly Waly'. Sometimes the arrangements seem wilfully artful ('The Ash Grove', for example), but his interest in folk-music, which took practical form in 1942, was another sign of the returning Odysseus' determination to put down roots into his English landscape. Thus, when someone who had heard his minor-key 'The Miller of Dee' pointed out that the text refers to 'a jolly miller', Britten replied: 'Jolly – old Suffolk word meaning miserable'. He enjoyed his folk-music and so can we.

He died leaving several tangible memorials, besides the Aldeburgh Festival. The gross value of his estate was £1,664,000, of which only £225,000 was realizable. In lieu of capital transfer tax, some of the manuscripts and scores, which had accounted for £1,200,000 of the estate, were accepted by the Treasury for the nation. These manuscripts, now belonging to the British Library, have been deposited on permanent loan to the Britten-Pears Library at The Red House.[1] Some of the residuary estate, after personal bequests, was held upon discretionary trusts for charitable purposes, particularly for the Aldeburgh Festival and for a project very near to his heart, the Britten-Pears School for Advanced Musical Studies, founded at Snape Maltings. There, master classes, special courses and expert tuition are available to the rising generation.

Britten lives on, too, in his recordings, not only of a large proportion of his own music, but of works by others for which he had particular affection and admiration. His playing of the piano part of Schubert's *Winterreise*, uncovering limitless subtleties of rhythm, rubato and expressiveness, is an illustration of Rostropovich's remark: 'Britten-the-pianist closely resembles Britten-the-composer'. This is equally true of his conducting, for instance his dramatic, quasi-operatic interpretation of Elgar's *The Dream of Gerontius*, so far a unique example of a major English composer recording his view of a major work by another major English composer. In (above all) Mozart and in Haydn and Schumann, too, there are insights available only to the composer-interpreter. Alas that he recorded no Mahler.

Yet of course it is his music which is his living memorial. Will it live? Will those who find its supreme craftsmanship too 'knowing' predominate and give, for a generation perhaps, credence to the witty gibe that Britten could prove to be the Saint-Saëns of the twentieth century? Was he himself aware of the reverse side of the coin of his prolific inventiveness when he confessed to a misgiving that perhaps he had 'less depth' than his friend Tippett? Will the admiration accorded to him beyond British shores prove to be as fickle as it was in the case of Elgar, who had a widespread continental reputation before 1914?

Such questions may be asked, but they require no answer beyond that which time will give. I have prefaced this book with Britten's remark to the effect that he did not compose for posterity. He was fortunate that, after the successful creation of the twin instruments of the English Opera Group and the Aldeburgh Festival, he was surrounded by dedicated and gifted fellow-creators who were his ideal interpreters and, in a major sense, his inspiration. There could be a danger – though I myself believe that the intrinsic quality of the music will avert it – that some of his later works were so intimately connected with these individuals, were so 'useful and to the living', that their successors may find it dauntingly unrewarding to attempt to re-create them. The Church Parables are a case in point. There may be significance in the fact that, in the first years after Britten's death, public interest tended to centre on the works of his youthful fecundity. But already a later generation of tenors is interpreting the songs in a less ascetic but musically valid way and several productions of his operas, notably *Death in Venice*, have shown that they are strong enough to survive away from the original Aldeburgh-inspired creations.

Benjamin Britten manipulated the symbols of music so that even people who do not know one note from the next sense the logic, drama and poetry of his art. In that, he is of the company of the elect. The peculiar potency of his vocal music seems often to derive from his ability to convey to his listeners the unexplored area of a text which was always there but which needed revelation through his imaginative vision. His operas exert their grip not only through a natural dramatist's sense of theatre, but because the scores are constructed on symphonic principles of thematic and harmonic development. But the syntax of musicology is too prosaic a medium with which to convey, at the last, the spell cast by Britten's music on so many of his contemporaries. Like him, they will be heedless of posterity's verdict and will prefer to turn again to Christopher Smart for the words to enshrine what they received 'from the hand of the artist inimitable, and from the echo of the heavenly harp in sweetness magnifical and mighty.'

28

After 1976

In the decade since this book first appeared in paperback, the Britten Estate has authorized the performance and publication – and, in some cases, the recording – of several of Britten's compositions which he either withdrew or never released. Not all have added to his reputation, though none has been wholly insignificant; it is doubtful, for example, if much good was served by the resurrection of the sketchy first movement of a proposed Clarinet Concerto for Benny Goodman. Perhaps the most astonishing are works written in his boyhood: the publication of *A Britten Source Book* (1987) enables us to see the prolific extent of Britten's composing activity between 1921, when he was eight, and, say, 1932.

Some of the posthumously unearthed works, like *Go play, boy, play*, were listed and mentioned in the first edition of this book, but I had not heard them (nor, of course, had anybody else). Others are now included for the first time, the *Quartettino*, for instance, composed early in 1930. This is a harmonically bold work influenced, one suspects, by Bridge's more radical style as exemplified in his Third String Quartet of 1927. There are grating dissonances which Britten was soon to expunge from his music. Especially interesting is the use of a short motif to bind the whole work together in a Schoenbergian fashion. Britten's reversion to more traditional and tonal methods is already evident in the *Phantasy* in F minor for string quintet which won him the Cobbett Prize in July 1932, after which he revised it for a performance outside the Royal College of Music. It is an engaging piece, a companion to the *Phantasy* oboe quartet. Another 1932 chamber work (composed 6–20 May) was the *Phantasy-Scherzo*, later re-named *Introduction and Allegro*, for piano trio. This waited until 22 November 1986 for its first performance and remains unpublished.

Although Britten composed a *Jubilate Deo* in 1961 to go with his 1934 *Te Deum*, the original companion-piece, *Jubilate Deo* in E flat, also written in August 1934, was published in 1984 and 'belongs' more obviously. The string quartet *Alla Quartetto Serioso: 'Go play, boy, play'* was composed in 1933 and was intended as a five-movement work (sketches exist of two incomplete movements, *Alla Romanza* and *Theme and 2 Variations*). Britten was dissatisfied by a performance in December 1933 of the three completed movements and withdrew them until he revised them in 1936 for performance by the Stratton Quartet as *Three Divertimenti*. The movements are called *March*, *Waltz* and *Burlesque* and are character-pieces in the style Britten employed in his *Suite* for violin and piano, op. 6, of 1935. New glissandi were introduced into the *March* in revision and the 3/8 *Burlesque* was re-written in 6/8. The *Waltz* is the most delightful and appealing movement. The quartet-movement *Alla Marcia*, also composed in February 1933, was intended as the first movement of *Go play, boy, play* but was discarded and, in April, was again pressed into service as the opening of a suite to be based on the novel *Emil and the Detectives* by Erich Kästner. Britten had seen the German film based on the novel on 28 March 1933 and been bowled over by it. The *Alla Marcia* was played privately at Frank Bridge's home on 26 February 1933, revised in mid-July, when it was labelled 'Emil to be', but was left in manuscript until 1939 when Britten expanded it as the accompaniment to 'Parade' in *Les Illuminations*. The first violinist at the Bridge performance was Britten's friend Antonio Brosa, for whom Britten wrote a brilliant showpiece, *Reveille*, for violin and piano, in 1937. This was an 'in-joke', Brosa being noted as a late riser. It was first performed by Brosa and Franz Reizenstein on 12 April 1937.

The Britten keyboard repertory, extraordinarily small for one who was a great pianist, has been enlarged through exploration of his unpublished archive by Donald Mitchell and Colin Matthews. The *Three Character Pieces* of 1930 were composed between September and December in Britten's first year at the Royal College of Music, when he was studying pianoforte with Arthur Benjamin. They are portraits of three Lowestoft friends – John Boyd, Daphne Black and Michael Tyler – and are in a sweetly subtle harmonic idiom. The third is brilliant in a manner that anticipates the piano concerto and quotes from John Ireland's *Ragamuffin*, the second of his *Three London Pieces*, and also quotes the theme of the second Britten piece. They received their first performance from Sarah Briggs at Chester on 28 July 1989. More experimental were the *12 Variations on a Theme* of 1931. Here some have detected the influence of Hindemith. The theme (*allegretto*) is certainly Hindemithian in its rather dry, sequential fashion, and as one listens to the final fugue it is clear that Britten at seventeen was interested in neoclassicism. An incomplete set of variations for piano, dating from March 1932, is of interest because Britten used the theme from Bridge's *Idyll* No. 2 for string quartet to which he turned again five years later for the *Variations on a Theme of Frank Bridge* for string orchestra. Britten the witty parodist is to the fore in *Two Lullabies*, for two pianos, written in 1936 for a BBC audition in company with Adolph Hallis. The first is like Chopin re-composed by Poulenc, while the second, *Lullaby for a Retired Colonel*, is a mockingly martial affair which alludes to *La Marseillaise*, *Men of Harlech*, and the *Last Post*. The *Sonatina Romantica* dates from 1940 when Britten and Pears were staying with the Mayers at Amityville. The director of the Long Island Home at which Dr Mayer was senior neurologist was Dr William B. Titley, who was an enthusiastic pianist. Britten interrupted his work on the *Sinfonia da Requiem* to compose the sonatina for Dr Titley to try to divert him from his struggles with Weber's *Invitation to the Waltz*. Britten was not pleased with the work and put it on one side after attempting to revise the *finale*. His executors have published the first two movements, which are relatively simple and fulfil their intended function of being useful for teaching.

A major addition to Britten's catalogue of unaccompanied choral pieces was the restoration of his *A.M.D.G.* (Ad Maiorem Dei Gloriam), composed in the United States between 7 and 30 August 1939 and given the opus number 17 (which was re-allocated to *Paul Bunyan* in 1976). Britten intended it for a group of singers – the Round Table Singers, headed by Peter Pears – to perform in London in the autumn. But both Pears and Britten stayed in America when the Second World War broke out and the seven four-part settings of poems by Gerard Manley Hopkins remained in sketch, requiring only a little 'tidying up' from Colin Matthews. Four of the songs were performed at the 1984 Aldeburgh Festival, and all seven were recorded in 1988. Britten left no order of performance and Matthews therefore chose his own: *Heaven-Haven*, *O Deus, ego amo te*, *Rosa Mystica*, *The Soldier*, *Prayer II* ('Thee God, I come from, to thee I go'), *God's Grandeur*, and *Prayer I* ('Jesus that dost in Mary Dwell'). They are of exceptional technical difficulty. All Britten's fertile inventiveness of the 1939–40 period is here at its most prolific. There is an extraordinary setting of *O Deus, ego amo te*, leaping with erotic religious fervour; in *Rosa Mystica* the women's voices first have the text and the melody against the chanting of the men; in *The Soldier* it is possible to recognize the future composer of the *War Requiem*, for it is in the jaunty mocking vein of some of the Owen settings; and *God's Grandeur* is a savagely exciting example of Britten at his most virtuosic. Two of the songs (*Prayer I* and *The Soldier*) are crossed through in the sketches, which caused some misgivings about the ethics of reviving them.

Another work salvaged from Britten's American years is the overture he composed in October 1941 for Artur Rodzinski and the Cleveland Orchestra. Why it was never performed is unclear – possibly the completed work, given the opus number 27, which Britten re-allocated to the *Hymn to St Cecilia*, was never delivered to those who had commissioned it. A photograph of the score was sent to Britten from America in 1967. He had forgotten it and only the evidence of the photograph convinced him it was his work. In 1972, the manuscript came to light in New York Public Library. Britten had originally called the work *Occasional Overture*, a good description of its brassy, excitable, nervy contents, which were first heard on 8 November 1983 in Birmingham when Simon Rattle conducted the City of Birmingham Symphony Orchestra. It was published in 1985 and re-titled *An American Overture* to distinguish it from the *Occasional Overture* (Britten's title again) composed in September 1946 for the launching on the 29th of the BBC Third Programme, when the BBC Symphony Orchestra, conducted by Sir Adrian Boult, gave its broadcast première. Perhaps the haste in which this later overture was written contributed to Britten's dissatisfaction, for it was withdrawn at once and probably not heard again until Rattle recorded it in 1984. It is not particularly distinguished, but it makes a bright start to a concert and it is, after all, by Britten. A 1982 publication, and also recorded, was *Men of Goodwill*, a set of not very sophisticated variations on the carol 'God rest you merry, gentlemen' which was composed for a Christmas Day radio programme in 1947.

Two other radio scores have been revived since Britten's death. *The Company of Heaven* (1937) was a broadcast feature of verse, prose and music devised for Michaelmas by R.E. Roberts and first broadcast on 29 September 1937. It was produced by Robin Whitworth who, over fifty years later, recalled that he had not regarded the score as suitable because Britten had not troubled to understand the programme but had 'ploughed his own furrow and provided a straightforward musical entity'. Roberts, on the other hand, considered that the music had given the feature 'unity of thought and feeling'. Britten had been brought into the programme through his friend Trevor Harvey, who was then assistant chorusmaster at the BBC. He began to sketch the music in August 1937 just after completing the *Variations on a Theme of Frank Bridge*, and completed it in September. Harvey conducted the first performance, in which Felix Aylmer was among the speakers and the vocal soloists were Sophie Wyss and Peter Pears. The work is in three parts, 'Angels before the Creation', 'Angels in Holy Scripture' and 'Angels in Common Life and at our Death'. Britten frankly said he could not see the significance of the programme and did not understand it. What interested him was that he had 'nice words to set': they included the 'War in Heaven' passage from *Revelations* and Emily Bronte's 'A thousand, thousand gleaming fires'. The latter is the first music Britten composed with Pears's voice in mind. Yet the finest piece in the work is the orchestral interlude *Funeral March for a Boy*, clearly influenced by Mahler.

The score of *The Company of Heaven* and that of its 1938 successor *The World of the Spirit*, which Harvey also conducted, remained in Harvey's keeping throughout the war. He made a concert version of *The Company of Heaven* which was broadcast on 20 May 1956. After that, none of the music was heard until the complete original work was performed on 12 June 1989 at the Aldeburgh Festival, conducted by Philip Brunelle, who later recorded it.

Among other recordings which restore to us a Britten 'occasion' is that of *The Heart of the Matter*, a sequence of words and music based on the works of Edith Sitwell and devised by Britten for the 1956 Aldeburgh Festival, when Dame Edith was the reader. The core of the sequence was the Canticle III, *Still Falls the Rain*, but there were three other fine settings which remain unpublished, 'Where are the Seeds of the Universal Fire?' 'We are the darkness' and, as epilogue, 'So out of the dark'. The sequence was revived in 1983 and recorded by the BBC in 1985, with Pears as speaker (his singing career had been ended by a stroke in 1982). The EMI recording was already planned, but Pears died and the BBC allowed their tapes of Sir Peter's readings to be used.

When Britten was writing a set of songs, he usually composed more items than he needed, excluding some because they did not fit into his final scheme. Thus, in the archive at Aldeburgh there are unpublished settings of Auden, Rimbaud, Michelangelo, Donne, Hardy, Blake, and Soutar. Some of these have now been released for performance. Most significant is the second Tennyson setting planned for the *Serenade* – 'Now sleeps the crimson petal'. This song, beautiful and erotic though it is, would not have fitted into the work, but it remarkably anticipates the mood and style of the 1958 *Nocturne*. The orchestration for horn and strings has been edited by Colin Matthews. Two Hardy settings were excluded from *Winter Words*, 'The Children and Sir Nameless' and the haunting 'If it's ever spring again'. The 1937 Auden settings 'To lie flat on the back' and 'Night covers up the rigid land' (both were addressed to Britten by the poet in his vain attempt to have a physical relationship with him) are treasure trove, as is the gorgeous 'Not even summer yet', Britten's only setting of words by Peter Burra. Three rhymes by William Soutar omitted from *Who are these children?* – 'Dawtie's Devotion', 'Tradition' and 'The Gully' – are also worthy of resurrection. They were composed in August 1969.

Some further manuscript songs were performed for the first time at the Aldeburgh Festivals of 1991 and 1992. The earliest, 'When you're feeling like expressing your affection', has a text almost certainly by Auden, belongs stylistically to the *Cabaret Songs*, and must have been composed in 1935 or 1936 for a short film about the telephone service which in the event was never made. It is also possible that Hedli Anderson had been intended as its first singer. 'The Red Cockatoo', composed on 24 January 1938, was Britten's first setting of an Arthur Waley translation of a Chinese poet (Po-Chu-i), not followed up until the *Songs from the Chinese* of 1957. Two splendid songs with texts by Thomas Lovell Beddoes, 'Wild with passion' and 'If thou wilt ease', were composed in April 1942 aboard the M.S. *Axel Johnson* while Britten and Pears were returning to England. The poems were in the anthology bought in Halifax, Nova Scotia, which contained the carols Britten set on the voyage as *A Ceremony of Carols*. In 1944, perhaps to encourage a Beddoes cycle, Pears bought Britten an edition of the collected poems. Among the songs left behind in America in 1942 was an unfinished setting of Louis MacNeice's 'Cradle Song for Eleanor'. Britten resumed his friendship with this poet at the BBC in 1942 and his setting of 'Sleep, my darling, sleep' dates from the autumn of that year. This, too, may have been meant for Hedli Anderson, whom MacNeice had married in 1942. After the *Sechs Hölderlin-Fragmente* in 1958, Britten was given an edition of Goethe's poetry by his friend Prince Ludwig of Hesse. He marked over 20 poems, which suggests he was considering a Goethe cycle. But only *Um Mitternacht* was composed, in 1959 or 1960. This is a strong setting in Britten's 'nocturnal' style, with 12 tolling chords in the piano accompaniment, each rooted on a different pitch of the chromatic scale.

If none of the above works alters the contours of the map of Britten's development as a composer, they all add features to the landscape which we would be the poorer not to know. Readers are referred to *Letters from a Life*, Vols. I and II, for tantalizing glimpses of projected works which were abandoned, among them a *Sonata for Orchestra* (1942), a theme from which was transformed into the round 'Old Joe has gone fishing' in *Peter Grimes*, and *The Bewitched Violin* (1941), intended for Georg Szell and the NBC Orchestra.

Notes to the text

1: Suffolk Childhood

1 B. Britten: *On Receiving the First Aspen Award* (Faber & Faber, 1964), p. 15.
2 From his speech on receiving the freedom of Lowestoft, 1951.
3 B. Britten: *On Receiving the First Aspen Award*, op. cit., p. 21.
4 Ibid., p. 20.
5 B. Britten: *The Composer and the Listener*, BBC schools broadcast talk, 7 November 1946.
6 D. Mitchell and J. Evans: *Benjamin Britten: Pictures from a Life 1913–1976* (Faber & Faber, 1978)
7 B. Britten: *The Composer and the Listener*, op. cit.
8 B. Britten: 'Britten Looking Back', *Sunday Telegraph*, 17 November 1963.

2: Frank Bridge

1 B. Britten: 'Britten Looking Back', op. cit.
2 Ibid.
3 Ibid.
4 Ibid.
5 Ibid.
6 M. Schafer: *British Composers in Interview* (Faber & Faber, 1963), p. 30.

3: At the College

1 M. Schafer: *British Composers in Interview*, op. cit., p. 114.
2 M. Kennedy: *The Works of Ralph Vaughan Williams* (O.U.P., 1964), p. 376.
3 B. Britten: 'Britten Looking Back', op. cit.
4 But this was far from being his first essay in the medium. By the age of twelve he had written six string quartets and ten piano sonatas.
5 M. Schafer: *British Composers in Interview*, op. cit.
6 Britten's diary entries as quoted in *Britten: The Early Years, 1*. BBC Radio 3, 4 April 1980.
7 B. Britten: 'Britten Looking Back', op. cit.

8 Quoted in D. Mitchell and J. Evans: *Benjamin Britten, Pictures from a Life 1913–1976*, illus. 353 (Faber & Faber, 1978).
9 B. Britten: 'Variations on a Critical Theme', *Opera*, March 1952.
10 *Britten in Retrospect*, discussion on BBC Radio 3 between D. Mitchell and Hans Keller, first broadcast 31 March 1979.

4: Auden & Co.

1 As originally published, the *Suite* had four movements – 'March', 'Moto Perpetuo', 'Lullaby', 'Waltz' – prefaced by a short Introduction. Shortly before he died, Britten suggested excluding the Introduction and Moto Perpetuo and the work was published in 1977 under the title *Three Pieces from Suite, Op. 6*.
2 An irrelevant personal aside: my first vicarious contact with Britten was made just before this date, playing cricket and football for a Rhyl preparatory school against Clive House.
3 B. Britten: *The Composer and the Listener*, op. cit.
4 M. Schafer: *British Composers in Interview*, op. cit., pp. 114–15.
5 J. Blades: *Drum Roll* (London, 1977).
6 Quoted in D. Mitchell and J. Evans, op. cit., illus. 103.
7 On Britten's relationship with Auden, I am indebted for invaluable information and stimulating comment to Donald Mitchell's *Britten and Auden in the Thirties: the year 1936*, lectures given at the University of Kent in November 1979 and first published in *The Times Literary Supplement*, 15 February 1980, and later by Faber.
8 M. Schafer: *British Composers in Interview*, op. cit., p. 117.
9 Quoted in D. Mitchell and J. Evans, illus. 92.
10 Quoted in *Britten: the Early Years 2*. BBC Radio 3, 11 April 1980.
11 *Sophie Wyss Remembers*: BBC Radio 3 talk, 4 December 1977.
12 Quoted in D. Mitchell's *Britten and Auden in the Thirties*, op. cit.
13 Ibid.
14 Ibid.
15 Letter in August 1958 to Mrs Vaughan Williams quoted in M. Kennedy: *The Works of Ralph Vaughan Williams*, op. cit., p. 253.
16 B. Britten: 'Britten Looking Back', op. cit.
17 Quoted by D. Mitchell in *Tempo*, no. 120.
18 Quoted in D. Mitchell's *Britten and Auden in the Thirties*, op. cit.

5: America

1 Quoted in D. Mitchell's *Britten and Auden in the Thirties*, op. cit.
2 Ibid.
3 Pears thought their first recital might have been in Cambridge in aid of Spanish War Relief. Others believe it was in the Master's Lodging at Balliol College, Oxford, on 17 February 1939.

4 B. Neel: 'The String Orchestra' in *Benjamin Britten: a commentary on his works...*, ed. Mitchell and Keller (Rockliff, 1952).
5 B. Britten: 'Britten Looking Back', op. cit.
6 Britten's programme-note in Aldeburgh Festival programme book, 1969.
7 B. Britten: *On Receiving the First Aspen Award*, op. cit., p. 21.
8 D. Mitchell: *Britten and Auden in the Thirties*, op. cit.
9 B. Britten: *On Receiving the First Aspen Award*, op. cit., p. 21.
10 *Peter Grimes:* Sadler's Wells Opera Books No. 3.
11 B. Britten: *On Receiving the First Aspen Award*, op. cit., p. 11.
12 D. Mitchell: *Britten and Auden in the Thirties*, op. cit.

6: The Return

1 *Tempo*, No. 46, 1957–8, pp. 5–6.
2 M. Schafer: *British Composers in Interview*, op. cit., p. 116.
3 M. Schafer: *British Composers in Interview*, op. cit.
4 R. Blythe: 'Peter Grimes – A Note' in *Scottish Opera* 1979–1980.

7: The Borough

1 I. Holst: *Britten* (Faber & Faber, 1966), p. 39.
2 'Conversation with Benjamin Britten', *Tempo*, February 1944.
3 E. Crozier: 'Peter Grimes', *Opera*, Vol. 16, No. 6, June 1965, pp. 412–16.
4 S. Goddard: 'Benjamin Britten' in *British Music of our Time* (Pelican, 1946) p. 217.
5 Programme of Royal Opera House memorial performance of *Peter Grimes*, 24 March 1977.
6 E. Walter White: *Benjamin Britten, his Life and Operas* (Faber & Faber, 1970), p. 42.
7 *The Gramophone*, interview with Alan Blyth, June 1970, p. 29.
8 Wilfred Blunt: *John Christie of Glyndebourne* (Geoffrey Bles, 1968), pp. 254–5.
9 Quoted in I. Holst: *Britten*, op. cit.
10 R. Duncan: *The Rape of Lucretia* (The Bodley Head, 1946).
11 Britten was fiercely insistent on this title and was irritated by Sir Malcolm Sargent's custom of referring to it by its sub-title *Variations and Fugue on a Theme of Purcell*, perhaps on the grounds that *Young Person's Guide* was in some way trivial.
12 E. Crozier: 'Staging First Productions, (1)' in *The Operas of Benjamin Britten*, ed. D. Herbert (Hamish Hamilton, 1979), pp. 29–30.

8: Aldeburgh

1 The composer's friend Henry Boys wrote as early as 1938 (in the *Monthly Musical Record*) that Britten, if he chose, 'could undoubtedly become the most original and probably the most successful maker of light music in England since Sullivan'.
2 I. Holst: *Britten*, op. cit., p. 50.
3 B. Britten: 'Three Premières', in *Kathleen Ferrier, a memoir*, ed. N. Cardus, (Hamish Hamilton, 1954), pp. 54–61.
4 B. Britten: 'A Note on the Spring Symphony', *Music Survey*, Spring 1950.
5 Reprinted in *The Listener*, 6 December 1951, p. 959.

9: Gloriana

1 Published by Rockliff, London, and reprinted in the U.S.A. in 1972 by the Greenwood Press.
2 Vol. XXXIV No. 2.
3 I. Holst: *Britten*, op. cit.
4 Britten wrote to Anthony Gishford of Boosey and Hawkes on 31 January 1954: 'I hope you liked the performance. I thought it was a great improvement, and hope that the reception at the end may prove that the tide is slightly turning'. (*Tempo*, No. 120, 1977).

10: Gamelan

1 M. Piper: 'Writing for Britten' in *The Operas of Benjamin Britten*, ed. Herbert (Hamish Hamilton, 1979), pp. 8–21.
2 I. Holst: *Britten*, op. cit., p. 55.
3 B. Coleman: 'Staging First Productions (2)' in *The Operas of Benjamin Britten*, op. cit., pp. 34–43.
4 *Edith Sitwell, Selected Letters*, ed. J. Lehmann and D. Parker (London 1970), p. 191.
5 Quoted in D. Mitchell and J. Evans, op. cit., illus. 297.
6 J. Cranko: 'Making a Ballet', *The Observer*, 13 and 20 January 1957.
7 Imogen Holst, in her *Britten*, op. cit., recounts: 'He had thought of having teacups hit with a teaspoon ... But he came round to me one afternoon saying that he'd tried it out at teatime and it wouldn't work. So I took him into my kitchen and showed him how a row of mugs could be strung on a length of string and hit with a large wooden spoon. We then went along the High Street to Mrs Beech's shop and bought a lot of mugs with "A Present from Aldeburgh" on them, and he took them the next day to the school at Woolverstone Hall where the boys were already rehearsing the percussion parts.'
8 K. Clark: 'The Other Side of the Alde' in *Tribute to Benjamin Britten* (Faber & Faber, 1963).

11: War Requiem

1 Britten himself preferred to spell 'obligato' with one b.
2 B. Britten: 'A New Britten Opera', *The Observer*, 5 June 1960.
3 C. Graham: 'Staging First Productions (3)' in *The Operas of Benjamin Britten*, op. cit., pp. 44–58.
4 Postcard dated 25 September 1960, kindly lent to the author by Mr Ward.
5 M. Rostropovich: 'Three Friends', *The Observer*, 27 November 1977.
6 M. Rostropovich: 'Three Friends', ibid.
7 B. Britten: *On Receiving the First Aspen Award*, op. cit., p. 11.
8 W. Owen: Preface to *Collected Poems* (p. 31 of 1963 edition, Chatto & Windus).
9 It should perhaps be recorded here that Britten's choral arrangement of the National Anthem for the 1961 Leeds Festival moved an Oxford resident to write to *The Listener* (2 November 1961): 'Britten has tampered with the music in a way that immediately struck one as amateurish... The basic horror is the inflation of the second half of the tune, which not only completely upsets the rightful balance, but also has a ridiculously pompous effect. It is to be sincerely hoped that this ungainly piece of misplaced Victoriana will be withdrawn immediately...'
10 B. Britten: 'Britten Looking Back', op. cit.
11 *Tempo*, no. 120.
12 I. Stravinsky: *Themes and Conclusions* (Faber & Faber, 1972), pp. 26–7.

12: Noh-Play in Orford

1 *Tempo*, No. 120, March 1977, p. 4.
2 *Tempo*, Autumn-Winter 1963, p. 32.
3 *Tribute to Benjamin Britten on his Fiftieth Birthday*, ed. Gishford (Faber & Faber, 1963).
4 Prince Ludwig of Hesse and the Rhine: 'Ausflug Ost 1956', from *Tribute to Benjamin Britten on his Fiftieth Birthday*, op. cit., p. 56.
5 B. Britten: Note in libretto of *Curlew River*, Faber 1964.
6 C. Graham: 'The Convention of *Curlew River*', article in booklet with Decca recording of *Curlew River*, issued 1966.
7 *The Gramophone*, June 1970, interview with Alan Blyth, p. 30.
8 B. Britten in *Faber Music News*, Autumn 1966.
9 B. Britten: *On Receiving the First Aspen Award*, op. cit.
10 Britten's recordings of his own works are especially valuable for this very reason – that they will show future performers the *style* of his performances.

13: Moscow and Maltings

1 P. Pears: *Armenian Holiday: August 1965*, privately printed 1965.
2 P. Pears: *Moscow Christmas: December 1966*, privately printed 1967.

3 J. Culshaw: 'Ben, a Tribute to Benjamin Britten', *The Gramophone*, February 1977, pp. 1251–2.
4 P. Pears: Preface to *The Operas of Benjamin Britten*, op. cit.

14: The Fire

1 M. Piper: 'Writing for Britten' in *The Operas of Benjamin Britten*, op. cit., pp. 8–21.
2 *The Gramophone*, June 1970, interview with Alan Blyth, p. 29.
3 Information from Mr James Day.
4 *The Daily Telegraph*, 2 June 1971.

15: Death in Suffolk

1 'Britten returns to composing': interview in *The Times*, 30 December 1974.
2 Interview in Tony Palmer's television film *A Time There Was*, screened on 6 April 1980.
3 *Tempo*, September 1973.
4 *The Times*, 30 December, 1974, op. cit.
5 Covent Garden memorial programme (*Peter Grimes*), 24 March 1977.
6 H. Keller: 'Death of a genius', *The Spectator*, 15 January 1977, pp. 27–8.
7 M. Tippett: *Benjamin Britten*, broadcast on BBC Radio 3, 4 December 1976, reprinted in *The Listener*, 16 December 1976, p. 791.

16: Pride and Prejudice

1 Covent Garden memorial programme (*Peter Grimes*), 24 March 1977.
2 *The Guardian:* Dennis Barker on Saturday, 11 June 1977.
3 J. Baker: 'Working with Britten', in *The Operas of Benjamin Britten*, op. cit., p. 2.
4 D. Mitchell and H. Keller (eds): *Benjamin Britten: a commentary on his works ...*, op. cit.
5 J. Piper: 'Designing for Britten' in *The Operas of Benjamin Britten*, op. cit., p. 6.
6 Interview with Alan Blyth in *The Gramophone*, June 1970, pp. 29–30.
7 Interview in Tony Palmer's television film *A Time There Was*, op. cit.
8 Interview with Shirley Fleming, *High Fidelity/Musical America*, 1979.
9 H. Keller: Introduction to *The Operas of Benjamin Britten*, op. cit., p. xxvi.
10 M. Schafer: *British Composers in Interview*, op. cit.
11 D. Mitchell in *Aldeburgh Anthology*, ed. R. Blythe (Snape Maltings Foundation, 1972), pp. 436–7.

17: 1923–35

1 P. Evans: *The Music of Benjamin Britten* (J.M. Dent & Sons, 1979, rev. 1989).

18: 1936–39

1 In the concert at Norwich the audience that day heard first Jane Scroop's lament for her sparrow in Vaughan Williams's *Five Tudor Portraits* (Skelton) and then this Britten-Auden lament for a monkey.
2 'Conversation with Benjamin Britten': *Tempo*, February 1944.
3 J.B. Priestley: *Margin Released* (Heinemann, 1962), p. 210.

20: 1942–45

1 B. Britten in *Peter Grimes* (Sadler's Wells Opera Books No. 3), ed. E. Crozier (The Bodley Head, 1945).
2 N. Maw in 'B. Britten: Tributes and Memories', *Tempo*, 1977.

22: 1949–54

1 B. Britten: 'A Note on the *Spring Symphony*', *Music Survey*, 1950, p. 237.
2 The 1960 revision of *Billy Budd* reduced it from four acts to two (thus incidentally eradicating three intervals, which tended to dissipate tension among the audience). It principally affected the original Acts I and II. Act I had ended with the crew mustering for an address by Vere; there was then a final chorus in praise of Vere, with solo contributions from Billy Budd. In merging the two acts, the muster becomes a change of watch, Vere is not seen but is spoken about, and the chorus is deleted. The action now goes from the quarterdeck to Vere's cabin. In addition, the original ended with an anticipation of Billy's lullaby. In the final version, the old cabin scene of Act III becomes Act II, scene 2, ending with the series of triads. Act IV has now become scenes 3 and 4 of Act II.
3 M. Piper: 'Some thoughts on the libretto of *The Turn of the Screw*', in *Tribute to Benjamin Britten on his fiftieth birthday*, op. cit., p. 80.
4 D. Mitchell: 'Britten's revisionary practice: practical and creative', *Tempo*, 1963, pp. 15–22.

23: 1955–60

1 Britten explained his attitude to the fairies in an article ('A New Britten Opera') in *The Observer*, 5 June 1960. Remarking that his fairies were 'very different from the innocent nothings that often appear in productions of Shakespeare', he added: 'I have always been struck by a kind of sharpness in Shakespeare's fairies: besides, they have some odd poetry to

speak ... They are, after all, the guards to Tytania: so they have, in places, martial music.' He retained the quarto spelling Tytania, which is thus pronounced with a long first syllable.

24: 1961–71

1 I discovered recently that Britten had a high regard for the *For the Fallen* movement which ends *The Spirit of England.* Writing in the Aldeburgh Festival programme-book for 1969, before a projected performance (cancelled because of the Maltings fire), he said: '[It] has always seemed to me to have in its opening bars a personal tenderness and grief, in the grotesque march, an agony of distortion, and in the final sequences a ring of genuine splendour'.
2 They are 'London', 'A Poison Tree' and 'Ah! Sunflower'.

25: 1970–73

1 On this episode in particular, and other facets of writing for television, interested readers are recommended to Myfanwy Piper's absorbing essay 'Writing for Britten' in *The Operas of Benjamin Britten*, op. cit., pp. 8–21.
2 J. Baker: 'Working with Britten' in *The Operas of Benjamin Britten*, op. cit., pp. 1–4.

26: 1973–76

1 H. Keller: Introduction to *The Operas of Benjamin Britten*, op. cit., xiii–xxxi.

27: Epilogue

1 This Library had been established by Britten and Pears in 1973 and embraced their own private collection of books and music in the large wing built for them ten years before. The Library is open to scholars and research students (by appointment only) and houses a unique Britten archive.

Appendix A

Calendar

Because Britten's birthday came nearly at the end of the year, his age throughout this calendar is shown as that of his previous birthday, i.e. 9 in 1923, not 10

Year	Age	Life	Contemporary Musicians and Events
1913		Edward Benjamin Britten born Nov. 22 in Lowestoft, Suffolk, son of Robert Victor Britten (1878–1934) and Edith Rhoda Britten (née Hockey) (1874–1937)	Lutoslawski born, Jan. 5; First perfs. of Schoenberg's *Gurrelieder*, Vienna, Feb. 23; Stravinsky's *The Rite of Spring*, Paris, May 29; Elgar's *Falstaff*, Leeds, Oct. 1.
1919	5	Begins composing and in next year or so writes play with incidental music, goes to pre-preparatory school and has piano lessons.	Leoncavallo (61) dies. First perfs. of Strauss's *Die Frau ohne Schatten*, Vienna, Oct. 10, and Elgar's Cello Concerto, London, Oct. 26.
1923	9	Enters South Lodge preparatory school. Writes waltzes for piano. Has viola lessons and begins to write for strings.	Ligeti born, May 28. First perfs. of Sibelius's Symphony No. 6, Helsinki, Feb. 19; Walton's String Quartet, London, July 5, and Salzburg, Aug. 4.
1924	10	Goes to Norwich Triennial Festival in Sept. and hears Bridge conduct *The Sea*.	Nono born, Jan. 29; Busoni (58) dies, July 27; Fauré (79) dies, Nov. 4; Puccini (65) dies, Nov. 29. First perfs. of Sibelius's Symphony No. 7, Stockholm, March 24; Schoenberg's *Erwartung*, Prague, June 6, *Serenade*, Donaueschingen, July 20, *Quintet*, Vienna, Sept. 13, *Die glückliche Hand*, Vienna, Oct. 14; Strauss's *Intermezzo*,

Dresden, Nov. 4; Bliss's 2-
piano concerto (orig. vers.),
Boston, Dec.

| 1927 | 13 | Hears Bridge conduct first perf. of *Enter Spring* at Norwich Triennial Festival in Sept. Meets Bridge and has first lesson with him. |

Boulez 2; Henze 1. First perfs.
of Berg's *Lyric Suite*, Vienna,
Jan. 8, and Chamber
Concerto, Berlin, March 27;
Krenek's *Jonny spielt auf*,
Leipzig, Feb. 11; Varèse's
Arcana, Philadelphia, April 8;
Stravinsky's *Oedipus Rex*,
Paris, May 30; Busoni's
Doctor Faustus, Frankfurt,
June 29; Bartók's Piano
Concerto No. 1, Frankfurt,
July 1; Bliss's Oboe Quintet,
Venice, Sept. 11; Schoenberg's
Third String Quartet, Vienna,
Sept. 19; Shostakovich's
Symphony No. 2, Leningrad,
Nov. 6; Janáček's *Glagolitic
Mass*, Brno, Dec. 5.

| 1928 | 14 | Regular lessons with Bridge in London and attends concerts with him. Piano lessons from Harold Samuel. *Victor ludorum* in last term at prep. school. Writes *Quatre chansons françaises* in July. Enters Gresham's School, Holt, in Sept. |

Barraqué born, Jan. 17;
Musgrave born, May 27;
Baird born, July 26;
Stockhausen born, Aug. 28;
Janáček (74) dies, Aug. 12.
First perfs. of Walton's
Sinfonia Concertante,
London, Jan. 5; Stravinsky's
Apollo Musagetes,
Washington, April 27;
Strauss's *Die ägyptische
Helena*, Dresden, June 6;
Janáček's String Quartet No.
2, Brno, Sept. 11; Webern's
String Trio, Siena, Sept. 12;
Ravel's *Boléro*, Paris, Nov.
22; Schoenberg's *Variations*,
Berlin, Dec. 2

| 1929 | 15 | Composes carol *A Wealden Trio* in April and song *The Birds* in June. |

Crumb born, Oct. 24;
Diaghilev (57) dies, Aug. 19.
First perfs. of Vaughan
Williams's *Sir John in Love*,
London, Mar. 21; Prokofiev's
Symphony No. 3, Paris, May

17; Walton's Viola Concerto London, Oct. 3; Webern's Symphony, New York, Dec. 8.

1930	16	Leaves Gresham's School July. Composes *Hymn to the Virgin* in July. Enters Royal College of Music in Sept. Composition lessons with John Ireland, piano with Arthur Benjamin.	Warlock (36) dies, Dec. 17. First perfs. of Shostakovich's *The Nose*, Leningrad, Jan. 18, Symphony No. 3, Leningrad, Jan. 21, *The Age of Gold*, Leningrad, Oct. 26; Janáček's *From the House of the Dead*, Brno, April 12; Berg's *Der Wein*, Königsberg, June 4; Elgar's *Severn Suite*, London, Sept. 27; Bliss's *Morning Heroes*, Norwich, Oct. 22; Vaughan Williams's *Job*, Norwich, Oct. 23; Stravinsky's *Symphony of Psalms*, Brussels, Dec. 13; first perf. in England of Mahler's Symphony No. 9, Manchester, Feb. 27
1931	17	Composes *Thy King's Birthday*, which includes motet *New Prince, New Pomp* and carol *Sweet was the Song the Virgin Sung*. Composes *String Quartet in D* May 8– June 2. Wins Farrar Prize for composition, R.C.M. in July.	M. Williamson born, Nov. 21; Nielsen (66) dies, Oct. 3; d'Indy (80) dies, Dec. 2. First perfs. of Shostakovich's *The Bolt*, Leningrad, April 8; Prokofiev's String Quartet No. 1, Washington, April 25; Elgar's *Nursery Suite*, London, May 23; Walton's *Belshazzar's Feast*, Leeds, Oct. 8.
1932	18	Composes *Sinfonietta*, June 20–July 9; *Phantasy Quartet* for oboe, Sept.–Oct. Begins *A Boy Was Born* in Nov. *Phantasy Quintet* for strings perf. at RCM July 22 and (revised) in London on Dec. 12 at same concert as his three 2-part settings of poems by de la Mare.	A. Goehr born, Aug. 10; Sousa (77) dies, March 6. First perfs. of Ravel's Piano Concerto in G, Paris, Jan. 14; Delius's *Songs of Farewell*, London, Mar. 21: Vaughan Williams's *Magnificat*, Worcester, Sept. 8.
1933	19	*Sinfonietta* perf. in London, Jan 31. Meets	Penderecki born, Nov. 23; Duparc (85) dies, Feb. 13.

Schoenberg, Feb. 8.
Phantasy Quintet broadcast
on Feb. 17. Hears
Schoenberg's *Pierrot Lunaire*
in Nov. Completes *A Boy Was
Born* in May. Composes *Two
Part-Songs*, on June 6 and 8.
Wins Farrar Prize again in
July. *Phantasy Quartet*
broadcast on Aug. 6. Part-
songs and unfinished String
Quartet *Go play, boy, play*,
performed in London on Dec.
11. Passes A.RC.M.
examination on Dec. 13.
Begins work on *Simple
Symphony* on Dec. 23.

First perfs. of Bartók's Piano
Concerto No. 2, Frankfurt,
Jan. 23; Vaughan Williams's
Piano Concerto, Feb. 1;
Varèse's *Ionisation*, New
York, March 6; Strauss's
Arabella, Dresden, July 1;
Shostakovich's Piano
Concerto No. 1, Leningrad,
Oct. 15; Hitler comes to
power in Germany, Jan. 30.

1934	20	Finishes *Simple Symphony* on Feb. 10 and conducts first perf. in Norwich on March 6. *A Boy Was Born* broadcast on Feb. 23, its first performance. Hears Berg's *Wozzeck* (concert performance) on March 14. Goes to Florence for performance of his *Phantasy Oboe Quartet* at I.S.C.M. concert on April 5. His father dies on April 6. Writes *Te Deum* on July 17 and *Holiday Diary* on Oct. 11. Visits Europe, including Vienna, in October and November. Meets Erwin Stein in Vienna. Begins *Suite* for violin and piano, three movements of which are played in London on Dec. 17. *Phantasy Oboe Quartet* played in London on Nov. 21. Brief meeting with Peter Pears during this year.	Birtwistle born, July 15; Maxwell Davies born, Sept. 8. Elgar (76) dies, Feb. 23; Schreker (56) dies, March 21; Holst (59) dies, May 25; Delius (72) dies, June 10. First perfs. of Shostakovich's *Lady Macbeth of the Mtensk District*, Leningrad, Jan. 22, and Cello Sonata, Leningrad, Dec. 25; Hindemith's suite, *Mathis der Maler*, Berlin, March 12; Stravinsky's *Perséphone*, Paris, April 30; Rakhmaninov's *Rhapsody on a Theme of Paganini*, Baltimore, Nov. 7; Berg's *Lulu-Symphonie*, Berlin, Nov. 30; Walton's Symphony No. 1 (without finale), London, Dec. 3.
1935	21	Works as composer of music for G.P.O. Film Unit. Completes *Friday Afternoons* (begun in 1933). *Violin Suite*	Maw born, Nov. 5; Dukas (69) dies, May 17; Berg (50) dies, Dec. 24. First perfs. of Shostakovich's *Bright Stream*,

completed in June. First meeting with W.H. Auden on July 4. Collaborates with Auden in films *Night Mail* and *Coal Face*.

Leningrad, April 4; Bartók's Quartet No. 5, Washington, April 8; Vaughan Williams's Symphony No. 4, London, April 10; Strauss's *Die-schweigsame Frau*, Dresden, June 24; Gershwin's *Porgy and Bess*, Boston, Sept. 30; Walton's Symphony No. 1 (complete), London, Nov. 6; Prokofiev's Violin Concerto No. 2, Madrid, Dec. 1.

1936   22   Signs publishing contract with Boosey and Hawkes on Jan. 3. First performance of *Te Deum* on Jan. 27 in London. Revised version of *Go play, boy, play* performed in London on Feb. 25. Joins staff of G.P.O. Film Unit in March. *Violin Suite* broadcast March 6. Hears concert performance of Shostakovich's *Lady Macbeth of the Mtsensk District* in March. Goes to Barcelona in April for I.S.C.M. festival at which *Violin Suite* is played. Hears first performance of Berg's Violin Concerto in Barcelona on April 19. Begins *Our Hunting Fathers* on May 13, finishing it on July 23. First performance of *Our Hunting Fathers* at Norwich on Sept. 25. Arranges Rossini pieces as *Soirées Musicales*. His *Temporal Variations* for oboe and piano first performed on Dec. 15 in London.

Richard Rodney Bennett Born, March 29; Cardew born, May 7; Amy born, Aug. 29; Glazunov (70) dies, March 21; Respighi (56) dies, April 18. Spanish Civil War begins, July 18. First perfs. of Berg's Violin Concerto, Barcelona, April 19; Prokofiev's *Peter and the Wolf*, Moscow, May 2; Vaughan Williams's *Five Tudor Portraits*, Norwich Sept. 25, and *Dona Nobis Pacem*, Huddersfield, Oct. 2.

1937   23   B's mother dies on Jan. 31 Incidental music for Auden-Isherwood *The Ascent of F6* performed in Feb. Friendship with P. Pears begins in March. Begins *Variations on a Theme*

Widor (92) dies, March 12; Szymanowski (52) dies, March 28; Gershwin (39) dies, 11 July; Roussel (68) dies, Aug. 23; Ravel (62) dies, Dec. 28. First perfs. of of *Frank Bridge* on June 5 and completes it on July 12. First public performance of *Variations* at Salzburg on Aug. 27. Buys Old Mill at Snape, Suffolk, in autumn. Composes Auden songs *On This Island* in October. First performance of *On This Island* on Nov. 19 (broadcast). Completes *Mont Juic* in collaboration with L. Berkeley.

Schoenberg's String Quartet No. 4, Los Angeles, Jan. 9; Bartók's *Music for strings, percussion and celesta*, Basle, Jan. 21; Stravinsky's *Jeu de Cartes*, New York, April 27; Berg's *Lulu*, Zürich, June; Orff's *Carmina Burana*, Frankfurt, June 8; Shostakovich's Symphony No. 5, Leningrad, Nov. 21.

1938 24 Settles fully at Snape in April. Composes Cabaret Songs. Completes *Piano Concerto* on July 26 and is soloist in first performance at Henry Wood Prom. on Aug. 18. Writes music for two BBC features and incidental music for Priestley's *Johnson Over Jordan*. In autumn composes *Advance Democracy*. Begins *Les Illuminations*.

First perfs. of Bartók's Sonata for 2 pianos and percussion, Basle, Jan. 16; Stravinsky's 'Dumbarton Oaks' concerto, Washington, May 8; Hindemith's *Mathis der Maler* (opera), Zürich, May 28; Strauss's *Friedenstag*, Munich, July 24, and *Daphne*, Dresden, Oct. 15; Webern's String Quartet, Pittsburgh, Sept. 22; Shostakovich's String Quartet No. 1, Leningrad, Oct. 10.

1939 25 Completes *Ballad of Heroes* on March 29, a week before first performance on April 5 in London. Sails with Pears for N. America in May, spends several weeks in Canada and arrives in late June. At Woodstock, N.Y., composes *Young Apollo* between July 23 and 29. *Young Apollo* performed in Toronto on Aug. 27. Two songs from *Les Illuminations* sung in Birmingham and in London (Aug. 17). B. first stays with Mayer family at Amityville, Long Island, from Aug. 21. Completes *Violin Concerto* on Sept. 28 in Quebec. Completes *Les Illuminations*

Holliger born, May 21. First perfs. of Bartók's Violin Concerto No. 2, Amsterdam, March 23; Bliss's Piano Concerto, New York, June 10; Shostakovich's Symphony No. 6, Leningrad, Nov. 5; Walton's Violin Concerto, Cleveland, Dec. 7. Second World War begins, Sept. 3.

at Amityville on Oct. 25.
Completes *Canadian Carnival*
on Dec. 10.

1940 26 First performance of complete
Les Illuminations in London
on Jan. 30. B. seriously ill in
New York in February.
Composes *Sinfonia da
Requiem*. Violin Concerto
first performed on March 28
at New York Philharmonic
concert. Orchestrates
Chopin's *Les Sylphides* for
N.Y. Ballet Theatre.
Diversions composed for
Wittgenstein in summer in
Maine. *Seven Sonnets of
Michelangelo* completed at
Amityville on Oct. 30.
Composes *Introduction and
Rondo alla burlesca* in
November. B. and Pears move
into Auden's 'commune' at 7,
Middagh Street, Brooklyn
Heights, N.Y., in November.
Begins *Paul Bunyan*.

First perfs. of Finzi's *Dies
Natalis*, London, Jan. 26;
Tippett's Double String
Concerto, London, April 21;
Bartók's *Divertimento*, Basle,
June 11; Stravinsky's
Symphony in C, Chicago,
Nov. 7; Shostakovich's Piano
Quintet, Moscow, Nov. 23;
Schoenberg's Violin
Concerto, Philadelphia, Dec.
6.

1941 27 *Sinfonia da Requiem* first
performed by New York
Philharmonic on March 29.
Paul Bunyan performed in
Columbia University, N.Y.,
on May 5. In July goes to
Escondido, Calif., to stay with
Ethel Bartlett and Rae
Robertson, for whom he
writes *Mazurka Elegiaca*.
Writes String Quartet No. 1
in July. Reads Forster article
on Crabbe's poetry while in
California and decides to
write opera on subject of Peter
Grimes. *Mazurka Elegiaca*
performed in New York in
winter. Arranges five more
Rossini pieces as *Matinées
Musicales* for American Ballet

Frank Bridge (61) dies, Jan.
10; Paderewski (80) dies, June
29. First perfs. of
Rakhmaninov's *Symphonic
Dances*, Philadelphia, Jan. 3;
Bartók's String Quartet No.
6, New York, Jan. 20;
Hindemith's Cello Concerto,
Boston, Feb. 7; Walton's
Scapino, Chicago, April 3.

Company. String Quartet No.
1 played in Washington on
Oct. 30. Completes *Scottish
Ballad* on Oct. 27 and Bartlett
and Robertson play it in
Cincinnati on Nov. 28.

1942	28	Hears Koussevitzky conduct *Sinfonia da Requiem* in Boston on Jan. 2. Wittgenstein gives first performance of *Diversions* in Philadelphia on Jan. 16. Koussevitzky Musical Foundation agrees to commission opera from Britten. B. and Pears board ship in New York to return to England on March 16. During voyage Britten finishes composing *Hymn to St Cecilia* and composes *A Ceremony of Carols*. Arrives in Liverpool on April 17. Appears before conscientious objectors' tribunal and is exempted from military service. First London performance of *Sinfonia da Requiem* on July 22. First performance of *Seven Sonnets of Michelangelo* at Wigmore Hall, London, on Sept. 23. First (broadcast) performance of *Hymn to St Cecilia* on Nov. 22. First performance of *A Ceremony of Carols* at Norwich Castle on Dec. 5.	Zemlinsky (69) dies, March 16. First perfs. of Stravinsky's *Danses Concertantes*, Los Angeles, Feb. 8; Shostakovich's Symphony No. 7, Kuibishev, March 5; Finzi's *Let us Garlands Bring*, London, Oct. 12; Strauss's *Capriccio*, Munich, Oct. 28.
1943	29	Works with M. Slater on libretto of *Peter Grimes*. Composes *Prelude and Fugue* for strings in May. B. and Pears give first performance of Tippett's *Boyhood's End* in London in June. Completes *Rejoice in the Lamb* on July 17. Composes *Serenade*, which is first performed in	Rakhmaninov (69) dies, March 28. First perfs. of Prokofiev's Piano Sonata No. 7, Moscow, Jan. 18; Tippett's String Quartet No. 2, London, March 27; Shostakovich's Piano Sonata No. 2, Moscow, June 6, and Symphony No. 8, Moscow, Nov. 4; Strauss's Horn Concerto No. 2,

London on Oct. 15. Writes music for radio drama *The Rescue*, broadcast in November. Completes *The Ballad of Little Musgrave and Lady Barnard* on Dec. 13.

Salzburg, Aug. 11; Vaughan Williams's Symphony No. 5, London, June 24.

1944	30	Begins composition of *Peter Grimes* in January. Composes *Festival Te Deum* on Nov. 8 and 9. Composes two short items for BBC feature *Poet's Christmas*, broadcast in December.	Tavener born, Jan. 28; Sinigaglia (75) dies, May 16. First perfs. of Schoenberg's Piano Concerto, New York, Feb. 6; Tippett's *A Child of our Time*, London, March 19; Vaughan Williams's String Quartet No. 2, London, Oct. 12; Shostakovich's String Quartet No. 2, Leningrad, Nov. 14; Bartók's *Concerto for Orchestra*, Boston, Dec. 1; Prokofiev's Piano Sonata No. 8, Moscow, Dec. 30.
1945	31	Completes *Peter Grimes* in February at Snape. First performance of *Peter Grimes* in London on June 7. Begins *The Holy Sonnets of John Donne*. Visits Belsen and other concentration camps as accompanist to Menuhin in summer. Completes *Donne Sonnets* on Aug. 19. Completes *Second String Quartet* on Oct. 14. Begins work on *The Rape of Lucretia*. Composes music for MacNeice's radio play, *The Dark Tower*.	Mascagni (81) dies, Aug. 2; Webern (61) dies, Sept. 15; Bartók (64) dies, Sept. 26. First perfs. of Prokofiev's Symphony No. 5, Moscow, Jan. 13; Shostakovich's Symphony No. 9, Leningrad, Nov. 3. Second World War ends, Aug. 15
1946	32	*The Dark Tower* broadcast on Jan. 21. Conducts 1st performance of revised *Piano Concerto* at Cheltenham on July 2. Completes *The Rape of Lucretia*, which has first performance at Glyndebourne on July 12. With Pears, Crozier and Joan Cross, forms English Opera Group.	Falla (69) dies, Nov. 14. First perfs. of Stravinsky's *Symphony in Three Movements*, New York, Jan. 24, and *Ebony Concerto*, Hollywood, Dec. 1; Strauss's *Metamorphosen*, Zürich, Jan. 25; Bartók's Piano Concerto No. 3, Philadelphia, Feb. 8; Prokofiev's *War and Peace*

Returns to U.S.A. for American première of *Peter Grimes* at Tanglewood in August. Composes *The Young Person's Guide to the Orchestra*. Writes organ work, *Prelude and Fugue on a Theme of Vittoria* on Sept. 18. Begins work on *Albert Herring*.

(first vers.), Leningrad, June 12; Shostakovich's String Quartet No. 3 Moscow, Dec. 16.

1947	33	B. and Pears move into Crag House, Crabbe Street, Aldeburgh. *Albert Herring*, first performance at Glyndebourne on June 20. In July goes with English Opera Group to Holland and Switzerland. Decides to hold festival at Aldeburgh. Completes Canticle I, *My beloved is mine*, at Crag House on Sept. 12. Writes *A Charm of Lullabies* in December. Works on version of Gay's *The Beggar's Opera*.	Casella (63) dies, March 5. First perfs. of Walton's String Quartet, London, May 4; Prokofiev's Symphony No. 6, Leningrad, Oct. 11.
1948	34	Conducts first performance of *The Beggar's Opera* at Cambridge on May 24. Completes *Saint Nicolas* on May 31. First Aldeburgh Festival opens on June 5 with performance of *Saint Nicolas*. Suggests *Billy Budd* to E.M. Forster and E. Crozier as subject for his next major opera. Begins work on *The Little Sweep* and *Spring Symphony*.	Wolf-Ferrari (72) dies, Jan. 21; Lehár (78) dies, Oct. 24. First perfs. of Vaughan Williams's Symphony No. 6, London, April 21; Stravinsky's Mass, Milan, Oct. 27; Schoenberg's *A Survivor from Warsaw*, Albuquerque, Nov. 4.
1949	35	Discusses *Billy Budd* libretto in January. First performance of *Let's Make an Opera!* (*The Little Sweep*) at Aldeburgh Festival on June 14. *Spring Symphony* first performed on July 9 in Amsterdam. Recital tour of N. America with Pears	Turina (66) dies, Jan. 14; Pfitzner (80) dies, May 22; Strauss (85) dies, Sept. 8; Skalkottas (45) dies, Sept. 19. First perfs. of Walton's Violin Sonata, Zürich, Sept. 30; Bartók's Viola Concerto, Minneapolis, Dec. 2;

		from October until December.	Shostakovich's *Song of the Forests*, Leningrad, Dec. 15.
1950	36	Works on composition of *Billy Budd*. Composes *Five Flower Songs* in March and *Lachrymae* in April. Aldeburgh Festival in June.	Cilèa (84) dies, Nov. 20; Moeran (55) dies, Dec. 1. First perfs. of Strauss's *Four Last Songs*, London, May 22; Webern's *Zweite Kantate*, Brussels, June 23.
1951	37	First performance of B.'s edition of *Dido and Aeneas* at Hammersmith on May 1. With Pears, gives first performance of Tippett's *The Heart's Assurance* in May. Composes *Six Metamorphoses after Ovid* for performance in open-air at Thorpeness on June 14. Hon. Freeman of Lowestoft on July 28. Conducts first performance of *Billy Budd* at Covent Garden on Dec. 1.	Schoenberg (76) dies, July 13; Lambert (45) dies, Aug. 21; Medtner (71) dies, Nov. 13. First perfs. of Vaughan Williams's *The Pilgrim's Progress*, London, April 26; Stravinsky's *The Rake's Progress*, Venice, Sept. 11.
1952	38	Composes Canticle II, *Abraham and Isaac*, in January. Ski-ing holiday in Austria in March during which idea for Coronation opera is born. Work on *Gloriana* continues for rest of year. Aldeburgh Festival in June. Imogen Holst becomes B.'s music assistant.	Accession of Queen Elizabeth II, Feb. 6. First perfs. of Stravinsky's *Cantata*, Los Angeles, Nov. 11; Shostakovich's 24 *Preludes and Fugues*, Leningrad, Dec. 23.
1953	39	Completes *Gloriana* on March 13. Created Companion of Honour on June 1. First performance of *Gloriana* at Covent Garden on June 8. Composes *Winter Words* in September. Begins work with Myfanwy Piper on libretto of *The Turn of the Screw*.	Prokofiev (61) dies, March 5; Bax (69) dies, Oct. 3. First perfs. of Vaughan Williams's *Sinfonia Antartica*, Manchester, Jan. 14; Tippett's *Fantasia Concertante on a Theme of Corelli*, Edinburgh, Aug. 29; Shostakovich's Symphony No. 10, Leningrad, Dec. 17.
1954	40	Begins composing music of *The Turn of the Screw* in February. Conducts first	First perfs. of Stravinsky's Septet, Washington, Jan. 23, and *In Memoriam Dylan*

performance in Venice on Sept. 14. Completes Canticle III, *Still Falls The Rain*, on Nov. 27.

Thomas, Los Angeles, Sept. 20; Schoenberg's *Moses and Aaron* (concert), Hamburg, March 12; Vaughan Williams's *Hodie*, Worcester, Sept. 8; Walton's *Troilus and Cressida*, London, Dec. 3. Boulez composes *Le marteau sans maître*.

1955	41	Gives recitals with Pears in Belgium and Switzerland before ski-ing holiday in Zermatt where he writes *Alpine Suite*. Aldeburgh Festival in June. Leaves on world tour with Pears in November.	Honegger (63) dies, Nov. 27. First perfs. of Tippett's *The Midsummer Marriage*, London, Jan. 27; Bliss's Violin Concerto, London, May 11. Finzi's Cello Concerto, Cheltenham, July 19; Shostakovich's Violin Concerto No. 1, Leningrad, Oct. 29. Stockhausen composes *Gruppen*.
1956	42	Hears *gamelan* music in Bali in January. Attends Japanese Noh play *Sumidagawa* in Tokyo in February. Completes *Antiphon* on March 30. Summer holiday in Switzerland. In autumn completes ballet *The Prince of the Pagodas*. Tours Germany with Pears giving recitals in November.	Finzi (55) dies, Sept. 27. First perfs. of Vaughan Williams's Symphony No. 8, Manchester, May 2; Stravinsky's *Canticum sacrum*, Venice, Sept. 13; Shostakovich's String Quartet No. 6, Leningrad, Oct. 7.
1957	43	Conducts first performance of *The Prince of the Pagodas* at Covent Garden on Jan. 1. Elected honorary member of American Academy of Arts and Letters in April. With English Opera Group on tour of Canada from August to October. Completes *Songs from the Chinese* in autumn. Begins *Noye's Fludde* on Oct. 22. Moves into The Red House, Aldeburgh, in November. Completes *Noye's Fludde* on Dec. 15.	Sibelius (91) dies, Sept. 20; Korngold (60) dies, Nov. 29. First perfs. of Walton's Cello Concerto, Boston, Jan. 25; Poulenc's *The Carmelites*, Milan, Jan. 26; Schoenberg's *Moses and Aaron* (stage), Zürich, June 6; Stravinsky's *Agon*, Los Angeles, June 17; Shostakovich's Piano Concerto No. 2, Moscow, May 10, and Symphony No. 11, Moscow, Oct. 30.

279

1958	44	*Noye's Fludde* first performed in Orford Church, during Aldeburgh Festival, on June 18. Composes *Nocturne* in summer. Composes *Sechs Hölderlin-Fragmente* and plays in first performance on Nov. 14.	Vaughan Williams (85) dies, Aug. 26. First perfs. of Tippett's Symphony No. 2, London, Feb. 5; Vaughan Williams's Symphony No. 9, London, April 2; Stravinsky's *Threni*, Venice, Sept. 23.
1959	45	Composes *Cantata Academica* in March. *Missa brevis* completed in June. Visits Venice in summer. In October begins to compose *A Midsummer Night's Dream*.	Bloch (78) dies, July 15; Martinů (68) dies, Aug. 28; Villa-Lobos (72) dies, Nov. 17. First perf. of Shostakovich's Cello Concerto No. 1, Leningrad, Oct. 4.
1960	46	Completes *A Midsummer Night's Dream* on April 15. Conducts its first performance in Aldeburgh on June 11. Revises *Billy Budd* from four acts to two. First meets Shostakovich and Rostropovich in September and begins to compose *Cello Sonata*. Revised *Billy Budd* broadcast on Nov. 13.	Benjamin (66) dies, April 10; Seiber (55) dies, Sept. 25. First perfs. of Stravinsky's *Movements*, New York, Jan. 10; Shostakovich's String Quartet No. 7, Leningrad, May 15, and No. 8, Leningrad, Oct 2; Walton's Symphony No. 2, Edinburgh, Sept. 2.
1961	47	Completes *Cello Sonata* in January. Composes *Jubilate Deo* in February. With Rostropovich, gives first performance of *Cello Sonata*, Aldeburgh, July 7. Composes *War Requiem*, which he completes on Dec. 20.	Grainger (78) dies, Feb. 20. First perfs. of Henze's *Elegy for Young Lovers*, Schwetzingen, May 20; Shostakovich's Symphony No. 12, Moscow, Oct 15.
1962	48	Completes *Psalm 150* on May 1. First performance of *War Requiem* in Coventry Cathedral on May 30. Made Hon. Freeman of Aldeburgh on Oct. 22. Completes *A Hymn of St Columba* on Dec. 29.	Ibert (71) dies, Feb. 5; Ireland (82) dies, June 12. First perfs. of Bliss's *The Beatitudes*, Coventry, May 25; Tippett's *King Priam*, Coventry, May 29; Stravinsky's *The Flood*, New York (TV), June 14; Shostakovich's Symphony No. 13, Moscow, Dec. 18.
1963	49	Visits Soviet Union for festival of British music in March.	Poulenc (64) dies, Jan. 30. Hindemith (68) dies, Dec. 28.

Composes *Cello Symphony*, completing it on May 3. Completes *Cantata Misericordium* on May 25 and *Nocturnal after John Dowland* on Nov. 11. On night of fiftieth birthday, Nov. 22, *Gloriana* has concert performance in London. Tippett's *Concerto for Orchestra* dedicated to Britten.

First perf. of Walton's *Variations on a Theme of Hindemith*, London, March 8.

1964   50   Visits Venice in February to work on *Curlew River*. Conducts first performance of *Cello Symphony* in Moscow on March 12. Completes *Curlew River* on April 2. First performance of it in Orford Church, during Aldeburgh Festival, on June 12. Goes to Aspen, Colorado, to receive first Aspen Award on July 31. Goes with English Opera Group to Russia in October for performances of three of his chamber operas. Awarded Gold Medal of Royal Philharmonic Society. Composes first *Cello Suite* in November and December.

First perfs. of Mahler's Symphony No. 10 (in Cooke performing vers.), London, Aug. 13; Stravinsky's *Abraham and Isaac*, Jerusalem, Aug. 21; Shostakovich's String Quartets Nos. 9 and 10, Moscow, Nov. 20.

1965   51   Appointed member of the Order of Merit on March 23. New works published by Faber henceforward. Visits India and begins to compose *Gemini Variations*, completing them in Aldeburgh in March. Completes *Songs and Proverbs of William Blake* on April 6. In July, writes *Voices For Today*. Flies on Aug. 3 to Armenia for holiday. Composes *The Poet's Echo*, completing it in Dilidjan on

First perfs. of R.R. Bennett's *The Mines of Sulphur*, London, Feb. 24; Henze's *The Young Lord*, Berlin, April 7.

Aug. 23.

1966	52	Has abdominal operation in February. Completes *The Burning Fiery Furnace* in Aldeburgh on April 5. Visits Austria for song recitals with Pears in May. First Russian performance of *War Requiem* on May 23. Rewrites *Sweet was the Song the Virgin Sung* (1931) for performance at Aldeburgh Festival on June 15. Completes *The Golden Vanity* on Aug. 26. *Gloriana* (slightly revised) revived with success at Sadler's Wells on Oct. 21. Completes *Hankin Booby* in Aldeburgh on Dec. 11. Goes to Moscow and Leningrad and spends Christmas with Shostakovich and Rostropovich.	First perfs. of Tippett's *The Vision of St Augustine*, London, Jan. 19; Shostakovich's String Quartet No. 11, Leningrad, May 28, and Cello Concerto No. 2, Moscow, Sept. 25; Henze's *The Bassarids*, Salzburg, Aug. 6; Barber's *Antony and Cleopatra*, New York, Sept. 16; Stravinsky's *Requiem Canticles*, Princeton, Oct. 8.
1967	53	Conducts opening concert at Queen Elizabeth Hall, London, including first performance of *Hankin Booby*, on March 1. Completes *The Building of the House* on March 16 and *The Oxen* on April 19. *The Prince of the Pagodas* performed in Vienna in May. The Queen opens The Maltings concert hall at Snape on June 2. B. completes *Second Cello Suite* on Aug. 17. Goes to Montreal with English Opera Group in September and then to New York and South America for recitals with Pears. Re-writes *The Sycamore Tree* and *A Wealden Trio* in November.	Kodály (84) dies, March 6. First perfs. of Walton's *The Bear*, Aldeburgh, June 3; Shostakovich's Violin Concerto No. 2, Moscow, Sept. 26.
1968	54	Visits Venice in March to work on *The Prodigal Son*. Returns to England, falls seriously ill, but completes	Castelnuovo-Tedesco (72) dies, March 15. First perfs. of Birtwistle's *Punch and Judy*, Aldeburgh, June 9;

The Prodigal Son on April 22. In summer re-writes *Tit for Tat* song-cycle. Many Britten performances at Edinburgh Festival in August and September. Completes *Children's Crusade* on Nov. 10.

Shostakovich's String Quartet No. 12, Leningrad, Sept. 14. Berio (43) composes *Sinfonia*; Stockhausen (40) composes *Aus den sieben Tagen*; Lutosławski (55) composes *Livre pour orchestre*.

1969   55   Conducts *Peter Grimes* for television in February. Begins to compose *Owen Wingrave*. Completes *Suite for Harp* on March 18 and re-writes *Five Walztes* for piano. The Maltings burns down on June 7, opening night of Aldeburgh Festival. Composes *Who are these children?* in summer. Gives recitals with Pears in New York and Boston in autumn in aid of rebuilding The Maltings.

First perfs. of Maxwell Davies's *Eight Songs for a Mad King*, London, April 22; Penderecki's *The Devils of Loudun*, Hamburg, June 20; Tavener's *Celtic Requiem*, London, July 16; Shostakovich's Symphony No. 14, Leningrad, Sept. 29. Cage composes *Cheap Imitation*.

1970   56   Buys Chapel House, Horham, as Suffolk retreat. Goes to Australia with English Opera Group in spring. Gives recitals with Pears in New Zealand. The Maltings reopened on June 7 for start of Aldeburgh Festival. Conducts first European performance of Shostakovich's 14th Symphony in The Maltings on June 14. Conducts television recording of *Owen Wingrave* in November.

Gerhard (73) dies, Jan. 5. First perfs. of Walton's *Improvisations on an Impromptu of Benjamin Britten*, San Francisco, Jan. 14; R.R. Bennett's *Victory*, London, April 13; Bliss's Cello Concerto, Aldeburgh, June 24 (cond. by Britten); Shostakovich's String Quartet No. 13, Leningrad, Sept. 13; Tippett's *Songs for Dov*, London, Oct. 12, and *The Knot Garden*, London, Dec. 2.

1971   57   Completes Canticle IV, *Journey of the Magi*, in January. *Third Cello Suite* composed between Feb. 23 and March 3. Accompanies Pears in first performance of seven of songs from *Who are these children?* at Cardiff on March 7. Visits Moscow and

Stravinsky (88) dies, April 6; Rawsthorne (66) dies, July 26. Ligeti (48) composes *Melodien*; Birtwistle (37) composes *The Fields of Sorrow*; Bedford (34) composes *Star Clusters, Nebulae and Places in Devon*.

Leningrad for British music
week in April. First complete
performance of *Who are these
children?* in Edinburgh on
May 4. *Owen Wingrave*
shown on BBC TV on May
16. Conducts Elgar's *The
Dream of Gerontius* at
Aldeburgh Festival on June 9
and later records it. Visit to
Venice in October, where he
begins serious work on *Death
in Venice.*

1972 58 Visits Schloss Wolfsgarten in
March to work on *Death in
Venice.* 25th Aldeburgh
Festival opens on June 11. B.
conducts *The Turn of the
Screw* on June 16. Conducts
recording of Schumann's
Scenes from Goethe's Faust in
September. Works on *Death
in Venice* in spite of increasing
ill-health.

First perfs. of Shostakovich's
Symphony No. 15, Moscow,
Jan. 8; Birtwistle's *The
Triumph of Time*, London,
June 1; Tippett's Symphony
No. 3, London, June 22;
Maxwell Davies's *Taverner*,
London, July 12.

1973 59 Visits Schloss Wolfsgarten in
March. Completes full score
of *Death in Venice* at home in
March. Operation to replace
heart valve in London on May
8. First stage performance of
Owen Wingrave at Covent
Garden on May 10. Leaves
hospital on June 1 to
convalesce at Horham. First
performance of *Death in
Venice* at The Maltings on
June 16. Hears broadcast of
performance of *Death in
Venice* on June 22. Sees *Death
in Venice* at The Maltings in
a special performance on Sept.
12. Goes to Wales with Pears
in October. Attends first
Covent Garden performance
of *Death in Venice* on Oct. 18.
Widespread tributes to him in

Malipiero (91) dies, Aug. 1.
First perfs. of Tippett's Piano
Sonata No. 3, Bath, May 26;
Shostakovich's String Quartet
No. 14, Leningrad, Nov. 12.

press and on radio and
television on his 60th birthday
on Nov. 22.

1974 60   Begins to revise String Quartet in D (1931). Attends recording of *Death in Venice* at The Maltings at Easter. Begins to revise *Paul Bunyan* (1941) in summer after holiday at Barcombe, Sussex. Composes Canticle V, *The Death of St Narcissus*, at Horham in July. Visits Schloss Wolfsgarten and begins to compose *Suite on English Folk Tunes*, completing it in Suffolk on Nov. 16. Awarded Ravel Prize. First performance of *Third Cello Suite* at Snape on Dec. 21. Begins *Sacred and Profane* in December.

Milhaud (81) dies, June 22; Frank Martin (84) dies, Nov. 21. First perfs. of Tavener's *Ultimos Ritos*, Haarlem, June 23; Shostakovich's String Quartet No. 15, Leningrad, Nov. 15.

1975 61   Completes *Sacred and Profane* in January. Completes *A Birthday Hansel* on March 21. Canal holiday in Oxfordshire in May. At Aldeburgh Festival in June, *Death in Venice* is performed. First public performance of 1931 String Quartet on June 7. First performance of *Suite on English Folk Tunes* on June 13. Goes to Covent Garden for *Death in Venice* on July 7 and *Peter Grimes* on July 9. Completes *Phaedra* on Aug. 12. First performance of *Sacred and Profane* at Snape on Sept. 14. Begins to compose *Third String Quartet* in October. Visits Venice in November and completes quartet.

Dallapiccola (71) dies, Feb. 19; Bliss (83) dies, April 26; Shostakovich (68) dies, Aug. 9. First perfs. of Shostakovich's *Suite on Verses of Michelangelo Buonarroti*, Leningrad, Jan. 23, and Moscow, Oct. 12 (with orch.), and Viola Sonata, Leningrad, Oct. 1; R.R. Bennett's *Spells*, Worcester, Aug. 28.

1976 62   BBC broadcasts revised *Paul Bunyan* on Feb. 1. B. arranges

First perfs. of Shostakovich's *The Dreamers*, Moscow, Jan.

(Britten was 63 on Nov. 22, twelve days before his death)

Lachrymae with orch. in February. First British stage performance of *Paul Bunyan* at The Maltings on June 4. Created life peer on June 12. First performance of *Phaedra* at Snape on June 16. Arranges *Eight Folk Songs* for voice and harp in summer. Goes to Bergen for holiday in summer and begins work on Sitwell cantata *Praise We Great Men.* Completes *Welcome Ode* in August. Amadeus Quartet play *Third String Quartet* to B. in library of The Red House on Sept. 28 and 29. Works on *Praise We Great Men* (left unfinished) in November. Reaches 63rd birthday on Nov. 22. Dies at The Red House on Dec. 4. Buried in Aldeburgh cemetery, near Parish Church, on Dec. 7. First performance of *Third String Quartet* at Snape on Dec. 19.

19; Burgon's *Requiem,* Hereford, Aug. 26

Appendix B

Classified list of works

(BH = Boosey & Hawkes; FM = Faber Music; N = Novello; OUP = Oxford University Press. Works unmarked are not published.)

Stage Works

(A) Operas

1940–1 *Paul Bunyan*, op. 17, operetta in 2 acts and prologue. Libretto by W.H. Auden. Rev. 1974. F.p. New York, 5 May 1941. F.p. rev. vers. BBC, 1 Feb. 1976; (stage) Snape, 4 June 1976, f. London p. 1 Sept. 1976. (FM)

1944–5 *Peter Grimes*, op. 33, opera in 3 acts and prologue. Libretto by Montagu Slater, based on poem by Crabbe. F.p. London, 7 June 1945. (BH)

1945–6 *The Rape of Lucretia*, op. 37, opera in 2 acts. Libretto by Ronald Duncan, after play by Obey. Rev. 1947. F.p. Glyndebourne, 12 July 1946, f.p. rev. vers., Glyndebourne, 7 July 1947. F. London p. 28 August 1946. (BH)

1947 *Albert Herring*, op. 39, comic opera in 3 acts. Libretto by Eric Crozier, freely adapted from story by Maupassant. F.p. Glyndebourne, 20 June 1947, f. London p. 6 Nov. 1957. (BH)

1949 *The Little Sweep*, op. 45, children's opera in 3 scenes. Libretto by Eric Crozier, being second part of *Let's Make an Opera!*, entertainment for young people. F.p. Aldeburgh, 14 June 1949, f. London p. 8 Oct. 1957. (BH)

1950–1 *Billy Budd*, op. 50, opera in 4 acts (orig. vers.). Libretto by E. M. Forster and Eric Crozier, from story by Herman Melville. Rev. as 2 acts 1960. F.p. (orig.) London, 1 Dec. 1951, f.p. rev. vers. BBC radio, 13 Nov. 1960; stage, London, 9 Jan. 1964. (BH)

1952–3 *Gloriana*, op. 53, opera in 3 acts. Libretto by William Plomer. Rev. 1966. F.p. London, 8 June 1953, f.p. rev. vers. London, 21 Oct. 1966. (BH)

1954 *The Turn of the Screw*, op. 54, opera in 2 acts and prologue.

Libretto by Myfanwy Piper, after story by Henry James. F.p. Venice, 14 Sept. 1954, f. Eng. p. London, 6 Oct. 1954. (BH)

1957   *Noye's Fludde*, op. 59, Chester Miracle Play set for adult and child performers in 1 act. F.p. Orford, 18 June 1958, f. London p. 14 Nov. 1958. (BH)

1959–60   *A Midsummer Night's Dream*, op. 64, opera in 3 acts. Libretto, adapted from Shakespeare, by Benjamin Britten and Peter Pears. F.p. Aldeburgh, 11 June 1960, f. London p. 2 Feb. 1961. (BH)

1970   *Owen Wingrave*, op. 85, opera in 2 acts. Libretto by Myfanwy Piper, after story by Henry James. F.p. (TV) 16 May 1971, f. stage p. London, 10 May 1973. (FM)

1971–3   *Death in Venice*, op. 88, opera in 2 acts. Libretto by Myfanwy Piper, after *novella* by Thomas Mann. F.p. Snape, 16 June 1973, f. London p. 18 Sept. 1973. (FM)

(B) Parables for Church Performance

1964   *Curlew River*, op. 71. Libretto by William Plomer. F.p. Orford, 12 June 1964, f. London p. 13 July 1964. (FM)

1966   *The Burning Fiery Furnace*, op. 77. Libretto by William Plomer. F.p. Orford, 9 June 1966; f. London p. 24 July 1967. (FM)

1968   *The Prodigal Son*, op. 81. Libretto by William Plomer. F.p. Orford, 10 June 1968, f. London p. 13 July 1968. (FM)

(C) Incidental Music

1. Plays

1935   *Timon of Athens* (Shakespeare). F.p. London, Westminster Theatre, 19 Nov. 1935.

Easter 1916 (M. Slater). F.p. Islington, Town Hall, 4 Dec. 1935.

1936   *Stay Down Miner* (Slater). F.p. London, Westminster Theatre, 10 May 1936.

The Agamemnon (Aeschylus, tr. L. MacNeice). F.p. London, Westminster Theatre, 1 Nov. 1936.

1937   *The Ascent of F6* (Auden and Isherwood). F.p. London, Mercury Theatre, 26 Feb. 1937 (includes *Funeral Blues*).

Pageant of Empire (Slater). F.p. London, Collins's Music Hall, 28 Feb. 1937.

Out of the Picture (MacNeice). F.p. London, Westminster Theatre,

5 Dec. 1937 (includes 'Sleep and Wake' for soprano and chorus in which soloist was Sophie Wyss).

1938   *Spain* (Slater). F.p. London, Mercury Theatre, 22 June 1938.

On the Frontier (Auden and Isherwood). F.p. Cambridge, Arts Theatre, 14 Nov. 1938. F. London p. Globe Theatre, 12 Feb. 1939.

They Walk Alone (Max Catto). Organ only. F.p. London, 'Q' Theatre, 21 Nov. 1938.

1939   *Johnson over Jordan* (J.B. Priestley). F.p. London, New Theatre, 22 Feb. 1939.

1945   *This Way to the Tomb* (R. Duncan). F.p. London, Mercury Theatre, 11 Oct. 1945.

1946   *The Eagle Has Two Heads* (J. Cocteau, tr. R. Duncan). F.p. Hammersmith, Lyric Theatre, 4 Sept. 1946.

The Duchess of Malfi (J. Webster, adapted by Auden). F.p. Providence, Rhode Island, Metropolitan Theatre, 20 Sept. 1946. F. New York p. Ethel Barrymore Theatre, 15 Oct. 1946.

1949   *Stratton* (Duncan). F.p. Brighton, Theatre Royal, 31 Oct. 1949.

1954   *Am Stram Gram* (André Roussin). F.p. London, Toynbee Hall Theatre, 4 Mar. 1954.

1955   *The Punch Revue* (compiled R. Duncan). F.p. London, Duke of York's Theatre, 28 Sept. 1955. Britten's contributions were two songs – *Tell me the truth about love* (1938, Auden) and *Old friends are best* (1955, W. Plomer) – and a waltz for piano based on the second song.

2. Films
1935   *The King's Stamp* (GPO Film Unit). April–May.

Coal Face (GPO Film Unit). Verses by M. Slater and by Auden, whose 'O lurcher-loving collier' Britten set. May–June.

Telegrams (GPO Film Unit). Not used. July.

The Tocher (GPO Film Unit). Rossini arrangements. July.

C.T.O. – the Story of the Central Telegraph Office (GPO Film Unit). July.

Gas Abstract (British Commercial Gas Assoc.). Not used. Aug.–Sept.

God's Chillun (GPO Film Unit). Sept.–Nov. Not used until *c.* 1937.

Men Behind the Meters (British Commercial Gas Assoc.). Sept.

Dinner Hour (British Commercial Gas Assoc.). Sept.

Title Music III (British Commercial Gas Assoc.). Not used. Sept.

How the Dial Works. (GPO Film Unit). Sept.

Conquering Space – the Story of Modern Communications (GPO Film Unit). Sept.

Sorting Office (GPO Film Unit). Not used. Sept.

The Savings Bank (GPO Film Unit). Sept.

The New Operator (Empire Marketing Board Film Unit/GPO Film Unit). Not used. Sept.

Night Mail (GPO Film Unit). Verse by Auden ('This is the night mail crossing the border') set by Britten. Nov. 1935–Jan. 1936.

1936   *Calendar of the Year* (GPO Film Unit). March, Sept.–Oct.

Peace of Britain (Strand Films). March.

Around the Village Green (Travel & Industrial Development Assoc.). April, Sept.–Oct.

Men of the Alps (GPO Film Unit/Pro Telephon, Zürich). Includes music by Rossini, arr. Britten, and Walter Leigh. Sept.–Oct.

Line to the Tschierva Hut (GPO Film Unit/Pro Telephon, Zürich). Sept.–Nov.

Message from Geneva (GPO Film Unit/Pro Telephon, Zürich). Sept.–Nov.

Four Barriers (GPO Film Unit/Pro Telephon, Zürich). Music also by J.H. Foulds. Sept.–Nov.

The Saving of Bill Blewitt (GPO Film Unit). Oct.

Love from a Stranger (Trafalgar Films). Britten's only score for a feature film, in which Ann Harding and Basil Rathbone acted. First shown, London, 7 Jan. 1937. Conductor, Boyd Neel.

The Way to the Sea (Strand Films). Verse by Auden. Dec.

1937   *Book Bargain* (GPO Film Unit).

1938   *Mony a Pickle* (GPO Film Unit). Music also by Foulds and Victor Yates.

Advance Democracy (Realistic Film Unit).

1945   *The Instruments of the Orchestra* (Crown Film Unit). Script by

Montagu Slater. Produced for Ministry of Education and first shown at Empire, Leicester Square, London, on 29 Nov. 1946. Music performed by LSO, cond. Sargent. Concert version, *The Young Person's Guide to the Orchestra*, has script by Eric Crozier.

3. Radio

1937   *King Arthur* (BBC, by D.G. Bridson). F.p. 23 April 1937, cond. Clarence Raybould. (Some of this score was used in 1945 in *Impromptu*, the substitute slow movement of the Piano Concerto). March–April.

Up the Garden Path (BBC, by W.H. Auden). 'Elaborate and light-hearted leg-pull' on bad verse and bad music. F.p. 13 June 1937.

The Company of Heaven (BBC, compiled by R. Ellis Roberts). F.p. 29 Sept. 1937. S. Wyss (sop.), P. Pears (ten.), BBC Chorus and Orch., cond. Trevor Harvey, Aug.–Sept.

Hadrian's Wall (BBC, by Auden). Includes setting of Auden's 'Roman Wall Blues'. F.p. 25 Nov. 1937, cond. Britten. Nov.

1938   *Lines on the Map* (BBC). Four programmes by various authors broadcast between Jan. and April. Jan.

The Chartists' March (BBC, by J.H. Miller). F.p. 13 May 1938, cond. Britten. April–May.

The World of the Spirit (BBC, compiled by R. Ellis Roberts). F.p. 5 June 1938. S. Wyss (sop.), A. Wood (cont.), E. Bebb (ten.), V. Harding (bass), BBC Singers & Orch., cond. Trevor Harvey. April–May.

1939   *The Sword in the Stone* (BBC, by M. Helweg from T.H. White's novel). F.p. in six episodes, 11 June–16 July 1939. BBC Singers & Orch., cond. Leslie Woodgate. April–May.

1940   *The Dark Valley* (CBS, New York, by Auden). F.p. 2 June 1940, cond. Bernard Herrmann. A monologue for Dame May Whitty.

The Dynasts (CBS, New York, by Thomas Hardy). F.p. late 1940. Score lost.

1941   *The Rocking-Horse Winner* (CBS, New York, by Auden and James Stern from D.H. Lawrence's story). F.p. 6 April 1941, cond. B. Herrmann.

1942   *Appointment* (BBC). F.p. 20 July 1942.

An American in England (CBS, New York/BBC, London). Six programmes by Norman Corwin, produced by Edward R. Murrow, telling America about wartime Britain. Music performed by RAF Orch., cond. R.P. O'Donnell (with Dennis Brain as first horn): 1. London by Clipper, 27 July 1942; 2. London to Dover, 10 Aug.; 3. Ration Island, 17 Aug.; 4. Women of Britain, 24 Aug.; 5. The Yanks are Here, 31 Aug.; 6. The Anglo-American Angle, 7 Sept.

The Man Born to be King (BBC, by Dorothy L. Sayers). Dramatized series on life of Christ for which Britten composed 'Bring me garlands, bring me wine' for male-voice chorus for episode 10, 'The Princes of the World' (broadcast 23 Aug. 1942) and song for female voice, 'Soldier, soldier, why will you roam?' for episode 11, 'King of Sorrows' (broadcast 20 Sept. 1942).

Lumberjacks of America (BBC London/New York, by R. MacDougall). F.p. 24 Aug. 1942, cond. Britten.

Britain to America (BBC London for NBC New York, by MacNeice). Twenty-two programmes in two series for which Britten composed music for I, No. 9 'Britain through American Eyes' (20 Sept. 1942, LSO/Mathieson), II, No. 4 'Where Do I Come In?' (7 Nov. 1942), II, No. 13 'Where Do We Go From Here?' (3 Jan. 1942).

1943   *The Four Freedoms: Pericles* (BBC, by MacNeice). F.p. 21 Feb. 1943.

The Rescue (BBC, by Edward Sackville-West). Epic drama in two parts based on Homer's *Odyssey*. F.p. 25 and 26 Nov. 1943, BBC Symphony Orch., cond. C. Raybould.

1944   *A Poet's Christmas* (BBC, by Auden, MacNeice, Day Lewis, E. Sitwell, etc.). Britten set two Auden texts, *A Shepherd's Carol* and *Chorale* (see under *Unaccompanied Chorus*). F.p. 24 Dec. 1944, BBC Singers, cond. L. Woodgate.

1946   *The Dark Tower* (BBC, by MacNeice). F.p. 21 Jan. 1946, cond. Walter Goehr.

1947   *Men of Goodwill: the Reunion of Christmas* (BBC, compiled by L. Gilliam and L. Cottrell). Set of variations on 'God rest you merry, gentlemen' (see under *Orchestral (D)*). F.p. 25 Dec. 1947, LSO cond. Goehr (FM).

(D) Ballet

1956   *The Prince of the Pagodas*, op. 57, ballet in 3 acts by John Cranko. F.p. London, 1 Jan. 1957. (BH).

Orchestral

(A) Symphonies

1932   *Sinfonietta*, op. 1. Chamber orchestra. F.p. London, 31 Jan. 1933. (BH).

1940   *Sinfonia da Requiem*, op. 20. F.p. New York, 29 Mar. 1941, f. London p. 22 July 1942. F.p. orig. version Birmingham, 2 Feb. 1989. (BH)

(B) For Strings

1933–4   *Simple Symphony*, op. 4. F.p. Norwich, 6 Mar. 1934. (OUP)

1937   *Variations on a Theme of Frank Bridge*, op. 10. F.p. Radio Hilversum, 25 Aug. 1937, f. public p. Salzburg, 27 Aug. 1937, f. London p. 5 Oct. 1937. (BH)

1943   *Prelude and Fugue* for 18-part string orchestra, op. 29. F.p. London, 23 June 1943. (BH)

(C) Solo Instrument and Orchestra

1938   Piano Concerto in D, op. 13. F.p. London, 18 Aug. 1938. Rev. (new 3rd movement) 1945. F.p. of rev. vers. Cheltenham, 2 July 1946. (BH)

1939   *Young Apollo*, op. 16, for pianoforte, string quartet and strings. F.p. Toronto, 27 Aug. 1939, f. Europ. p. Snape, 20 June 1979. (FM) Violin Concerto, op. 15. F.p. New York, 28 Mar. 1940, f. London p. 6 Apr. 1941. Rev. 1950 (f.p. London, 12 Dec. 1951) and 1958. (BH)

1940   *Diversions*, op. 21. Pianoforte (left hand) and orchestra. F.p. Philadelphia, 16 Jan. 1942, f. Eng. p. Bournemouth, 14 Oct. 1950, F. London p. 29 Oct. 1950. Rev. 1954. (BH)

1941   *Scottish Ballad*, op. 26. Two pianofortes and orchestra, F.p. Cincinnati, 28 Nov. 1941, f. Eng. p. London, 10 July 1943. (BH)

1962–3   *Symphony for Cello and Orchestra*, op. 68. F.p. Moscow, 12 Mar. 1964; f. Eng. p. Aldeburgh, 18 June 1964, f. London p. 15 July 1964. (BH)

1976   *Lachrymae*, op. 48a. Viola and small string orchestra. Arr. of work for viola and piano (1950, see *Chamber Music*). F.p. Recklinghausen, 3 May 1977, f. Eng. p. Snape, 21 June 1977, f. London p. 12 Oct. 1977. (BH)

(D) Miscellaneous

1928   *Humoreske in C.* F.p. (BBC broadcast) 2 Oct. 1985.

1936   *Soirées Musicales*, op. 9, Suite from Rossini. (BH)
        Russian Funeral, march for brass and percussion. F.p. London 8
        Mar. 1936. (FM)

1937   *Mont Juic*, op. 12 (with Lennox Berkeley whose op. 9 it is). Suite
        of Catalan Dances. F.p. (broadcast) London, 8 Jan. 1938. (BH)

1939   *Canadian Carnival (Kermesse Canadienne)*, op. 19. F.p. (broadcast)
        Bristol, BBC, 6 June 1940, f. concert p. Cheltenham, 13 June 1945.
        (BH)

1941   *Matinées Musicales*, op. 24, 2nd Suite from Rossini. (Written for
        Balanchine ballet.) (BH)
        Overture, Paul Bunyan (not used in New York production). Orch.
        Colin Matthews. F. concert p. London, 6 Aug. 1978. (FM)
        An American Overture. F.p. Birmingham, 8 Nov. 1983. (FM)

1945   *Four Sea Interludes* from *Peter Grimes*, op. 33a (1. Dawn. 2. Sunday
        Morning. 3. Moonlight. 4. Storm.) F. concert p. Cheltenham, 13
        June 1945. (BH)
        Passacaglia from *Peter Grimes*, op. 33b. (BH)

1946   *The Young Person's Guide to the Orchestra*, op. 34, Variations and
        Fugue on a Theme of Henry Purcell, for speaker and orchestra,
        or orchestra alone. (See also *Stage Works* (C) Incidental Music
        (Films)). F.p. Liverpool, 15 Oct. 1946, f. London p. 17 Nov. 1946.
        (BH)
        Occasional Overture in C, op. 38 (withdrawn), for orchestra. F.p.
        London (BBC broadcast) 29 Sept. 1946. (FM)

1947   *Men of Goodwill: Variations on a Christmas Carol.* See under *Stage
        Works* (C) Incidental Music (Films). (FM)

1953   *Variation 4* of *Variations on an Elizabethan Theme (Sellenger's
        Round)* composed by six contemporary British composers to mark
        coronation of Elizabeth II. Other variations on the theme (Byrd)
        were by Arthur Oldham (Var. 1), Tippett (Var. 2), L. Berkeley
        (Var. 3), Searle (Var. 5), Walton (Var. 6). F.p. Aldeburgh, 20 June
        1953 (cond. Britten). Britten's variation, 'Quick and gay', includes
        quotation from *Gloriana*.

1953–4 *Symphonic Suite 'Gloriana'*, op. 53a. Orchestra and opt. tenor solo.
        (1. The Tournament. 2. The Lute Song – tenor solo may be
        replaced by oboe. 3. The Courtly Dances – may be performed
        separately. 4. Gloriana moritura.) F.p. Birmingham, 23 Sept. 1954.
        (BH)

1956   *Pas de Six* from *'The Prince of the Pagodas'*, op. 57a. F.p.
        Birmingham, 26 Sept. 1957. (BH)

1967   *The Building of the House*, op. 79, overture with or without chorus.
        F.p. Snape, 2 June 1967, f. London p. 16 Jan. 1968. (FM)

1974   *Suite on English Folk Tunes, 'A Time There Was...'*, op. 90. (1.
        Cakes and Ale. 2. The Bitter Withy. 3. Hankin Booby. 4. Hunt
        the Squirrel. 5. Lord Melbourne.) F.p. Snape, 13 June 1975, f.
        London p. 17 Sept. 1975. F.p. of No. 3, London, 1 Mar. 1967.
        (FM)

Chorus and Orchestra

1937   *Pacifist March*. Text by R. Duncan. (Peace Pledge Union).

1939   *Ballad of Heroes*, op. 14. Tenor (or soprano), chorus and orchestra.
        Text by R. Swingler and W.H. Auden. (1. Funeral March. 2.
        Scherzo (Dance of Death). 3. Recitative and Choral. 4. Epilogue
        (Funeral March).) F.p. London, 5 Apr. 1939. (BH)

1948   *Saint Nicolas*, op. 42, cantata for tenor, chorus, women's semi-
        chorus, 4 boy singers, strings, piano duet, percussion, and organ.
        F.p. Aldeburgh, 5 June 1948, f. London p. 23 June 1949. (BH)

1949   *Spring Symphony*, op. 44. Soprano, alto and tenor, chorus, boys'
        choir and orchestra. (1. Introduction – The Merry Cuckoo –
        Spring – The Driving Boy – The Morning Star. 2. Welcome, Maids
        of Honour – Waters above – Out on the lawn. 3. When will my
        May come – Fair and fair – Sound the Flute. 4. Finale: London,
        to thee I do present.) F.p. Amsterdam, 9 July 1949, f. London p.
        9 Mar. 1950. (BH)

1959   *Cantata Academica, Carmen Basiliense*, op. 62. Soprano, alto, tenor
        and bass, chorus and orchestra. Latin text compiled by Bernhard
        Wyss. F.p. Basle, 1 July 1960, f. London p. 10 Mar. 1961. (BH)

1961   *War Requiem*, op. 66. Soprano, tenor and baritone, chorus,
        orchestra, chamber orchestra, boys' choir and organ. Text from
        Latin Mass for the Dead and poems of Wilfred Owen. F.p.
        Coventry, 30 May 1962, f. London p. 6 Dec. 1962. (BH)

1962   *Psalm 150*, op. 67. Two-part children's voices and instruments. F.
        public p. Aldeburgh, 24 June 1963. (BH)

1963   *Cantata Misericordium*, op. 69. Tenor and baritone, small chorus,
        string quartet, string orchestra, piano, harp and timpani. Latin
        text by Patrick Wilkinson. F.p. Geneva, 1 Sept. 1963, f. London p.
        12 Sept. 1963. (BH)

1967   *The Building of the House*, op. 79. Overture for orchestra with or without chorus. Text: Psalm 127 (adapted). F.p. Snape, 2 June 1967, f. London p. 16 Jan. 1968. (FM)

1968   *Children's Crusade (Kinderkreuzzug)*, op. 82. Ballad for children's voices, percussion, 2 pianos and organ. Text by Brecht. F.p. London, 19 May 1969. (FM)

1976   *Welcome Ode*, op. 95. Young people's chorus and orchestra. Text: 17th and 18th cent. English lyrics. F.p. Ipswich, 11 July 1977. F. London p. 31 Oct. 1977. (FM)

Solo Voice and Orchestra

1928   *Quatre chansons françaises*. High voice and orchestra. 1. Nuits de Juin (Hugo). 2. Sagesse (Verlaine). 3. L'enfance (Hugo). 4. Chant d'automne (Verlaine). F.p. BBC broadcast, 30 Mar. 1980; f. public perf. Snape, 10 June 1980. (FM)

1936   *Our Hunting Fathers*, op. 8. Symphonic cycle for high voice. Text devised by W.H. Auden. (Prologue. 1. Rats Away! 2. Messalina. 3. Dance of Death, Epilogue and Funeral March.) F.p. Norwich, 25 Sept. 1936, f. London p. 30 Apr. 1937. (BH)

1939   *Les Illuminations*, op. 18. High voice and strings. Text by A. Rimbaud. (1. Fanfare. 2. Villes. 3(a) Phrase, (b) Antique. 4. Royauté. 5. Marine. 6. Interlude. 7. Being beauteous. 8. Parade. 9. Départ.) F. complete p. London, 30 Jan. 1940; Nos. 7 and 5 were performed separately in Birmingham 1939 and in London 17 Aug. 1939. (BH)

1943   *Serenade*, op. 31. Tenor, horn and strings. (Prologue. 1. Pastoral (Cotton). 2. Nocturne (Tennyson). 3. Elegy (Blake). 4. Dirge (Anon). 5. Hymn (Jonson). 6. Sonnet (Keats). Epilogue.) F.p. London, 15 Oct. 1943. (BH)
        Discarded setting: *Now Sleeps the Crimson Petal* (ed. C. Matthews). F.p. London, Friends' House, 3 April 1987. (FM)

1953–4 *Symphonic Suite, 'Gloriana'*, op. 53a. Orchestra and optional tenor solo in 2nd movement 'The Lute Song'. See under Orchestral (D).

1958   *Nocturne*, op. 60. Tenor, 7 obbligato instruments and strings. Texts by Shelley, Tennyson, Coleridge, Middleton, Wordsworth, Owen, Keats and Shakespeare. F.p. Leeds, 16 Oct. 1958, f. London p. 30 Jan. 1959. (BH)

1960   *Bottom's Dream* from *A Midsummer Night's Dream*, op. 64. Bass-baritone and orchestra (or piano). (BH)

1975   *Phaedra*, op. 93. Dramatic cantata for mezzo-soprano and small orchestra. Text, Robert Lowell's translation of Racine. F.p. Snape, 16 June 1976, f. London p. 7 Aug. 1977. (FM)

Unaccompanied Chorus

1929   *A Wealden Trio: The Song of the Women*. Carol for women's voices. See under 1967.

1930   *A Hymn to the Virgin*. Anthem for mixed voices. Text: Anon. F.p. Lowestoft, 5 Jan. 1931. Rev. 1934. (BH)
        I saw three ships. Carol. F.p. Lowestoft, 5 Jan. 1931. Rev. 1967 as *The Sycamore Tree*. (See 1967, below.)

1931   *Sweet was the song the Virgin sung*, Christmas Suite, *Thy King's Birthday*, which incorporated Carol for women's voices, rev. 1966 (See below) and *New Prince, New Pomp*, motet for soprano and chorus. Text: R. Southwell and the Bible.

1932–3   *A Boy Was Born*, op. 3. Choral variations for men's, women's and boys' voices (organ opt.). Text: Anon, C. Rossetti, T. Tusser, F. Quarles. F.p. London (BBC broadcast), 23 Feb. 1934; f. concert p. London, 17 Dec. 1934. Rev. 1955. (OUP)
        See also *Corpus Christi Carol* under Chorus and Instruments.

1938   *Advance Democracy*. Eight-part chorus. Text by R. Swingler. (BH)

1939   *A.M.D.G.* Four-part chorus. Text by G. Manley Hopkins. (1. Prayer I. 2. Rosa Mystica. 3. God's Grandeur. 4. Prayer II. 5. O Deus, ego amo te. 6. The Soldier. 7. Heaven-Haven.) F.p. of 1, 2, 5, and 7, Beccles Church, 18 June 1984; f. complete p. London, Purcell Room, 21 Aug. 1984. (FM)

1941–2   *Hymn to St Cecilia*, op. 27. Five-part chorus and solos. Text by Auden. F.p. London, 22 Nov. 1942. (BH)

1944   *A Shepherd's Carol* and *Chorale*. Mixed voices. Text by Auden. F.p. in BBC feature 'Poet's Christmas' 1944. F. concert p. London, 17 Oct. 1962. (N). *Chorale*. (FM)

1950   *Five Flower Songs*. Mixed voices. (1. To Daffodils. 2. The Succession of the Four Sweet Months. 3. Marsh Flowers. 4. The Evening Primrose. 5. The Ballad of Green Broom.) F.p. (broadcast) 24 May 1951, f. London p. June 1951. (BH)

1953   *Six Choral Dances from 'Gloriana'*. Mixed voices. (1. Time. 2. Concord. 3. Time and Concord. 4. Country Girls. 5. Rustics and Fishermen. 6. Final Dance of Homage.) (BH)

1965 *Voices for Today*, op. 75. Anthem for men's, women's and children's voices, with organ opt. F.p. simultaneously New York, Paris and London, 24 Oct. 1965. (FM)

1966 *Sweet was the song the Virgin sung.* Carol for women's voices. Text from W. Ballet's Lute Book. Composed early 1931. Re-written 1966. F.p. Aldeburgh, 15 June 1966. (FM)

1967 *The Sycamore Tree.* Carol for mixed voices. Composed Aug. 1930 as *I saw three Ships* (see 1930). Re-written 1967. F.p. of rev. vers., Aldeburgh, 19 June 1968. (FM)

   A Wealden Trio: The Song of the Women. Carol for women's voices. Text by Ford Madox Ford. Composed April 1929. Re-written 1967. F.p. of rev. vers. Aldeburgh, 19 June 1968. (FM)

1974–5 *Sacred and Profane*, op. 91. Eight mediaeval lyrics for five-part chorus. (1. St Godric's Hymn. 2. I mon waxe wod. 3. Lenten is come. 4. The long night. 5. Yif ic of luve can. 6. Carol. 7. Ye that pasen by. 8. A death.) F.p. Snape, 14 Sept. 1975, f. London p. 30 Dec. 1977. (FM)

Chorus and Instrument(s)

1932 *Three 2-part Songs.* Boys' or women's voices and piano. Texts by Walter de la Mare. (1. The Ride-by-Nights. 2. The Rainbow. 3. The Ship of Rio.) F.p. London, 12 Dec. 1932. (OUP) For *The Ship of Rio* see also *Voice and Piano.*

1933 *Two Part-Songs.* Mixed chorus and piano. 1. I lov'd a lass (G.Wither). 2. Lift Boy (R. Graves). F.p. London, 11 Dec. 1933. (BH)

1933–5 *Friday Afternoons*, op. 7. Children's voices and piano. (1. Begone, dull care. 2. A Tragic Story. 3. Cuckoo! 4. Ee-oh! 5. A New Year Carol. 6. I must be married on Sunday. 7. There was a man of Newington. 8. Fishing Song. 9. The Useful Plough. 10. Jazz-Man. 11. There was a monkey. 12. Old Abram Brown.) (BH)

1934 *May.* Unison song with piano. (The Year Book Press.)

   Te Deum in C. Choir (treble solo) and organ (or strings, and harp or piano). F.p. (organ) London, St Michael's, Cornhill (Harold Darke) 13 Nov. 1935; f.p. (orch.) London, 27 Jan. 1936. (OUP)

   Jubilate Deo in E flat. Choir and organ. (FM) See also 1961 *Jubilate Deo.*

1942 *A Ceremony of Carols*, op. 28. Treble voices and harp. (1. Procession. 2. Wolcum Yole! 3. There is no rose. 4(a) That Yongë child. (b) Balulalow. 5. As dew in Aprille. 6. This little Babe. 7. Interlude. 8. In freezing winter night. 9. Spring Carol. 10. Deo

Gracias. 11. Recessional.) F.p. Norwich, 5 Dec. 1942, f. London p. 21 Dec. 1942. Rev. 1943. Also arr. for mixed chorus and harp or piano by Julius Harrison, 1948. (BH)

1943   *Rejoice in the Lamb (Jubilate Agno)*, op. 30. Festival cantata for mixed chorus (treble, alto, tenor and bass solos), and organ. Text by Christopher Smart. F.p. Northampton, 21 Sept. 1943. Also arr. for chorus and orchestra by Imogen Holst. (BH)
    The Ballad of Little Musgrave and Lady Barnard. Male voices and piano. Text: Anon. F.p. Eichstätt, Germany (prisoner-of-war camp), Feb. 1944. (BH)

1944   *Festival Te Deum*, op. 32. Mixed chorus and organ. F.p. Swindon, 24 Apr. 1945. (BH)
    Old Joe has gone fishing (Peter Grimes). Mixed chorus and piano; *Song of the Fishermen (Peter Grimes)*, mixed chorus and piano. (BH)

1949   *A Wedding Anthem (Amo Ergo Sum)*, op. 46. Soprano, tenor, mixed chorus and organ. Text by R. Duncan. F.p. London, 29 Sept. 1949. (BH)

1955   *Hymn to St Peter*, op. 56a. Mixed chorus (treble solo) and organ. Text from Gradual of Feast of St Peter and St Paul. (BH)
    Antiphon, op. 56b. Mixed chorus and organ. Text by G. Herbert. (BH)

1958   *Einladung zur Martinsgans.* Eight-part canon. Voices and piano. For 60th birthday of Martin Hürlimann.

1959   *Missa brevis* in D, op. 63. Boys' voices and organ. F.p. London (Westminster Cathedral), 22 July 1959. (BH)

1961   *Jubilate Deo.* Mixed chorus and organ. F.p. Leeds, 8 Oct. 1961. (OUP) See also 1934, *Te Deum.*
    Venite Exultemus Domino. Choir and organ. F.p. Westminster Abbey, 2 Oct. 1983. (FM)
    Fancie. Unison voices and piano. Text by Shakespeare. (BH)
    Corpus Christi Carol, arr. from Var. 5 of *A Boy Was Born* for treble solo or unison voices and organ. (OUP)

1962   *A Hymn of St Columba (Regis regum rectissimi).* Mixed chorus and organ. Text attrib. to St Columba. F.p. (pre-recorded tape) Garton, Co. Donegal, 2 June 1963. (BH)

1966   *The Golden Vanity*, op. 78. Vaudeville for boys' voices and piano. Text by C. Graham, based on English ballad. F.p. Snape, 3 June 1967, f. London p. 24 Nov. 1967. (FM)

1967   *The Oxen.* Carol for women's voices and piano. Text by T. Hardy.
        (FM)

1971   *A New Year Carol*, arr. from No. 5 of *Friday Afternoons*, op. 7.
        Women's voices and piano. (BH)

Solo Voice(s) and Piano

1922–3 *Beware!* Text by H. W. Longfellow. (FM)
1928–31 *Tit for Tat.* Re-written 1968. See 1968 for details.

1929   *The Birds.* Medium voice. Text by H. Belloc. Rev. 1934. (BH)

1935–6? *When you're feeling like expressing your affection.* High voice. Text
        by Auden. F.p. Blythburgh, Holy Trinity Church, 15 June 1992.

1936   *Two Ballads.* Two voices. (1. Mother Comfort (M. Slater). 2.
        Underneath the abject willow (Auden).) F.p. London, 31 Dec.
        1936. (BH)
        On This Island, op. 11. High voice. Text by Auden. (1. Let the
        florid music praise! 2. Now the leaves are falling fast. 3. Seascape.
        4. Nocturne, 5. As it is, plenty.) F.p. London (BBC broadcast) 19
        Nov. 1937. (BH)
        Fish in the unruffled lakes. High voice. Text by Auden. (BH)
        To lie flat on the back. High voice. Text by Auden. F.p. London
        (BBC broadcast), 22 Nov. 1985.
        Night covers up the rigid land. High voice. Text by Auden. F.p.
        London, 22 Nov. 1985.
        The sun shines down on the ships at sea. High voice. Text by Auden.
        Not even summer yet. High voice. Text by Peter Burra. F.p. 1937.

1937–9 *Four Cabaret Songs.* Contralto. Text by Auden. (1. Tell me the
        truth about love. 2. Funeral Blues. 3. Johnny. 4. Calypso.) (FM)

1938   *The Red Cockatoo.* High voice. Text from Chinese of Po-Chu-i,
        tr. A. Waley. F.p. Snape, Maltings, 17 June 1991.

1940   *Seven Sonnets of Michelangelo*, op. 22. Tenor. Texts, in Italian, by
        Michelangelo (Sonnets XVI, XXXI, XXX, LV, XXXVIII,
        XXXII and XXIV). F.p. privately in America in 1940. F. public
        p. London, 23 Sept. 1942. (BH)

1942   *Wild with passion* and *If Thou wilt ease.* High voice. Text by T.L.
        Beddoes. F.p. Blythburgh, Holy Trinity Church, 15 June 1992.
        Sleep, my darling, sleep. High voice. Text by L. MacNeice. F.p.
        Blythburgh, Holy Trinity Church, 15 June 1992.

1945   *Three Arias from Peter Grimes.* Text by M. Slater. 1. Peter's Dreams
        (tenor). 2. Embroidery Aria (soprano). 3. Church Scene (soprano).
        May be sung with orchestra. (BH)

The Holy Sonnets of John Donne, op. 35. High voice. (1. O my blacke Soule. 2. Batter my heart. 3. O might those sighes and teares. 4. Oh, to vex me. 5. What if this present. 6. Since she whom I loved. 7. At the round earth's imagined corners. 8. Thou hast made me. 9. Death, be not proud.) F.p. London, 22 Nov. 1945. (BH). Discarded song: *Perchance he for whom the bell tolls be so ill.*

1946   *Three Arias from The Rape of Lucretia*. Text by R. Duncan. (1. Flower Song (contralto). 2. The Ride (tenor). 3. Slumber Song (mezzo).) May be sung with orchestra. (BH)

1947   *Canticle I, My Beloved is Mine*, op. 40. High voice. Text by F. Quarles. F.p. London, 1 Nov. 1947. (BH)
A Charm of Lullabies, op. 41. Mezzo-soprano. (1. A Cradle Song. 2. The Highland Balou. 3. Sephestia's Lullaby. 4. A Charm. 5. The Nurse's Song.) F.p. The Hague, 3 Jan. 1948, f. London p. 8 Feb. 1949. (BH). Discarded songs: 1. Somnus the humble god. 2. Come, little Babe.

1952   *Canticle II, Abraham and Isaac*, op. 51. Alto or counter-tenor and tenor. Text from Chester Miracle Play. f.p. Nottingham, 21 Jan. 1952, f. London p. 3 Feb. 1952. (BH)

1953   *Winter Words*, op. 52. Lyrics and ballads of Thomas Hardy. High voice. (1. At day-close in November. 2. Midnight on the Great Western. 3. Wagtail and Baby. 4. The little old table. 5. The choirmaster's burial. 6. Proud songsters. 7. At the railway station, Upway. 8. Before life and after.) F.p. Leeds (Harewood House) 8 Oct. 1953, f. London p. (broadcast) 28 Nov. 1953; f. public p. in London, 24 Jan. 1954. (BH) Discarded songs: *The Children and Sir Nameless* and *If it's ever Spring again*. F.p. London (BBC broadcast) 23 Apr. 1985.

1954   *Canticle III, Still falls the rain – The raids, 1940, Night and Dawn*, op. 55. Tenor and horn (with piano). Text by E. Sitwell. F.p. London, 28 Jan. 1955. (BH)

1958   *Sechs Hölderlin-Fragmente*, op. 61. Text in German. (1. Menschenbeifall – The Applause of Men. 2. Die Heimat – Home. 3. Sokrates und Alcibiades. 4. Die Jugend – Youth. 5. Hälfte des Lebens – The middle of life. 6. Die Linien des Lebens – The line of life.) F.p. (broadcast) 14 Nov. 1958, f. London p. 1 Feb. 1960. (BH)

1959 or   *Um Mitternacht*. Text by Goethe. F.p. Blythburgh, Holy Trinity
1960   Church, 15 June 1992.

1965   *Songs and Proverbs of William Blake*, op. 74. Baritone. Text selected by P. Pears. (Proverb I – London. Proverb II – The chimney-sweeper. Proverb III – A Poison Tree. Proverb IV – The Tyger. Proverb V – The Fly. Proverb VI – Ah, Sunflower! Proverb VII – Every Night and Every Morn.) F.p. Aldeburgh, 24 June 1965, f. London (Croydon) p. 6 Dec. 1965. (FM)
The Poet's Echo, op. 76. High voice. Text, in Russian, by A. Pushkin. English version by P. Pears (1. Echo. 2. My heart... 3. Angel. 4. The Nightingale and the Rose. 5. Epigram. 6. Lines written during a sleepless night.) F. complete p. Moscow, 2 Dec. 1965, f. London p. 2 July 1966. (F.p. in West, New York, 19 Dec. 1965.) (FM)

1968   *Tit for Tat*. Five settings from boyhood of poems by Walter de la Mare. Composed 1928–31, re-written 1968. (1. A Song of Enchantment, 1929. 2. Autumn, 1931. 3. Silver, 1928. 4. Vigil, 1930. 5. Tit for Tat, 1928.) F.p. Aldeburgh, 23 June 1969. (FM)

1969   *Who Are These Children?* op. 84. Lyrics, rhymes and riddles by William Soutar. Tenor. (1. A Riddle (The Earth). 2. A Laddie's Sang. 3. Nightmare. 4. Black Day. 5. Bed-time. 6. Slaughter. 7. A Riddle (The Child you were). 8. The Larky Lad. 9. Who are these children? 10. Supper. 11. The Children. 12. The Auld Aik.) F.p. (incomplete: Nos. 1, 2, 3, 4, 7, 9, and 12), Cardiff, 7 Mar. 1971, f. complete p. Edinburgh, 4 May 1971, f. London p. 27 Sept. 1971. (FM). Discarded songs: 1. Dawtie's devotion. 2. Tradition. 3. The Gully.

1971   *Canticle IV, Journey of the Magi*, op. 86. Counter-tenor, tenor and baritone. Text by T.S. Eliot. F.p. Snape, 26 June 1971, f. London p. 28 May 1972. (FM)

1975   *Four Burns Songs*, being Nos. 3, 4, 5 and 6 from *A Birthday Hansel*, op. 92. (See Voice and Harp, 1975.) (1. Afton Water. 2. Wee Willie Gray. 3. The Winter. 4. My Hoggie.) Piano acc. arr. by C. Matthews. (FM)

Voice and Guitar

1957   *Songs from the Chinese*, op. 58. High voice. Text from Chinese poets, tr. A.Waley. (1. The Big Chariot. 2. The Old Lute. 3. The Autumn Wind. 4. The Herd-Boy. 5. Depression. 6. Dance Song.) F.p. Great Glemham House, Suffolk, 17 June 1958. (BH)

Voice and Harp

1974   *Canticle V, The Death of Saint Narcissus*, op. 89. Tenor. Text by T.S. Eliot. F.p. Schloss Elmau, Upper Bavaria, 15 Jan. 1975. F. British p. Croydon, 23 Jan. 1975, f. London p. 14 Jan. 1976. (FM)

1975   *A Birthday Hansel*, op. 92. Text by Burns. (1. Birthday song. 2. My Early Walk. 3. Wee Willie Gray. 4. My Hoggie. 5. Afton Water. 6. The Winter. 7. Leezie Lindsay.) F. public p. Cardiff, 19 Mar. 1976, f. London public p. 1 Feb. 1977. (FM) See also Voice and piano, *Four Burns Songs*, 1975.

        For many unpublished settings, see *A Britten Source Book* (Aldeburgh, 1987).

Chamber Music

(A) Quartets, etc.

1929   *Rhapsody*, for string quartet. F.p. Manchester, Royal Northern College of Music, 6 Nov. 1985.

1930   *Quartettino*, for string quartet. F.p. London, Barbican Centre, 23 May 1983. (FM)
        Bagatelle, violin, viola and piano. F.p. Holt, Norfolk, Gresham's School, 1 Mar. 1930 (Britten played viola).

1931   *String Quartet* in D. See 1974.

1932   *Phantasy*, string quintet. F.p. London, 22 July 1932 (FM)
        Phantasy, op. 2. Oboe, violin, viola, cello. F.p. London (BBC broadcast), 6 Aug. 1933, f. concert p. Florence, 5 Apr. 1934, f. London p. 21 Nov. 1934. (BH)
        Introduction and Allegro (orig. *Phantasy Scherzo*). Piano, viola and cello. F.p. London, Wigmore Hall, 22 Nov. 1986.
        Alla Marcia, for string quartet. Withdrawn and used in *Les Illuminations*. Orig. version recorded 1982. (FM)

1933   *Three Divertimenti (Alla quartetto serioso)*. Three movements from unfinished suite for string quartet, 'Go play, boy, play'. 1. March. 2. Waltz. 3. Burlesque. F.p. London, 11 Dec. 1933, f.p. of rev. version, London, 25. Feb. 1936. (FM)

1941   *String Quartet* No. 1 in D, op. 25. F.p. Washington, D.C., Library of Congress, 30 Oct. 1941, f. London p. 28 Apr. 1943. (BH)

1945   *String Quartet* No. 2 in C, op. 36. F.p. London, 21 Nov. 1945. (BH)

1965   *Gemini Variations*, op. 73. (12 Variations and Fugue on an Epigram
        of Kodály.) Quartet for 2 players (flute, violin and piano, 4 hands).
        F.p. Aldeburgh, 19 June 1965. Also version for 4 players. (FM)

1974   *String Quartet* in D. Composed 1931, revised 1974. F. public p.
        Snape, 7 June 1975. (FM)

1975   *String Quartet* No. 3, op. 94. F.p. Snape, 19 Dec. 1976, f. London
        p. 1 Feb. 1978. (FM)

(B) Instrument and Piano

1934–5 *Suite*, op. 6. Violin and piano. (Introduction. 1. March. 2. Moto
        perpetuo. 3. Lullaby. 4. Waltz.) F.p. of 3 movements, London, 17
        Dec. 1934, f. complete p. London (BBC broadcast) 6 Mar. 1936,
        f. complete public p. Barcelona, 21 Apr. 1936. (BH) Re-published
        1978 as *Three Pieces* (1. March. 2. Lullaby. 3. Waltz). (BH)

1935   *Two Insect Pieces*. Oboe and piano. (1. The Grasshopper. 2. The
        Wasp.) F.p. Manchester, 7 Mar. 1979, f. London p. (BBC
        broadcast), 3 Apr. 1980. (FM)

1936   *Temporal Variations*. Oboe and piano. Theme (Andante rubato).
        1. Oration. 2. March. 3. Exercises. 4. Commination. 5. Chorale.
        6. Waltz. 7. Polka. 8. Resolution. F.p. London, 15 Dec. 1936, f.
        broadcast p. 3 Apr. 1980. (FM)

1937   *Reveille*. Violin and piano. F.p. London, Wigmore Hall, 12 Apr.
        1937. (FM)

1950   *Lachrymae*, op. 48. (Reflections on a song of John Dowland.) Viola
        and piano. F.p. Aldeburgh, 20 June 1950. Arr. for viola and strings
        1976 (See Orchestral (C) 1976 for details). (BH)

1955   *Timpani Piece for Jimmy* (James Blades). Timpani and piano.

1961   *Sonata* in C, op. 65. Cello and piano. F.p. Aldeburgh, 7 July 1961.
        (BH)

(C) Solo Cello (ed. M. Rostropovich)

1964   *Suite*, op. 72. F.p. Aldeburgh, 27 June 1965, f. London p. 30 June
        1966. (FM)

1967   *Second Suite*, op. 80. F.p. Snape, 17 June 1968, f. London p. 12
        Sept. 1968. (FM)

1971   *Third Suite*, op. 87. F.p. Snape, 21 Dec. 1974, f. London p. 11 Oct.
        1977. (FM)

1976   *Tema* ... SACHER. Written for Paul Sacher's 70th birthday as theme for variations by other composers. F.p. Zürich, Tonhalle, 2 May 1976. (FM)

(D) Two Pianos

1936   *Two Lullabies.* 1. Lullaby. 2. Lullaby for a Retired Colonel. F.p. London (BBC audition), Concert Hall, Broadcasting House, 19 March 1936; f. concert p. Snape, Maltings, 22 June 1988. (FM)

1940   *Introduction and Rondo alla burlesca*, op. 23, no. 1. F.p. New York, 5 Jan. 1941, f. British p. Cambridge, 25 Apr. 1943, f. London p. 29 Mar. 1944. (BH)

1941   *Mazurka elegiaca*, op. 23, no. 2. F.p. New York, 9 Dec. 1941, f. British p. Cambridge, 25 Apr. 1943, f. London p. 29 Mar. 1944. (BH)

(E) Wind Instruments

1951   *Six Metamorphoses after Ovid*, op. 49. (1. Pan. 2. Phaeton. 3. Niobe, 4. Bacchus. 5. Narcissus. 6. Arethusa.). F.p. Thorpeness, 14 June 1951. (BH)

1953   *Morris Dance from 'Gloriana'*, arr. for 2 descant recorders. (BH)

1955   *Alpine Suite.* Recorder trio (2 descant, 1 treble). (1. Arrival at Zermatt. 2. Swiss Clock. 3. Nursery Slopes. 4. Alpine Scene. 5. Moto perpetuo: Down the Piste. 6. Farewell to Zermatt.) (BH) *Scherzo.* Recorder quartet (descant, treble, tenor, bass or 2nd tenor). (BH)

1959   *Fanfare for St Edmundsbury.* 3 trumpets. F.p. precincts of Bury St Edmunds Cathedral, June 1959. (BH)

1960   *Fanfare for S.S. Oriana.* F.p. at launching, 3 Nov. 1960.

1966   *Hankin Booby.* Folk dance for wind and drums. F.p. London, 1 Mar. 1967. (See *Orchestral* (D) 1974, *Suite on English Folk Tunes*, op. 90. (FM)

(F) Solo Instruments (excluding Cello – see (C) above.)

1. Piano

1923–5   *Five Walztes (Waltzes).* (1. Rather fast and nervous, 1925. 2. Quick, with wit, 1924. 3. Dramatic, 1925. 4. Rhythmic; not fast, 1924. 5. Variations: quiet and simple, 1923.) Re-written 1969. (FM)

Britten

1930 *Three Character Pieces.* (1. John. 2. Daphne. 3. Michael). F.p. Chester, Town Hall, 28 July 1989. (FM)

1931 *12 Variations on a Theme.* F.p. Snape, Maltings, 22 June 1986. (FM)

1934 *Holiday Diary*, op. 5. Suite. (1. Early morning bathe. 2. Sailing. 3. Funfair. 4. Night.) (BH)

1940 *Sonatina Romantica.* F. public p. Snape, Maltings, 16 June 1988, of first and second movements only, *Moderato* and *Nocturne.* (FM)

1963 *Night Piece (Notturno).* Written for first Leeds International piano competition 1963. (BH)

   2. Organ

1946 *Prelude and Fugue on a Theme of Vittoria.* F.p. Northampton, 21 Sept. 1946. (BH)

   3. Guitar (ed. J. Bream)

1963 *Nocturnal after John Dowland*, op. 70. Reflections on 'Come, heavy sleep'. F.p. Aldeburgh, 12 June 1964, f. London p. 19 Nov. 1965. (FM)

   4. Harp (ed. O. Ellis)

1969 *Suite*, op. 83. (1. Overture. 2. Toccata. 3. Nocturne. 4. Fugue. 5. Hymn (St Denio). F.p. Aldeburgh, 24 June 1969, f. London p. 28 Sept. 1969. (FM)

Miscellaneous

1938 *The Tocher* (Silhouette film, prod. by Lotte Reiniger. Music by Rossini, arr. Britten). (*Tocher* means dowry, i.e. savings book.)

1940 *The Dark Valley.* Monologue by W.H. Auden for Dame May Whitty with two songs by Britten. (C.B.S.)

Arrangements and Realizations of Works by Other Composers (including folk songs)

(Except where otherwise stated, dates in this section are those of publication. Some of the Purcell settings date from Britten's years in America)

Bach J.S.

Five Spiritual Songs (Geistliche Lieder). High voice and piano (Eng. tr. by P. Pears). (1. Gedenke doch, mein Geist, zurücke. 2. Komm, Seelen, dieser Tag.

3. Liebster Herr Jesu. 4. Komm, süsser Tod. 5. Bist du bei mir.) F.p. Aldeburgh, 18 June 1969. (FM) SATB vers. also published in the *New Catholic Hymnal* of nos. 3 and 4.

Chopin, Fryderyk

Les Sylphides. Arr. for small orchestra for Ballet Presentations Inc. (Ballet Theater), New York, 1940. Score Lost.

Folk Songs (with dates of publication)

(a) British
Voice and piano:
Vol. 1. (High or medium voice.) The Salley Gardens (also unison voices and piano). Little Sir William. The Bonny Earl o' Moray. O can ye sew cushions? The trees they grow so high. The ash grove. Oliver Cromwell (also unison voices and piano). (BH, 2 June 1943.)
Vol. 3. (High or medium voice.) The Plough Boy. There's none to soothe. Sweet Polly Oliver. The Miller of Dee. The foggy foggy dew. O Waly, Waly. Come you not from Newcastle? (BH, 31 Dec. 1947.)
Vol. 5. The brisk young widow. Sally in our alley. The Lincolnshire poacher. Early one morning. Ca' the yowes. (BH, 14 Feb. 1961.)
Voice and guitar (Ed. J. Bream):
Vol. 6. (High voice.) I will give my love an apple. Sailor-boy. Master Kilby. The soldier and the sailor. Bonny at morn. The shooting of his dear. (BH, 8 Nov. 1961)
Voice and harp (or piano):
Eight Folk Song Arrangements. 1. Lord, I married me a wife. 2. She's like the swallow. 3. Lemady. 4. Bonny at morn. 5. I was lonely and forlorn. 6. David of the White Rock. 7. The False Knight. 8. Bird scarer's song. Arr. in summer of 1976. (FM)
Unaccompanied Mixed Chorus: The Holly and the Ivy, 1957. (BH)
Unison voices and piano: King Herod and the Cock. (BH, 7 Oct. 1965).
Voice and orchestra: The bonny Earl o' Moray. Come you not from Newcastle? Little Sir William. O can ye sew cushions? Oliver Cromwell. The Plough Boy. The Salley Gardens. O Waly, Waly. (BH)
(b) French
Voice and piano:
Vol. 2. (High or medium voice, with Eng. tr. by Iris Rogers.) La noël passée. Voici le printemps. Fileuse. Le roi s'en va-t'en chasse. La belle est au jardin d'amour. Il est quelqu'un sur terre. Eho! Eho! Quand j'étais chez mon père. (BH, 31 Dec. 1946)
Voice and orchestra: La belle est au jardin d'amour. Eho! Eho! Fileuse. La noël passée. Quand j'étais chez mon père. Le roi s'en va-t'en chasse. (BH)

(c) Irish (Moore's Irish Melodies)
Voice and Piano:
Vol. 4. Avenging and bright. Sail on, sail on. How sweet the answer. The minstrel boy. At the mid hour of night. Rich and rare. Dear harp of my country. Oft in the stilly night. The last rose of summer. O the sight entrancing. (BH, 10 May 1960)

Gay, John

The Beggar's Opera, op. 43.* Ballad-opera (1728), realized from original airs by B. Britten. F.p. Cambridge, 24 May 1948, f. London p. 15 July 1967. New prelude to Act 3 composed 1963. (BH)

Haydn, Joseph

Cadenzas to Cello Concerto in C (Hob. VII 6:1), F.p. Blythburgh, 18 June 1964. (BH)

Mahler, Gustav

What the Wild Flowers Tell Me, 2nd movement of Symphony No. 3, arr. for reduced orchestra in 1941. (BH, 1950)

Mozart, Wolfgang Amadeus

Cadenzas to Piano Concerto No. 22 in E flat (K.482). F.p. Tours, July 1966. (FM)

National Anthem

For chamber orchestra (*Rape of Lucretia*): F.p. Glyndebourne, 12 July 1946.
Orchestra: F.p. Snape, 13 June 1971. (FM)
Mixed chorus and orchestra: F.p. Leeds, 7 Oct. 1961. With reduced orchestration: F.p. London, 1 Mar. 1967. (BH)

Purcell, Henry

Dido and Aeneas (1689), opera in 3 acts, realized and ed. by Britten and I. Holst. Orch. for strings and continuo. F.p. London (Hammersmith) 1 May 1951. (BH)
The Fairy Queen. Masque for soloists, mixed chorus and orchestra, shortened for concert performance by P. Pears, edited and realized by Britten and I. Holst, harpsichord part realized by P. Ledger. (1. Oberon's birthday. 2. Night

---

* Britten opus number.

and silence. 3. The sweet passion. 4. Epithalamium.) F.p. Aldeburgh, 25
June 1967. (FM)
When night her purple veil had softly spread, secular cantata.
Baritone, 2 violins, continuo. F.p. of this arr. Aldeburgh, 24 June 1965. (FM)
Chacony in G minor. String quartet or string orchestra. (BH, 25 May 1965.)
The Golden Sonata. 2 violins, cello, piano. (BH)
Orpheus Britannicus. (Realized and ed. Britten and Pears):
5 Songs for voice: I attempt from love's sickness to fly. I take no pleasure.
Hark the ech'ing air! Take not a woman's anger ill. How blest are Shepherds.
(BH, 6 Sept. 1960).
6 Songs for high, or medium, voice and piano: Mad Bess. If music be the food
of love (1st vers.). There's not a swain of the plain. Not all my torments.
Man is for the woman made. Sweeter than roses. (BH, 25 Mar. 1948.)
7 Songs for high, or medium, voice and piano: Fairest Isle. If music be the
food of love (3rd vers.). Turn then thine eyes. Music for a while. Pious
Celinda. I'll sail upon the dog-star. On the brow of Richmond Hill. (BH,
24 Jan. 1947).
6 Duets for high and low voices and piano: Sound the trumpet. I spy Celia.
Lost is my quiet. What can we poor females do? No, no, resistance is but
vain. Shepherd, leave decoying. (BH, 24 May 1961.)
Suite of Songs for high voice and orchestra: Let sullen discord smile. Why
should men quarrel? So when the glittering Queen of Night. Thou tun'st
this world. 'Tis holiday – sound fame thy brazen trumpet. (BH, 3 Feb. 1956.)
3 Songs for high voice and orchestra: Hark the ech'ing air! Not all my
torments. Take not a woman's anger ill. (BH)
Harmonia Sacra (realized and ed. by Britten and Pears):
The Blessed Virgin's Expostulation (15 Apr. 1947), *Job's Curse* (3 Mar. 1950),
2 Divine Hymns and Alleluia (high voice and piano) (7 Sept. 1960), *Saul and
the Witch at Endor* (soprano, tenor, bass and piano) (24 Dec. 1947), *3 Divine
Hymns* (high, or medium, voice and piano) (24 Dec. 1947). (BH)
Odes and Elegies (realized and ed. by Britten and Pears):
The Queen's Epicedium (*Elegy on the death of Queen Mary*, 1965).
(High voice and piano.) (BH, 14 June 1946.)

Rossini, Gioacchino

1935   *The Tocher.* (GPO silhouette film contained Rossini music arr.
        Britten.) Full score, entitled *Rossini-Suite*, was recorded in 1988.
        Parts of it were re-orchestrated as *Soirées musicales* and *Matinées
        musicales.* See below.

1936   *Soirées musicales*, op. 9. Suite of 5 movements (1. March. 2.
        Canzonetta. 3. Tirolese. 4. Bolero. 5. Tarantella.) (BH)
        Men of the Alps. (GPO documentary film contained Rossini music
        arr. Britten and W. Leigh.)

Britten

1941   *Matinées musicales*, op. 24. 2nd Suite of 5 movements. (1. March. 2. Nocturne. 3. Waltz. 4. Pantomime. 5. Moto perpetuo (Solfeggi e Gorgheggi)). (BH)

Schubert, Franz

Song, *Ach, neige, du Schmerzenreiche* (D. 564), completed by B.B. F.p. Cambridge, Arts Theatre, 25 Apr. 1943.
Song, *Die Forelle* (D. 550) arr. for voice and small orch. *c.*1942.

Schumann, Robert

Song, *Frühlingsnacht* arr. for voice and small orch. *c.*1942.

Appendix C

Personalia

(Dates refer to year of composition or of performance, as relevant in the context)

Ashton, Sir Frederick (1904–88), English choreographer and producer who produced Britten's *Albert Herring* at its first performance at Glyndebourne, 1947, and choreographed the 'dances of Apollo' for first performance of *Death in Venice*, Aldeburgh 1973.

Auden, Wystan Hugh (1907–73), English-born poet (later American citizen) with whom Britten collaborated in late 1930s in several works (documentary films, plays, and radio features) and whom he followed to the United States in 1939. Librettist of operetta *Paul Bunyan* (1941) and author of poems which Britten set as *Hymn to St Cecilia* in 1942. Britten's *On This Island* (1937) consists of settings of Auden. *Our Hunting Fathers* (1936) has a text compiled by Auden.

Baker, Dame Janet (b. 1933), English mezzo-soprano, a distinguished interpreter of Lucretia in *The Rape of Lucretia*. Britten wrote the role of Kate Julian in *Owen Wingrave* (1970) for her and the dramatic cantata *Phaedra* (1975), which is dedicated to her. Has written about working with Britten.

Barbirolli, Sir John (1899–1970), English conductor who, when conductor of the Philharmonic-Symphony Orchestra of New York, conducted the first performances of Britten's Violin Concerto (1940) and *Sinfonia da Requiem* (1941).

Bartlett, Ethel (1900–78), English pianist who settled in America with her husband, Rae Robertson, with whom she played music for two pianos. For them Britten composed his *Scottish Ballad* (1941) and the *Introduction and Rondo alla burlesca* (1940) and *Mazurka elegiaca* (1941).

Bedford, Steuart (b. 1939), English conductor and pianist, who conducted first stage performance of *Owen Wingrave* (1973), and first performances of Britten's *Death in Venice* (1973), the *Suite on English Folk Tunes* (1975), *Phaedra* (1976), and the revised version of *Paul Bunyan* (1976). An artistic director of Aldeburgh Festival since 1974.

Benjamin, Arthur (1893–1960), Australian composer and pianist who was Britten's piano teacher at the Royal College of Music. Wrote operas, symphony, concertos and film music. Britten's *Holiday Diary* (1934) is dedicated to him.

Berg, Alban (1885–1935), Austrian composer, a pupil of Schoenberg and admirer of Mahler, whose music, in an unorthodox 12-note idiom, Britten admired. Britten attended the first performance of the Violin Concerto at Barcelona in 1936.

Berkeley, Sir Lennox (1903–89), English composer whose friendship with Britten began in 1936 when they were both in Barcelona for festival of the International Society for Contemporary Music. Collaborated with Britten in orchestral suite *Mont Juic* (1936–7), each contributing two movements. Wrote operas, symphonies, choral music, chamber works, etc. Britten's Piano Concerto (1938) is dedicated to him.

Blades, James (1901–99), English percussion player who first worked with Britten on documentary films in 1930s and later helped devise many percussion effects in his operas and other works while playing in English Opera Group orchestra.

Boughton, Joy (1913–63), English oboist, daughter of the composer Rutland Boughton. Britten wrote his *Six Metamorphoses After Ovid* (1951) for her. She is the oboist in Britten's recording of his opera *The Turn of the Screw*.

Boult, Sir Adrian (1889–1983), English conductor and champion of British music who conducted first London performance of Britten's *Our Hunting Fathers* in 1937.

Boys, Henry (1910–92), English teacher and critic who met Britten when he was at the Royal College of Music and encouraged his interest in the music of Schoenberg and Stravinsky. Britten's Violin Concerto (1939) is dedicated to him. Arranged vocal scores of *The Rape of Lucretia* (1946) and *Albert Herring* (1947). One of the first 'musical assistants' of English Opera Group.

Brain, Dennis (1921–57), English horn-player of supreme virtuosity and artistry who was first player of horn part in Britten's *Serenade* for tenor, horn and strings (1943) and Canticle III, *Still Falls the Rain*, for tenor, horn and piano (1955). Britten first met him in 1942 when Brain was principal horn of RAF Orchestra, which performed some of Britten's incidental music for radio features. Killed in car crash.

Brannigan, Owen (1908–73), English bass-baritone who created the Britten roles of Swallow in *Peter Grimes* (1945), Collatinus in *The Rape of Lucretia* (1946), Noye in *Noye's Fludde* (1958), and Bottom in *A Midsummer Night's Dream* (1960). Sings in several of Britten's opera recordings.

Bream, Julian (b. 1933), English guitarist and lutenist who has edited much early music for his instruments and who is largely responsible for present-day revival of popularity of lute music by Dowland, etc. Britten wrote his

Nocturnal after John Dowland (1963) for guitar for him (first performance at 1964 Aldeburgh Festival), and the *Songs from the Chinese* (1957) were written for Bream's guitar accompaniment. Also accompanied Peter Pears in song recitals.

Bridge, Frank (1879–1941), English composer, conductor, viola-player and teacher, who gave Britten private lessons in composition from 1927. Britten's *Sinfonietta* (1932) and *Variations on a Theme of Frank Bridge* (1937) are dedicated to him, the latter 'a tribute with affection and admiration'. Britten greatly admired his music and included much of it in Aldeburgh Festival concerts. Works include *The Sea, Summer, Enter Spring*, all for orchestra, the cello concerto *Oration*, piano sonata, string quartets and songs.

Brosa, Antonio (1894–1979), Spanish violinist who settled in England in 1914. Was first to play Britten's *Suite* for violin and piano in its complete (1936) version, and was soloist in first performance of the Violin Concerto in New York, 1940.

Coleman, Basil (b. 1916), English opera producer who worked with the English Opera Group. Producer for first stagings of Britten's *The Little Sweep* (1949), *Billy Budd* (1951), *Gloriana* (1953), and *The Turn of the Screw* (1954). Producer Sadler's Wells revival of *Peter Grimes* (1963) and *Billy Budd* for BBC television (1966). Also produced first American performance of Britten's *A Midsummer Night's Dream* (San Francisco, 1961) and first South American performance (Buenos Aires, 1962).

Cranko, John (1928–73), South African choreographer and theatrical producer. Settled in England 1946. Choreographed dances in Britten's *Gloriana* (1953) and directed new Covent Garden production of *Peter Grimes* later same year. Choreographed ballet *Variations on a Theme* (1954), to music of Britten's *Variations on a Theme of Frank Bridge* in version scored for small orchestra by James Bernard. Wrote scenario for and choreographed Britten's full-length ballet *The Prince of the Pagodas* (1956). Produced première of Britten's *A Midsummer Night's Dream* (Aldeburgh 1960). Became ballet director at Stuttgart and died in aircraft on flight from New York to Stuttgart.

Cross, Joan (1900–93), English soprano, opera director, producer and translator. Artistic director of Sadler's Wells Opera 1942–6 and largely responsible for decision to produce *Peter Grimes* in 1945. Created Britten roles of Ellen Orford in *Peter Grimes*, Female Chorus in *The Rape of Lucretia* (1946), Lady Billows in *Albert Herring* (1947), Elizabeth I in *Gloriana* (1953), and Mrs Grose in *The Turn of the Screw* (1954). One of co-founders of English Opera Group, 1946.

Crozier, Eric (1914–94), English writer, librettist and opera producer. One of first BBC television producers. Co-founder of English Opera Group, 1946. Librettist for Britten in *Albert Herring* (1947), *Saint Nicolas* (1948), *Let's Make an Opera! (The Little Sweep)* (1949), and *Billy Budd* (with E.M. Forster)

(1951). Producer for first performances of *Peter Grimes* (1945) and *The Rape of Lucretia* (1946). Wrote commentary for concert version of *The Young Person's Guide to the Orchestra* (1946).

Culshaw, John (1924–80), English writer, critic, opera and recording producer and administrator. While working for Decca was responsible for recording most of Britten's works and when Head of BBC TV Music supervised televised recordings of several Britten operas, including *Peter Grimes* and *Owen Wingrave*, and other works. Author of book on Rakhmaninov and about recording *The Ring* (Wagner) with Solti in Vienna.

de la Mare, Walter (1873–1956), English poet and author, some of whose poems Britten set in his boyhood and published as *Tit for Tat* in 1969. His son Richard (b. 1899) was chairman of Britten's publishers, Faber Music, 1966–71, and *Tit for Tat* is dedicated to him.

Duncan, Ronald (1914–82), Rhodesian-born English poet and dramatist. Britten first collaborated with him in 1937 on a *Pacifist March* for Peace Pledge Union and later wrote incidental music for his play *This Way to the Tomb* (1945). Wrote libretto of *The Rape of Lucretia* (1946) and verses for *A Wedding Anthem* (1949). Some other projects with Britten, such as an opera based on Jane Austen's *Mansfield Park*, came to nothing. Author of *Working with Britten* (1981).

Ellis, Osian (b. 1928), Welsh harpist and singer, former principal harpist of London Symphony Orchestra. Britten admired his playing and wrote the *Suite*, op. 83 (1969) for him, Canticle V, *The Death of St Narcissus* (1974) for voice and harp, *A Birthday Hansel* (1975) for voice and harp, and arranged folk-songs for voice and harp for performance by Pears and Ellis.

Evans, Nancy (b. 1915), English contralto and wife of Eric Crozier. She sang Lucretia in the second cast at Glyndebourne, 1946, gave first performance of *A Charm of Lullabies* (1947), which is dedicated to her, and created the role of Nancy in *Albert Herring* (1947).

Ferrier, Kathleen (1912–53), English contralto for whom Britten wrote the role of Lucretia, which she created at Glyndebourne, 1946, and the contralto part in Canticle II, *Abraham and Isaac* (1952), which is dedicated to her and Peter Pears.

Fischer-Dieskau, Dietrich (b. 1925), German concert and operatic baritone for whom Britten wrote the baritone part in *War Requiem* (1962). Sang in first performance at Coventry 1962 and in first performance of *Cantata Misericordium*, Geneva, 1963. *Songs and Proverbs of William Blake* (1965) written for and dedicated to him.

Forster, Edward Morgan (1879–1970), English novelist and essayist. His 1941 broadcast on the poet George Crabbe, reprinted in *The Listener*, was instrumental in causing Britten to decide to return to England from America in 1942 and led directly to the choice of *Peter Grimes* as an opera subject. Co-librettist with Eric Crozier of *Billy Budd* (1951). Britten dedicated *Albert Herring* (1947) to him 'in admiration'.

Goehr, Walter (1903–60), German-born conductor and composer who while on the staff of Morley College, London, conducted the first performance in 1943 of Britten's *Serenade* for tenor, horn and strings. Father of composer Alexander Goehr (b. 1932).

Goodall, Sir Reginald (1901–90), English conductor who directed first performance of Britten's *Te Deum* in 1936 and other early performances of his music. Conducted première of *Peter Grimes* at Sadler's Wells in 1945 and second cast in *The Rape of Lucretia* at Glyndebourne, 1946 (Ansermet conducted first cast).

Graham, Colin (b. 1931), English opera producer, librettist and designer. Director of productions, English Opera Group, 1961–75 and made an artistic director of Aldeburgh Festival in 1969. Assistant producer to Basil Coleman on *The Turn of the Screw* (1954). Produced premières of Britten's *Noye's Fludde* (1958, also designed setting), *Curlew River* (1964), *The Burning Fiery Furnace* (1966), *The Prodigal Son* (1968), revival of *Gloriana* (1966), *Owen Wingrave* (1971), *Death in Venice* (1973) and *Paul Bunyan* (rev. vers., 1976). Also designed sets for the three church parables. Wrote libretto of projected Britten opera *Anna Karenina* and of *The Golden Vanity* (1966).

Grainger, Percy (1882–1961), Australian composer, pianist and folk-song collector whose compositions and arrangements Britten much admired. Several Grainger performances were given in Aldeburgh and recordings of his music were made by Britten and colleagues. Britten's *Suite on English Folk Tunes* (1974) is 'lovingly and reverently' dedicated to Grainger's memory.

Hawkes, Ralph (1898–1950), chairman of publishers Boosey and Hawkes. Great musical 'talent-spotter'. Gave Britten his first publishing contract 1936. One of first directors of English Opera Group. Britten's *Our Hunting Fathers* (1936) is dedicated to him.

Holst, Imogen (1907–84), English conductor, musicologist and writer, daughter of composer Gustav Holst (1874–1934). Music assistant to Britten 1952–64 and an artistic director of Aldeburgh Festival 1957–77. Co-editor with Britten of version of Purcell's *Dido and Aeneas* (1951) and of concert version of Purcell's *The Fairy Queen* (1967); co-author with Britten of *The Story of Music* (1958, re-issued 1968 as *The Wonderful World of Music*). Arranged vocal scores of *Gloriana* (1953), *The Turn of the Screw* (1954), *Noye's Fludde* (1957), *Nocturne* (1958), *Cantata Academica* (1959), *A Midsummer Night's Dream* (1960, with Martin Penny), *War Requiem* (1961) and *Cantata Misericordium* (1963). Author of *Britten* (1966, rev. 1970, rev. 1980) in Faber 'Great Composers' series. Britten's *The Prince of the Pagodas*

(1956) is jointly dedicated to her and Ninette de Valois. His *The Sycamore Tree* (1967) is dedicated to her.

Ireland, John (1879–1962), English composer, pianist and teacher who was one of Britten's composition teachers at the Royal College of Music.

Keller, Hans (1919–85), Austrian-born violinist, music critic and musicologist. British citizen from 1948. On BBC staff 1949–79. Co-editor with Donald Mitchell, 1952, of symposium on Britten's works. Dedicatee of 3rd String Quartet. Made German translations of *The Poet's Echo* (1965), *The Golden Vanity* (1966), *The Prodigal Son* (1968) and *Death in Venice* (1973, with Claus Henneberg) and English translation of *Children's Crusade* (1968).

Koussevitzky, Serge (1874–1951), Russian-born conductor who settled in Paris after the Revolution and later in the United States. Conductor of the Boston Symphony Orchestra 1924–49. Notable champion of 20th century music. Arranged for Koussevitzky Music Foundation to commission *Peter Grimes* and commissioned *Spring Symphony* (1949) for Boston, though he ceded first performance to Holland Festival.

Ledger, Philip (b. 1937), English organist, pianist, conductor and harpsichordist, who was first director of music at University of East Anglia, 1965–73. Director of music and organist, King's College, Cambridge, 1974–82. Took part as keyboard player in many Aldeburgh Festival performances and in several of Britten's recordings. Organist in first performances and recordings of the three Church Parables. An artistic director of Aldeburgh Festival 1968–89. Principal, Royal Scottish Academy of Music and Drama from 1982.

Ludwig, Prince of Hesse and the Rhine (1908–68), German patron and benefactor, with his wife Princess Margaret (a Scotswoman), of the Aldeburgh Festival. Travelled abroad several times with Britten and Pears, including the visit to the Far East when the idea for *Curlew River* was born. He wrote *Ausflug Ost*, a privately printed memoir (1956) of this tour. Britten often stayed at the Prince's home near Darmstadt, Schloss Wolfsgarten. The *Sechs Hölderlin-Fragmente* (1958) were dedicated to him on his fiftieth birthday. The *Songs from the Chinese* (1957) are dedicated to the Prince and Princess. As 'Ludwig Landgraf', the Prince translated into German the libretti of *The Turn of the Screw* (1954), *Noye's Fludde* (1957), *Nocturne* (1958), *War Requiem* (1962, Owen poems, with Fischer-Dieskau), *Curlew River* (1964) and *The Burning Fiery Furnace* (1966).

Macnaghten, Anne (1908–2000), English violinist and founder of string quartet. With Iris Lemare founded series of concerts in 1930s which promoted works by young British composers. Several of Britten's early works were first performed at Lemare-Macnaghten concerts, including *Sinfonietta* (1933) and *A Boy Was Born* (1934, first concert performance).

McPhee, Colin (1901–64), American composer who lived in Bali from 1934 to 1939 and met Britten in America in 1939. He and Britten recorded transcriptions for two pianos of Balinese ceremonial music. This was Britten's first introduction to Balinese music, an interest which further developed after he had visited Bali in 1956.

Malcolm, George (1917–97), English organist, pianist, harpsichordist and conductor. Master of the Music at Westminster Cathedral, 1947–59. Britten wrote his *Missa brevis* (1959) for Malcolm's choristers.

Mayer, Dr William (1887–1956), German-born psychiatrist who settled in U.S.A. in 1936 and became medical director of the Long Island Home, Amityville. In its grounds was his house, Stanton Cottage, to which many promising and significant personalities in the arts were invited, such as Auden. In 1939–40 Britten and Pears made it their home. Dr Mayer's wife Elizabeth (1884–1970) was a devotee of the arts and a 'second mother' to Britten. With Pears, she made an English translation of the *Sechs Hölderlin-Fragmente* (1958). The *Hymn to St Cecilia* (1942) is dedicated to her.

Mitchell, Donald (b. 1925), English publisher, critic and writer. Joint editor, with Hans Keller, of symposium on Britten's music (1952) and, with Philip Reed, of Britten's diaries and letters. Music critic for *Musical Times* 1953–7, *Daily Telegraph* 1959–64. Editor of *Tempo* 1958–62. Authority on Mahler, being author and editor of books about him. Managing director of Faber Music 1965–71, chairman 1977–86. *The Burning Fiery Furnace* (1966) is dedicated to Mitchell and his wife Kathleen.

Neel, Boyd (1905–81), English conductor (trained as doctor of medicine) who in 1933 founded Boyd Neel String Orchestra and performed many works by English composers. For visit to Salzburg Festival 1937 commissioned Britten's *Variations on a Theme of Frank Bridge*. Britten wrote his *Prelude and Fugue* for strings for orchestra's tenth anniversary in 1943.

Oldham, Arthur (b. 1926), English composer, pianist and chorus-master. Studied privately with Britten, for whom he made the vocal scores of *Saint Nicolas* (1948), *The Beggar's Opera* (1948), *Spring Symphony* (1949) and *The Little Sweep* (1949). Adapted Arne's *Love in a Village* for 1952 Aldeburgh Festival. Trained chorus for several Britten performances, including that for Britten's recording of Elgar's *The Dream of Gerontius*. Was chorus-master of Scottish Opera, 1966–74.

Pears, Sir Peter (1910–86), English tenor whose musical partnership with Britten began in 1937 and lasted to the end of the composer's life. Was member of BBC Singers 1934–7. Went to America with Britten 1939–42. Member of Sadler's Wells Opera 1943–6. Created several important roles in Britten's operas: title-roles in *Peter Grimes* (1945) and *Albert Herring* (1947), Male Chorus in *The Rape of Lucretia* (1946), Captain Vere in *Billy Budd* (1951), Essex in *Gloriana* (1953), Quint in *The Turn of the Screw* (1954), Flute in *A Midsummer Night's Dream* (1960), Madwoman in *Curlew*

River (1964), *Nebuchadnezzar* in *The Burning Fiery Furnace* (1966), Tempter
in *The Prodigal Son* (1968), Sir Philip Wingrave in *Owen Wingrave* (1971)
and Aschenbach in *Death in Venice* (1973). Gave first performances of many
of Britten's song-cycles, etc.: *Seven Sonnets of Michelangelo* (1942), *Serenade*
(1943), *Holy Sonnets of John Donne* (1945), Canticle I, *My Beloved is Mine*
(1947), *Winter Words* (1953), Canticle III, *Still Falls the Rain* (1954), *Sechs
Hölderlin-Fragmente* (1958), *Songs from the Chinese* (1958), *Who are these
children?* (1971), Canticle V, *The Death of St Narcissus* (1975), and *A
Birthday Hansel* (1975). Sang tenor part in first performances of *Saint Nicolas*
(1948), *Spring Symphony* (1948), *A Wedding Anthem* (1949), Canticle II,
Abraham and Isaac (1952), *Nocturne* (1958), *Cantata Academica* (1960), *War
Requiem* (1962), *Cantata Misericordium* (1963) and Canticle IV, *Journey of
the Magi* (1971). Directed first performance of *Sacred and Profane* (1975).
Provided English translation (with Elizabeth Mayer) of *Sechs Hölderlin-
Fragmente* (1958) and of *The Poet's Echo* (1966). Selected and arranged text
of song-cycle *Songs and Proverbs of William Blake* (1965). Britten works
dedicated exclusively to him are *Seven Sonnets of Michelangelo* (1940), *The
Holy Sonnets of John Donne* (1945), and *Death in Venice* (1973). Canticle II
Abraham and Isaac (1952) is dedicated to Pears and Kathleen Ferrier, Canticle
IV *Journey of the Magi* (1971) to James Bowman, John Shirley-Quirk and
Pears, and *Sacred and Profane* (1974–5) 'to P.P. and the Wilbye Consort'.
Sang Macheath in first performance of Britten's version of *The Beggar's
Opera* (1948). Sang Johnny Inkslinger in revised version (radio) of *Paul
Bunyan* (1976). Wrote chapter on Britten's vocal music in 1952 Mitchell-
Keller symposium. Co-adapter with Britten of libretto for *A Midsummer
Night's Dream* (1960). Co-arranger with Britten of Purcell songs, etc.
Recorded Gerontius in Elgar's *The Dream of Gerontius* conducted by Britten
and sang in recordings of other works by composers other than Britten
which Britten conducted. Gave many recitals of Purcell, Schubert (notably
Winterreise), Bach, etc. with Britten as accompanist. Created role of Pandarus
in Walton's *Troilus and Cressida* (1954). Co-founder of English Opera Group
1946 and of Aldeburgh Festival 1948. Commissioned and gave first
performances of many works by contemporary composers other than British
(including Lutoslawski's *Paroles tissées*).

Piper, John (1903–92), English artist and stage designer whose association
with Britten began in 1932. Designed sets for the following Britten stage
works: *The Rape of Lucretia* (1946), *Albert Herring* (1947), *Billy Budd* (1951),
Gloriana (1953), *The Turn of The Screw* (1954), *The Prince of the Pagodas*
(1957), *A Midsummer Night's Dream* (1960, assisted by Carl Toms), *Owen
Wingrave* (1971), *Death in Venice* (1973). Britten's song-cycle *Winter Words*
is dedicated to Piper and his wife Myfanwy. Designer of Britten memorial
window in Aldeburgh Parish Church.

Piper, Myfanwy (1911–97), librettist, wife of John Piper. Wrote three libretti
for Britten: two adaptations of Henry James, *The Turn of the Screw* (1954)

and *Owen Wingrave* (1971) and one of Thomas Mann, *Death in Venice* (1973). Has written interesting essay on writing for Britten.

Plomer, William (1903–73), South African-born poet and novelist who wrote the following libretti for Britten: *Gloriana* (1953) and the three church parables *Curlew River* (1964), *The Burning Fiery Furnace* (1966) and *The Prodigal Son* (1968). Canticle V, *The Death of Saint Narcissus* (1974) was written 'in loving memory' of Plomer.

Robertson, Rae (1893–1956), Scottish pianist who formed piano duo with his wife Ethel Bartlett. Britten wrote three works for them. (See Bartlett, Ethel, for details.)

Rostropovich, Mstislav (b. 1927), Russian cellist, pianist and conductor, deprived of his Soviet citizenship in 1978 because of his support for Russian dissidents such as the novelist Solzhenitsyn (it was restored by the Gorbachev régime and he returned to Russia). Shostakovich wrote several works for him and it was after playing the 1st Cello Concerto in London in 1960 that he first met Britten, the start of a firm and lasting friendship. He played on several occasions at the Aldeburgh Festival. Britten wrote five works for him, Rostropovich giving the first performances in the years indicated: Sonata in C (1961), *Symphony* (1964), Suite No. 1 (1965), No. 2 (1968), No. 3 (1974). Played piano accompaniment in first complete performance in Moscow, 1965, of Britten's *The Poet's Echo*, written for his wife, the soprano Galina Vishnevskaya, and dedicated to them both. An artistic director of Aldeburgh Festival 1978–91. At the time of his death, Britten was writing a choral work for Rostropovich to conduct in Washington, D.C.

Samuel, Harold (1879–1937), English pianist, specialist in keyboard music of Bach, and professor of piano at Royal College of Music for many years. Britten had private lessons from him from about the age of 15.

Schoenberg, Arnold (1874–1951), Austrian-born composer and teacher who became American citizen in 1941. One of the most influential figures in 20th-century music, this mainly because of his 'method of composing with 12 notes' from which serialism was developed. His earlier 'expressionist' works also had a marked influence, notably his *Pierrot Lunaire* (1912) which greatly impressed Britten in 1933. Though never an atonalist, Britten in his music showed awareness of Schoenberg's harmonic and structural procedures.

Shirley-Quirk, John (b. 1931), English baritone who created several Britten operatic roles in English Opera Group productions, i.e. the Ferryman in *Curlew River* (1964), Ananias in *The Burning Fiery Furnace* (1966), the Father in *The Prodigal Son* (1968), Coyle in *Owen Wingrave* (1971) and seven roles in *Death in Venice* (1973). Gave first performance of revised version of song-cycle *Tit for Tat* (Aldeburgh 1969) and sang in first performance of *Journey of the Magi* (Aldeburgh 1971) of which he is a dedicatee.

Shostakovich, Dmitri (1906–75), Russian composer and pianist, whose 15 symphonies, 15 string quartets, operas, concertos, song-cycles and other works represent the most eminent artistic achievement of the Soviet Union, with the authorities of which, however, he was frequently in disfavour. Warm friendship with Britten developed in 1960s during visits by each of them to Britain or Russia, particularly through mutual friendship with cellist Rostropovich. Britten admired Shostakovich's music from his first acquaintance with it in the 1930s and was strongly influenced by it. Shostakovich dedicated his 14th Symphony (1969) to Britten, who conducted the first English performance at Aldeburgh, 1970, and Britten dedicated *The Prodigal Son* (1968) to Shostakovich.

Slater, Montagu (1902–56), English poet and dramatist, whose collaboration with Britten began with incidental music for Slater's plays *Stay Down Miner* (1936) and *The Seven Ages of Man* and *Spain* (1938). His poem *Mother Comfort* was set by Britten in 1937 for soprano, contralto and piano. Wrote libretto for *Peter Grimes* (1942–3, music composed 1944–5). Britten's *Ballad of Heroes* (1939) is dedicated to Slater and his wife, Enid.

Stein, Erwin (1886–1958), Austrian-born music critic who settled in London and became British citizen. Pupil of Schoenberg. In 1938 joined staff of Boosey and Hawkes where he met and befriended Britten, about whom he wrote many valuable articles. Arranged vocal scores of *Peter Grimes* (1945) and *Billy Budd* (1950). Wrote on some of Britten's operas in Mitchell-Keller symposium, 1952. *The Rape of Lucretia* (1946) is dedicated to him. His daughter Marion (b. 1927) also became close friend of Britten.

Strode, Rosamund (b. 1927), English musician, trained at Royal College of Music (singing and viola) and Dartington Hall (pupil of Imogen Holst). Joined Purcell Singers in 1952. Succeeded Imogen Holst as music assistant to Britten, 1964–76. Secretary and archivist to Britten Estate until 1992.

Swingler, Randall (1909–67), English poet, journalist and amateur musician, at one time literary editor of Communist *Daily Worker* (now *Morning Star*). Britten set his poem *Advance Democracy* in 1938. Part of the text of Britten's *Ballad of Heroes* (1939) was by Swingler.

Tippett, Sir Michael (1905–98), English composer of operas, symphonies, oratorios, concertos, string quartets, song-cycles, etc., whose music was admired by Britten. In 1943 Pears and Britten gave first performance of his song-cycle *Boyhood's End*. Tippett's *Concerto for Orchestra* (1963) is dedicated to Britten and Britten's *Curlew River* (1964) to Tippett "in friendship and admiration". Contributed movement to the *Variations on an Elizabethan Theme* (*Sellenger's Round*) devised by Britten for Aldeburgh Festival 1953.

Vishnevskaya, Galina (b. 1926), Russian soprano, wife of Mstislav Rostropovich and, like him, deprived of Soviet citizenship 1978 until it was restored by the Gorbachev régime. Britten wrote the soprano part of *War*

Requiem (1962) for her, although she could not sing in the first performance (later she recorded it with Britten). First singer and joint dedicatee with Rostropovich of Britten's Pushkin song-cycle *The Poet's Echo*, Moscow 1965.

Vyvyan, Jennifer (1925–74), English soprano, whose solo operatic career began with role in Britten's 1948 version of *The Beggar's Opera* for the English Opera Group. Created roles of Lady Rich in *Gloriana* (1953), the Governess in *The Turn of the Screw* (1954), Tytania in *A Midsummer Night's Dream* (1960), and Mrs Julian in *Owen Wingrave* (1971).

Walton, Sir William (1902–83), English composer of two symphonies, two operas, the oratorio *Belshazzar's Feast*, four concertos, chamber music, songs and film music. His one-act opera *The Bear* was first performed at the Aldeburgh Festival 1967. In 1969 wrote *Improvisations on an Impromptu of Benjamin Britten* for orchestra, theme being taken from Britten's Piano Concerto (first European performance at The Maltings, Snape, 1970).

Wittgenstein, Paul (1887–1961), Austrian pianist who lost arm in First World War and commissioned concertos or similar works for left hand from Strauss, Schmidt, Prokofiev, Ravel and others. In 1939 settled in the United States and commissioned work from Britten, the result being *Diversions* (1940), of which he gave the first performance in 1942 in Philadelphia. Also gave first performances in England in 1950 in Bournemouth and London.

Wyss, Sophie (1897–1983), Swiss soprano who settled in England in 1925 and championed British music. Was soloist in first performance of Britten's *Our Hunting Fathers* at Norwich in 1936 and at first London performance 1937. Gave first performance of *On This Island* in 1937 and of *Les Illuminations*, London 1940, having previously sung two of the songs in the latter separately in Birmingham and London in 1939. (It is dedicated to her.)

Zorian, Olive (1916–65), English violinist whose string quartet, formed in 1942, gave first or early performances of works by young British composers, including Britten and Tippett. First performance of Britten's 2nd String Quartet was given by Zorian Quartet, 1945. She was leader of English Opera Group orchestra 1952–7.

Appendix D

Select bibliography

(A) Writings etc., by Britten

1940 'An English composer sees America', *Tempo*, New York, i.
1942 'On behalf of Gustav Mahler', *Tempo*, New York, ii.
1944 'Conversation with Benjamin Britten', *Tempo* (London, Feb. 1944).
1946 *The Composer and the Listener*, BBC talk (7 Nov. 1946).
1950 'A Note on the *Spring Symphony*', *Music Survey* (Spring 1950).
1951 Contribution to 'Verdi: a symposium', in *Opera* (Feb. 1951). Reprinted in *The Opera Bedside Book*, ed. H. Rosenthal (London, 1965), pp. 196–7.
1952 'Variations on a Critical Theme', *Opera* (Mar. 1952). Reprinted in *The Opera Bedside Book*, ed. H. Rosenthal (London, 1965), pp. 15–18.
1954 'Three Premières', in *Kathleen Ferrier, a Memoir*, ed. N. Cardus (London, 1954).
1958 *The Story of Music*, with Imogen Holst (London, 1958); re-issued 1968 as *The Wonderful World of Music*.
1959 'On realising the continuo in Purcell's songs': in *Henry Purcell 1659–1695*, ed. I. Holst (London, 1959).
1963 'Benjamin Britten' (answers to questions), in M. Schafer, *British Composers in Interview* (London, 1964).
'Britten looking back', *Sunday Telegraph*, 17 Nov.
1966 'Frank Bridge 1879–1941', *Faber Music News* (Autumn 1966).

(B) Books on Britten

Auden, W.H., *Paul Bunyan: the Libretto of the Operetta by Benjamin Britten* (with essay by Donald Mitchell) (London, 1988).
Banks, Paul, ed., *The Making of Peter Grimes*: I Facsimile of composition draft, II Notes and Commentaries by P. Banks, P. Brett, B. Britten, E. Crozier, D. Mitchell, P. Pears, P. Reed, R. Strode (Woodbridge, 1996).
—— ed., *Britten's Gloriana: Essays and Sources* (Woodbridge, 1993).
Blades, James, *Drum Roll* (London, 1977).
Blyth, Alan, ed., *Remembering Britten* (Contributors: Frederick Ashton, Janet Baker, Steuart Bedford, Lennox Berkeley, Basil Cameron, Joan Cross, Clifford Curzon, Norman Del Mar, Colin Graham, Keith Grant, Lord Harewood, Imogen Holst, Miss Hudson, Graham Johnson, Hans Keller, Colin Matthews, Donald Mitchell, Peter Pears, Murray Perahia, John and

Myfanwy Piper, Mary Potter, Stephen Reiss, Mstislav Rostropovich, Peter
Schidlof, William Servaes, Rosamund Strode, Robert Tear, Marion Thorpe,
Michael Tippett, Beth Welford) (London, 1981).

Blythe, Ronald, ed., *Aldeburgh Anthology* (Snape Maltings Foundation, 1972).

Brett, Philip ed., *Benjamin Britten: Peter Grimes* (Cambridge, 1983).

Britten, Beth, *My Brother Benjamin* (Bourne End, 1986).

Carpenter, Humphrey, *Benjamin Britten: a Biography* (London, 1992).

Cooke, Mervyn, *Britten: War Requiem* (Cambridge, 1996).

—— *Britten and the Far East: Asian Influences in the Music of Benjamin
Britten* (Woodbridge, 1998).

—— and Reed, Philip, *Benjamin Britten: Billy Budd* (Cambridge, 1993).

Duncan, Ronald, *Working with Britten: a Personal Memoir* (London, 1981).

Evans, John, ed., with Reed, Philip and Wilson, Paul, *A Britten Source Book*
(Aldeburgh, 1987). See also under Mitchell, Donald.

Evans, Peter, *The Music of Benjamin Britten* (London, 1979); rev. 1989.

Ford, Boris, ed., *Benjamin Britten's Poets* (Manchester, 1994).

Foreman, Lewis, ed., *From Parry to Britten: British Music in Letters
1900–1945* (London, 1987).

Garnham, Maureen, *As I Saw It: Basil Douglas, Benjamin Britten and the
English Opera Group 1955–1957* (London, 1998).

Gishford, Anthony, ed., *Tribute to Benjamin Britten on his fiftieth birthday*
(London, 1963).

Godsalve, William H. L., *Britten's A Midsummer Night's Dream: Making an
Opera from Shakespeare's Comedy* (Cranbury, NJ, 1995).

Headington, Christopher, *Britten* (London, 1981).

—— *Peter Pears: a Biography* (London, 1992).

Herbert, David, ed., *The Operas of Benjamin Britten* (London, 1979).
(Contains librettos of operas, church parables, *Noye's Fludde* and *The
Golden Vanity*, also essays by Janet Baker, Basil Coleman, Eric Crozier,
Colin Graham, Hans Keller, Peter Pears, John Piper, Myfanwy Piper,
Andrew Porter.)

Holst, Imogen, *Britten* ('Great Composers' series) (London, 1966); 2nd edn.
1970, 3rd edn. 1980.

Howard, Patricia, *The Operas of Benjamin Britten* (London, 1969).

—— ed., *Benjamin Britten: The Turn of the Screw* (Cambridge, 1985).

Hurd, Michael, *Benjamin Britten* (London, 1966).

Keller, Hans. See under Mitchell, Donald.

Lindler, H., *Benjamin Britten: das Opernwerk* (Bonn, 1955).

Mitchell, Donald, *Britten and Auden in the Thirties – The Year 1936* (London, 1981).

—— ed. *Benjamin Britten: Death in Venice* (Cambridge, 1987).

—— and Evans, John, eds., *Benjamin Britten: Pictures from a life 1913–1976*
(London, 1978).

—— and Keller, Hans, eds., *Benjamin Britten: a commentary on his works
from a group of specialists.* (Contributors: G. Auric, L. Berkeley, N. Del
Mar, A. E. F. Dickinson, P. Hamburger, Ld. Harewood, I. Holst, H. Keller,

G. Malcolm, W. Mann, D. Mitchell, B. Neel, A. Oldham, P. Pears, H. F. Redlich, E. Stein) (London, 1952; Greenwood Press, U.S.A., 1972).

Mitchell, Donald and Reed, Philip, eds., *Letters From a Life: Selected Letters and Diaries of Benjamin Britten, Vol. I 1923–39, Vol. II 1939–45* (London, 1991).

Oliver, Michael, *Benjamin Britten* (London, 1996).

Palmer, Christopher, ed., *The Britten Companion.* (Contributors: P. Brett, J. Culshaw, J. Evans, C. Headington, R. Holloway, I. Holst, G. Johnson, H. Keller, D. Matthews, W. Mellers, A. Milner, D. Mitchell, C. Palmer, P. Pears, P. Porter, E. Roseberry, E. Stein, R. Strode) (London, 1984).

Reed, Philip and Cooke, Mervyn, *Benjamin Britten: Billy Budd* (Cambridge, 1993).

Strode, Rosamund, *Music of Forty Festivals* (Aldeburgh, 1987).

White, Eric Walter, *Benjamin Britten: a sketch of his life and works* (London, 1948); Ger. tr. by B. & M. Hürlimann, Zürich, 1948; rev. and enlarged edn. London, 1954.

—— *Benjamin Britten: his life and operas* (London, 1970); 2nd edn ., ed. J. Evans, London, 1983.

Wilcox, Michael, *Benjamin Britten's Operas* (Bath, 1997).

Young, Percy M., *Benjamin Britten* ('Masters of Music' series) (London, 1966).

(C) Important Articles etc., on Britten

Baker, Janet, 'Working with Britten', in *The Operas of Benjamin Britten*, ed. Herbert (London, 1979), pp. 1–4.

Berkeley, Lennox, 'Britten's *Spring Symphony*', *Music and Letters* xxxi (1950), p. 216.

Blyth, Alan, 'Britten returns to composing', *The Times* (30 Dec. 1974).

Boys, Henry, 'Benjamin Britten', *Monthly Musical Record*, lxviii (1938), p. 234.

Brett, Philip, 'Britten and Grimes', *The Musical Times*, vol. 118, No. 1618, pp. 995–1000.

Coleman, Basil, 'Staging First Productions – 2', in *The Operas of Benjamin Britten*, ed. Herbert (London, 1979), pp. 34–43.

Crozier, Eric, 'Staging First Productions – 1', in *The Operas of Benjamin Britten*, ed. Herbert (London, 1979), pp. 24–33.

—— ed., *Peter Grimes* (Sadler's Wells Opera Books No. 3) (London, 1945).

—— ed., *The Rape of Lucretia: a symposium* (London, 1947).

Culshaw, John, 'Ben: a tribute to Benjamin Britten', *The Gramophone* (Feb. 1977), pp. 1251–2.

Evans, Peter, 'Sonata structures in early Britten', *Tempo* 82 (1967), p. 2.

—— 'Britten's *War Requiem*', *Tempo* 61/62 (1962), p. 20.

—— 'Britten's *Cello Symphony*', *Tempo* 66/67 (1963), p. 2.

—— 'Britten's *Death in Venice*', *Opera* xxiv (1973), p. 490.

—— 'Britten's Fourth Creative Decade', *Tempo* 106 (1973), p. 8.

Goddard, Scott, 'Benjamin Britten', in *British Music of our Time*, ed. Bacharach (London, 1946), pp. 209–18.

Graham, Colin, 'Staging First Productions – 3', in *The Operas of Benjamin Britten*, ed. Herbert (London, 1979), pp. 44–58.

Keller, Hans, 'Benjamin Britten's Second Quartet', *Tempo* 18 (1947), p. 6.

—— 'Death of a genius', *The Spectator* (15 Jan. 1977), pp. 27–8.

—— 'Britten's last masterpiece', *The Spectator* (2 June 1979), pp. 27–8.

—— 'Introduction: Operatic Music and Britten', in *The Operas of Benjamin Britten*, ed. Herbert (London, 1979), pp. xiii–xxxi.

Mason, Colin, 'Britten: another view', *Monthly Musical Record* lxxiii, (1943), p. 153

Matthews, Colin, 'Britten's Indian Summer', *Soundings* vi (1977), p. 44.

Mitchell, Donald, 'A Note on *St Nicolas*: some points of Britten's style', *Music Survey* ii (1950), p. 220.

—— 'More off than on *Billy Budd*', *Music Survey* iv (1952), p. 286.

—— 'Britten's Revisionary Practice: practical and creative', *Tempo* 66/67 (1963), pp. 15–22.

Music Survey, Britten issue, vol. ii, no. 4 (1950).

Noble, Jeremy, 'Britten's *Songs from the Chinese*', *Tempo* 52 (1959), p. 25.

Opera, Britten issue, vol. ii (1951).

Payne, Anthony, 'Dramatic use of tonality in *Peter Grimes*', *Tempo* 66/67 (1963), p. 22.

Pears, Peter, 'The Vocal Music' in *Benjamin Britten: a commentary on his works . . .*, ed. Mitchell-Keller (London, 1952).

—— *Armenian Holiday: August 1965*, privately printed 1965.

—— *Moscow Christmas: December 1966*, privately printed 1967.

Piper, John, 'Designing for Britten', in *The Operas of Benjamin Britten*, ed. Herbert (London, 1979), pp. 5–7.

Piper, Myfanwy, 'Writing for Britten', in *The Operas of Benjamin Britten*, ed. Herbert (London, 1979), pp. 8–21.

Porter, Andrew, 'Britten's *Billy Budd*', *Music and Letters* xxxiii (1952), p. 111.

—— 'The First Opera', in *The Operas of Benjamin Britten*, ed. Herbert (London, 1979), pp. 22–3. (Originally published in the *New Yorker* and reprinted in A. Porter's *Music of Three Seasons*, New York and London, 1975.)

—— 'The Last Opera', in *The Operas of Benjamin Britten*, ed. Herbert (London 1979), pp. 59–62. (Originally published in the *New Yorker* and reprinted in A. Porter's *Music of Three Seasons*, New York and London, 1975.)

Robertson, Alec, 'Britten's *War Requiem*', *The Musical Times* ciii (1962), p. 308.

Roseberry, Eric, 'The Music of *Noye's Fludde*', *Tempo* 49 (1958), p. 2.

—— 'Britten's *Missa Brevis*', *Tempo* 53/54 (1960), p. 11.

Stein, Erwin, 'Opera and *Peter Grimes*', *Tempo* 12 (1945), p. 2.

—— 'Benjamin Britten's Operas', *Opera* i (1950), p. 16.

—— 'Britten's *Spring Symphony*', *Tempo* 15 (1950), p. 19.

Stein, Erwin, '*The Turn of the Screw* and its musical idiom', *Tempo* 34 (1955), p. 6.

—— 'Britten's new opera for children: *Noye's Fludde*', *Tempo* 48 (1958), p. 7.

Tempo, Britten issue (*Billy Budd*), No. 21 (1952).

—— Britten 50th birthday issue, No. 66/67 (1963).

—— Britten 60th birthday issue, No. 106 (1973).

—— Britten memorial issue, No. 120 (1977).

Tippett, Michael, 'First Encounters' (1963), in *Music of the Angels*, essays and sketchbooks of M. Tippett, ed. Meirion Bowen (London, 1980), pp. 77–8.

—— 'Britten at fifty', *The Observer* (17 Nov. 1963); reprinted in *Music of the Angels*, ed. Bowen (London, 1980), pp. 77–81.

—— 'Obituary', BBC (4 Dec. 1976); reprinted in *The Listener* xcix, (16 Dec. 1976), and in *Music of the Angels*, ed. Bowen (London, 1980), pp. 82–4.

Warrack, John, 'Britten's *Cello Symphony*', *The Musical Times* cv (1964), p. 418.

Westrup, J. A., 'The Virtuosity of Benjamin Britten', *The Listener* xxviii (1942), p. 93.

White, Eric W., 'Britten in the theatre: a provisional catalogue', *Tempo* 107 (1973), p. 2.

Appendix E

Discography

Compiled by Ray Crick

Benjamin Britten, as an adjunct to his life as a composer, enjoyed a truly remarkable career as a recording artist, spanning some thirty-six years. The fruits of these years remain as a legacy of unparalleled richness, and are set out below in a discography that lists all recordings which have been made commercially available. The chronological listings feature Britten's recordings as conductor and pianist (and viola player!), interpreting both his own and thirty-seven other composers' music. The numbers preceding each title entry allow cross reference from an alphabetical repertoire index on pp. 348–50.

The discography lists all *published* material. In the eight years since the last edition there have been many additions, notably an extensive series of *Britten – The Performer* on BBC Legends, and the oldest recording now available is some five years earlier: Britten's 1936 soundtrack of *The Way to the Sea*. Extensive collections of unpublished recordings are held by the BBC, the National Sound Archive, and The Britten–Pears Library.

Note on record numbers. Unless otherwise indicated all numbers refer to compact discs. Where a Britten recording has yet to appear on CD, the LP number is quoted. In some cases the recordings have only ever been issued on 78s. All the recordings were made for Decca apart from those indicated. Whilst virtually all the CDs listed are available at the time of going to press, other formats are now deleted.

I Britten as Conductor

(A) Conducting his own works

	Date and location of recording, work, and artists	Record numbers
1	December 1936, Imperial Studio, Borehamwood. *The Way to the Sea* (1936). Geoffrey Tandy, narrator; chamber ensemble.	1PD 14 (Beulah)
2	May, 1941, New York (ISCM Festival recording). *Les Illuminations*, Op. 18 (1939). Peter Pears, tenor; CBS Symphony Orchestra.	NMC D030 (NMC)
3	May & October 1944, Kingsway Hall, London. *Serenade for Tenor, Horn & Strings*, Op. 31 (1943). Peter Pears, tenor; Dennis Brain, horn; Boyd Neel String Orchestra.	468 801–2 425 996–2 GEMMCD 9177 (Pearl)

	Date and location of recording, work, and artists	Record numbers
4	October 1946, Holland. *The Rape of Lucretia*, Op. 37 (1946), excerpts. Kathleen Ferrier, Peter Pears, Joan Cross, Otakar Kraus, Owen Brannigan etc.; English Opera Group Orchestra.	CD 901 (Music & Arts)
5	December 1951, Royal Opera House, Covent Garden. *Billy Budd*, Op. 50 (1951), original version. Theodor Uppman, Peter Pears, Frederick Dalberg, Hervey Alan, Geraint Evans, Michael Langdon etc.; Royal Opera House Orchestra & Chorus, Covent Garden.	VAIA 1034 (Video Artists International)
6	June 1953, Aldeburgh Parish Church (Aldeburgh Festival recording). *Variations on an Elizabethan Theme* (by Oldham, Tippett, Berkeley, Britten, Searle & Walton). Aldeburgh Festival Orchestra.	LXT 2798 (LP)
7	September 1953, Copenhagen. *A Ceremony of Carols*, Op. 28 (1942). Copenhagen Boys' Choir; Enid Simon, harp.	436 394–2
8	September 1953, Copenhagen. *Sinfonia da Requiem*, Op. 20 (1940). Danish State Radio Symphony Orchestra.	LXT 2981 (LP)
9	July 1954, Kingsway Hall. *Diversions*, Op. 21 (1940 rev. 1954). Julius Katchen, piano (left hand); London Symphony Orchestra.	421 855–2
10	January 1955, Decca Recording Studios, West Hampstead, London. *The Turn of the Screw*, Op. 54 (1954). Peter Pears, Jennifer Vyvyan, Joan Cross, Arda Mandikian, David Hemmings & Olive Dyer; English Opera Group Orchestra.	425 672–2
11	April 1955, Aldeburgh Parish Church. *Saint Nicolas*, Op. 42 (1948). Peter Pears, tenor; David Hemmings, treble; Aldeburgh Festival Orchestra & Choir.	425 714–2
12	October 1955, Decca Recording Studios. *The Little Sweep (Let's make an Opera)*, Op. 45 (1949). Jennifer Vyvyan, April Cantelo, Nancy Thomas, David Hemmings, Peter Pears, Trevor Anthony etc.; English Opera Group Orchestra; Alleyn's School Choir.	436 393–2

	Date and location of recording, work, and artists	Record numbers
13	December 1956, Baden Baden. *Sinfonia da Requiem*, Op. 20 (1940). Sinfonieorchester des Südwestfunks.	0629 029 (Deutsche Grammophon LP)
14	January 1957, Decca Recording Studios. *A Boy was Born*, Op. 3 (1933 rev. 1955). Purcell Singers.	436 394–2
15	February 1957, Walthamstow Assembly Hall. *The Prince of the Pagodas*, Op. 57 (1956), abridged version. Royal Opera House Orchestra, Covent Garden.	421 855–2
16	April 1957, All Souls' Church, Langham Place, London. *Rejoice in the Lamb*, Op. 30 (1943). Purcell Singers; George Malcolm, organ.	425 714–2
17	December 1958, Walthamstow Assembly Hall. *Peter Grimes*, Op. 33 (1945). Peter Pears, Claire Watson, Owen Brannigan, Geraint Evans, James Pease, David Kelly etc.; Royal Opera House Orchestra & Chorus, Covent Garden (Sea Interludes & Passacaglia*).	467 682–2 *425 659–2
18	September 1959, Walthamstow Assembly Hall. *Nocturne*, Op. 60 (1958). Peter Pears, tenor; London Symphony Orchestra.	436 395–2
19	November 1960, Kingsway Hall. *Spring Symphony*, Op. 44 (1949). Jennifer Vyvyan, soprano; Norma Procter, contralto; Peter Pears, tenor; Royal Opera House Orchestra & Chorus, Covent Garden.	436 396–2
20	June 1961, BBC Studio No. 1, Maida Vale (broadcast recording). *Our Hunting Fathers*, Op. 8 (1936). Peter Pears; London Symphony Orchestra.	BBCB 8014–2 (BBC Legends)
21	December 1961, Kingsway Hall. *The National Anthem* (arr. Britten). London Symphony Orchestra & Chorus.	436 403–2
22	April 1962, Vancouver. *Nocturne*, Op. 66 (1958), includes rehearsal sequence. Peter Pears, tenor; CBC Vancouver Chamber Orchestra.	69420 (Video Arts International video)

Date and location of recording, work, and artists	Record numbers
23	January 1963, Kingsway Hall. *War Requiem*, Op. 66 (1961), includes rehearsal sequence. Galina Vishnevskaya, soprano; Peter Pears, tenor; Dietrich Fischer-Dieskau, baritone; Bach Choir; London Symphony Orchestra & Chorus; Melos Ensemble.	414 383–2
24	May 1963, Kingsway Hall. *Serenade for Tenor, Horn & Strings*, Op. 31 (1943). Peter Pears, tenor; Barry Tuckwell, horn; London Symphony Orchestra.	436 395–2
25	May 1963, Kingsway Hall. *The Young Person's Guide to the Orchestra*, Op. 34 (1945). London Symphony Orchestra.	417 509–2 425 659–2
26	December 1963, Kingsway Hall. *Cantata misericordium*, Op. 69 (1963). Peter Pears, tenor; Dietrich Fischer-Dieskau, baritone; London Symphony Orchestra & Chorus.	468 811–2 425 100–2
27	March 1964, Great Hall, Moscow Conservatory. *Symphony for Cello and Orchestra*, Op. 68 (1963). Mstislav Rostropovich, cello; Moscow Philharmonic Orchestra.	CZS 572 016–2 (EMI) RV 10100 (Revelation) RD CD 11108 (Russian Disc)
28	April 1964, Jubilee Hall, Aldeburgh. *Albert Herring*, Op. 39 (1947). Peter Pears, Sylvia Fisher, Owen Brannigan, Joseph Ward, Catherine Wilson, April Cantelo, Sheila Rex etc.; English Chamber Orchestra.	421 849–2
29	July 1964, Kingsway Hall. *Symphony for Cello and Orchestra*, Op. 68 (1963). Mstislav Rostropovich, cello; English Chamber Orchestra.	425 100–2
30	December 1964, Kingway Hall. *Sinfonia da Requiem*, Op. 20 (1940). New Philharmonia Orchestra.	425 100–2
31	June 1965, Orford Parish Church. *Curlew River*, Op. 71 (1964). Peter Pears, John Shirley-Quirk, Harold Blackburn, Bryan Drake, Bruce Webb etc.; seven instrumentalists; with Viola Tunnard, assistant conductor.	421 858–2

	Date and location of recording, work, and artists	Record numbers
32	May 1966, King's College Chapel, Cambridge. *Voices for Today*, Op. 75 (1965). King's College & Cambridge University Musical Society Choirs; with David Willcocks, conductor (NB This work involves two conductors).	ZRG 947 (Argo LP)
33	July 1966, Decca Recording Studios. *Friday Afternoons*, Op. 7 (1934), 11 songs. Downside School Choir, Purley; Viola Tunnard, piano.	436 394–2
34	July 1966, Kingsway Hall. *Psalm 150*, Op. 67 (1962). Boys of Downside School, Purley.	436 394–2
35	September & October 1966, Walthamstow Assembly Hall. *A Midsummer Night's Dream*, Op. 64 (1960). Alfred Deller, Elizabeth Harwood, Peter Pears, Thomas Hemsley, Josephine Veasey, Heather Harper, John Shirley-Quirk, Helen Watts, Owen Brannigan, Stephen Terry etc.; London Symphony Orchestra.	425 663–2
36	December 1966, Kingsway Hall. *Les Illuminations*, Op. 18 (1939). Peter Pears, tenor; English Chamber Orchestra.	436 395–2
37	December 1966, Kingsway Hall. *Variations on a Theme of Frank Bridge*, Op. 10 (1937). English Chamber Orchestra.	417 509–2
38	March 1967, Queen Elizabeth Hall, London (inaugural concert) *Gloriana*, Op. 53: Dances; *Hankin Booby*. Peter Pears, tenor; Osian Ellis, harp; Ambrosian Singers.	BBCB 8009–2 (BBC Legends)
39	May 1967, Orford Parish Church. *The Burning Fiery Furnace*, Op. 77 (1966). Peter Pears, Bryan Drake, John Shirley-Quirk, Robert Tear, Stafford Dean etc.; 8 instrumentalists; with Viola Tunnard, assistant conductor.	414 663–2
40	June 1967, The Maltings, Snape (Aldeburgh Festival recording of the royal inaugural concert). *The Building of the House*, Op. 79; *Gloriana*, Op. 53 (1953): Fanfare*; *The*	BBCB 8007–2 (BBC Legends) *5BB 119/20 (2 LPs)

Date and location of recording, work, and artists	Record numbers

National Anthem* (arr. Britten). Chorus of
East Anglian Choirs; English Chamber
Orchestra.

41 June 1967, The Maltings, Snape (Aldeburgh — AS 324 (AS Disc)
Festival recording). *Piano Concerto*, Op. 13
(1938 rev. 1945). Sviatoslav Richter, piano;
English Chamber Orchestra.

42 November 1967, Queen Elizabeth Hall, London. — BBCB 8013–2
Nocturne, Op. 60 (1958). Peter Pears, tenor; — (BBC Legends)
English Chamber Orchestra.

43 December 1967, Kingsway Hall. *Billy Budd,* — 417 428–2
Op. 50 (1951 rev. 1960). Peter Glossop,
Peter Pears, Michael Langdon, John
Shirley-Quirk, Owen Brannigan, Bryan
Drake etc.; London Symphony Orchestra.

44 May 1968, The Maltings, Snape. *Simple Symphony,* 417 509–2
Op. 4 (1934). English Chamber Orchestra. — 436 990–2
— 448 569–2

45 April 1969, Royal Albert Hall, London. — BBCL 4046–2
War Requiem, Op. 66 (1961). Stefania — (BBC Legends)
Woytowicz, soprano; Peter Pears, tenor;
Hans Wilbrink, baritone; Wandsworth School
Boys' Choir; New Philharmonia Chorus &
Orchestra; Carlo Maria Giulini, conductor;
Melos Ensemble (conducted by Britten).

46 May 1969, Orford Parish Church. *The Prodigal* 425 713–2
Son, Op. 81 (1968). Robert Tear, Peter Pears,
John Shirley-Quirk, Bryan Drake etc.; 8
instrumentalists; with Viola Tunnard,
assistant conductor.

47 October 1969, St John's, Smith Square, London. 436 393–2
Children's Crusade, Op. 82 (1969). — 468 811–2
Wandsworth School Boys' Choir; with
Russell Burgess, conductor.

48 July 1970, The Maltings, Snape. *The Rape of* — 425 666–2
Lucretia, Op. 37 (1946 rev. 1947). Janet
Baker, Benjamin Luxon, Peter Pears, Heather
Harper, John Shirley-Quirk, Bryan Drake etc.;
English Chamber Orchestra.

Date and location of recording, work, and artists	Record numbers
49 July 1970, The Maltings, Snape. *Violin Concerto*, Op. 15 (1939 rev. 1958). Mark Lubotsky, violin; English Chamber Orchestra.	417 308–2
50 December 1970, Kingsway Hall. *Owen Wingrave*, Op. 85 (1970). Benjamin Luxon, Janet Baker, Peter Pears, John Shirley-Quirk, Sylvia Fisher, Heather Harper etc.; English Chamber Orchestra.	433 200–2
51 December 1970, The Maltings, Snape. Piano Concerto, Op. 13 (1938 rev. 1945). Sviatoslav Richter, piano; English Chamber Orchestra.	417 308–2
52 September 1971, The Maltings, Snape. *Prelude and Fugue*, Op. 29 (1943). English Chamber Orchestra.	448 569–2

I Britten as Conductor

(B) Conducting the works of others

53 June 1956, Jubilee Hall, Aldeburgh (Aldeburgh Festival recording). HAYDN: Symphonies Nos. 45 'Farewell', & 55 'The Schoolmaster'. With Aldeburgh Festival Orchestra.	458 869–2
54 September 1959, BBC Studio (BBC Transcription Service recording). PURCELL: *Dido & Aeneas*. Claire Watson, Jeannette Sinclair, Arda Mandikian, Patricia Clark, Rosemary Philips, Peter Pears, John Hahessy, Michael Ronayne; George Malcolm, harpsichord; Purcell Singers; English Opera Group Orchestra.	BBCB 8003–2 (BBC Legends)
55 July 1961, Orford Parish Church (Aldeburgh Festival recording). HOLST: *Egdon Heath*. London Symphony Orchestra.	BBCB 8007–2 (BBC Legenda)
56 July 1961, Orford Parish Church (Aldeburgh Festival recording). MAHLER: Symphony No. 4. Joan Carlyle, soprano; London Symphony Orchestra.	BBCB 8004–2 (BBC Legends)

57	July 1961, Orford Parish Church (Aldeburgh Festival recording). SCHUMANN: Cello Concerto. Mstislav Rostropovich, cello; London Symphony Orchestra.	RR 500 (Discocorp LP)
58	May 1962, Drottningholmsteater, Stockholm (Drottningholm Festival recording). PURCELL: *Dido and Aeneas*, excerpts. Janet Baker, John Lawrenson, Jeannette Sinclair; English Opera Group Chorus & Orchestra.	CD 295 (Denon)
59	June 1962, BBC Studios. MOZART: Symphony No. 39, K543; *Per pietà, non ricercata*, K420*; *Si mostra la sorte*, K209*. * Peter Pears, tenor; English Chamber Orchestra.	466 820–2
60	June 1962, BBC Studio, Maida Vale (broadcast recording). TCHAIKOVSKY: *Legend 'Christ in his Garden'*; Suite 'Mozartiana'. *Peter Pears, tenor; English Chamber Orchestra.	BBCB 8002–2 (BBC Legends)
61	July 1964, Kingsway Hall. HAYDN: Cello Concerto in C. Mstislav Rostropovich, cello; English Chamber Orchestra.	430 633–2
62	June 1965, Blythburgh Church (Aldeburgh Festival recording). BACH: Cantata No. 102 *'Herr, deine Augen sehen nach dem Glauben'*. Janet Baker, mezzo-soprano; Peter Pears, tenor; Dietrich Fischer-Dieskau, baritone; Aldeburgh Festival Singers; English Chamber Orchestra.	466 819–2
63	June 1965, Blythburgh Church (Aldeburgh Festival recording). HAYDN: Symphony No. 95. English Chamber Orchestra.	BBCB 8008–2 (BBC Legends)
64	June 1965, Blythburgh Church (Aldeburgh Festival recording). MOZART: Piano Concerto No. 27, K. 595. Sviatoslav Richter, piano; English Chamber Orchestra.	BBCB 8005–2 (BBC Legends)
65	June 1965, Blythburgh Church (Aldeburgh Festival recording). SCHUMANN: *Introduction & Allegro Appassionato*. Sviatoslav Richter, piano; English Chamber Orchestra.	AS 329 (AS)
66	June 1966, Blythburgh Church (Aldeburgh Festival recording). BEETHOVEN: *Coriolan* Overture; DEBUSSY: *Prelude à l'après midi d'un Faune*. English Chamber Orchestra.	BBCB 8008–2 (BBC Legends)

Date and location of recording, work, and artists	Record numbers
67	June 1966, Blythburgh Church (Aldeburgh Festival recording). MOZART: Symphony No. 41 '*Jupiter*', K551. English Chamber Orchestra.	466 820–2
68	March 1967, Queen Elizabeth Hall. PURCELL: Birthday Ode for Queen Mary, '*Celebrate this festival*'. Heather Harper, soprano; Josephine Veasey, mezzo-soprano; James Bowm.	466 819–2
69	June 1967, The Maltings, Snape (Aldeburgh Festival recording). BRIDGE: *Enter Spring*. New Philharmonia Orchestra.	BBCB 8007–2 (BBC Legends)
70	June 1967, The Maltings, Snape (Aldeburgh Festival recording of the royal opening concert). HANDEL: *Ode for St Cecilia's Day*. Heather Harper, soprano; Peter Pears, tenor; Philip Ledger, organ; Julian Bream, lute; Richard Adeney, flute; Philip Jones, trumpet; Keith Harvey, cello; Chorus of East Anglian Choirs; English Chamber Orchestra.	BBCB 8009–2 (BBC Legends)
71	June 1967, The Maltings, Snape (Aldeburgh Festival recording). MOZART: *Adagio & Fugue*, K. 546; Piano Concerto No. 22, K. 482*. *Sviatoslav Richter, piano; English Chamber Orchestra.	BBCB 8010–2 (BBC Legends)
72	November 1967, Queen Elizabeth Hall, London. MOZART: *Sinfonia Concertante*, K. 364. Norbert Brainin, violin; Peter Schidlof, viola; English Chamber Orchestra.	BBCB 8010–2 (BBC Legends)
73	May 1968, The Maltings, Snape. MOZART: Symphony No. 40, K. 550; *Serenata Notturna*, K. 239. English Chamber Orchestra.	444 323–2
74	June 1968, The Maltings, Snape (Aldeburgh Festival recording). TCHAIKOVSKY: *Nocturne*; Serenade for Strings*. *Mstislav Rostropovich, cello; English Chamber Orchestra.	BBCB 8002–2 (BBC Legends)
75	June 1968, The Maltings, Snape (Aldeburgh Festival recording). TCHAIKOVSKY: *Romeo and Juliet*. English Chamber Orchestra.	BBCB 8012–2 (BBC Legends)

	Date and location of recording, work, and artists	Record numbers
76	December 1968, The Maltings, Snape BACH: *Brandenburg Concertos*, BWV 1046/51. English Chamber Orchestra.	443 847–2 466 209–2
77	December 1968, St. Andrew's Church, Holborn, London. BACH: Cantata No. 151 '*Süsser Trost, mein Jesus kommt*'. Heather Harper, soprano; Helen Watts, contralto; Peter Pears, tenor; John Shirley-Quirk, baritone; Wandsworth School Boys' Choir; English Chamber Orchestra.	466 819–2
78	December 1968, The Maltings, Snape. BRIDGE: *Sir Roger de Coverley*; DELIUS: *Two Aquarelles*; ELGAR: Introduction & Allegro for Strings; PURCELL: *Chacony*. English Chamber Orchestra.	448 569–2
79	December 1968, The Maltings, Snape. GRAINGER: Shepherd's Hey; Willow willow; I'm seventeen come Sunday; Bold William Taylor; There was a pig went out to dig; My Robin is to the greenwood gone; Lord Maxwell's Goodnight; The Duke of Marlborough Fanfare; Scotch Strathspey & Reel; Lisbon; The lost lady found; Shallow Brown ('Salute to Percy Grainger'). Peter Pears, tenor; John Shirley-Quirk, baritone; Ambrosian Singers; English Chamber Orchestra.	425 159–2
80	June 1969, The Maltings, Snape (Aldeburgh Festival recording). MAHLER: *Des Knaben Wunderhorn*: 2 songs. Elly Ameling, soprano; English Chamber Orchestra.	BBCB 8004–2 (BBC Legends)
81	June 1969, Blythburgh Church (Aldeburgh Festival recording). MOZART: *Exsultate Jubilate*. Elly Ameling, soprano; English Chamber Orchestra.	BBCB 8005–2 (BBC Legends)
82	June 1970, The Maltings, Snape (Aldeburgh Festival recording). BLISS: *Concertino* for Cello & Orchestra. Mstislav Rostropovich, cello; English Chamber Orchestra.	INCD 7151 (Intaglio)
83	June 1970, The Maltings, Snape (Aldeburgh Festival recording). SHOSTAKOVICH: Symphony No. 14, Op. 135. Galina Vishnevskaya, soprano; Mark Rezhetin, bass; English Chamber Orchestra.	BBCB 8013–2 (BBC Legends)

	Date and location of recording, work, and artists	Record numbers
84	July 1970, The Maltings, Snape. MOZART: Symphony No. 38, K. 504, *'Prague'*. English Chamber Orchestra.	444 323–2
85	September 1970, The Maltings, Snape. MOZART: Piano Concertos Nos. 20, K. 466 & 27, K. 595. Clifford Curzon, piano; English Chamber Orchestra.	417 288–2
86	September 1970, The Maltings, Snape. PURCELL: *The Fairy Queen*. Jennifer Vyvyan, James Bowman, Peter Pears, Owen Brannigan, John Shirley-Quirk, etc.; English Chamber Orchestra.	433 163–2
87	February 1971, The Maltings, Snape. MOZART: Symphony No. 29, K. 201. English Chamber Orchestra.	433 323–2
88	April 1971, The Maltings, Snape. BACH: *St John Passion*, BWV 245: highlights. Peter Pears, Robert Tear, Heather Harper, Alfreda Hodgson, John Shirley-Quirk, Gwynne Howell etc.; Wandsworth School Boys' Choir; English Chamber Orchestra.	443 859–2
89	June 1971, The Maltings, Snape (Aldeburgh Festival recording). BRIDGE: *The Sea*. English Chamber Orchestra.	*450 010–2 BBCB 8007–2 (BBC Legends)
90	June 1971, The Maltings, Snape (Aldeburgh Festival recording). TCHAIKOVSKY: *Francesca da Rimini*. English Chamber Orchestra.	BBCB 8012–2 (BBC Legends)
91	June 1971, The Maltings, Snape (Aldeburgh Festival recording). MENDELSSOHN: *Hebrides* Overture. English Chamber Orchestra.	BBCB 8008–2 (BBC Legends)
92	July 1971, The Maltings, Snape. ELGAR: *The Dream of Gerontius*. Peter Pears, tenor, Yvonne Minton, mezzo-soprano; John Shirley-Quirk, baritone; London Symphony Orchestra & Chorus.	421 381–2 448 170–2
93	September 1971, The Maltings, Snape. MOZART: Symphony No. 25, K. 183. English Chamber Orchestra.	444 323–2
94	September 1971, The Maltings, Snape. SCHUBERT: Symphony No. 8, 'Unfinished'. English Chamber Orchestra.	436 407–2

	Date and location of recording, work, and artists	Record numbers
95	June 1972, The Maltings, Snape (Aldeburgh Festival recording). FALLA: *El Amor Brujo*. Anna Reynolds, mezzo-soprano; Steuart Bedford, piano; English Chamber Orchestra.	BBCB 8012–2 (BBC Legends)
96	June 1972, The Maltings, Snape (Aldeburgh Festival recording). MAHLER: *Lieder eines fahrenden Gesellen*. Anna Reynolds, mezzo-soprano; English Chamber Orchestra.	BBCB 8004–2 (BBC Legends)
97	June 1972, The Maltings, Snape (Aldeburgh Festival recording). MOZART: Symphony No. 35, '*Haffner*', K. 385. English Chamber Orchestra.	BBCB 8008–2 (BBC Legends)
98	September 1972, The Maltings, Snape. SCHUMANN: *Scenes from Goethe's 'Faust'*. Dietrich Fischer-Dieskau, Elizabeth Harwood, John Shirley-Quirk, Peter Pears, Jennifer Vyvyan etc.; English Chamber Orchestra.	425 705–2

II *Britten as Pianist*. Accompanying Peter Pears, tenor (unless otherwise stated)

(A) Playing his own works

99	Early 1941, New York(?) (private recording). *Seven Sonnets of Michelangelo*, Op. 22 (1940).	NMCD 030 (NMC)
100	November 1942, EMI Recording Studios, Abbey Road, London. *Seven Sonnets of Michelangelo*, Op. 22 (1940).	CDC 754 605–2 (EMI) GEMMCD 9177 (Pearl)
101	May 1943, Decca Recording Studios. *Folksongs* (arr. Britten): Voici le printemps; Fileuse; Le roi s'en va-t'en chasse; La belle est au jardin d'amour; Quand j'étais chez mon père. Accompanying Sophie Wyss, soprano.	CMS 764 727–2 (EMI)
102	January 1944, Kingsway Hall. *Introduction & Rondo alla Burlesca*, Op. 23 No. 1 (1940); *Mazurka Elegiaca*, Op. 23 No. 2 (1941). With Clifford Curzon, piano.	GEMMCD 9177 (Pearl) 1PD 14 (Beulah)
103	January 1944, Kingsway Hall. *Folksongs* (arr. Britten): The Ash Grove; Little Sir William; Oliver Cromwell; The Salley gardens.	CMS 764 727–2 (EMI) GEMMCD 9177 (Pearl)

	Date and location of recording, work, and artists	Record numbers
104	June 1945, Decca Recording Studios. *Folksongs* (arr. Britten): The Bonny Earl o'Moray; Quand j'étais chez mon père (Heigh ho! Heigh hi!).	CMS 764 727–2 (EMI)
105	January 1946; Decca Recording Studios. *Folksongs* (arr. Britten): Sweet Polly Oliver; There's none to soothe.	CMS 764 727–2 (EMI)
106	August 1947, EMI Recording Studios. *Folksongs* (arr. Britten): Come you not from Newcastle?; The Foggy, Foggy Dew; The Plough Boy (Shield).	CMS 764 727–2 (EMI)
107	August & December 1947, EMI Recording Studios. *The Holy Sonnets of John Donne*, Op. 35 (1945).	CDC7 54805–2 (EMI)
108	September 1950, EMI Recording Studios. *Folksong* (arr. Britten): Le roi s'en va-t'en chasse (The king is gone a-hunting—sung in English).	CMS 764 727–2 (EMI)
109	November 1950, EMI Recording Studios. *Folksong* (arr. Britten): O Waly, Waly.	CMS 764 727–2 (EMI)
110	March 1954, Decca Recording Studios. *Winter Words*, Op. 52 (1953).	425 996–2
111	March 1954, Decca Recording Studios. *Folksongs* (arr. Britten): The Ash Grove; The Bonny Earl o' Moray; The Brisk Young Widow; Little Sir William; The Miller of Dee; Oliver Cromwell; The Salley gardens; Sweet Polly Oliver; There's none to soothe.	LW 5122 (10≤LP)
112	July 1954, Kingsway Hall. *Seven Sonnets of Michelangelo*, Op. 22 (1940).	425 996–2
113	September & October 1955, Decca Recording Studios. *On This Island*, Op. 11 (1937): Let the florid music praise.	ECS 545 (LP)
114	June 1956, Aldeburgh Parish Church. *Canticle III, Still falls the rain*, Op. 55 (1954). With Peter Pears, tenor; Dennis Brain, horn.	BBCB 8014–2 (BBC Legends)
115	March 1957, Decca Recording Studios. *Canticle II, Abraham and Isaac*, Op. 51 (1952). Acc. Norma Proctor, contralto; Peter Pears, tenor.	468 811–2

	Date and location of recording, work, and artists	Record numbers
116	June 1959, Jubilee Hall, Aldeburgh. *Folksongs* (arr. Britten): The Foggy, Foggy Dew; The Lincolnshire Poacher; Sally in our alley (Carey); Tom Bowling (Dibdin).	BBCB 8006–2 (BBC Legends)
117	October 1959, Kingsway Hall. *Folksongs* (arr. Britten): The Foggy, Foggy Dew; The Lincolnshire Poacher; Sally in our alley (Carey); Tom Bowling (Dibdin).	430 063–2
118	January & April 1961, Kingsway Hall. *Canticle I, My beloved is mine*, Op. 40 (1947); *Canticle II, Abraham and Isaac*, Op. 51 (1952); *Canticle III, Still falls the rain*, Op. 55 (1954). Acc. John Hahessy, boy alto; Peter Pears, tenor; Barry Tuckwell, horn.	425 716–2
119	January & April 1961, Kingsway Hall. *Friday Afternoons*, Op. 7 (1934), 5 songs; *The Birds* (1929 rev. 1934), *Corpus Christi carol* (1961). Acc. John Hahessy, boy alto (Michael Berkeley, treble, also sings on *Cuckoo!* from *Friday Afternoons*).	ZFA 18 (Argo 7≤45)
120	July 1961, Kingsway Hall. *Cello Sonata*, Op. 65 (1961). With Mstislav Rostropovich, cello.	421 859–2 452 895–2
121	November 1961, Kingsway Hall. *Six Hölderlin Fragments*, Op. 61 (1958).	468 811–2 433 200–2
122	November 1961, Kingsway Hall. *Folksongs* (arr. Britten): The Ash Grove; Avenging and bright; La belle est au jardin d'amour; The Bonny Earl o' Moray; The Brisk Young Widow; Ca' the yowes; Come you not from Newcastle?; Early one morning; How sweet the answer; The last rose of summer; The Miller of Dee; The Minstrel Boy; O Waly, Waly; Oft in the stilly night; The Plough Boy (Shield); Le roi s'en va-t'en chasse; Sweet Polly Oliver.	430 063–2
123	March 1962 (BBC broadcast recording). *A Charm of Lullabies*, Op. 41 (1947). Acc. Helen Watts, contralto.	REGL 417 (BBC LP)

	Date and location of recording, work, and artists	Record numbers
124	March 1963, Grand Hall of the Leningrad Philharmonic Society (live recording). *Folksong* (arr. Britten): I wonder as I wander; *Winter Words*. Op. 52.	M10 46091 009 (Melodiya LP)
125	May 1963, BBC Studios. *Lachrymae*, Op. 48 (1950). With Margaret Major, viola.	BBCB 8014–2 (BBC Legends)
126	December 1965, Kingsway Hall. *Songs & Proverbs of William Blake*, Op. 74 (1964). Acc. Dietrich Fischer-Dieskau, baritone.	417 428–2
127	March 1966, Grand Hall of the Leningrad Philharmonic Society (live recording). *Folksongs* (arr. Britten): The Ash Grove; Le roi s'en va-t'en chasse.	M10 46091 009 (Melodiya LP)
128	June 1967, The Maltings, Snape (Aldeburgh Festival recording). *Introduction and Rondo alla Burlesca*, Op. 23 No. 1 (1940). With Sviatoslav Richter, piano.	CD 709 (Music & Arts)
129	November 1967, The Maltings, Snape. *The Holy Sonnets of John Donne*, Op. 35 (1945).	417 428–2
130	June 1969, Blythburgh Church (Aldeburgh Festival recording). *On This Island*, Op. 11 (1937).	BBC 8015–2 (BBC Legends)
131	October 1969, St John's, Smith Square, London. *The Golden Vanity*, Op. 78 (1966). Acc. Wandsworth School Boys' Choir; with Russell Burgess, conductor.	436 397–2
132	September 1971, The Maltings, Snape. *Who are these Children?*, Op. 84 (1969).	BBCB 8014–2 (BBC Legends)
133	June 1972, The Maltings, Snape (Aldeburgh Festival recording). *Folksongs* (arr. Britten): The Salley Gardens.	BBCB 8015–2 (BBC Legends)
134	September 1972, The Maltings, Snape (Aldeburgh Festival recording). *Folksongs* (arr. Britten): The Foggy, Foggy, Dew; The Miller of Dee; The Plough Boy (Shield); *Winter Words*, Op. 52 (1953).	AF 001 (Aldeburgh Festival LP)
135	November 1972, The Maltings, Snape. *Canticle IV: Journey of the Magi*, Op. 86 (1971). Acc.	425 716–2

	Date and location of recording, work, and artists	Record numbers
	James Bowman, countertenor; Peter Pears, tenor; John Shirley-Quirk, baritone.	
136	November 1972, The Maltings, Snape. *Tit for Tat* (1928/31, rev. 1968). Acc. John Shirley-Quirk, baritone.	SXL 6608 (LP)
137	November 1972, The Maltings, Snape. *Who are these Children?*, Op. 84 (1969).	SXL 6608 (LP)

II Britten as Pianist. Accompanying Peter Pears, tenor (unless otherwise stated)

(B) Playing the works of others

138	1941, New York. *Balinese Ceremonial Music* (arr. McPhee): Pemungkah; Rebong; Gambangan; Lagu delem; Tabu telu. With Cohn McPhee, piano.	GEMMCD 9177 (Pearl)
139	July 1945, London. VAUGHAN WILLIAMS: *On Wenlock Edge*. With Peter Pears, tenor; Zorian Quartet.	GEMS 0062 (Pearl)
140	August 1947, EMI Recording Studios. PURCELL: *The Queen's Epicedium*.	RLS 748 (2 EMI LPs)
141	September & November 1950, EMI Recording Studios. COPLAND: *Old American Songs*: The boatman's dance; Long time ago; The dodger; Simple gifts; I bought me a cat; GRAINGER: *Folksongs*: The jolly sailor song; Six dukes went a-fishin'; SCHUBERT*: *Auf der Bruck; Im Frühling*.	RLS 748 (2 EMI LPs) *also on CHS 566 154–2 (EMI)
142	February 1952 (BBC broadcast recording). SCHUBERT: Ganymed; Du liebst mich nicht; Lachen und Weinen. Acc. Kathleen Ferrier, contralto.	433 471–2
143	June 1955, Aldeburgh Parish Church (Aldeburgh Festival recording). BEETHOVEN: Quintet for Piano and Wind. With The Dennis Brain Quintet.	IGI 370 (Educational Media Associates LP)
144	September & October 1955, Decca Recording Studios. BERKELEY: How love come in; BRIDGE: Go not, happy day; Love went a-riding;	ECS 545 (LP)

342

Date and location of recording, work, and artists	Record numbers

BUTTERWORTH: Is my team ploughing?; HOLST: Humbert Wolfe Songs: Persephone; IRELAND: I have twelve oxen; MOERAN: In youth is pleasure; OLDHAM: *Three Chinese Lyrics*; WARLOCK: Yarmouth Fair.

145 June 1956, Jubilee Hall, Aldeburgh (Aldeburgh Festival recording). MOZART: Piano Concerto No. 12, K. 414. With Aldeburgh Festival Orchestra. — 458 869–2

146 June 1958, Jubilee Hall, Aldeburgh (Aldeburgh Festival recording). FAURÉ: La Bonne Chanson; SCHUBERT: Auflösung; Nachtviolen; Die Sterne; SCHUMANN: Liederkreis, Op. 39. — BBCB 8006–2 (BBC Legends)

147 February 1959 (BBC broadcast recording). SCHUBERT: Abendbilder; Der Winterabend; WOLF: Frühling übers Jahr; Sankt Nepomuks Vorabend. — REGL 410 (BBC LP)

148 April 1959, Kingsway Hall. SCHUBERT: An die Laute; Du bist die Ruh**; Der Einsame; Geheimes*; Gesang des Harfners—Wer sich der Einsamkeit ergibt**; Der Musensohn**; *Schwanengesang*: Die Stadt*; Die Taubenpost. — 452 402–2 *SEC 5984 (7≤45) **BR 3066 (10≤LP)

149 June 1959, Jubilee Hall, Aldeburgh. PURCELL: I attempt from love's sickness to fly; I'll sail upon the Dogstar; Man is for the woman made; Not all my torments; There's not a swain of the plain. — BBCB 8006–2 (BBC Legends)

150 October 1959, Kingsway Hall. SCHUBERT: *Die schöne Müllerin*. — 452 402–2

151 April 1960 (BBC broadcast recording). WOLF: Ganymed; Beherzigung; Spottlied; Der Scholar; Der Gärtner; Bei einer Trauung; Schlafendes Jesuskind; Die du Gott gebarst; Fuhr' mich, Kind; Wie sollt' ich heiter bleiben; Wenn ich dein gedenke. — REGL 410 (BBC LP)

152 June 1960, Jubilee Hall (Aldeburgh Festival recording). MOZART: Sonata for two pianos, K. 448. With Clifford Curzon, piano. — BBCL 4037–2 (BBC Legends)

	Date and location of recording, work, and artists	Record numbers
153	July 1961, Kingsway Hall. DEBUSSY: Cello Sonata; SCHUMANN: *Fünf Stücke im Volkston*. With Mstislav Rostropovich, cello.	452 895–2 460 974–2
154	November 1961, Kingsway Hall. HAYDN: *Six Canzonets*.	SDD 197 (LP)
155	October 1963, Kingsway Hall. BRIDGE: Goldenhair; Journey's end; So perverse; 'Tis but a week; When you are old; IRELAND: Friendship in misfortune; *The Land of Lost Content*: 6 songs; Love and friendship; The one hope; The trellis.	461 550–2
156	October 1963, Kingsway Hall. SCHUBERT: *Winterreise*.	452 402–2 466 382–2
157	October 1963, Kingsway Hall. SCHUMANN: *Dichterliebe*.	443 933–2
158	January 1964 (BBC broadcast recording). SCHUBERT: Ihr Grab; Das war ich; Die Götter Griechenlands; Der blinde Knabe; Das Lied im Grünen.	REGL 410 (BBC LP)
159	June 1964, Jubilee Hall (Aldeburgh Festival recording). SCHUBERT: *Variations*, D. 813. With Sviatoslav Richter, piano.	466 822–2
160	June 1964, Aldeburgh Parish Church (Aldeburgh Festival recording) SHOSTAKOVICH: Cello Sonata, Op.40. With Mstislav Rostropovich, cello.	466 823–2
161	December 1964, Kingsway Hall. TIPPETT: *Songs for Ariel*.	461 550–2
162	June 1965, Aldeburgh Parish Church (Aldeburgh Festival recording). JANACEK: *Pohadka*. With Mstislav Rostropovich, cello.	466 823–2
163	June 1965, Jubilee Hall (Aldeburgh Festival recording). PURCELL: When night her purple veil has softly spread. With Dietrich Fischer-Dieskau, baritone; Alberni String Quartet.	BBCB 8003–2 (BBC Legends)
164	June 1965, Jubilee Hall (Aldeburgh Festival recording). SCHUBERT: *Andantino Varié*, D. 823. With Sviatoslav Richter, piano.	466 812–2

	Date and location of recording, work, and artists	Record numbers
165	June 1965, Jubilee Hall (Aldeburgh Festival recording). SCHUBERT: *Grand Duo*, D. 812; *Fantasia*, D. 940. With Sviatoslav Richter, piano.	466 822–2
166	June 1966, Aldeburgh Parish Church (Aldeburgh Festival recording). MOZART: Piano Sonata (four hands), K. 521. With Sviatoslav Richter, piano.	466 812–2
167	June 1966, Aldeburgh Parish Church (Aldeburgh Festival recording). SCHUMANN: *Bilder aus Osten*. With Sviatoslav Richter, piano.	KICC 2271 (King Records)
168	June 1967, The Maltings, Snape (Aldeburgh Festival recording). BRIDGE: *Phantasy*. With Norbert Brainin, violin; Peter Schidlof, viola; Martin Lovett, cello.	466 823–2
169	June 1967, The Maltings, Snape (Aldeburgh Festival recording). DEBUSSY: *En Blanc et Noir*; MOZART: Sonata for two pianos, K. 448. With Sviatoslav Richter, piano.	466 812–2
170	June 1967, The Maltings, Snape (Aldeburgh Festival recording). SCHUMANN: *Bilder aus Osten*. With Sviatoslav Richter, piano.	CD 709 (Music & Arts)
171	November 1967, The Maltings, Snape. HOLST: *Humbert Wolfe Songs*.	ZRG 512 (Argo LP)
172	June 1968, The Maltings, Snape (Aldeburgh Festival recording). BRAHMS: *Liebeslieder Waltzes*. With Heather Harper, soprano; Janet Baker, contralto; Peter Pears, tenor; Thomas Hemsley, baritone; with Claudio Arrau, piano.	BBCB 8001–2 (BBC Legends)
173	June 1968, The Maltings, Snape (Aldeburgh Festival recording). SHOSTAKOVICH: *Romances on Verses by Alexander Blok*, Op. 127. With Galina Vishnevskaya, soprano; Emanuel Hurwitz, violin; Mstislav Rostropovich, cello.	466 823–2
174	July 1968, The Maltings, Snape. BRIDGE: Cello Sonata. With Mstislav Rostropovich, cello.	443 575–2
175	July 1968, The Maltings, Snape. SCHUBERT: *Arpeggione Sonata*. With Mstislav Rostropovich, cello.	443 575–2 452 393–2 460 974–2

Date and location of recording, work, and artists	Record numbers
176	December 1968, The Maltings, Snape. GRAINGER: Let's dance gay in green meadow*; The pretty maid milkin' her cow; The sprig of thyme ('Salute to Percy Grainger'). *With Viola Tunnard, piano.	425 159–2
177	December 1968, The Maltings, Snape. SCHUBERT: Abendstern; An die Entfernte; Auf dem Wasser zu singen; Auflösung; Im Frühling; Nachtstück; Nacht und Träume.	443 933–2
178	June 1969, Blythburgh Church (Aldeburgh Festival recording). SCHUBERT: Abendstern; An die Entfernte; Atys; Auflösung; Ganymed; Der Musensohn; Nähe des Geliebten.	BBCB 8015–5 BBC Legends)
179	June 1971, The Maltings, Snape (Aldeburgh Festival recording). ROSSINI: Four Duets; TCHAIKOVSKY: Four Duets. Acc. Heather Harper, soprano; Janet Baker, contralto.	BBCB 8001–2 (BBC Legends)
180	June 1971, The Maltings, Snape (Aldeburgh Festival recording) WOLF: *Mörike* Lieder— Auf ein altes Bild; Schlafendes Jesuskind; *Three Poems of Michelangelo*; Spanish Songbook*: Nun wandre, Maria. *Acc. John Shirley-Quirk, baritone.	BBCB 8011–2 (BBC Legends)
181	September 1971, The Maltings, Snape. MOZART: Piano Quartet in G minor, K. 478. With Kenneth Sillito, violin; Cecil Aronowitz, viola; Kenneth Heath, cello.	BBCB 8005–2 (BBC Legends)
182	June 1972, The Maltings, Snape (Aldeburgh Festival recording). ARNE: Come away, death; Under the Greenwood Tree; QUILTER: Fear no more the heat of the sun; O Mistress mine; TIPPETT: *Songs for Ariel*: Come unto these yellow sands; WARLOCK: Take, o take those lips away; WOLF: *Mörike Lieder*: Jägerlied; An eine Aeolsharfe; Im Frühling; Heimweh; Denk'es, o Seele!; Lied eines Verliebten; Bei einer Trauung.	BBCB 8015–2 (BBC Legends)
183	June 1972, The Maltings, Snape (Aldeburgh Festival recording). SCHUBERT: An die Freunde; Auf der Donau; Aus Heliopolis II; Fischerweise; Freiwilliges Versinken; Gruppe aus dem Tartarus;	BBCB 8011–2 (BBC Legends)

Date and location of recording, work, and artists	Record numbers

Prometheus; Der Strom; Der Wanderer; Der Wanderer an den Mond. Acc. Dietrich Fischer-Dieskau, baritone.

184   June 1972, The Maltings, Snape (Aldeburgh Festival recording). SCHUBERT: Der Hirt auf dem Felsen. With Heather Harper, soprano; Thea King, clarinet.   BBCB 8011–2 (BBC Legends)

185   November 1972, The Maltings, Snape. PURCELL: Sweeter than roses. Acc. James Bowman, countertenor.   443 393–2

186   November 1972, The Maltings, Snape. SCHUBERT: Atys; Der Einsame; Der Geistertanz; Lachen und weinen; *Schwanergesang*: Das Fischermädchen; Sprache der Liebe.   443 933–2

III   *Britten as Viola Player*

187   November 1946, EMI Recording Studios. PURCELL: *Fantasia upon one note*. With the Zorian Quartet.   RLS 748 (2 EMI LPs)

IV   *Britten Anthologies*

'The World of Benjamin Britten': excerpts from *Billy Budd*; *A Ceremony of Carols*; Folksong Arrangements; *A Hymn to the Virgin*; *Noye's Fludde*; *Peter Grimes*; *Serenade for Tenor, Horn & Strings*; *Simple Symphony*; *Spring Symphony*; *War Requiem*; *The Young Person's Guide to the Orchestra*. Benjamin Britten, piano & conductor; with various artists.   436 990–2

'25 Years at the Aldeburgh Festival': excerpts from *Albert Herring*; Cello Sonata; *Curlew River*; *Gloriana*; *The Little Sweep*; *Mazurka Elegiaca*; *A Midsummer Night's Dream*; *Noye's Fludde*; Piano Concerto; *The Rape of Lucretia*; *Saint Nicolas*; *Songs & Proverbs of William Blake*; Suite for Harp; *Voices for Today*; plus music by Bridge, Dowland, Elgar, Handel, Holst, Mozart, Purcell, Scarlatti, & Schubert. Benjamin Britten, piano & conductor; with various artists.   5BB 119/20 (2 LPs)

V *Britten's Voice on Record*

(BBC broadcast recording).   REGL 368
Kathleen Ferrier—A Portrait of a Well-loved Singer: (BBC LP)
1. Benjamin Britten describes the first time he heard
Kathleen singing in *Messiah*; 2. Gerald Moore &
Britten talking about Kathleen's singing of
folksongs; 3. Britten recalls Kathleen's singing of the
role of Lucretia in his opera *The Rape of Lucretia*;
4. Britten sums up the qualities of her voice; 5. Britten
talks of Kathleen singing his canticle *Abraham and
Isaac*.

January 1963, Kingsway Hall. *War Requiem*, Op. 66   414 383–2
(1961)—rehearsal sequence.

VI *Britten's Recorded Repertory*
The numbers refer to the main body of the discography.

ARNE: Shakespeare Songs (182)
BACH: *Brandenburg* Concertos (76); Cantatas 102 (62) & 151 (77), *St John
Passion* (88)
BEETHOVEN: *Coriolan* Overture (59); Quintet for Piano & Wind (123)
BERKELEY: How love came in (144); Variation on an Elizabethan Theme (6)
BLISS: Concertino (82)
BRAHMS: *Liebeslieder* Waltzes (172)
BRIDGE: Cello Sonata (174); *Enter Spring* (69); *Phantasy* (168); *The Sea* (89); *Sir
Roger de Coverley* (78); Songs (144, 155)
BRITTEN: *Albert Herring* (28); *Billy Budd* (5, 43); *The Birds* (119); *A Boy was
Born* (14); *The Building of the House* Overture (40); *The Burning Fiery
Furnace* (39); *Cantata misericordium* (26); 4 Canticles (114, 115, 118, 135);
Cello Sonata (120); *A Ceremony of Carols* (7); *A Charm of Lullabies* (123);
Children's Crusade (47); Corpus Christi Carol (119); *Curlew River* (31);
Diversions (9); Folksong arrangements (101, 103–6, 108, 109, 111, 116, 117,
122, 124, 127, 134); *Friday Afternoons* (33, 119); *Gloriana* (38, 40); *The
Golden Vanity* (131); *Hankin Booby* (38); 6 Hölderlin Fragments (121); *The
Holy Sonnets of John Donne* (107, 129); *Les Illuminations* (2, 36);
Introduction & Rondo Alla Burlesca (102, 128); *Lachrymae* (125); *The Little
Sweep* (12); *Mazurka Elegiaca* (102); *A Midsummer Night's Dream* (35);
The National Anthem (21, 40); Nocturne (18, 22, 42); *On This Island* (113,
130); *Our Hunting Fathers* (20); *Owen Wingrave* (50); *Peter Grimes* (17);
Piano Conerto (41, 51); Prelude & Fugue (52); *The Prince of the Pagodas*
(15); *The Prodigal Son* (46); *Psalm* 150 (34); *The Rape of Lucretia* (4, 48);
Rejoice in the Lamb (16); *Saint Nicolas* (11); Serenade for Tenor, Horn &
Strings (3, 24); *Simple Symphony* (44); *Sinfonia da Requiem* (8, 13, 30);

Songs & Proverbs of William Blake (126); *Sonnets of Michelangelo* (99, 100, 112); *Spring Symphony* (19); Symphony for Cello & Orchestra (27, 29); *Tit for Tat* (136); *The Turn of the Screw* (10); Variation on an Elizabethan Theme (6); *Variations on a Theme of Frank Bridge* (37); Violin Concerto (49); *Voices for Today* (32); *War Requiem* (23, 45); *The Way to the Sea* (1); *Who are these Children?* (132, 137); *Winter Words* (110, 124, 134); *The Young Person's Guide to the Orchestra* (25)

BUTTERWORTH: Is my team ploughing? (144)

CAREY: Sally in our alley (116, 117)

COPLAND: *Old American Songs* (141)

DELIUS: *2 Aquarelles* (78)

DEBUSSY: Cello Sonata (153); En Blanc et Noir (169); *Prelude à l'après midi d'un Faune* (66)

DIBDIN: Tom Bowling (116, 117)

ELGAR: *The Dream of Gerontius* (92); Introduction & Allegro for Strings (78)

FALLA: *El Amor Brujo* (95)

FAURÉ: La Bonne Chanson (146)

GRAINGER: Folksongs (141); 'Salute to Percy Grainger' (79, 176)

HANDEL: *Ode for St Cecilia's Day* (70)

HAYDN: 6 Canzonets (154); Cello Concerto in C (61); Symphonies 45, 55 (53) & 95 (63)

HOLST: *Egdon Heath* (55); Humbert Wolfe Songs (144, 171)

IRELAND: *The Land of Lost Content* (155); Songs (144, 155)

JANACEK: *Pohadka* (162)

MAHLER: *Des Knaben Wunderhorn* (80); *Lieder eines fahrenden Gesellen* (96); Symphony No. 4 (56)

MCPHEE: Balinese Ceremonial Music (138)

MENDELSSOHN: *Hebrides* Overture (91)

MOERAN: In youth is pleasure (144)

MOZART: Adagio & Fugue (71); Arias (59); *Exsultate Jubilate* (81); Piano Concertos 12 (145), 20 (85), 22 (71) & 27 (64, 85); Piano Quartet K.478 (181); Piano Sonata, 4-hands K. 521 (166); *Serenata Notturna* (73); Sinfonia Concertante K. 364 (72); Sonata for 2 Pianos K. 448 (152, 169); Symphonies 25 (93), 29 (87), 35 (97), 38 (84), 39 (59), 40 (73) & 41 (67)

OLDHAM: *3 Chinese Lyrics* (144); Variation on an Elizabethan Theme (6)

PURCELL: Birthday Ode for Queen Mary (68); *Chacony* (78); *Dido & Aeneas* (54, 58); *The Fairy Queen* (86); Fantasia upon one note (187); *The Queen's Epicedium* (140); Songs (149); Sweeter Than Roses (185); When night her purple veil has softly spread (163)

QUILTER: Shakespeare Songs (182)

ROSSINI: Duets (179)

SCHUBERT: *Andantino Varié* (164); *Arpeggione* Sonata (175); Fantasia (165); *Grand Duo* (165); Der Hirt auf dem Felsen (184); Lieder (141, 142, 146–8, 158, 177, 178, 183, 186); *Die schöne Müllerin* (150); *Schwanengesang* (148, 186); Symphony 8 (94); *Variations* (159); *Winterreise* (156)

Index

Index

Index

354

Index

Index